At Your Service?
The Promise of Services-Led Development

At Your Service?
The Promise of Services-Led Development

Gaurav Nayyar, Mary Hallward-Driemeier,
and Elwyn Davies

 WORLD BANK GROUP

Contents

Boxes

Figures

Tables

Foreword

Manufacturing-led development has provided the traditional model for creating jobs and prosperity. But in the past three decades a new structural transformation, in which the services sector has grown faster than the manufacturing sector, has been unfolding in many developing economies. In 2019, the services sector accounted for an average of 55 percent of GDP and 45 percent of employment in developing economies.

Does this simply signal a slowdown in manufacturing? Or could the services sector help low- and middle-income countries catch up with high-income countries while also expanding good job opportunities? *At Your Service? The Promise of Services-Led Development* assesses the prospects for services-led development. Its findings and their implications lie squarely at the center of the World Bank Group's "better jobs for more people" Jobs and Economic Transformation agenda.

At Your Service? shows how the winds of change are blowing. The digital economy is expanding access to markets and opportunities for innovation in the services sector. Services are also becoming increasingly important as enablers for a wide range of sectors, as is best illustrated by the blurring lines between services and manufacturing. The choice for policy makers is no longer whether to support services or manufacturing, but how to best leverage the potential of the services sector to deliver productivity growth and jobs.

Analyses of productivity, employment, and enterprises in the services sector are rare, at least in part because of the paucity of data as a result of the sector's exclusion from, or unimportance in, censuses and surveys. By collating and analyzing data from dispersed sources, *At Your Service?* makes a valuable contribution to the evidence on the topic. The book also shows that government agencies and private sector organizations should prioritize collecting better data on services, because economic development depends so much on them.

In assessing where the potential for productivity growth and job creation lies, the authors emphasize the heterogeneity of the "services sector"—shorthand for a diverse range of economic activities that span the full gamut of production and distribution beyond farms and factories. The services sector is not monolithic—a reality that is fundamental to the policy debate that pits "services-led development" against "manufacturing-led development" strategies.

As the global economy recovers from the COVID-19 (coronavirus) pandemic, governments around the world are looking for ideas to strengthen economic dynamism and speed up job creation. While some services have been hit particularly hard in the current economic crisis, the framework and evidence presented in this book suggest a range of possibilities. There is no easy formula for success, but the book argues that the essential ingredients include expanding services *trade* to widen market access, fostering *technology* adoption and *training* workers to upgrade skills, and *targeting* services that provide benefits to the wider economy for public support.

Focusing on services is timely, given the rapid adoption of industrial automation in advanced economies and mounting worries about the slow pace of industrialization in many developing economies. For decades, the services sector has been treated as the residual economy. Now it deserves a seat at the high table. *At Your Service?* will convince policy makers that being complacent about this agenda is no longer an option.

Indermit S. Gill
Vice President
Equitable Growth, Finance, and Institutions
World Bank Group

Preface

Productivity accounts for half of the differences in GDP per capita across countries. Identifying policies to stimulate it is thus critical to alleviating poverty and fulfilling the rising aspirations of global citizens. Yet productivity growth has slowed globally in recent decades, and the lagging productivity performance in developing economies constitutes a major barrier to convergence with advanced-economy levels of income.

The World Bank Productivity Project seeks to bring frontier thinking on the measurement and determinants of productivity, grounded in the developing-country context, to global policy makers. Each volume in the series explores a different aspect of the topic through dialogue with academics and policy makers and through sponsored empirical work in our client countries. The Productivity Project is an initiative of the Vice Presidency for Equitable Growth, Finance, and Institutions.

This fifth volume in the series, *At Your Service? The Promise of Services-Led Development* (www.worldbank.org/services-led-development), offers a truly fresh exploration of one of the central development questions of our time: As manufacturing's share of GDP and employment recedes across low- and middle-income countries, can services—traditionally thought to be a sector with low productivity growth—offer a new development path promising good jobs and facilitating convergence with advanced economies? The task is challenging, as most data collection and frameworks for productivity analysis have focused on the manufacturing sector. Nonetheless, the authors of this volume bring together a wealth of evidence and, through original analysis, offer a surprisingly optimistic assessment, albeit one with important caveats. Unpacking the variety of activities classified as *services*, they identify many that increasingly share the growth-generating features thought unique to manufacturing. For instance, the acceleration of digital technologies is bringing new opportunities for scale and innovation. And expanding links with other sectors, particularly the servicification of manufacturing, is reinforcing the scope for spillovers. That said, the volume stresses the need for reforms and substantial investments to enable countries to leverage this potential through reducing barriers to services trade, mastering new technologies, raising skill levels, and targeting potential links to related sectors.

This volume is a product of the Vice Presidency for Equitable Growth, Finance, and Institutions.

William F. Maloney
Chief Economist
Equitable Growth, Finance, and Institutions
World Bank Group

Other Titles in the World Bank Productivity Project

Harvesting Prosperity: Technology and Productivity Growth in Agriculture. 2020. Keith Fuglie, Madhur Gautam, Aparajita Goyal, and William F. Maloney. Washington, DC: World Bank.

High-Growth Firms: Facts, Fiction, and Policy Options for Emerging Economies. 2019. Arti Grover Goswami, Denis Medvedev, and Ellen Olafsen. Washington, DC: World Bank.

Productivity Revisited: Shifting Paradigms in Analysis and Policy. 2018. Ana Paula Cusolito and William F. Maloney. Washington, DC: World Bank.

The Innovation Paradox: Developing-Country Capabilities and the Unrealized Promise of Technological Catch-Up. 2017. Xavier Cirera and William F. Maloney. Washington, DC: World Bank.

All books in the World Bank Productivity Project are available free of charge at https://openknowledge .worldbank.org/handle/10986/30560.

Acknowledgments

This book project was undertaken by a team led by Gaurav Nayyar, Senior Economist, and Mary Hallward-Driemeier, Senior Economic Adviser, in the Equitable Growth, Finance, and Institutions Vice Presidency of the World Bank. Other core team members were Elwyn Davies, Reyes Aterido, and Besart Avdiu. Excellent research support was provided by João Bevilaqua T. Basto, Dominic Scarcelli, and Andrea Atencio. The work was carried out under the guidance of Denis Medvedev, Practice Manager, Firms, Entrepreneurship and Innovation in the Equitable Growth, Finance, and Institutions Vice Presidency; William Maloney, Chief Economist, Equitable Growth, Finance, and Institutions Vice Presidency; and Caroline Freund, Global Director, Trade, Investment, and Competitiveness.

The following background papers served as important inputs:

- Alfaro, Laura, and Marcela Eslava. 2020. "Development and the Comparative Advantage of Services." Unpublished manuscript, Harvard Business School, Boston, MA, and Uniandes, Bogotá, Colombia.

- Artuc, Erhan, and Paulo Bastos. 2020. "Learning by Working in High-Skill Industries: Manufacturing versus Services in Brazil." Unpublished manuscript, World Bank, Washington, DC.

- Aterido, Reyes, Elwyn Davies, Mary Hallward-Driemeier, and Gaurav Nayyar. 2021. "Revisiting the Size-Productivity Relationship in Services." Unpublished manuscript, World Bank, Washington, DC.

- Avdiu, Besart, Karan S. Bagavathinathan, Ritam Chaurey, and Gaurav Nayyar. 2021. "Services Trade, Gender and Jobs: Evidence from India." Unpublished manuscript, World Bank, Washington, DC.

- Avdiu, Besart, Banu Demir, Umut Kilinc, and Gaurav Nayyar. 2021. "Does the Services Sector Benefit from a Manufacturing Core? Firm-Level Evidence from Turkey." Unpublished manuscript, World Bank, Washington, DC.

- Brolhato de Oliveria, Sara, Xavier Cirera, Ana P. Cusolito, and Eric Jardim. 2020. "Business Dynamism across Sectors: Evidence Using Employer-Employee Data in Brazil." Unpublished manuscript, World Bank, Washington, DC.

- Cusolito, Ana P., and Fausto Patiño Peña. 2020. "How Digital-Technology Adoption Affects the Skill Composition of the Workforce: Firm-Level Evidence for Manufacturing vs. Service Sectors in Developing Countries." Unpublished manuscript, World Bank, Washington, DC.

- Grover, Arti, and Aaditya Mattoo. 2020. "Why Do Manufacturing Firms Sell Services? Evidence from India." Policy Research Working Paper 9701, World Bank, Washington, DC.
- Lopez-Cordova, Ernesto. 2020. "Digital Platforms and the Demand for International Tourism Services." Policy Research Working Paper 9147, World Bank, Washington, DC.
- Syverson, Chad. 2020. "Measuring Productivity in Services." Unpublished manuscript, University of Chicago, Booth School of Business.

We are also grateful to Alison Cathles, Adriana Conconi, Sonia Plaza, and Katherine Stapleton for their inputs.

The team has benefited enormously from discussions with, and feedback from, Laura Alfaro, Richard Baldwin, Stefan Dercon, Mark Dutz, Michael Ferrantino, Poonam Gupta, Bradford Jensen, Aaditya Mattoo, and Chad Syverson. We are also grateful to Andrew Beath, Luc Christiaensen, Xavier Cirera, Marcio Cruz, Marcela Eslava, Alvaro Gonzalez, Arti Grover, Justin Hill, Leonardo Iacovone, Umut Kilinc, Peter Kusek, Yan Liu, Jose Ernesto Lopez-Cordova, Valerie Mercer-Blackman, Dino Merotto, Theresa Osborne, Carlos Rodriguez Castelan, Federica Saliola, Abhishek Saurav, Jan von der Goltz, and Michael Weber for their comments and suggestions.

Conversations with Kay Atanda, Gerlin Catangui, Alexandru Cojocaru, Ileana Cristina Constantinescu, Bernard Hoekman, Etienne Raffi Kechichian, Martha Martinez Licetti, Maryla Maliszewska, Alen Mulabdic, Karen Muramatsu, Pierre Sauve, Victor Steenbergen, Jonathan Timmis, Trang Thu Tran, Huanjun Zhang, and Juni Tingting Zhu are also deeply appreciated.

We thank our publishing team—Patricia Katayama, Michael Harrup, Cindy Fisher, Debra Malovany, and Orlando Mota—for the design and production of this book; Mary Anderson for her editorial services; and our communications team, Elizabeth Price and Melissa Knutson, for their creative energy in promoting the book.

Financial support from the Competitive Industries and Innovation Program (CIIP) and the Facility for Investment Climate Advisory Services (FIAS) Trust Funds is gratefully acknowledged.

About the Authors

Gaurav Nayyar is a Senior Economist in the Equitable Growth, Finance, and Institutions Vice Presidency at the World Bank, which he joined as a Young Professional in 2013. Previously, he was an Economics Affairs Officer in the Economic Research Division of the World Trade Organization, where he co-led the World Trade Report 2013, *Factors Shaping the Future of World Trade*. Gaurav's research interests lie primarily in the areas of economic growth, structural transformation, trade, industrialization, and firm productivity, and he has published in a variety of academic journals on these issues. His previous books include *Trouble in the Making? The Future of Manufacturing-Led Development* (with Mary Hallward-Driemeier, published by the World Bank), *The Service Sector in India's Development* (published by Cambridge University Press), and *Europe 4.0: Addressing the Digital Dilemma* (with Mary Hallward-Driemeier, Wolfgang Fengler, Anwar Aridi, and Indermit Gill, published by the World Bank). Gaurav holds a DPhil in Economics from the University of Oxford, where he was a Dorothy Hodgkin Scholar. His other alma maters include the London School of Economics and Political Science, the University of Cambridge, and St. Stephen's College, University of Delhi.

Mary Hallward-Driemeier is the Senior Economic Adviser in the Equitable Growth, Finance, and Institutions Vice Presidency at the World Bank, overseeing its analytical agenda on competitiveness and private sector development. A Canadian national, she joined the World Bank in 1997 as a Young Professional. She has published widely on entrepreneurship, firm productivity and firm dynamics, the impact of financial crises, and women's economic empowerment. She leads the Jobs and Economic Transformation special theme for the International Development Association (IDA), supporting low-income countries. She has served as an adviser to the Chief Economist of the World Bank, a co-manager of the Jobs Group, and the Deputy Director for *World Development Report 2005: A Better Investment Climate for Everyone*, and is a founding member of the Microeconomics of Growth Network. Her previous books include *Trouble in the Making? The Future of Manufacturing-Led Development* (with Gaurav Nayyar, published by the World Bank), *Enterprising Women: Expanding Economic Opportunities in Africa* (published by the World Bank), and *Europe 4.0: Addressing the Digital Dilemma* (with Gaurav Nayyar, Wolfgang Fengler, Anwar Aridi, and Indermit Gill, published by the World Bank). Mary received her AB from Harvard University; her MSc in Development Economics from Oxford University, where she was a Rhodes Scholar; and her PhD in Economics from the Massachusetts Institute of Technology.

Elwyn Davies is an Economist in the Equitable Growth, Finance, and Institutions Vice Presidency at the World Bank, where he works on firm capabilities, productivity, and innovation in a wide range of countries, mostly in Sub-Saharan Africa and Central and Eastern Europe. A Dutch and British national, Elwyn joined the World Bank in 2017 as a Young Professional. Elwyn's research studies constraints to firm growth and productivity—in particular, the impact of management and incentives—as well as the drivers of growth. Before joining the World Bank, Elwyn worked at the Directorate-General for Trade of the European Commission and was a Lecturer in Economics at the Queens College, University of Oxford. Elwyn holds BSc and BA degrees from Utrecht University, where he majored in Physics and Economics, and an MPhil and DPhil in Economics from the University of Oxford.

Abbreviations

4Ts	trade, technology, training, and targeting
AI	artificial intelligence
ASEAN	Association of Southeast Asian Nations
BLS	Bureau of Labor Statistics (US)
BoP	balance of payments
BPO	business process outsourcing
BPS	Business Pulse Survey (World Bank)
CAGR	compound annual growth rate
CPI	consumer price index
EAC	East African Community
EC	European Commission
EU	European Union
EU-15	European Union, 15 members (specifically, the 15 countries that were members of the EU before May 1, 2004)
EVAD	Export Value Added Database (World Bank)
FAT	Firm-Level Adoption of Technology survey (World Bank)
FATS	Foreign Affiliates Statistics (EU)
FDI	foreign direct investment
FTA	free trade agreement
FY	fiscal year
GATS	General Agreement on Trade in Services
GDP	gross domestic product
GGDC	Groningen Growth and Development Centre
GNI	gross national income
GPT	general purpose technology
GVC	global value chain
HICs	high-income countries
I2D2	International Income Distribution Dataset (World Bank)
ICT	information and communication technology
IDA	International Development Association (World Bank)
ILO	International Labour Organization
ILOSTAT	ILO Statistics
IMF	International Monetary Fund

IoT	Internet of Things
ISCO	International Standard Classification of Occupations
ISIC	International Standard Industrial Classification of All Economic Activities (UN)
IT	information technology
ITU	International Telecommunication Union
LMICs	low- and middle-income countries
LVA	labor value added
ML	machine learning
MOPS	Management and Organizational Practices Survey (US Census Bureau)
MPS	Material Product System
O*NET	Occupational Information Network database (US Department of Labor)
OECD	Organisation for Economic Co-operation and Development
PMR	product market regulation
PPI	producer price index
PPP	purchasing power parity
PTA	preferential trade agreement
R&D	research and development
RPA	robotic process automation
SMEs	small and medium enterprises
SML	suitability for machine learning
SOEs	state-owned enterprises
STAN	STructural ANalysis database (OECD)
STI	science, technology, and innovation
STPs	software technology parks
STRI	Services Trade Restrictiveness Index
TFP	total factor productivity
TFPQ	quantity TFP
TFPR	revenue TFP
TiSMoS	Trade in Services Data by Mode of Supply
TiVA	Trade in Value Added database (OECD)
UK	United Kingdom
UN	United Nations
UNCTAD	UN Conference on Trade and Development
UNIDO	United Nations Industrial Development Organization
US	United States
VA	value added
WMS	World Management Survey
WTO	World Trade Organization

1 Of Goods and Services: Inside the Black Box

Introduction

Some of the biggest development gains in history have been associated with industrialization.[1] Those economies that led the Industrial Revolution are now among the richest in the world. More recently, the "economic takeoff" circa 1960 that resulted in East Asia's growth miracle coincided with the rapid growth of the manufacturing sector, reinforcing the development community's attention on the manufacturing export-led development model. The few countries that have reached high income levels without developing a manufacturing base have done so through either natural resource extraction or the exploitation of specific locational or other advantages.

At the same time, conventional wisdom has held that the services sector contributes little to productivity growth. For classical economists such as Adam Smith (1776), services were products of labor that perished the moment the labor was performed, seldom leaving any trace or quantifiable value behind, and thereby amounted to unproductive economic activities. Similarly, the Marxist-Leninist theory of social production considered most services as nonmaterial production and hence unproductive (Lequiller and Blades 2014).

An Unconventional Structural Transformation

To the extent that economists' attention has historically focused on manufacturing, the past three decades of structural change in low- and middle-income countries (LMICs) do not conform to the pattern established by now-industrialized economies. The literature on structural change during the 1960s documented canonical shifts of output and labor—first from agriculture to industry and later from industry to services—in the structural transformation of today's high-income countries (Kaldor 1967; Kuznets 1971). Since the 1980s, however, the peak shares of manufacturing in value added and employment across a range of low- and middle-income economies were both lower and occurred at lower levels of per capita income than in their high-income, early-industrializer precursors (Rodrik 2016).

In most countries, this phenomenon largely reflects the faster growth of services relative to manufacturing. Those worried about "premature deindustrialization" have called on governments and the development community to support efforts to expand manufacturing in lower-income countries. Beyond whether this is feasible, however, an important question is whether it is especially desirable.

Evidence suggests that manufacturing-led development in the past delivered the twin gains of productivity growth and large-scale job creation for the relatively unskilled. Underlying these were economies of scale, access to international markets, innovation, and supply chain linkages with other sectors, combined with the ability to leverage relatively unskilled labor with capital. Although services are labor intensive, they often require simultaneous production and consumption that precludes accessing larger markets. Their more limited ability to use capital to improve labor productivity also limits both scale economies and incentives to innovate. Conventional wisdom is therefore pessimistic about the prospects for services-led development.

This book seeks to test that conventional wisdom. To that end, there are two guiding questions. The first concerns whether the services sector has the potential to expand opportunities for poor people within LMICs and whether these jobs can raise their productivity over time. Much of the discussion here focuses on the opportunities to create jobs for low-skilled workers.[2]

The second question is the extent to which the services sector can help lower-income countries catch up with the productivity and wealth of higher-income countries. Much of the discussion here focuses on the opportunities for productivity growth.

The prospect for services-led development invites a comparison with manufacturing, but that comparison must take a dynamic perspective. Comparison of productivity and jobs across sectors is an important starting point, but *growth*—and how the prospects for future growth are changing—is also important. This is especially true given that the landscape for manufacturing-led growth today is different from what it was several decades ago. To begin with, that several countries, most notably China, have reached significant scale can make it harder for new countries to break into global markets and match the leading countries' efficiency. Second, greater industrial robotization in high-income countries is reducing the importance of low labor costs in determining competitiveness.

These trends may potentially narrow the paths for lower-income countries to industrialize, especially when the splintering of production in global value chains (GVCs) means there is far more competition for locations to attract manufacturing activity. A more detailed discussion of the shifting prospects for manufacturing-led development is provided in the companion book, *Trouble in the Making? The Future of Manufacturing-Led Development* (Hallward-Driemeier and Nayyar 2018).

This book contributes to the literature on services-led development in five ways:

- It meaningfully categorizes the services sector based on the same features that have characterized the manufacturing-led development model: scale, innovation, spillovers, and job creation for low-skilled labor.

- It compiles and analyzes firm-level data from 20 low- and middle-income economies to generate a new set of stylized facts on firm growth and productivity across these categories in the services sector. Given a historical paucity of firm censuses and surveys relative to the manufacturing sector, this makes an important contribution to the evidence base.[3] While helping to fill this gap, the book also proposes ways to improve data collection on services firms for further research.

- It provides new insights on how digital technologies are changing some of the underlying characteristics of services—such as their reliance on physical proximity for delivery and their limited ability to combine labor with technology and capital—and how these changes can expand their potential for scale, innovation, and job creation.

- It questions assumptions about the traditional linear path for structural transformation (particularly as the line between manufacturing and services becomes increasingly blurred) and examines the potential for growth opportunities in the services sector without having to rely on a manufacturing base.

- It provides a framework for countries to identify policy priorities that can help leverage the potential of the services sector for jobs and economic transformation.

The rest of chapter 1 examines the extent to which the services sector has contributed to economic inclusion within and across countries. Importantly, the sector is not monolithic, and its ability to provide meaningful economic transformation depends on whether the services subsectors that are expanding have the potential to achieve scale economies, innovation, and positive spillovers. It proceeds as follows:

- The next section establishes some aggregate stylized facts that highlight how the services sector has driven both job creation and catch-up in productivity growth across LMICs since the mid-1990s.

- The chapter then considers a framework for revisiting the "uniqueness" of manufacturing by analyzing the longer-term potential of services-led structural transformation. It explores the sector's potential to achieve scale, innovation, and spillovers as well as create jobs for low-skilled workers—characteristics previously considered unique to the manufacturing sector.

- A subsequent discussion of the heterogeneity of services regarding these characteristics demonstrates that the sector is anything but monolithic.
- After discussing the implications of services-led growth for economic inclusion in lower-income countries, the chapter concludes with a summary of these findings and highlights the key issues to be analyzed in subsequent chapters.

Chapter 2, "Productivity and Jobs in Services: Mind the Gaps," analyzes the underlying firm dynamics to show that although some services subsectors have higher productivity than manufacturing on average, those that have contributed to job creation in LMICs have experienced limited productivity growth.

Chapters 3 and 4—"Will Technology Make the Twain Meet? A Changing Productivity-Jobs Dichotomy in Services" and "Services Before Manufacturing? Look Before You Leap"—take a more forward-looking perspective at how technology and intersectoral linkages, respectively, are shifting the potential for services-led development. They particularly examine changes in the dichotomy between productivity growth and job creation across different services subsectors.

Chapter 5, "Boosting Productivity to Keep Up the Good Work: Policy Imperatives," develops a policy framework that emphasizes trade, technology, training, and targeting (the 4Ts) to leverage the ability of the services sector to achieve greater scale economies, raise the productivity of labor through innovation, and take advantage of greater spillovers through linkages.

Chapter 6, "Conclusion: In the Service of Development?" summarizes the book's main takeaways and outlines a future data agenda to strengthen the evidence base that can further inform the prospects of services-led development.

As these chapters establish, services that are already highly productive—such as information and communication technology (ICT) and professional services—stand to benefit more than others from technological changes. And although some of the least productive services (such as accommodation and food, retail, and personal services) can use digital tools to expand access to more consumers, they are less able than highly productive services to innovate in service delivery. On the one hand, this disparity risks raising income inequality. On the other hand, services benefiting the most from scale and innovation are those characterized by the highest linkages with other sectors.

Therefore, although raising skills makes more workers eligible to work in higher-productivity services, the spillovers and rising demand as incomes rise should still benefit less-skilled or poorer workers. For policy makers in LMICs, it should not be a question of whether to support manufacturing *or* services but a recognition that the potential for services to contribute to productivity and jobs is growing—and they should act to take advantage of it.

Services, Jobs, and Economic Transformation

Economic development has been historically associated with structural changes in national economies. The pioneering work of Fisher (1935), Clark (1940), Chenery (1960), and Kuznets (1971) postulates a set of stylized facts from empirical evidence relating to the now-industrialized countries. They suggest that in the early stages of economic development, the agriculture sector's share in both output and employment is overwhelmingly large. Subsequently, as industrialization proceeds, the agriculture sector's share falls, and the industrial sector's share rises. Once countries have industrialized and reached an advanced stage of economic development, the industrial sector's share declines, and the services sector's share increases.

However, recent trends in structural transformation in LMICs show they are not following the same path of industrialization that most of today's high-income countries did when they developed and achieved their high-income status. A key question is what to make of the shares of manufacturing in employment and value added in hitherto less industrialized countries having peaked at lower levels and at lower per capita gross domestic product (GDP) than what occurred in the past in the now-industrialized countries (Dasgupta and Singh 2007; Rodrik 2016).[4]

The resulting concerns about "premature deindustrialization" focus on seemingly truncated manufacturing growth in LMICs. Does it simply reflect the faster growth of services, which have absorbed a larger share of the workforce? And what does it mean for overall productivity growth?

Structural Transformation and Job Creation

For almost 30 years (from 1991 to 2018), the industrial sector's share of total employment across LMICs remained almost unchanged, averaging 20 percent.[5] As a result, the increase in the services sector's share of total employment, from 40 percent to 50 percent, offset almost the entire decline in the agriculture sector's share (figure 1.1, panel a).

Similar trends held true for the changing sectoral shares of GDP. In fact, the share of industry in GDP marginally declined, on average, across LMICs from 33 percent in 1991 to 30 percent in 2018 (figure 1.1, panel b). This implies that the services sector, whose share of GDP increased from 49 percent in 1991 to 59 percent in 2018, offset the entire decline in the GDP shares of the agriculture and industrial sectors over this period. It is not that the industrial sector shrank; it is that the services sector grew relatively faster.

This pattern of structural change was consistent across regions as well. The share of industry in total employment between 1995 and 2018 increased marginally among LMICs in East Asia, South Asia, and the Middle East and North Africa; declined marginally in Eastern Europe and Central Asia as well as in Latin America and the Caribbean; and remained almost constant in Sub-Saharan Africa (figure 1.2, panel a).

Much of the Decline in Agriculture's Share of Employment and GDP in LMICs since the 1990s Has Been Offset by Services

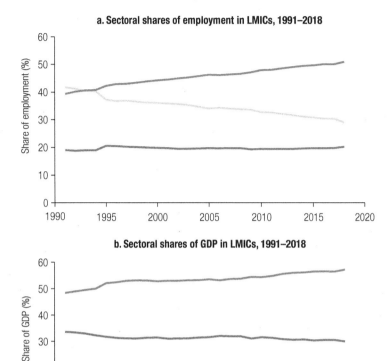

a. Sectoral shares of employment in LMICs, 1991–2018

b. Sectoral shares of GDP in LMICs, 1991–2018

Services ⸺⸺⸺ Agriculture ⸺⸺⸺ Industry

Source: World Development Indicators database.

Note: Data for the "industry" sector include not only manufacturing but also mining, utilities, and construction. "Low- and middle-income countries" (LMICs), by World Bank income group classifications, had 1994 gross national income (GNI) of less than US$8,955.

Similarly, the share of industry in GDP between 1995 and 2018 increased marginally among LMICs in East Asia and South Asia, but it declined marginally in Eastern Europe and Central Asia, Latin America and the Caribbean, the Middle East and North Africa, and Sub-Saharan Africa (figure 1.2, panel b).

The share of agriculture in GDP and employment declined in every region—a decline offset almost entirely by the services sector's increasing share over the past three decades.

Labor Productivity Growth

Labor productivity in services still lags that of industry across LMICs, on average, but the productivity differential between the industrial and services sectors has shrunk since

At Your Service? The Promise of Services-Led Development

FIGURE 1.2 **Consistently across Regions, Services Have Offset Much of Agriculture's Decline in Share of Employment and GDP in LMICs since the 1990s**

a. Sectoral shares of employment in LMICs, by region and relative to high-income countries, 1995 and 2018

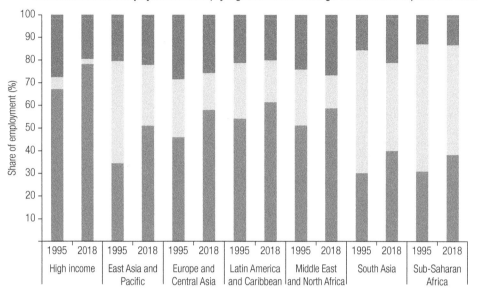

b. Sectoral shares of GDP in LMICs, by region and relative to high-income countries, 1995 and 2018

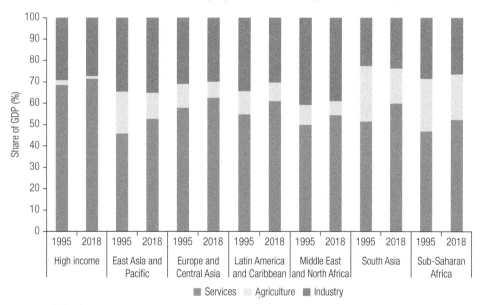

■ Services ▨ Agriculture ■ Industry

Source: World Development Indicators database.

Note: Data for the "industry" sector include not only manufacturing but also mining, utilities, and construction. "Low- and middle-income countries" (LMICs), by World Bank income group classifications, had 1994 gross national income (GNI) of less than US$8,955. "High-income countries" had GNI exceeding US$8,955 in 1994.

FIGURE 1.3 **Labor Productivity in Services Has Increased Consistently in LMICs since the 1990s**

Value added per worker in LMICs, by sector, 1991–2018

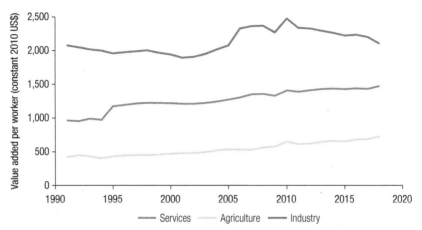

Source: World Development Indicators database.

Note: Data for the "industry" sector include not only manufacturing but also mining, utilities, and construction. "Low- and middle-income countries" (LMICs), by World Bank income group classifications, had 1994 gross national income (GNI) of less than US$8,955.

the 1990s. Although the average value added per worker in the services sector consistently increased across LMICs between 1991 and 2018, industrial labor productivity was more volatile, sharply declining after the 2008–09 Global Financial Crisis (figure 1.3).[6]

In fact, among LMICs between 1995 and 2018, only those in the East Asia and Pacific region as well as Eastern Europe and Central Asia—on average—matched the experience of high-income countries in that their industrial labor productivity growth exceeded that of services.[7] In contrast, labor productivity growth in the services and industrial sectors across South Asia, Sub-Saharan Africa, the Middle East and North Africa, and Latin America and the Caribbean was roughly comparable over the same period (figure 1.4).

These regional differences are not surprising given that export-led manufacturing has been the cornerstone of economic growth in East Asia since 1990—especially in China, whose share of global manufacturing value added increased fivefold, from less than 5 percent in 1990 to 25 percent in 2015 (Hallward-Driemeier and Nayyar 2018). Similarly, the offshoring of labor-intensive production from Western European countries benefited manufacturers in the Czech Republic, Hungary, and Poland. However, countries in Sub-Saharan Africa never broke into manufacturing production to a significant extent, while many Latin American and South Asian countries saw progress stall after a transitory pickup of economic growth.

What is also striking is that labor productivity growth in services in LMICs across all regions between 1995 and 2018—except in the Middle East and North Africa—exceeded that of high-income countries (figure 1.4). These narrowing productivity

At Your Service? The Promise of Services-Led Development

FIGURE 1.4 **Labor Productivity Growth in Services Has Matched That in Industry across LMICs in Many Regions since the 1990s, Typically Exceeding That of HICs**

Growth in value added per worker in LMICs, by broad sector and relative to high-income countries, 1995–2018

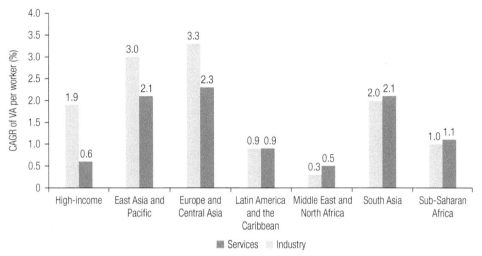

Source: Calculations based on World Development Indicators database.

Note: Value-added (VA) data are in constant prices. "Low- and middle-income countries" (LMICs), by World Bank income group classifications, had 1994 gross national income (GNI) of less than US$8,955. "High-income countries" (HICs) had GNI exceeding US$8,955 in 1994. Data for the "industry" sector include not only manufacturing but also mining, utilities, and construction. CAGR = compound annual growth rate.

gaps are encouraging evidence that services growth can contribute to lower-income countries' ability to catch up. There is, in fact, evidence of unconditional convergence of productivity to the frontier: countries starting from lower labor productivity in the services sector grew faster between 1975 and 2012 than those with higher initial labor productivity in that sector (Enache, Ghani, and O'Connell 2016; Kinfemichael and Morshed 2019).

Of course, countries vary in the extent to which they are benefiting. Chapter 5 examines some of the policy choices that can help expand opportunities for services.

Contributions to Overall Productivity Growth

The question, then, is the extent to which these sectoral productivity and structural change patterns have affected overall labor productivity. An economy can increase labor productivity either through productivity growth within sectors or through labor movement from low-productivity to high-productivity sectors. The former "within" effect is scaled by the sectors' importance in overall employment at the beginning of the period under consideration, while the latter "between" effect is scaled by the sectors' productivity at the end of this period (McMillan and Rodrik 2011).

Contribution of Within-Sector Change

Looking at three broad sectors—agriculture, industry, and services—across a large cross-section of LMICs between 1995 and 2018, we find that within-sector increases explain at least two-thirds of labor productivity growth, on average, in every region of the world (figure 1.5).[8] This finding reinforces other evidence that highlights opportunities to enhance productivity growth within sectors. For example, Herrendorf, Rogerson, and Valentinyi (2013) show that, for most high-income and transition economies, productivity growth has largely occurred within sectors. McMillan, Rodrik, and Verduzco-Gallo (2014) also support this finding, concluding that growth accelerations in Latin American, Asian, and Sub-Saharan African countries were based on rapid within-sector labor productivity growth.

Strikingly, except in East Asia and the Pacific, productivity growth within the services sector contributes more than productivity growth within industry to aggregate productivity growth. In South Asia, the percentage contribution of productivity increases within the services sector (34 percent) was more than double that of industry. Similarly, in Sub-Saharan Africa, the percentage contribution of productivity increases within the services sector (33 percent) was four times that of industry (figure 1.5). This is not entirely surprising because, despite higher rates of industrial labor productivity

FIGURE 1.5 **Among LMICs in Most Regions, Services Have Contributed More Than Industry to Aggregate Labor Productivity Growth since the 1990s**

Decomposition of aggregate productivity growth "within" and "between" sectors in LMICs, by region and relative to high-income countries, 1995–2018

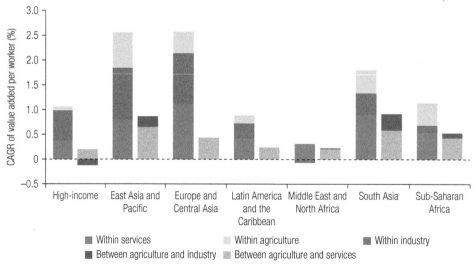

Source: Calculations based on World Development Indicators database.

Note: Data for the "industry" sector include not only manufacturing but also mining and construction. "Low- and middle-income countries" (LMICs), by World Bank income group classifications, had 1994 gross national income (GNI) of less than US$8,955. "High-income countries" had GNI exceeding US$8,955 in 1994. CAGR = compound annual growth rate. For the underlying methodology of the decomposition analysis, see annex 1B.

growth, its contribution to overall productivity growth is stunted by its low share in total employment across regions at the beginning of the period (in 1995).

Contribution of Between-Sector Change

As a corollary, structural change across LMICs between 1995 and 2018, on average, contributed no more than one-third to overall labor productivity growth in any region (figure 1.5). Its contribution ranged from 14 percent in Eastern Europe and Central Asia and 19 percent in Latin America and the Caribbean to 25 percent in East Asia and the Pacific, 32 percent in Sub-Saharan Africa, and 34 percent in South Asia.[9] This positive but relatively small contribution of structural change reinforces the findings of McMillan, Rodrik, and Verduzco-Gallo (2014)—that overall productivity accelerations in several regions were based on rapid within-sector productivity growth—although the magnitude of the contributions shown here is somewhat larger.

We further disaggregate this "between" component to distinguish between the movement of labor in and out of industry and services.[10] Although the literature has emphasized structural transformation from agriculture to manufacturing as the central dynamic to understanding productivity growth in LMICs, we find that the increasing share of services in total employment accounts for the bulk of the contribution of structural change in each region (figure 1.5).

This finding reinforces evidence from recent case studies showing that when productivity-enhancing structural change kicked in during the 2000s in Sub-Saharan Africa (specifically in Botswana, Ghana, Nigeria, and Zambia), the bulk of this contribution was accounted for by the movement of labor from agriculture into services (McMillan, Rodrik, and Sepúlveda 2017). In fact, the contribution of structural transformation from agriculture into industry to overall labor productivity growth was close to zero in Eastern Europe and Central Asia and even negative in Latin America and the Caribbean (figure 1.5). This is not surprising given the patterns of structural change described earlier. Despite positive productivity growth within industry in these regions, there was a negligible increase or even a decline in industry's share of employment.

This implies two things: First, industry has played a special, dominant role in East Asia (and to a smaller extent in Eastern Europe), whereas LMICs in other regions, on average, have not benefited as much from industry as a central driver of their development. Second, it is not the case that industry inherently outperforms services. For many LMICs, therefore, the choice between manufacturing- and services-led development is not of dire importance. The data show that services can deliver productivity growth—in several cases, growth that is *higher* than that of industry. What matters for the longer-term potential of services-led development is whether the features of industrialization that have enabled scale, innovation, and spillovers along with job creation for unskilled labor—as in East Asia—are increasingly shared by the services sector.

Scale, Innovation, Spillovers, and Job Creation: Revisiting the "Uniqueness" of Manufacturing

The patterns presented in the previous section show that industry's share of output and employment across LMICs since 1990 has stagnated and that the industrial and services sectors have experienced comparable productivity growth. Does this imply that the countries that have not yet industrialized will be unable to replicate East Asia's success in manufacturing-led development?

This question risks misplacing the emphasis of what is important. It is not necessarily the production of "goods" or "services" per se that matters but *how* these are produced. Expanding a sector with potential for growth or for positive spillovers does not necessarily imply that the growth or spillovers will automatically occur (Baldwin 1969; De Ferranti et al. 2002; Lederman and Maloney 2010; Rodríguez-Clare 2007). Countries have expanded manufacturing production but without significant contributions to productivity or longer-term growth, as in the case of Latin America's import substitution efforts (further discussed below). So, what made manufacturing special in the case of East Asia? And does the services sector have similar underlying features?

Key Features of Manufacturing

Manufacturing-led development, particularly as exemplified by East Asia's success in export-led growth, has highlighted how a sector's key characteristics shape its potential to drive development. The experience with manufacturing underscores the sector's contributions from (a) access to larger markets; (b) the scope to augment labor with capital and technology; and (c) linkages with other sectors—that is, the contributions of *economies of scale*, *innovation*, and *spillovers*.

"Kaldor's growth laws," based on data from present-day high-income economies in the 1960s, reflect these contributions of innovation, scale, and spillovers in delineating the manufacturing sector as the main engine of growth for an economy (Kaldor 1966). These laws document three positive associations: (a) between growth of manufacturing output and *average GDP growth* (explained via a transfer of surplus labor from agriculture to manufacturing, where it can be combined with capital and technology); (b) between growth of manufacturing output and *manufacturing productivity* (attributable to static and dynamic economies of scale); and (c) between growth of manufacturing output and *overall productivity* of the economy (owing to spillover effects).

Based on data from LMICs between 1995 and 2018, Kaldor's three growth laws remain valid for the broad industrial sector.[11] These dynamics, as further described below, have led to productivity growth and substantial job creation for unskilled workers.

Economies of scale. Manufactured goods are storable and transferable, so that production can be separated from consumption. This enabled the manufacturing sector to achieve enormous gains from *scale*, particularly when goods were traded and thus able to access demand beyond the domestic market. Although the agriculture sector was also traded, it typically faced price volatility in international markets.

Demand-side dynamics also underlie the global expansion of markets for manufactured goods (Szirmai 2012): as per capita incomes rise, the share of agricultural products in total expenditure declines, while the share of manufactured goods increases in accordance with a hierarchy of needs (Engel's law). The production of tradable manufactured goods facilitates scale economies, technology diffusion, and greater competition which, in turn, underlie the "catch-up" that labor productivity in (formal) manufacturing exhibits across countries (Rodrik 2012).[12]

Innovation. The movement of surplus labor from (rural) agriculture to (urban) manufacturing and capital accumulation in the latter (Lewis 1954) was integral to *innovation* dynamics in the manufacturing-led development model. Much of the innovation was focused on improving and deepening capital investment—most of which raises labor productivity (although automation can serve to replace labor, too, beyond a threshold) while also providing the benefits of scale economies.

This innovation through labor-augmenting capital accumulation is reflected in large, systematic differences in labor productivity between the agriculture and manufacturing sectors, and these intersectoral labor productivity gaps are wider in the poorest countries (Caselli 2006; Herrendorf, Rogerson, and Valentinyi 2013; Restuccia, Yang, and Zhu 2008).[13]

Spillovers. Linkages between manufacturing subsectors also helped expand the productivity and growth dynamics of manufacturing through *spillovers*—for example, from basic metals to machinery and equipment—whereby manufactured goods could in turn help make more, and more sophisticated, goods.

Job creation. The production process in the manufacturing sector has therefore typically absorbed large numbers of relatively unskilled workers from agriculture at a substantial productivity premium and subsequently placed that labor on a productivity path that rises up to the global frontier (Rodrik 2012) owing to opportunities for scale, innovation, and spillovers.

However, the contrast between the industrialization experiences in East Asia and Latin America is important here. Labor-intensive, export-oriented industrialization in East Asia integrated the countries with world markets, enabling them to achieve scale, face competition, and acquire foreign technology while creating jobs for unskilled labor. In contrast, import substitution industrialization in Latin American countries—an inward-oriented strategy in the mid-twentieth century that used trade barriers to strengthen local producers and often employed capital-intensive techniques that did not conform with a country's comparative advantage—did not deliver similar growth benefits (Gereffi and Wyman 2014).

The simultaneity of consumption and production, the intrinsic role of labor, and limited linkages to other activities have typically affected the services sector's potential for scale, innovation, and spillovers. These salient characteristics that distinguished services from manufactured goods have thus traditionally led many to question the sector's potential to lead productivity growth and enable LMICs to catch up, especially when compared with manufacturing. However, the advent of digital technologies and increased tradability suggests that this potential has been changing.

Analog Services (Pre-ICT Era)

The "simultaneity of production and consumption" and "nonstorability and perishability" that traditionally characterized services emphasized the physical proximity between producers and consumers (Griliches 1992; Hill 1977). This importance of face-to-face interactions, in turn, constrained service providers from achieving scale by accessing demand beyond the local market, including through international trade. This meant that producers in lower-income countries could not exploit the rising demand for services in higher-income countries.[14] Unlike goods, the consumption of services could not be detached from their production because they cannot be stored.[15]

Subsequent to this early conceptualization, however, many studies have highlighted the restrictiveness of this definition with a view that not all services are same. For instance, many "noncontact" services allow for the separation of production and consumption across space (Bhagwati 1984; Kohn 1989). Similarly, that services cannot be put into stock may have little to do with their physical durability; many services such as education are not only permanent but also irreversible (Hill 1977).

Early characterizations of the services sector also outlined the "intrinsic role of labor" as a constraint to labor-augmenting capital accumulation and technology adoption. Baumol (1967) argued that the productivity of many services sector activities cannot be readily increased through capital accumulation, innovation, or economies of scale because of their relatively labor-intensive nature: whereas labor was simply an incidental requisite for the attainment of the final product in manufacturing, it was an important end in itself for services.

Baumol's classic example of this is that although it took a string quartet exactly the same amount of time to play a piece in 1965 as it did when Mozart wrote it in 1865, musicians in 1965 made a lot more money than musicians in 1865. Rising worker productivity in the manufacturing sector allowed factories to cut prices and raise wages at the same time. But when wages rise, live music venues have no alternative but to raise ticket prices to cover the higher costs of labor-intensive orchestra performances.[16]

The increasing share of services in total output may therefore be attributable to the increasing relative prices of services.

This argument became known as Baumol's "cost disease" hypothesis and had implications far beyond the arts. It implies that in a world of rapid technological progress, we should expect the cost of manufactured goods (cars, smartphones, T-shirts, bananas, and so forth) to fall and the cost of labor-intensive services (schooling, health care, childcare, haircuts, legal services, and so forth) to rise.

Last but not least, the potential role of providing spillovers—defined as the multiplier effects of linkages across sectors—applied to only a limited number of services (such as transportation and distribution) that were closely linked to the production of agricultural commodities and manufactured goods. This point abstracts from a larger literature on spillovers that looks at broader sources of externalities and market failures that have often resulted in the public provision of many services, such as telecommunications, finance, education, and health care.[17]

Digitally Enhanced Services

The features of manufacturing that were once considered uniquely special for productivity growth might be increasingly shared by some service sectors, especially given the advent of ICT (table 1.1). There is now greater scope for services firms to achieve efficiency gains through scale, labor-augmenting innovation, and backward or forward linkages with other sectors.

Gaining scale through access to international markets. Digital electronic content has made services more storable, codifiable, and transferable, which in turn has meant that physical proximity between consumers and producers no longer constrains the scaling-up of many services-related transactions—telephone and online banking, computer programming, and education services being cases in point (Ghani and Kharas 2010). Freund and Weinhold (2002) provided the earliest assessment of this relationship between digital technologies and scale in services, finding that the growth in US service exports and imports increased by 1.1 percentage points as internet penetration in a partner country increased by 10 percent.

Many services now have trade costs comparable to manufacturing industries (Gervais and Jensen 2019). In fact, compound annual growth in world exports has been higher in services than in manufacturing since 2000, with the highest rates in modern, more digitally enabled, services (Loungani et al. 2017).

Accumulating capital and adopting technologies for labor-augmenting innovation. Capital accumulation that augments labor is not uncommon to transportation and telecommunications services. Take the example of data centers, which require high levels of fixed assets and for which costs rapidly decrease with scale (Fontagné, Mohnen, and Wolff 2014).

TABLE 1.1 **Key Characteristics of Services Have Distinguished Them from Manufactured Goods in Their Implications for Productivity and Jobs, but These Are Changing with the Advent of Digital Technologies**

Sectors' key characteristics and their implications for productivity and jobs

Sectors and effects		Market size and location (What is produced and for whom?)	Ability to leverage labor with capital and technology (How do firms operate?)	Linkages (With whom do firms operate?)
Key characteristics	Manufacturing	Storable, transferable, tradable goods so production can be separated from consumption	Amenable to mechanization	Inputs into other manufactured goods
	Analog services (pre-ICT)	Simultaneity of production and consumption	Inherent role for labor	Important enablers for goods-producing sectors
	Digitally enhanced services	Reduced need for proximity	Labor-augmenting potential	Expanded roles for economywide enabling services
Implications	Productivity	Scale	Innovation	Spillovers
	Jobs (number, skill mix)	Number of jobs	Skill mix demanded	Multipliers that boost job creation and skill mix

Source: Summary based on chapter 1.

Note: Arrows indicate which of the three key characteristics contribute to scale, innovation, and spillovers. ICT = information and communication technology.

Firms in the services sector are also innovating more than before. The increase in research and development (R&D) since the 1990s has been largely concentrated within ICT multinationals through software patents (Branstetter, Glennon, and Jensen 2018). When innovation is defined to take forms other than R&D—including management techniques, organizational practices, marketing procedures, and adoption of existing technologies—the share of innovating firms is relatively similar across manufacturing and services in most countries (Pires, Sarkar, and Carvalho 2008). Based on data from six LMICs, Nayyar, Cruz, and Zhu (2018) classify both information technology (IT) services and the manufacture of electronics as "high" in their extent of product and process innovation.[18] The diffusion of ICT and related intangible capital is also expanding the ability of services firms to innovate (as further discussed in chapter 3).

Spillovers from growing linkages with other sectors. The share of services in world gross exports has remained about 20 percent since 1980. In terms of value added, however, services accounted for 43 percent of world exports in 2009, rising from 31 percent in 1980. In fact, more than two-thirds of the growth in services value added in exports between 1995 and 2011 was due to an increase in services embodied in other exports

(Heuser and Mattoo 2017). This suggests that services such as transportation, telecommunications, finance, and business services are increasingly used as intermediate inputs in the production and export of goods.

In France, Germany, Italy, the United Kingdom, and the United States, services contribute more than half the total value added embodied as inputs in exports. Even in China, traditionally viewed as an exporter of manufactures, more than a third of the value added in its exports comes from services (World Bank 2020). Furthermore, evidence indicates that services embodied as inputs improve the productivity of downstream manufacturing (as discussed in chapter 4).

The Question of Jobs in Services

The extent to which the manufacturing sector combined scale, innovation, and spillovers with employment, especially for low-skilled workers, was also central to its potential advantages for development. However, the services sector's emphasis on human capital might constrain the ability of dynamic services to absorb surplus labor from agriculture. It is easier to turn a rice farmer into a garment factory worker than a software engineer, entailing a manageable investment in physical capital but without significant investment in human capital. This limitation raises the concern that, unlike manufacturing, a given services subsector might not deliver the twin gains of productivity growth and job creation together.

The counterfactual scenario—the job-creation prospects for manufacturing export-led development—must also take a dynamic view. The nature of international competition and sources of comparative advantage are changing. Established centers of manufacturing, characterized by dense ecosystems of suppliers and rising industrial automation, are raising the bar in terms of what it will take for hitherto less-industrialized countries to enter GVCs (Hallward-Driemeier and Nayyar 2018). Therefore, LMICs stand to lose considerable potential for generating low-skilled manufacturing jobs as high-income countries adopt new technologies and keep more manufacturing within their own borders.

Alternatively, if the only way LMICs can compete in global manufacturing is by adopting quality-enhancing and labor-saving processes, that, too, will eliminate potential jobs. Rodrik (2014) argues that employment deindustrialization is virtually inevitable in middle-income countries as well. Similarly, Stiglitz (2018) argues that the declining share of manufacturing in global employment means that the sector's growth will not suffice to meet the needs for new jobs, especially in Sub-Saharan Africa with its burgeoning population.

In sum, although manufacturing will likely continue to deliver on productivity, scale, trade, and innovation, its unique desirability in terms of the twin wins of productivity and large-scale job creation for low-skilled labor is eroding.

The growth and productivity benefits associated with scale, innovation (mechanization that augments low-skilled labor), spillovers across sectors, and low skill intensity can be summarized in the combination of six indicators of these pro-development characteristics—which can, in turn, be used to categorize services subsectors:

- *Trade intensity:* The share of a sector's value added that is exported[19] indicates the potential to access larger markets.[20]

- *Offshorability:* Services are traded through different modes that either enable remote cross-border transactions or require that producers or consumers travel to a joint location (box 1.1). Whether a sector is amenable to offshoring through cross-border transactions is indicative of additional opportunities to achieve scale because it eliminates the need for physical proximity between consumers and producers. Survey-based estimates of such "offshorability" are based on the prevalence of tasks that require such face-to-face interactions.

- *R&D intensity:* The share of businesses' R&D expenditure in value added indicates their investment in the expansion of knowledge, technology, and productivity.

- *Capital intensity:* Measured as gross capital stock per worker, *capital intensity* combines with *R&D intensity* to proxy the scope for innovation and for contributing to scale economies by leveraging labor's contributions.

- *Linkages:* A sector's linkages, measured as the share of its output from (domestic) sales to other sectors in the economy, indicates the scope for spillovers.

- *Low skill intensity:* The share of low-skilled workers in a sector's employment (based on occupation-level data) reflects its skill bias or the lack thereof.

These measures are quantified using data from European Union (EU-15) countries[21] and the United States—high-income countries that are at more advanced stages of structural transformation than LMICs and where there are fewer policy distortions. The aim is to show the upside potential for scale, innovation, and linkages, since these countries have more-sophisticated services sectors that are more traded internationally; are home to firms where much of the business R&D takes place; and are characterized by stronger, more numerous linkages between sectors, owing to diversified production structures. As for skill intensity, these high-income countries provide a lower bound; if a sector's jobs are predominantly filled by unskilled workers in the United States, they are almost certainly likely to be intensive in low-skilled labor in lower-income countries.[22]

Table 1.2 illustrates the differences between agriculture, manufacturing, and services in terms of these pro-development characteristics, as commonly perceived. The manufacturing sector stands out in its absorption of unskilled labor combined with its trade intensity in international markets, R&D intensity, capital intensity, and linkages with other sectors. The services sector has lower levels of capital intensity and R&D intensity, is less traded internationally, is more skill-biased, and has fewer linkages with other sectors.

BOX 1.1

Trade in Services: A Tale of Four Modes

Trade in services can assume many forms, including international transactions as varied as a consumer buying a foreign movie to watch on a computer, a shipping company transporting goods over the sea, a tourist buying a meal abroad, a supermarket chain selling products through a foreign branch, or a management consultant advising a customer abroad. The most common classification of services trade is the one applied in the World Trade Organization (WTO) treaty, the General Agreement on Trade in Services (GATS), which breaks down services trade into four "modes":

- *Mode 1: Cross-border supply.* A provider delivers these services to a customer in another country without any movement of persons or commercial presence. This mode includes digital delivery to a customer abroad.
- *Mode 2: Consumption abroad.* The customer obtains services after traveling to the provider's country. This mode includes services provided to foreign tourists as well as for medical tourism and students studying abroad.
- *Mode 3: Commercial presence.* These are services provided through commercial presence in the consumer's country, such as through foreign direct investment (FDI) that establishes a local subsidiary or affiliate company.
- *Mode 4: Movement of natural persons.* Under this mode, service delivery involves the travel of a service provider (an employee or the business owner) to the consumer's country.

Because of their intangible nature, services trade volumes can be hard to measure. Statistics usually rely on balance of payments (covering modes 1, 2, and 4) and FDI (covering mode 3) data that have been compiled from firm surveys, bank transactions, and administrative records. However, data availability and collection practices vary between countries. Furthermore, trade statistics usually follow GATS definitions. For example, mode 4 statistics usually follow the narrow view of what counts as "movement of persons" (mode 4) trade in services, excluding most forms of employment abroad and out-migration. The challenges in measuring trade in services are further explored in "Spotlight: Bringing Services to the Surface: The Measurement Challenge," following chapter 2.

Based on an experimental dataset—Trade in Services Data by Mode of Supply (TiSMoS)[a]—the WTO estimates that across countries and sectors, on average, the dominant mode of services trade is commercial presence (mode 3), which accounted for 59 percent of world services trade in 2017 (WTO 2019). The corresponding shares of other modes were 28 percent for cross-border supply (mode 1), 10 percent for consumption abroad (mode 2), and 3 percent for movement of natural persons (mode 4).

a. TiSMoS is an experimental dataset produced by the WTO and funded by the Directorate-General for Trade of the European Commission.

The difference in trade intensity between the manufacturing and services sectors reflects the latter's physical proximity burden between producers and consumers, which results in disproportionately high trade costs (Anderson, Milot, and Yotov 2014; Fontagné, Guillin, and Mitaritonna 2011; Francois and Hoekman 2010; Gervais 2018; Miroudot, Sauvage, and Shepherd 2013). And even though the services sector experienced a cumulative decline in trade costs of about 9 percent between 2000 and 2017 (comparable to the manufacturing sector), it still accounted for only about 20 percent of cross-border trade in 2017 (WTO 2019).

TABLE 1.2 **The Scope for Scale, Innovation, Spillovers, and Low-Skill Jobs Has Been Lower in Services Than in Manufacturing**

Sectoral comparison of trade intensity, R&D intensity, capital intensity, intersectoral linkages, and low skill intensity in the United States and EU-15, circa 2015

Sector	Share of value added that is exported[a] (US 2015, %)	Share of offshorable jobs[b] (US, %)	R&D intensity[c] (EU-15 2017, share of value added, %)	Capital stock per worker[d] (EU-15 2017, constant 2015 US$, thousands)	Share of sales to other sectors[e] (EU-15 2015, %)	Share of low-skilled workers in total sector employment[f] (US 2018, %)
Agriculture	24.02	n.a.	0.43	505.3	58.86	91.81
Manufacturing	35.40	32.60	7.20	360.6	49.20	70.58
Services	7.04	29.20	0.85	207.5[g]	37.66	51.11

Sources: Blinder and Krueger 2013; OECD's TiVA, R&D Sources and Methods, and STAN databases; US Department of Labor's O*NET database.

Note: Sectors are defined by the three broad sectors in the International Standard Industrial Classification of All Economic Activities (ISIC) Rev. 4. EU-15 comprises the 15 pre-2004 European Union member states: Austria, Belgium, Denmark, Finland, France, Germany, Greece, Ireland, Italy, Luxembourg, the Netherlands, Portugal, Spain, Sweden, and the United Kingdom (which has since exited the EU). OECD = Organisation for Economic Co-operation and Development; R&D = research and development; n.a. = not applicable.

a. The share of value added that is exported—based on the OECD's Trade in Value-Added (TiVA) database—indicates a sector's trade intensity and therefore its potential to access larger markets.

b. A sector's percentage of offshorable jobs indicates its potential to achieve scale by reducing the need for physical proximity between consumers and producers. It is measured here by survey questions in Blinder and Krueger (2013) that assess the extent to which worker tasks (a) involve face-to-face contact with people other than coworkers; (b) can be done without being physically present; and (c) will experience a decline in quality if they can be delivered remotely.

c. R&D intensity—the share of businesses' R&D expenditure in value added, taken from the OECD's R&D Sources and Methods database—proxies the sector's scope for innovation.

d. Capital stock per worker—from the OECD's STructural ANalysis (STAN) database—measures a sector's "capital intensity," a proxy for contributing to scale economies and innovation by leveraging labor's contributions.

e. The share of sales to other sectors in a sector's output—taken from the OECD's STAN database—indicates the extent of its linkages within the economy and therefore its scope for positive spillovers.

f. The share of low-skilled workers in a sector's employment—measured by the share of workers in manual-task-intensive occupations among 23 major occupational groups in the US Department of Labor's Occupational Information Network (O*NET) database—reflects its skill intensity and hence its job creation potential for low-skilled or unskilled workers. The occupations identified as being manual-labor-intensive include community and social services; health care support; protective services; food preparation and serving; buildings and grounds cleaning; personal care; sales-related occupations; farming-related occupations; construction and extraction; installation, maintenance, and repair; production; transportation; and material moving.

g. Capital stock per worker in the services sector excludes the real estate subsector because the value of the buildings greatly skews the overall average.

That almost one-third of jobs in the services sector are offshorable shows that the diffusion of ICT has allowed firms to disentangle service delivery from consumption and to exploit labor cost differences between higher-income and lower-income countries (Blinder 2009). That the manufacturing sector has a similar share of offshorable jobs might reflect the substantial offshoring that had already taken place for manufacturing jobs in the United States by 2015, but not for services jobs.

The Services Sector Is Not Monolithic

In the literature on the subject so far, economists have treated the services sector as a black box, much as they long treated technology. They often see services as a residual after accounting for agricultural and industrial activity. Sometimes, services are also seen as a composite category that is diverse, yet homogenous enough for economic analysis. The resulting paucity of or imprecision in data collection has limited empirical analysis of the services sector (as further discussed in the "Spotlight" after chapter 2).

To the contrary, the services sector constitutes a highly heterogeneous category of economic activity with no uniform definition. Under the United Nations (UN) International Standard Industrial Classification of All Economic Activities (ISIC), the broad categories of services include, among others, wholesale and retail trade; accommodation and food; transportation, storage, and warehousing; information and communication technology (ICT) services; financial services; real estate; professional, scientific, and technical services; public administration and defense; education and research; health services; arts, entertainment, and recreational services; administrative and support services; and other social, community, and personal services (UN 1993; also see annex 1A). Mining; utilities such as electricity, gas, and water; and construction are typically classified within "industry," together with manufacturing.[23]

A Typology for the Services Sector

Unsurprisingly, therefore, the services sector is not monolithic, and its subsectors vary in the extent to which they combine the dimensions of scale, innovation, spillovers, and jobs for low-skilled labor. This space of intersecting trade intensity, offshorability, R&D intensity, capital intensity, linkages, and low skill intensity exhibits great heterogeneity and thus the potential for dynamic gains across services. It is not that any single subsector embodies all six dimensions; they combine varying degrees of different dimensions—which is why it is important to look at services in more disaggregated terms.

Services Subsectors: The Four Categories
On the basis of data from the EU-15 and the United States, 12 services subsectors (by ISIC Revision [Rev.] 4 one-digit classification) can be grouped into four categories based on the clustering of the six pro-development characteristics defined earlier (table 1.3). Within each characteristic, the subsectors are also grouped based on the

TABLE 1.3 **The Scope for Scale, Innovation, Spillovers, and Low-Skill Jobs Varies across Services Subsectors**

Services subsectors in the United States and EU-15, grouped by combination of trade intensity, offshorability, R&D intensity, capital intensity, intersectoral linkages, and low skill intensity

Subsectors, by category	ISIC Rev. 4 two-digit industry code	Share of value added that is exported[a] (US 2015, %)	Share of offshorable jobs[b] (US, %)	R&D intensity[c] (EU-15 2017, share of value added, %)	Capital stock per worker[d] (EU-15 2017, constant 2015 US$, thousands)	Share of sales to other sectors[e] (EU-15 2015, %)	Share of low-skilled workers in total sector employment[f] (US 2018, %)
Global innovator services							
Professional, scientific, and technical services	69–75	12.09	57.4	5.3	119.9	72.0	10.8
Information and communication	58–63	9.37	53.6	4.5	380.8	45.8	28.6
Finance and insurance	64–66	10.33	58.2	1.7	290.7	62.8	16.1
Low-skill tradable services							
Transportation and storage	49–53	22.15	22.9	0.3	563.1	42.5	69.3
Wholesale trade	45–46	22.0	20.8	0.8	173.2	54.7	59.2
Accommodation and food	55–56	11.12	3.4	0.1	95.7	20.4	93.4
Skill-intensive social services							
Education	85	2.69	14.1	0.1	227.3	2.3	16.6
Health	86–88	0.23	19.8	0.1	117.3	25.7	43.9
Low-skill domestic services							
Retail trade	47	0.41	20.8	0.8	89.5	28.4	74.5
Administrative and support	77–82	0.01	20.0	0.0	134.1	—	64.6
Arts, entertainment, and recreation	90–93	3.10	21.9	0.1	143.3	18.6	72.0
Other social, community and personal services	94–99	0.0	—	0.2	91.3	0.0	68.5

Table continues on the following page

TABLE 1.3 The Scope for Scale, Innovation, Spillovers, and Low-Skill Jobs Varies across Services Subsectors (continued)

Services subsectors in the United States and EU-15, grouped by combination of trade intensity, offshorability, R&D intensity, capital intensity, intersectoral linkages, and low skill intensity

Subsectors, by category	ISIC Rev. 4 two-digit industry code	Share of value added that is exported[a] (US 2015, %)	Share of offshorable jobs[b] (US, %)	R&D intensity[c] (EU-15 2017, share of value added, %)	Capital stock per worker[d] (EU-15 2017, constant 2015 US$, thousands)	Share of sales to other sectors[e] (EU-15 2015, %)	Share of low-skilled workers in total sector employment[f] (US 2018, %)
Thresholds used for shading							
n.a.	n.a.	>10	>50	>3	>35	>40	>50
		<10	<50	<3	20–35	<40	30–50
					<20		<30

Sources: Blinder and Krueger 2013; OECD's TiVA, R&D Sources and Methods, and STAN databases; US Department of Labor's O*NET database.

Note: Subsectors are defined by International Standard Industrial Classification of All Economic Activities (ISIC) Rev. 4 "section-level" (1-digit) headings. EU-15 comprises the 15 pre-2004 European Union member states: Austria, Belgium, Denmark, Finland, France, Germany, Greece, Ireland, Italy, Luxembourg, the Netherlands, Portugal, Spain, Sweden, and the United Kingdom (which has since exited the EU). OECD = Organisation for Economic Co-operation and Development; R&D = research and development; n.a. = not applicable; — = not available.

a. The share of value added that is exported—based on the OECD's Trade in Value-Added (TiVA) database—indicates a sector's trade intensity and therefore its potential to access larger markets. Wholesale trade is distinguished from retail trade based on assumptions derived from the World Input-Output Database.

b. A sector's percentage of offshorable jobs indicates its potential to achieve scale by reducing the need for physical proximity between consumers and producers. It is measured here by survey questions in Blinder and Krueger (2013) that assess the extent to which worker tasks (a) involve face-to-face contact with people other than coworkers; (b) can be done without being physically present and; (c) will experience a decline in quality if they can be delivered remotely. Wholesale and retail trade cannot be separated in this indicator.

c. R&D intensity—the share of businesses' R&D expenditure in value added, taken from the OECD's R&D Sources and Methods database—proxies the sector's scope for innovation. Wholesale and retail trade cannot be separated in this indicator.

d. Capital stock per worker—from the OECD's STructural ANalysis (STAN) database—measures a sector's "capital intensity," a proxy for contributing to scale economies and innovation by leveraging labor's contributions.

e. The share of sales to other sectors in a sector's output—taken from the OECD's STAN database—indicates the extent of its linkages within the economy and therefore its scope for positive spillovers. In this indicator, whole-sale trade is distinguished from retail trade based on assumptions derived from the World Input-Output Database.

f. The share of low-skilled workers in a sector's employment—measured by the share of workers in manual-task-intensive occupations among 23 major occupational groups in the US Department of Labor's Occupational Information Network (O*NET) database—reflects its skill intensity and hence its job creation potential for unskilled workers. The occupations identified as being manual-labor-intensive include community and social services; health care support; protective services; food preparation and serving; buildings and grounds cleaning; personal care; sales-related occupations; farming-related occupations; construction and extraction; installation, maintenance, and repair; production; transportation; and material moving.

distribution of values (indicated by the shading within each column, which reflects threshold values reported across the bottom of the table). The sectors are then sorted into the four categories based on the common sets of rankings across the dimensions.

Among these results, two characteristics—the share of low-skilled workers and trade intensity (the share of exports in value added)—demonstrated the greatest variation, so those measures form the y- and x-axes, respectively, of figure 1.6.[24] And because of the significant correlation between trade intensity and the share of intermediate sales to other sectors, the bubble shading indicates the relative importance of linkages (low-linkage services in blue, high-linkage services in green). Offshorability and R&D intensity stood out in only a few subsectors, as indicated with the white dots inside the bubbles and a red outer circle, respectively. Capital intensity—the stock of capital

FIGURE 1.6 Services Subsectors Vary in Their Scope for Scale, Innovation, Spillovers, and Low-Skill Jobs

Services subsectors in the EU-15 and United States, grouped by trade intensity, offshorability, R&D intensity, capital intensity, intersectoral linkages, and low skill intensity

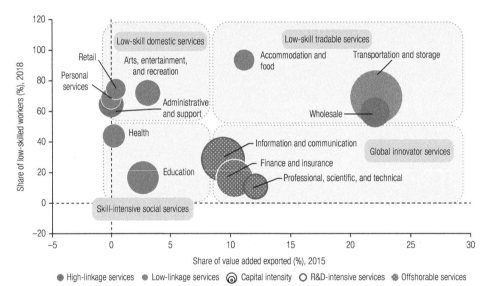

Sources: Calculations based on Blinder and Krueger 2013; OECD's Trade in Value-Added (TiVA), R&D Sources and Methods, and STructural ANalysis (STAN) databases; and US Department of Labor's Occupational Information Network (O*NET) database.

Note: Data from latest available year. Bubble sizes indicate relative gross capital stock per worker. Bubbles shaded with dots refer to sectors with high offshorability (above 75th percentile). Red outlines designate sectors with high research and development (R&D) intensity (above 75th percentile). The data on exports exclude services provided through "commercial presence" such as the establishment of affiliates abroad (mode 3 of services trade in the General Agreement on Trade in Services [GATS]). The share of low-skilled workers in a sector's employment is measured by the share of workers in manual-task-intensive occupations. The indicators on low-skilled workers, exports, and offshorability are based on US data; those on R&D, linkages, and capital intensity are based on EU-15 data. EU-15 countries comprise the 15 pre-2004 European Union member states: Austria, Belgium, Denmark, Finland, France, Germany, Greece, Ireland, Italy, Luxembourg, the Netherlands, Portugal, Spain, Sweden, and the United Kingdom (which has since exited the EU). OECD = Organisation for Economic Co-operation and Development.

At Your Service? The Promise of Services-Led Development

relative to workers employed—is represented by the size of the bubbles in the figure rather than being used as a way of categorizing the subsectors.

Taking the clustering of these characteristics together, the services subsectors can be analyzed in four groups: global innovator services, low-skill tradable services, skill-intensive social services, and low-skill domestic services (figure 1.6). The groups sort into two levels of trade and skill intensity—as also reflected in the group names—but are further differentiated within each level by offshorability, R&D intensity, capital intensity, and/or linkages. The comparison of trends within this sector typology can indicate ways in which countries may be able to benefit from producing in these subsectors.

Global innovator services. Professional, scientific, and technical services; ICT services; and financial and insurance services are highly traded in international markets, and the large majority of employees in these industries are skilled workers. Furthermore, these services are traded in international markets through remote cross-border supply and are therefore amenable to offshoring (and thus similarly shaded in figure 1.6).[25] Of these services, ICT and professional, scientific, and technical services are also characterized by high R&D intensity, while ICT and finance are relatively capital intensive. Collectively, these services subsectors also have greater linkages with other sectors.

Low-skill tradable services. Within the services subsectors that are more traded internationally, most of the employees in transportation and warehousing services, wholesale trade, and accommodation and food services are low-skilled workers. Further, transportation and warehousing services have a distinctly higher ratio of exports to value added—even higher than the subsectors making up the high-skill global innovators group—and are relatively capital intensive.

Of these three subsectors, transportation and warehousing services and wholesale trade also have greater linkages with other sectors.[26] This, in turn, is relevant for their amenability to offshoring. Transportation services and wholesale and retail services can be traded without people or capital moving across national borders, to an extent that they enable the export and import of goods. Accommodation and food services are typically exported through consumption abroad by tourists.

Skill-intensive social services. Among the services subsectors that are less traded internationally, education and health employ a relatively low share of low-skilled workers. The share of low-skilled workers is about 40 percent in health services, owing to large numbers of workers employed in health care support occupations. This share falls to about 20 percent if home health aides, nursing assistants, occupational therapy assistants, physical therapy assistants, massage therapists, pharmacy aides, dental assistants, and the like are categorized as (semi-)skilled jobs instead, which might be closer to the reality in lower-income countries.

Although typically less traded internationally with respect to the overall size of the sector, education and health services are indeed tradable. For example, education services can be exported through FDI or the enrollment of foreign students. Similarly, health services can be exported through "medical tourism" or remittances of individuals who migrate across international borders. These services also incorporate a sizable component of public provision in many countries.

Low-skill domestic services. Among the services subsectors that are less traded internationally, retail trade; administrative and support services; arts, entertainment, and recreation; and other community and personal services all employ relatively high shares of low-skilled workers. Except for administrative and support services, these services have few linkages with other sectors. And except for arts, entertainment, and recreation services, they are also generally less internationally traded.

Based on data for high-income countries, this typology suggests that the most internationally traded global innovator services are typically also relatively skill intensive. These highly traded services also share greater linkages with other sectors domestically, providing greater scale and scope for spillovers. In contrast, many low-skilled services—such as arts, entertainment, and recreation; retail trade; and personal services—provide little by way of productivity-enhancing potential through trade, innovation, and linkages.[27] Among the services subsectors, however, figure 1.6 shows that transportation and warehousing services, accommodation and food services, and wholesale trade are perhaps exceptions to this general pattern in that they are both internationally traded *and* create jobs for unskilled labor. Transportation and wholesale trade services are also highly linked to other sectors.[28]

The Subsector Groups, by Mode of Trade

These subsector groups are reinforced by differences in how they are traded and thus the potential entry points for LMICs. Services can be exported through four modes: (1) "cross-border supply"; (2) "consumption abroad"; (3) "commercial presence"; or (4) "movement of natural persons" (as further defined in box 1.1).

Exports through mode 3—by establishing "commercial presence," such as through affiliates abroad—is the most prominent form of trade across most services subsectors (figure 1.7). Accommodation and food services and education are the exceptions to this norm, being typically exported through tourism and the "consumption abroad" of foreign students (mode 2). Medical tourism provides similar opportunities, even though its share in global exports of health services is lower. Cross-border trade (mode 1) is most widespread among (a) the global innovator services that can be delivered digitally, as well as (b) transportation and distribution services (low-skill tradables) because they are closely linked to merchandise trade. The movement of individual service providers abroad (mode 4) is the least widespread mode of trade, although there is evidence of some exports through this mode among the global innovators and skill-intensive social services.

FIGURE 1.7 **The Most Prominent Mode of Exporting Services Is Establishing "Commercial Presence" Abroad, but "Cross-Border Supply" and "Consumption Abroad" Matter for Some Subsectors**

Decomposition of global services exports, by mode of supply and subsector, 2017

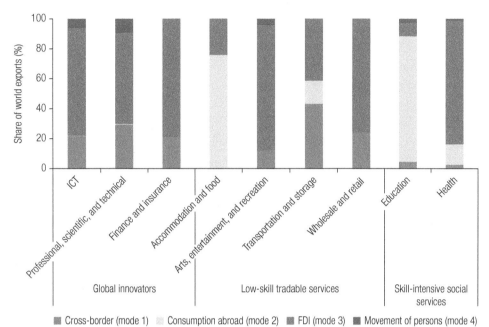

Source: Trade in Services by Mode of Supply (TiSMoS) database, World Trade Organization (WTO).

Note: TiSMoS is an experimental dataset that relies on imputations or assumptions for the breakdown of services trade in most countries between modes 1 (cross-border supply), 2 (consumption abroad), and 4 (movement of persons). Mode 3 trade (commercial presence through foreign direct investment [FDI] that establishes company affiliates in consumers' countries) is determined from the Foreign Affiliates Statistics (FATS) of the European Union's statistical office, Eurostat, and can be identified separately for most countries. For further details, see Wettstein et al. (2019). ICT = information and communication technology.

In principle, all services—including low-skill domestic services that are predicated on face-to-face interactions between producers and consumers—can be exported through the movement of producers across borders. This, however, shifts the discussion from services trade using mode 4 to prospects for longer-term migration.

Among services that share linkages with other sectors, many are also "embodied" as inputs in the export of goods—a practice often dubbed "mode 5" trade. These services typically include R&D, engineering, design, software, and logistics services that add value during the production of manufactured goods and agricultural commodities and are therefore exported indirectly. For example, with 10 million lines of computer programming code, software-related services constituted 40 percent of the value of General Motors' 2010 Chevy Volt model, compared with some 5 percent of the value of their cars in the 1980s. For most countries, these embodied services inputs represent about one-third of the total value of their manufactured exports (Antimiani and Cernat 2018). This "servicification" of manufacturing is discussed further in chapter 4.

The extent to which the scope for scale, innovation, spillovers, and jobs for low-skilled workers is *innate* to sectors—rather than reflecting policies, technology, or other trends—can be inferred from the extent to which they vary over time or across countries.

Changes in Characteristics over Time

Based on data from the EU-15 and the United States, there is little evidence to suggest that the magnitude of these pro-development characteristics across services subsectors has changed dramatically over time. The share of low-skilled workers in different services subsectors remained largely constant between 2001 and 2018, with professional, scientific, and technical services; ICT; and finance remaining the most skill-intensive subsectors, and accommodation and food services the least (figure 1.8, panel a). Health services was the only subsector that experienced a discernible increase in the share of low-skilled workers, from about 30 percent in 2001 to 40 percent in 2018.

The physical capital intensity of a given services subsector similarly remained largely unchanged between 2010 and 2017 across all services subsectors, with wholesale and retail trade becoming relatively more labor intensive over the period (figure 1.8, panel b). The extent of linkages with other sectors also remained largely unchanged between 2005 and 2015 across all services subsectors. In this regard, the share of intermediate sales in total output remained the highest in professional, scientific, and technical services and the lowest in education services during this period (figure 1.8, panel c).

The increased trade intensity of certain services in international markets is one of the more significant changes in the set of pro-development characteristics. Finance; information and communication; and professional, scientific, and technical services saw large increases in the share of value added that was exported between 2005 and 2015. This reflects, at least in part, their increased international tradability owing to the ICT revolution that enabled market exchange without physical proximity. At the same time, traditional services such as transportation and wholesale and retail trade also increased their international trade intensity, reflecting the role of policy changes such as the relaxation of restrictions on FDI (figure 1.8, panel d).

Differences in Characteristics across Countries

The characteristics of scale, innovation, and spillovers associated with a services subsector may also vary across countries, often reflecting differences in policies, skills, and technology use between high-income economies (such as the United States and Western European countries) and low- and middle-income economies.

Except in accommodation and food services, the export-to-output ratio is higher in high-income countries than in LMICs across all services subsectors (figure 1.9, panel a). Among low-skill tradable services, the lower export intensity of wholesale trade and

FIGURE 1.8 **The Skill Intensity, Capital Intensity, Intersectoral Linkage Intensity, and Trade Intensity across Services Subsectors Has Not Changed Dramatically over Time**

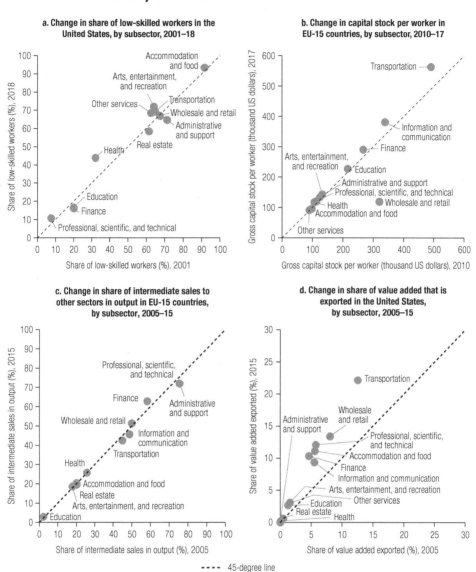

a. Change in share of low-skilled workers in the United States, by subsector, 2001–18

b. Change in capital stock per worker in EU-15 countries, by subsector, 2010–17

c. Change in share of intermediate sales to other sectors in output in EU-15 countries, by subsector, 2005–15

d. Change in share of value added that is exported in the United States, by subsector, 2005–15

- - - - 45-degree line

Sources: Calculations based on OECD's TiVA and STAN databases; US Department of Labor's O*NET database.

Note: EU-15 countries comprise the 15 pre-2004 European Union member states: Austria, Belgium, Denmark, Finland, France, Germany, Greece, Ireland, Italy, Luxembourg, the Netherlands, Portugal, Spain, Sweden, and the United Kingdom (which has since exited the EU). OECD = Organisation for Economic Co-operation and Development. The share of low-skilled workers in a subsector's employment is measured by the share of workers in manual-task-intensive occupations among 23 major occupational groups in the US Department of Labor's Occupational Information Network (O*NET) database.

FIGURE 1.9 The Export and Skill Intensity of Services Subsectors in HICs Are Higher Than in LMICs

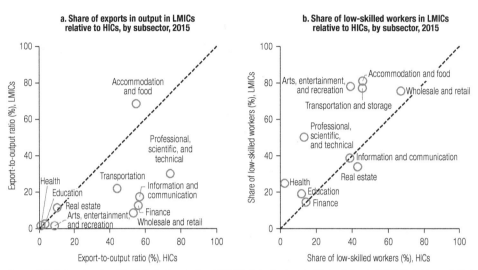

a. Share of exports in output in LMICs relative to HICs, by subsector, 2015

b. Share of low-skilled workers in LMICs relative to HICs, by subsector, 2015

Source: Calculations based on World Trade Organization (WTO) Trade in Services by Mode of Supply (TiSMoS) database; United Nations National Accounts; World Bank's International Income Distribution Dataset (I2D2).

Note: The dataset included 25 high-income countries (HICs) and 55 low- and middle-income countries (LMICs) in panel a; and 2 HICs (Australia and United States) and 43 LMICs in panel b. The I2D2 is a global harmonized household survey dataset. LMICs, by World Bank income group classifications, had 1994 gross national income (GNI) of less than US$8,955. HICs had GNI exceeding US$8,955 in 1994. The share of low-skilled workers in a subsector's employment is measured here as the share of workers in 4 of the 10 major occupational groups in the International Standard Classification of Occupations (ISCO), as shown in the World Bank's I2D2: (a) service and sales workers; (b) machine operators; (c) elementary occupations; and (d) craft workers.

transportation and storage services in LMICs may reflect either (a) a subpar logistics performance that hinders firms' competitiveness to export goods, or (b) a plethora of smaller, less-productive businesses that do not establish affiliates abroad.

Among global innovator services, the notably lower export-to-output ratios in LMICs likely reflect their lack of comparative advantage due to the relative scarcity of skilled labor. In fact, the share of low-skilled workers is higher in LMICs than in high-income countries across all services subsectors (figure 1.9, panel b).

The export and skill intensity of services in high-income countries therefore represent an upper and lower bound, respectively, for LMICs.

Implications for Inclusion in Lower-Income Countries

As noted earlier, the services sector in the aggregate has dominated both job creation and productivity growth across LMICs, on average, over the past two to three decades primarily because it has facilitated the structural transformation of these economies away from agriculture. This transformation has expanded job opportunities within lower-income countries and narrowed their productivity gaps with higher-income countries.

But the longer-term of potential of services-led development depends on whether a given services subsector can employ lower-skilled workers and enable them to raise their productivity over time.

The typology of services presented in the previous section used the share of low-skill employment, based on occupation-level data from high-income countries, as one pro-development characteristic in its categorization. The subsectors classified as low-skill (tradable and domestic) services indeed do employ disproportionately large shares of unskilled workers (those who have completed primary education at most) across LMICs.

In LMICs, on average, close to three-fourths (72 percent) of workers in wholesale and retail trade and hotels and restaurants and almost two-thirds (63 percent) in transportation services have completed only primary education, compared with three-fourths of workers (74 percent) in financial and business services who have completed postsecondary education (figure 1.10, panel a). In fact, wholesale and retail trade as well as hotels and

FIGURE 1.10 **In LMICs, Commerce, Hospitality, and Transportation Services Rely More on Unskilled Labor, While Financial and Business Services Rely More on Skilled Labor**

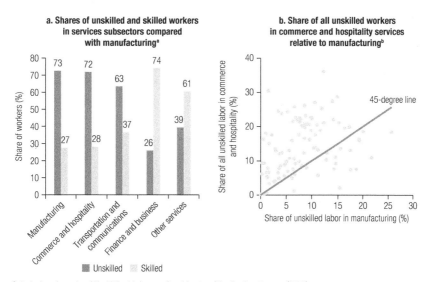

a. Shares of unskilled and skilled workers in services subsectors compared with manufacturing[a]

b. Share of all unskilled workers in commerce and hospitality services relative to manufacturing[b]

Source: Calculations based on World Bank's International Income Distribution Dataset (I2D2).

Note: The I2D2 is a global harmonized household survey database. Data are from the latest available year (between 2005 and 2017). "Unskilled" workers are those with no or only primary education. "Skilled" are those with at least some postsecondary education. "Commerce" refers to both wholesale and retail trade. "Hospitality" refers to hotels and restaurants. "Low- and middle-income countries" (LMICs), by World Bank income group classifications, had 1994 gross national income (GNI) of less than US$8,955. Other services comprise education; health; arts, entertainment, and recreation; administrative and support; and other social, community, and personal services.

a. Subsector employment data are aggregated from 107 LMICs.

b. Subsector employment data are aggregated from 101 LMICs.

restaurants—that is, commerce and hospitality-related services—employ a vast share of all unskilled workers in LMICs, even more so than manufacturing (figure 1.10, panel b).

Low-Skill Services: Where the Jobs Are

Low-skill domestic services (retail trade; personal services; arts, entertainment, and recreation; and administrative and support services) represent about two-thirds of services employment in lower-income countries compared with about 30 percent in high-income countries (figure 1.11, panel c). By contrast, global innovator services (finance, ICT, and professional services) account for 5–10 percent of services employment in lower-income countries compared with 15–20 percent in high-income countries (figure 1.11, panel b). The employment share of skill-intensive social services is also more prominent in higher-income countries (figure 1.11, panel d).

Among low-skill tradable services (accommodation and food as well as transportation services), there is an inverted U-shaped relationship between this subsector group's share in services employment and countries' per capita income levels, even though there is considerable variation across countries (figure 1.11, panel a).

Among low-skill domestic services, the inverse relationship with per capita income levels is driven by retail trade, whose share of services employment ranges from 12 percent in high-income countries to 39 percent in low-income countries (figure 1.12). Among low-skill tradable services, the employment share of transportation also tends to decrease as income increases, while this trend is less clear for wholesale trade and accommodation and food services. Among the global innovators, the pattern of a higher share of services employment at higher levels of per capita income seems to be universal for the three subsectors (finance, ICT, and professional services). Among skill-intensive social services, the share of education in services employment is similar across income groups, while that of health increases with per capita income.

Low-Skill Services: Where Most Jobs Have Been Created

Much of the increase in the services sector's employment share among LMICs is attributable to low-skill (tradable and domestic) services. The collective share of several of these subsectors—wholesale and retail trade, accommodation and food, and transportation and communications services (encompassing post and telecommunications)—in total employment across LMICs, on average, increased from 18 percent in 1991 to 26 percent in 2018.

At the same time, the share of global innovator services—finance, information, and professional services—almost doubled, from about 3 percent of total employment in 1991 to 5 percent in 2018, albeit from a very low base. The share of skill-intensive social services (education and health) in total employment remained almost unchanged at about 9 percent throughout this period (figure 1.13).

FIGURE 1.11 **Lower-Income Countries See More Employment in Low-Skill Services, While Higher-Income Countries See More in Global Innovator Services and Skill-Intensive Social Services**

Share of services subsector groups in total services employment, by country income level, most recent year available

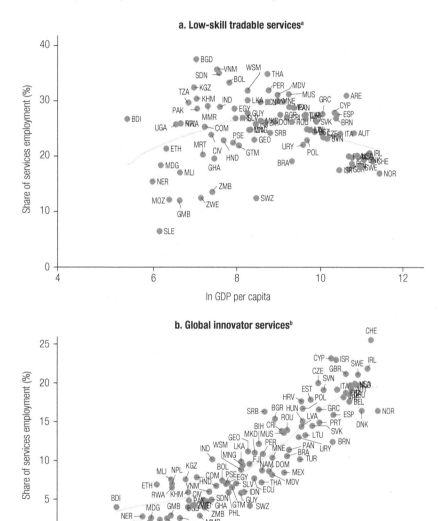

a. Low-skill tradable services[a]

b. Global innovator services[b]

Figure continues on the following page

FIGURE 1.11 **Lower-Income Countries See More Employment in Low-Skill Services, While Higher-Income Countries See More in Global Innovator Services and Skill-Intensive Social Services** *(continued)*

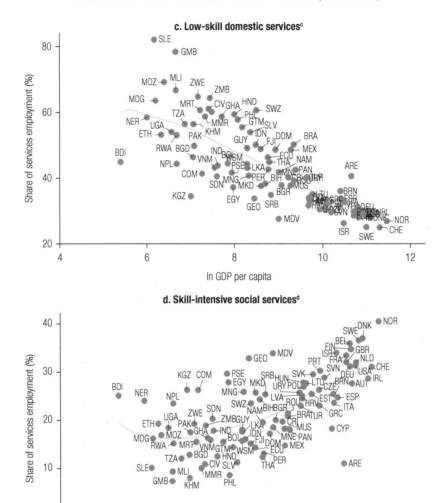

Source: Calculations based on International Labour Organization (ILO) and World Development Indicators data.

Note: Country data are for the most recent available year (between 2011 and 2019), covering 90 countries. Countries are labeled using the International Organization for Standardization's alpha-3 codes. ln = natural log.

a. Low-skill tradable services include wholesale trade, transportation and storage, and accommodation and food services.

b. Global innovator services include finance, information and communication technology (ICT), and a variety of professional, scientific, and technical services.

c. Low-skill domestic services include retail; arts, entertainment, and recreation; administrative and support services; and other social, community, and personal services.

d. Skill-intensive social services include education and health services.

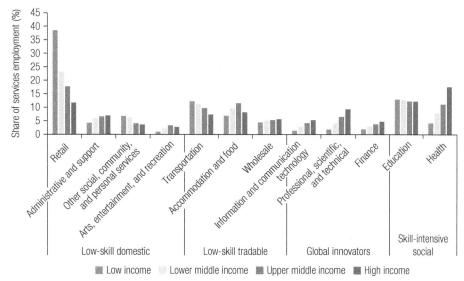

FIGURE 1.12 **The Inverse Relationship between Low-Skill Services and Per Capita Income Is Driven by Retail Trade**

Share of services employment in selected subsectors, by subsector group and country income level

Source: Calculations based on International Labour Organization (ILO) and World Development Indicators database.

Note: Data from 104 countries are for the most recent available year (between 2011 and 2019). Low-income, lower-middle-income, and upper-middle-income countries follow World Bank classifications by 1994 income level. "High-income countries" are those whose gross national income per capita was at least US$8,955 in 1994. ICT = information and communication technology.

These patterns of employment expansion are consistent with the two waves of services sector output growth (as identified in Eichengreen and Gupta 2011) based on a large cross-section of low-, middle-, and high-income countries between 1950 and 2005. That much of the services sector's increased share of employment among LMICs between 1991 and 2018 is attributable to low-skill services conforms to the first wave, consisting primarily of traditional services as a country moves from "low" toward "middle" income status.

The second wave consists of modern, knowledge-intensive services (in finance, communication, and business) as a country moves from "middle" toward "high" income status. This wave started at lower levels of per capita income after 1990 than in the preceding four decades.[29] Across LMICs, it is reflected in the increasing share of global innovator services in total employment—almost doubling between 1991 and 2018 on average, albeit from a low base.

Employment expansion in the services sector across LMICs has therefore been concentrated in services subsectors that are intensive in the use of low-skilled labor. This has important implications for economic inclusion because cross-country evidence

FIGURE 1.13 **Much of the Increase in the Services Sector's Share of Employment in LMICs since the 1990s Is Attributable to Low-Skill Services**

Share of services subsector groups in total employment of LMICs, 1991–2018

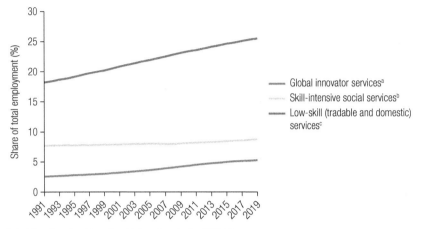

Source: Calculations based on International Labour Organization (ILO) data.

Note: The data cover 148 low- and middle-income countries (LMICs), which, by World Bank income group classifications, had 1994 gross national income (GNI) of less than US$8,955. Low-skill services here include communications, because the ILO data do not separate communications from transportation.

a. Global innovator services include finance and business services.

b. Skill-intensive social services include education and health.

c. Low-skill services include wholesale and retail trade, accommodation and food, and transportation and communication services.

shows that poverty reduction is stronger when growth has a labor-intensive inclination (Loayza and Raddatz 2010). The evidence suggests, for example, that the poverty-reducing effects of growth in wholesale and retail trade and transportation services are close to the effects of equal growth in either the agriculture or manufacturing sectors, at times even exceeding them (Dorosh and Thurlow 2018). The effects are further strengthened by the inclusion in these low-skill services of informal-economy workers and women.

Low-Skill Services Are Most Likely to Employ Informal Workers

A large part of the employment expansion in low-skill services is linked to the informal sector, which poses minimal barriers to entry for workers. The share of regular wage employment is least prevalent in wholesale and retail trade and in hotels and restaurants across Latin American countries (Hovhannisyan et al. 2021). Even in a larger set of LMICs, evidence suggests that about three-fourths of workers in these commerce- and hospitality-related services are either self-employed or wage labor without contracts (figure 1.14). The corresponding share in transportation services is about two-thirds.

Notably, the share of workers without contracts is even higher in manufacturing, on average, across a range of LMICs, although the self-employed are few and far between

FIGURE 1.14 **Low-Skill Services Are More Likely Than Global Innovator Services to Employ Informal Workers**

Share of workers with and without contracts in selected sectors of LMICs

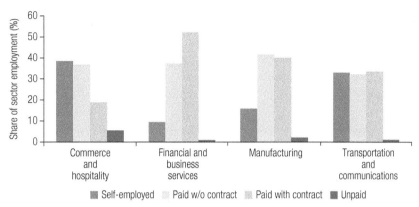

Source: Calculations based on World Bank's International Income Distribution Dataset (I2D2).

Note: The I2D2 is a global harmonized household survey database. The data are from 101 low- and middle-income countries (LMICs) for the most recent available year (between 2005 and 2017). "Commerce and hospitality" includes, respectively, wholesale and retail trade and hotels and restaurants. "Communications" includes post and telecommunication services. LMICs, by World Bank income group classifications, had 1994 gross national income of less than US$8,955.

(figure 1.14). This is perhaps indicative of a large informal segment within manufacturing where workers do not benefit from a wage premium owing to efficiency wages or institutional factors such as minimum wages, labor codes, and union bargaining (Jaumotte and Osorio Buitron 2015; Söderbom and Teal 2004; Verhoogen 2008).

The relatively large shares of self-employed and wage employees without contracts in the *low-skill (tradable and domestic) services* subsectors (trade, hotels, and restaurants, as well as transportation and communications) raises concerns about the extent to which these subsectors can raise the living standards of low-skilled workers. Informal employment arrangements are typically not characterized by access to minimum wages, labor codes, retirement plans, paid holidays and sick leave, and health and life insurance. They also tend to provide relatively unstable arrangements, relying more than the formal sector on part-time or temporary contracts. The returns to experience for a worker in the informal sector are also lower than in the formal sector (World Bank 2019).

Yet although many jobs in these *low-skill services* are in the informal sector and the productivity dynamics over time are not that high, these jobs still provide a higher and often more stable form of income for large numbers of people, especially those moving out of agriculture and off the farm. For example, evidence from India shows that labor productivity in the informal services sector was consistently higher than in agriculture since 1990 (Nayyar 2012).[30] In addition, household enterprises in retail, food, and accommodation services—as well as transportation services, particularly in secondary cities—have been important contributors to poverty reduction (Christiaensen and Kanbur 2017; Christiaensen and Martin 2018). And they provide opportunities to improve skills and earnings profiles over time (Beegle and Christiaensen 2019; World Bank 2012).

Moreover, recent experimental evidence from Ethiopia indicates that not all manufacturing jobs are better than self-employment in services: in the studied factories, there is no evidence of an industrial wage premium, and there are significant concerns about worker health and the safety of working conditions (Blattman and Dercon 2016).

Low-Skill Services Are Also Most Likely to Employ Women

Women have particularly benefited from the expansion of low-skill (domestic and tradable) services. The share of female workers in wholesale and retail trade, hotels, and restaurants is about 45 percent, compared with 38 percent in the manufacturing sector, on average, across LMICs (figure 1.15, panel a). In Sub-Saharan Africa, the share of female workers in these commerce and hospitality-related services was as high as 59 percent, compared with just over 42 percent in the manufacturing sector (figure 1.15, panel b).

Female workers also account for approximately 44 percent of employment in the global innovator services, on average, across LMICs (represented by financial and business services in figure 1.15, panel a). In fact, the share of female workers in financial and business services exceeded that in commerce and hospitality-related services in Eastern Europe and Central Asia (60 percent versus 57 percent) and was not too far behind the commerce and hospitality subsectors in both East Asia and the Pacific (47 percent in finance and business versus 56 percent in commerce and hospitality) and Latin America and the Caribbean (42 percent versus 50 percent) (figure 1.15, panel b).[31] However, women are typically employed in lower-paid occupations in finance and business services and therefore earn less than men in these subsectors (see chapter 2).

In addition, female entrepreneurs tend to be predominantly in retail services (World Bank 2019) and are more likely than men to operate in the informal sector (Hallward-Driemeier 2013). In recent World Bank Enterprise Surveys of four LMICs, 58 percent of informal retail firms had majority female ownership, compared with only 33 percent of formal retail firms (figure 1.16).

Prospects for Productivity Growth

Over time, increases in productivity will be central to creating better-paying jobs. The increase in the share of *low-skill services* in value added has not been commensurate with that in employment. The share of wholesale and retail trade, hotels, and restaurants in total employment across 25 LMICs, on average, almost doubled, from 11 percent in 1985 to 20 percent in 2010, while their corresponding average share of GDP increased marginally, from 15 percent in 1985 to 17 percent in 2010.[32] This evidence suggests that

FIGURE 1.15 **The Shares of Female Workers in Low-Skill Commerce and Hospitality Services—and in Global Innovator Services—Typically Exceed the Share in Manufacturing**

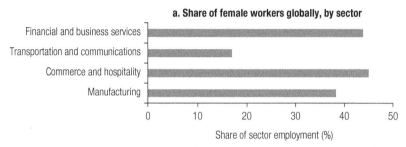

a. Share of female workers globally, by sector

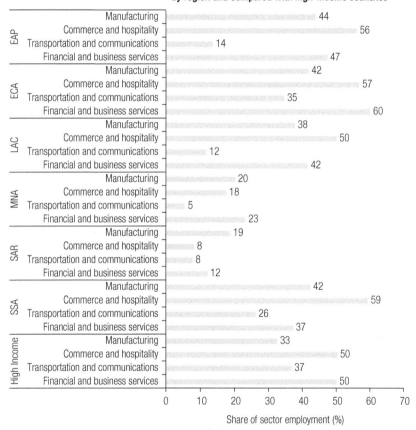

b. Share of female workers in selected sectors of LMICs, by region and compared with high-income countries[a]

Source: Calculations based on World Bank's International Income Distribution Dataset (I2D2).

Note: The I2D2 is a global harmonized household survey database. The data are from 101 low- and middle-income countries (LMICs) and 8 high-income countries for the latest available year (between 2005 and 2017). LMICs, by World Bank income group classifications, had 1994 gross national income (GNI) of less than US$8,955. "High-income countries" are those whose 1984 GNI per capita was at least US$8,955. "Commerce and hospitality" includes wholesale and retail trade and hotels and restaurants. "Communications" includes post and telecommunications services.

a. EAP = East Asia and Pacific; ECA = Eastern Europe and Central Asia; LAC = Latin America and the Caribbean; MNA = Middle East and North Africa; SAR = South Asia; SSA = Sub-Saharan Africa.

FIGURE 1.16 **The Share of Firms with Majority Female Ownership Is Highest in Low-Skill Retail Services, Especially in the Informal Sector**

Share of firms with majority female ownership in selected sectors of four LMICs, by formality status, 2018–19

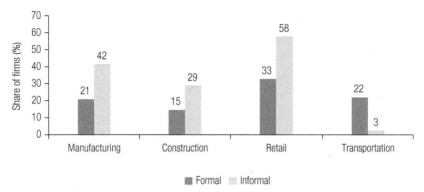

Source: Calculations based on World Bank Enterprise Surveys.

Note: These data cover the Lao People's Democratic Republic, Mozambique, Somalia, and Zambia, where the most recent round of Enterprise Surveys included the informal sector.

the large expansion of services sector employment across LMICs attributable largely to low-skill services has perhaps not been associated with large increases in productivity.

Cross-country evidence suggests that labor productivity growth in low-skill services such as wholesale and retail trade, although not large, has enabled lower-income countries to catch up (Kinfemichael and Morshed 2019). Yet gaps in labor productivity between lower- and higher-income countries tend to be larger among low-skill (domestic and tradable) services. For example, the labor productivity of commerce and hospitality services in low-income countries was little more than 5 percent of the level in high-income countries, but financial and business services in low-income countries had 10 percent of the labor productivity of those services in high-income countries (figure 1.17). And although these gaps are potentially discouraging, they indicate a potential for services in LMICs that is yet unrealized. Much will depend on the underlying firm dynamics, technological change, and intersectoral linkages. These issues are analyzed in the chapters that follow.

At the same time, wider productivity benefits may come from the further expansion of *global innovator services*—whose increasing share in value added has been commensurate with that of employment in LMICs[33] and whose labor productivity shows evidence of converging with the global frontier (Kinfemichael and Morshed 2019). The export orientation of the global innovator services has been associated with job creation in LMICs. For instance, the number of jobs (and wages) supported by the export of business services exceeds that of manufactured goods in Brazil, China, India, the Russian Federation, and South Africa (figure 1.18).

FIGURE 1.17 **Labor Productivity Gaps between Lower- and High-Income Countries Tend to Be Wider among Low-Skill Personal, Commerce, and Hospitality Services Compared with Global Innovator Services and Manufacturing**
Labor productivity in LMICs relative to HICs in selected sectors, 2010

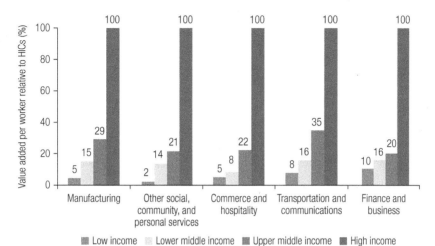

Source: Calculations based on the Groningen Growth and Development Centre (GGDC) 10-Sector Database.

Note: The data cover 40 countries across all income groups (classified by the World Bank based on 1994 gross national income). Percentages reported are simple averages across the countries in each income group. "Commerce and hospitality" includes wholesale and retail trade and hotels and restaurants. "Communications" includes post and telecommunications services. HICs = high-income countries; LMICs = low- and middle-income countries. For more information on the GGDC 10-Sector Database, see Timmer, DeVries, and DeVries (2015).

FIGURE 1.18 **The Shares of Jobs and Wages in Business Services Exports Exceed Those in Manufactured Goods' Exports in Many Large LMICs**
Shares of jobs and wages embodied in gross exports of manufactured goods and business services, selected LMICs and United States, 2015

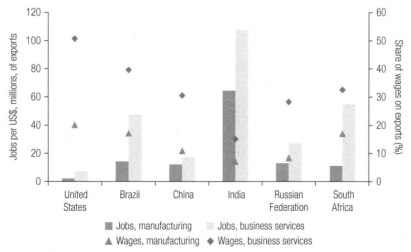

Source: Calculations based on Trade in Employment Database, Organisation for Economic Co-operation and Development.
Note: Business services here refer to professional, scientific, and technical services.

However, evidence, including from India and the Philippines, also shows that the export of these services has benefited skilled workers more than unskilled workers (Amoranto, Brooks, and Chun 2010; De and Raychaudhuri 2008; Mehta and Hasan 2012). As a result, the poverty-reducing effects have been limited so far (Dorosh and Thurlow 2018), and there is a concern that income inequality could increase.[34] The productivity benefits of global innovator services could be spread more widely through linkages with sectors that are more intensive in low-skilled labor (low-skill tradable services, industry, and agriculture) or by raising the demand for other goods and services, including low-skill domestic services (see chapter 4).

Conclusion

The stable or declining share of manufacturing in value added and employment across several LMICs over the past two decades largely reflects the faster growth of services. In fact, the services sector has provided the twin gains of productivity growth and large-scale job creation, much like manufacturing-led development—the hitherto dominant development paradigm—has done in the past.

Importantly, however, these twin gains have not been realized jointly in any given services subsector. The global innovators (such as finance, ICT, and professional services) that exhibit the potential for scale, innovation, and spillovers are more likely to be skill-biased. On the flip side, low-skill domestic services (such as retail and personal services) are likely to provide few opportunities for scale, innovation, and spillovers. Low-skill tradable services (such as wholesale trade, accommodation and food, and transportation) combine these "productivity-enhancing" characteristics with the absorption of low-skilled workers to some extent. Yet many of these growth opportunities, especially for transportation and distribution services, are based on linkages with goods-producing sectors.

Low-skill (tradable and domestic) services account for much of the services employment in lower-income countries. The important question, therefore, is whether the services sector has the longer-term potential to enable workers and firms in these countries to raise their productivity over time and to catch up with higher-income countries. Chapter 2 will examine the underlying firm dynamics to assess the extent to which different services subsectors have thus far combined the twin gains of productivity growth and job creation in LMICs. In doing so, it will also consider the importance of differences between narrowly defined industries within services subsectors and differences between firms within narrowly defined industries.

Chapters 3 and 4, respectively, will analyze the potential for technological change and intersectoral linkages to reduce some of the productivity-jobs dichotomy illustrated here. Digital technologies are enabling some low-skill services to achieve scale, innovation, and spillovers. At the same time, low-skilled labor can become more embedded in global innovator services through linkages with other sectors that spread the productivity and demand benefits more widely.

Annex 1A Classifications of Economic Activities in the Services Sector

The classifications used in this chapter follow Revision 4 of the United Nations International Standard Industrial Classification of All Economic Activities (ISIC), which is the most commonly used classification of economic activities. Often countries use classifications that are derived from this classification, such as the European NACE classification (NACE stands for *nomenclature statistique des Activités économiques dans la Communauté européenne*). In Canada, Mexico, and the United States, the North American Industry Classification System (NAICS) is used instead. Concordance tables are available between industrial classifications.

The ISIC classification (table 1A.1) is grouped into sections (indicated with a letter, sometimes colloquially indicated as a "one-digit" sector) and then into divisions (indicated with a two-digit number), groups (three-digit), and classes

TABLE 1A.1   Service Subsectors, by UN ISIC Rev. 4 Classification

Section (UN ISIC Rev. 4)	Included activities (UN ISIC Rev. 4 division number in parentheses)
Global innovator services	
Information and communication (J)	Publishing (58), audio and video production (59), television and radio broadcasting (60), telecommunications (61), computer programming and consulting (62), and information services (63). Information services include webhosting, web portals, and data processing, as well as news agencies.
Finance and insurance (K)	Financial services (64), insurance and pensions (65), and auxiliary financial and insurance services (66). Auxiliary services include insurance agents, brokerage of security and commodity contracts, and fund management activities.
Professional, scientific, and technical activities (M)	Legal services and accounting (both under 69), activities of head offices and management consultancy (both under 70), architecture and engineering (71), scientific R&D (72), advertising (73), veterinary (75), and other professional services such as specialized design, photographic activities, and translation activities (74).
Low-skill tradable services	
Wholesale (part of section G)	Wholesale (46).
Transportation and storage (H)	Various forms of transportation, including land (49), water (50), and air (51) transportation. Also includes logistical services such as storage, warehousing, and transport support (52), as well as postal and courier services (53).
Accommodation and food services (I)	Hotels and other forms of accommodation (55), as well as food and beverage services (56). Note that establishments selling food products produced at the facility but not consumed on location (such as bakeries) are usually classified as food manufacturing (10), even though takeaway services are still classified under this section.

Table continues on the following page

TABLE 1A.1   Service Subsectors, by UN ISIC Rev. 4 Classification (continued)

Section (UN ISIC Rev. 4)	Included activities (UN ISIC Rev. 4 division number in parentheses)
Low-skill domestic services	
Retail (part of section G)	Retail (47) and vehicles trade (45).
Real estate (L)	Buying and selling of real estate, renting and leasing activities, real estate agencies, and management of real estate (all under 68).
Administrative and support services (N)	Rental and leasing activities such as of goods, equipment, or vehicles (77); employment activities such as employment agencies (78); travel agencies and tour operators (79); security services (80); building support and landscaping activities (81); and office support services (82). Building support activities include cleaning activities as well as facility management. Office support services include office administration, call centers, conventions and trade shows, collection agencies, and credit bureaus.
Arts, entertainment, and recreation (R)	Performing arts and the creation of art (both under 90); libraries, museums, and zoos (91); gambling (92); and sports activities such as sports clubs and fitness facilities, as well as amusement and theme parks (93).
Other services (S)	Activities of membership organizations, such as trade unions, professional organizations, and political parties (94); repair of computers and personal and household goods (95); and personal services (96). Personal services include hairdressers and beauty treatments as well as laundry services.
Skill-intensive social services	
Public administration and defense (O)	Mostly nonmarket services provided by the government as well as social security (all under division 84).
Education (P)	Includes both education services often publicly provided (such as primary schools), as well as private training such as sports instruction, music classes, and driving schools (all under division 85).
Health and social work (Q)	Hospitals, doctors, and specialized medicine (all under 86); residential care (87); and social work activities without accommodation (88).

Note: Some service-related activities are classified under different sections. For example, the repair and installation of equipment (division 43) is classified under manufacturing (section C), and mining support services (division 9) are classified under mining and quarrying (section B). Also, some other sectors, such as construction (section F) as well as public utilities (section D and E), are occasionally aggregated within the services sector.

(four-digit). Most of the analysis in this book has been conducted at either the section or division level.

The fourth revision (Rev. 4) of the ISIC was adopted in March 2006, replacing the third revision, which had been in use since 1989 (with a minor revision in 2002). Some data sources—especially those including time series—still report data on services according to this older classification. There are some key differences between the two revisions: for example, in the third revision, telecommunications was grouped together with transportation, and IT services were grouped with business services, whereas Rev. 4 groups both telecommunications and IT services within ICT services.

The classification of groups in this chapter according to pro-development characteristics—the scope for scale, innovation, spillovers, and low-skill jobs—has been done at the section level (with wholesale and retail being separated wherever possible). Nevertheless, significant heterogeneity exists within sections, and particular subsectors might always not fully share all the characteristics of the larger group. (For example, in water and air transportation, high-skilled workers such as captains and pilots play an important role.)

Annex 1B Adapting the McMillan-Rodrik Decomposition to Show Sectoral Reallocation

McMillan and Rodrik (2011) decompose labor productivity growth into two components, with the first one representing within-sector productivity growth and the second one representing reallocation between sectors. The decomposition is expressed as follows:

$$\Delta Y = \Sigma_i \theta_{i,0} \Delta y_i + \Sigma_i y_{i,1} \Delta \theta_i. \tag{1B.1}$$

In equation (1B.1), ΔY represents the change in aggregate labor productivity ($\Delta Y = Y_1 - Y_0$). Aggregate labor productivity Y_t is a weighted average of sectoral labor productivity $y_{i,t}$, using sectoral employment shares $\theta_{i,t}$ as weights, with i denoting sector and t the time period ($Y_t = \Sigma_i \theta_{i,t} y_{i,t}$).

Equation (1B.1) splits the change in aggregated labor productivity, ΔY, into (a) a term representing the growth in sectoral productivity while keeping shares constant (the "within" component); and (b) a term representing changes in employment shares while keeping labor productivity at their final level (the "between" component).

It underlies figure 1.5, which illustrates a productivity decomposition for three sectors (agriculture, industry, and services). The "between" component—the second term in equation (1B.1)—is further split into (a) a component reflecting employment share changes in industry relative to agriculture, and (b) a component reflecting employment share changes in services relative to agriculture.

Let A_1, I_1, and S_1 be the labor productivity of respectively agriculture, industry, and services at the final time period ($t = 1$). Let $\Delta\alpha$, $\Delta\iota$, and $\Delta\sigma$ be the change in employment shares of respectively agriculture, industry, and services (that is, $\Delta\alpha = \alpha_1 - \alpha_0$). The second term can be written as

$$\Sigma_i y_{i,1} \Delta \theta_i = \Delta\alpha * A_1 + \Delta\iota * I_1 + \Delta\sigma * S_1. \tag{1B.2}$$

Given that the employment shares—by definition—add up to 1 ($\alpha + \iota + \sigma = 1$), and the sum of $\Delta\alpha$, $\Delta\iota$, and $\Delta\sigma$ needs to be zero ($\Delta\alpha + \Delta\iota + \Delta\sigma = 0$), we can rewrite this term as

$$\Sigma_i y_1 \Delta\theta = \Delta\alpha * A_1 + \Delta\iota * I_1 + \Delta\sigma * S_1 = (-\Delta\iota - \Delta\sigma) * A_1 + \Delta\iota * I_1 + \Delta\sigma * S_1. \tag{1B.3}$$

And, finally,

$$\Sigma_i y_1 \Delta\theta = \Delta\iota * (I_1 - A_1) + \Delta\sigma * (S_1 - A_1) \tag{1B.4}$$

This term consists of two components: one representing the labor productivity gain of increasing industry employment relative to agriculture (or loss, if $I_1 < A_1$), and one representing the labor productivity gain of increasing services employment relative to agriculture (or loss, if $S_1 < A_1$).

Annex 1C Estimating Kaldor's Laws for the Industry Sector, 1995–2018

Dependent variable → Explanatory variable ↓	GDP growth (1)	GDP growth (2)	Industry's productivity growth (3)	Industry's productivity growth (4)	Economywide productivity growth (5)	Economywide productivity growth (6)
Industry's value-added growth	0.363***		0.842***		0.363***	
	(0.006)		(0.008)		(0.008)	
Industry's value-added growth in preceding year		0.116***		0.116***		0.101***
		(0.008)		(0.016)		(0.010)
Constant	2.173***	3.172***	−1.711***	1.325***	0.286***	1.367***
	(0.068)	(0.091)	(0.083)	(0.178)	(0.080)	(0.104)
Observations	4,266	4,132	3,381	3,336	3,187	3,146
R^2	0.442	0.046	0.787	0.016	0.430	0.034
Country fixed effects	Yes	Yes	Yes	Yes	Yes	Yes

Source: Calculations based on World Development Indicators database.

Note: Industry includes manufacturing, mining, construction, and utilities; rates of growth are year-on-year rates of growth. Standard errors in parentheses.

*** = statistically significant at the 1 percent level of significance.

Notes

1. Throughout this book, the term "industrialization" refers only to manufacturing, except when specified otherwise.

2. This focus is aligned with the World Bank Group's "Jobs and Economic Transformation" agenda to generate "better jobs for more people." This agenda is being championed by the World Bank's International Development Association (IDA), which is the donor community's largest source of financial and technical support for low-income countries, with thematic priorities reached in agreement with borrowing countries. For more information, see

the IDA's Jobs and Economic Transformation web page: http://ida.worldbank.org/theme/jobs-and-economic-transformation.

3. In expanding the evidence base, this book builds on the preceding volume in this productivity flagship series—*Productivity Revisited: Shifting Paradigms in Analysis and Policy* (Cusolito and Maloney 2018)—to extend our understanding of productivity growth in the services sector.

4. Controlling for population size and per capita GDP in a sample of 42 economies between 1950 and 2012, Rodrik (2016) finds that the share of manufacturing in employment steadily declined, as reflected in the magnitudes of coefficients of decadal time dummy variables, which are negative and larger over time.

5. Note that the available data are of the "industrial sector," not "manufacturing." Thus, mining and construction are also included in this reference to the industrial sector.

6. Other evidence also suggests that average productivity growth in services has recently exceeded that of manufacturing in many LMICs, including China, India, and some Sub-Saharan African countries (IMF 2018).

7. Sorbe, Gal, and Millot (2018) also show that labor productivity growth in services was half that of manufacturing between 1980 and 2016 (1.3 percent against 3.0 percent annually) among Organisation for Economic Co-operation and Development (OECD) countries.

8. In this reference, "industry" encompasses manufacturing, mining, construction, and utilities.

9. The Middle East and North Africa experienced negligible labor productivity growth over the period.

10. The "between" component is equal to (a) the change in share in industry (including construction, utilities, and mining) multiplied by the difference in productivity between industry and agriculture; and (b) the change in share in services multiplied by the difference in productivity between services and agriculture. For the methodology, see annex 1B.

11. This finding draws on regressions where country fixed effects are accounted for and the explanatory variable is also lagged by one year (see annex 1C).

12. Rodrik (2012) finds that unlike evidence on per capita income levels or aggregate labor productivity, labor productivity in lagging manufacturing sectors, such as those in low- and middle-income economies, tends to rise and eventually converge with the global frontier regardless of policy or institutional determinants. Duarte and Restuccia (2010) also show that high productivity growth in the manufacturing sector explains about 50 percent of the catch-up in relative aggregate productivity across countries.

13. For example, across a sample of 11 African economies, agriculture (at 35 percent of average productivity) has the lowest productivity by far; manufacturing productivity is 1.7 times as high (Diao, McMillan, and Rodrik 2019).

14. Services consumption grows more than proportionally as income per capita increases, in accordance with a hierarchy of needs (Engel's law).

15. The only exceptions to this norm in the case of goods are highly perishable commodities, which cannot be put in stock and must be consumed as they are produced.

16. An arts institution that insisted on paying musicians 1860s wages in a 1960s economy would find their musicians were constantly quitting to take other jobs. Arts institutions—at least those that could afford it—therefore had to raise their wages to attract and retain the best musicians (Baumol 1967).

17. Telecommunications services are associated with market failures in the traditional form of public goods, externalities (including network externalities), and decreasing costs (leading to natural monopolies). Financial markets classically fail in the face of information asymmetries or inadequate collateral (Besley 1994). The social rates of return are thought to exceed private rates of return for primary and secondary education, owing to positive externalities (Acemoglu and Angrist 1999; Moretti 1999). Educated workers may raise the productivity of less-educated

coworkers or, more generally, an economy with a higher average level of human capital may lead to a higher incidence of learning from others.

18. Industries in which the share of firms that introduced new products and production methods was more than 0.67 standard deviation above the mean (across all industries) are classified as "high" in product and process innovation.

19. The share of a sector's value added that is exported is calculated as the domestic value added in gross exports as a share of value added in a sector.

20. Services production is less fragmented than manufacturing, and the distinction between domestic value added in exports and gross exports is therefore less pronounced. On average, the domestic value added in services constitutes 81 percent of services exports; imported services inputs account for 9 percent of services exports; and the domestic value added in other sectors accounts for the remaining 10 percent (WTO 2019).

21. The "EU-15" comprises the 15 pre-2004 EU member states: Austria, Belgium, Denmark, Finland, France, Germany, Greece, Ireland, Italy, Luxembourg, the Netherlands, Portugal, Spain, Sweden, and the United Kingdom. The data examined for this volume include all 15 countries, although as of January 31, 2020, the United Kingdom left the European Union.

22. The US data are also desirable because they provide the most detailed breakdown of tasks and skills needed by sectors.

23. The ISIC and the World Bank's World Development Indicators database adopt identical definitions of "services" and "industry."

24. These trade-intensity ratios are downward-biased because the OECD-WTO Trade in Value Added (TiVA) statistics do not readily identify trade through a "commercial presence" in the consumer's country (mode 3).

25. As a result of their offshorability, production of these global innovator services is increasingly being fragmented across countries, such as when preliminary architectural designs and tax returns are performed in one country and finalized and delivered to customers in another (World Bank 2020).

26. Wholesale and retail trade are two distinct segments: wholesalers sell to retailers, which in turn sell directly to consumers.

27. These patterns—whereby the more-dynamic services subsectors are also more skill intensive—reinforce the findings of Nayyar (2013) and Amirapu and Subramanian (2015) for India as well as Nayyar, Cruz, and Zhu (2018), which assesses firm-level data from six LMICs (Brazil, China, the Arab Republic of Egypt, India, Nigeria, and the Russian Federation).

28. The share of value added exported for different services subsectors is consistent with the literature, which finds the largest trade costs in retail trade and the smallest trade costs in transportation and logistics, wholesale trade, professional activities, telecommunications, and financial intermediation, with accommodation and food services somewhere in between (Jensen and Kletzer 2005).

29. Before 1990, the share of the services sector in output began to rise again in a second wave at a level of per capita income of about US$4,000 (in 2000 purchasing power parity [PPP] terms). However, India—which, for example, has experienced a dramatic growth of its software and business services sector during the decades since 1980—had a per capita income level of about US$3,300 (in 2000 PPP terms) as late as 2009.

30. The higher labor productivity in informal services was attributable, at least in part, to urban areas' more widespread and higher-quality infrastructure, such as roads, electricity, and hospitals.

31. In contrast, the share of female workers is strikingly low across all sectors in South Asia and Middle East and North Africa.

32. Estimates are based on the 10-sector database of the Groningen Growth and Development Center (GGDC) (Timmer, DeVries, and DeVries 2015).

33. The share of finance and business services in total employment across 25 LMICs, on average, increased from 2 percent in 1985 to 5 percent in 2010, while their corresponding share in GDP increased from 6 percent in 1985 to 10 percent in 2010. These estimates are based on the GGDC 10-sector database.

34. The skill requirements of global innovator services, combined with possibilities for remote delivery, make it advantageous for firms to agglomerate in major cities (Brinkman 2014; Diodato, Neffke, and O'Clery 2018). In the United States, tradable services are located primarily in densely populated coastal areas (Gervais and Jensen 2019). In India, services are more urbanized than manufacturing (Ghani, Grover, and Kerr 2016). This regional concentration could widen the rural-urban divide by boosting employment and wages in cities.

References

Acemoglu, Daren, and Joshua Angrist. 1999. "How Large Are the Social Returns to Education? Evidence from Compulsory Schooling Laws." Working Paper 7444, National Bureau of Economic Research, Cambridge, MA.

Amirapu, Amrit, and Arvind Subramanian. 2015. "Manufacturing or Services? An Indian Illustration of a Development Dilemma." Working Paper 409, Center for Global Development, Washington, DC.

Amoranto, Glenita, Douglas H. Brooks, and Natalie Chun. 2010. "Services Liberalization and Wage Inequality in the Philippines." Economics Working Paper 239, Asian Development Bank, Manila.

Anderson, James E., Catherine A. Milot, and Yoto V. Yotov. 2014. "How Much Does Geography Deflect Services Trade? Canadian Answers." *International Economic Review* 55 (3): 791–818.

Antimiani, Alessandro, and Lucian Cernat. 2018. "Liberalizing Global Trade in Mode 5 Services: How Much Is It Worth?" *Journal of World Trade* 52 (1): 65–83.

Baldwin, Robert E. 1969. "The Case against Infant-Industry Tariff Protection." *Journal of Political Economy* 77 (3): 295–305.

Baumol, William J. 1967. "Macroeconomics of Unbalanced Growth: The Anatomy of Urban Crisis." *American Economic Review* 57 (3): 415–26.

Beegle, Katherine, and Luc Christiaensen, eds. 2019. *Accelerating Poverty Reduction in Africa.* Washington, DC: World Bank.

Besley, Timothy. 1994. "How Do Market Failures Justify Interventions in Rural Credit Markets?" *World Bank Research Observer* 9 (1): 27–47.

Bhagwati, Jagdish N. 1984. "Why Are Services Cheaper in the Poor Countries?" *Economic Journal* 94 (374): 279–86.

Blattman, Christopher, and Stefan Dercon. 2016. "Occupational Choice in Early Industrializing Societies: Experimental Evidence on the Income and Health Effects of Industrial And Entrepreneurial Work." Working Paper 22683, National Bureau of Economic Research, Cambridge, MA.

Blau, Francine D., and Lawrence M. Kahn. 2017. "The Gender Wage Gap: Extent, Trends, and Explanations." *Journal of Economic Literature* 55 (3): 789–865.

Blinder, Alan S. 2009. "How Many US Jobs Might be Offshorable?" *World Economics* 10 (2): 41–78.

Blinder, Alan S., and Alan B. Krueger. 2013. "Alternative Measures of Offshorability: A Survey Approach." *Journal of Labor Economics* 31 (S1): S97–S128.

Borrowman, Mary, and Stephan Klasen. 2020. "Drivers of Gendered Sectoral and Occupational Segregation in Developing Countries." *Feminist Economics* 26 (2): 62–94.

Branstetter, Lee, Britta Glennon, and J. Bradford Jensen. 2018. "Knowledge Transfer Abroad: The Role of US Inventors within Global R&D Networks." Working Paper 24453, National Bureau of Economic Research, Cambridge, MA.

Brinkman, Jeffrey. 2014. "The Supply and Demand of Skilled Workers in Cities and the Role of Industry Composition." Working Paper 14-32, Federal Reserve Bank of Philadelphia.

Caselli, Francesco. 2006. "Accounting for Cross-Country Income Differences." In *Handbook of Economic Growth Vol 1A*, edited by Philippe Aghion and Steven N. Durlauf, 679–741. Amsterdam: Elsevier North-Holland.

Chenery, Hollis B. 1960. "Patterns of Industrial Growth." *American Economic Review* 50 (4): 624–54.

Christiaensen, Luc, and Ravi Kanbur. 2017. "Secondary Towns and Poverty Reduction: Refocusing the Urbanization Agenda." *Annual Review of Resource Economics* 9 (1): 405–19.

Christiaensen, Luc, and Will Martin. 2018. "Agriculture, Structural Transformation and Poverty Reduction: Eight New Insights." *World Development* 109: 413–16.

Clark, John M. 1940. "Toward a Concept of Workable Competition." *American Economic Review* 30 (2): 241–56.

Cusolito, Ana Paula, and William F. Maloney. 2018. *Productivity Revisited: Shifting Paradigms in Analysis and Policy*. Washington, DC: World Bank.

Dasgupta, Sukti, and Ajit Singh. 2007. "Manufacturing, Services and Premature Deindustrialization in Developing Countries: A Kaldorian Analysis." In *Advancing Development: Core Themes in Global Economics*, edited by George Mavrotas and Anthony Shorrocks, 435–54. London: Palgrave Macmillan.

De, Prabir, and Ajitava Raychaudhuri. 2008. "Is India's Services Trade Pro-Poor? A Simultaneous Approach." Working Paper 16, United Nations Economic and Social Commission for Asia and the Pacific (UNESCAP), Bangkok.

De Ferranti, David, Guillermo E. Perry, Daniel Lederman, and William E. Maloney. 2002. *From Natural Resources to the Knowledge Economy: Trade and Job Quality*. Washington, DC: World Bank.

Diao, Xinshen, Margaret McMillan, and Dani Rodrik. 2019. "The Recent Growth Boom in Developing Economies: A Structural-Change Perspective." In *The Palgrave Handbook of Development Economics: Critical Reflections on Globalisation and Development*, edited by Machiko Nissanke and José Antonio Ocampo, 281–334. Cham, Switzerland: Palgrave Macmillan.

Diodato, Dario, Frank Neffke, and Neave O'Clery. 2018. "Why Do Industries Coagglomerate? How Marshallian Externalities Differ by Industry and Have Evolved over Time." *Journal of Urban Economics* 106: 1–26.

Dorosh, Paul, and James Thurlow. 2018. "Beyond Agriculture versus Non-Agriculture: Decomposing Sectoral Growth–Poverty Linkages in Five African Countries." *World Development* 109: 440–51.

Duarte, Margarida, and Diego Restuccia. 2010. "The Role of the Structural Transformation in Aggregate Productivity." *Quarterly Journal of Economics* 125 (1): 129–73.

Eichengreen, Barry, and Poonam Gupta. 2011. "The Service Sector as India's Road to Economic Growth." Working Paper 16757, National Bureau of Economic Research, Cambridge, MA.

Enache, Maria, Ejaz Ghani, and Stephen O'Connell. 2016. "Structural Transformation in Africa: A Historical View." Policy Research Working Paper 7743, World Bank, Washington, DC.

Fisher, A. G. B. 1935. *The Clash of Progress and Society*. London: Macmillan.

Fontagné, Lionel, Amélie Guillin, and Cristina Mitaritonna. 2011. "Estimations of Tariff Equivalents for the Services Sectors." Working Paper 2011-24, Centres d'Etudes Prospectives et d'Informations Internationales (CEPII), Paris.

Fontagné, Lionel, Pierre Mohnen, and Guntram Wolff. 2014. "No Industry, No Future." *Notes du conseil d'analyse économique* 13 (3): 1–12.

Francois, Joseph, and Bernard Hoekman. 2010. "Services Trade and Policy." *Journal of Economic Literature* 48 (3): 642–92.

Freund, Caroline, and Diana Weinhold. 2002. "The Internet and International Trade in Services." *American Economic Review* 92 (2): 236–40.

Gereffi, Gary, and Donald L. Wyman, eds. 2014. *Manufacturing Miracles: Paths of Industrialization in Latin America and East Asia.* Princeton, NJ: Princeton University Press.

Gervais, Antoine. 2018. "Estimating the Impact of Country-Level Policy Restrictions on Services Trade." *Review of International Economics* 26 (4): 743–67.

Gervais, Antoine, and J. Bradford Jensen. 2019. "The Tradability of Services: Geographic Concentration and Trade Costs." *Journal of International Economics* 118: 331-50.

Ghani, Ejaz, and Homi Kharas. 2010. "The Service Revolution." *Economic Premise*, issue 14, World Bank, Washington, DC.

Ghani, Syed Ejaz, Arti Grover, and William Robert Kerr. 2016. "Spatial Development and Agglomeration Economies in Services: Lessons from India." Policy Research Working Paper 7741, World Bank, Washington, DC.

Griliches, Zvi. 1992. "The Search for R&D Spillovers." *Scandinavian Journal of Economics* 94 (Suppl.): S29-S47.

Hallward-Driemeier, Mary. 2013. *Enterprising Women: Expanding Economic Opportunities in Africa.* Washington, DC: World Bank.

Hallward-Driemeier, Mary, and Gaurav Nayyar. 2018. *Trouble in the Making? The Future of Manufacturing-Led Development.* Washington, DC: World Bank.

Herrendorf, Berthold, Richard Rogerson, and Ákos Valentinyi. 2013. "Two Perspectives on Preferences and Structural Transformation." *American Economic Review* 103 (7): 2752–89.

Heuser, Cecilia, and Aaditya Mattoo. 2017. "Services Trade and Global Value Chains." Policy Research Working Paper 8126, World Bank, Washington, DC.

Hill, T. Peter. 1977. "On Goods and Services." *Review of Income and Wealth* 23 (4): 315–38.

Hovhannisyan, Shoghik, Veronica Montalva-Talledo, Tyler Remick, Carlos Rodriguez-Castelan, and Kersten Stamm. 2021. "A Global Job Quality Index." Unpublished manuscript, World Bank, Washington, DC.

IMF (International Monetary Fund). 2018. *World Economic Outlook, April 2018: Cyclical Upswing, Structural Change.* Washington, DC: IMF.

Jaumotte, Florence, and Carolina Osorio Buitron. 2015. "Inequality and Labor Market Institutions." IMF Staff Discussion Note 15/14, International Monetary Fund, Washington, DC.

Jensen, J. Bradford, and Lori G. Kletzer. 2005. "Tradable Services: Understanding the Scope and Impact of Services Outsourcing." Working Paper 05-9, Peterson Institute for International Economics, Washington, DC.

Kaldor, Nicholas. 1966. *Causes of the Slow Rate of Economic Growth of the United Kingdom: An Inaugural Lecture.* London: Cambridge University Press.

Kaldor, Nicholas. 1967. *Strategic Factors in Economic Development.* Ithaca, NY: School of Industrial and Labor Relations, Cornell University.

Kinfemichael, Bisrat, and A. K. M. Mahbub Morshed. 2019. "Unconditional Convergence of Labor Productivity in the Service Sector." *Journal of Macroeconomics* 59: 217–29.

Kohn, Melvin. 1989. *Class and Conformity: A Study in Values—With a Reassessment, 1977.* Midway Reprint ed. Chicago: University of Chicago Press.

Kuznets, Simon. 1971. *Economic Growth of Nations: Total Output and Production Structure.* Cambridge, MA: Harvard University Press.

Lederman, Daniel, and William F. Maloney. 2010. "Does It Matter What LAC Produces and Exports?" Semiannual Report of the Office of the Regional Chief Economist, Latin America and the Caribbean Region, World Bank, Washington, DC.

Lequiller, François, and Derek W. Blades. 2014. *Understanding National Accounts.* 2nd ed. Paris: Organisation for Economic Co-operation and Development.

Lewis, William Arthur. 1954. "Economic Development with Unlimited Supplies of Labour." *Manchester School of Economic and Social Studies* 22 (2): 139–91.

Loayza, Norman V., and Claudio Raddatz. 2010. "The Composition of Growth Matters for Poverty Alleviation." *Journal of Development Economics* 93 (1): 137–51.

Loungani, Prakash, Saurabh Mishra, Chris Papageorgiou, and Ke Wang. 2017. "World Trade in Services: Evidence from a New Dataset." Working Paper 17/77, International Monetary Fund, Washington, DC.

McMillan, Margaret S., and Dani Rodrik. 2011. "Globalization, Structural Change and Productivity Growth." Working Paper 17143, National Bureau of Economic Research, Cambridge, MA.

McMillan, Margaret S., Dani Rodrik, and C. Sepúlveda. 2017. "Structural Change, Fundamentals, and Growth: A Framework and Case Studies." Working Paper 23378, National Bureau of Economic Research, Cambridge, MA.

McMillan, Margaret, Dani Rodrik, and Íñigo Verduzco-Gallo. 2014. "Globalization, Structural Change, and Productivity Growth, with an Update on Africa." *World Development* 63: 11–32.

Mehta, Aashish, and Rana Hasan. 2012. "The Effects of Trade and Services Liberalization on Wage Inequality in India." *International Review of Economics & Finance* 23: 75–90.

Miroudot, Sébastien, Jehan Sauvage, and Ben Shepherd. 2013. "Measuring the Cost of International Trade in Services." *World Trade Review* 12 (4): 719–35.

Moretti, Enrico. 1999. "Estimating the External Return to Education: Evidence from Repeated Cross-Sectional and Longitudinal Data." Unpublished manuscript, University of California, Berkeley.

Nayyar, Gaurav. 2012. *The Service Sector in India's Development.* New York: Cambridge University Press.

Nayyar, Gaurav. 2013. "Inside the Black Box of Services: Evidence from India." *Cambridge Journal of Economics* 37 (1): 143–70.

Nayyar, Gaurav, Marcio Cruz, and Linghui Zhu. 2018. "Does Premature Deindustrialization Matter? The Role of Manufacturing versus Services in Development." Policy Research Working Paper 8596, World Bank, Washington, DC.

Pires, Cesaltina Pacheco, Soumodip Sarkar, and Luísa Carvalho. 2008. "Innovation in Services: How Different from Manufacturing?" *Service Industries Journal* 28 (10): 1339–56.

Restuccia, Diego, Dennis Tao Yang, and Xiaodong Zhu. 2008. "Agriculture and Aggregate Productivity: A Quantitative Cross-Country Analysis." *Journal of Monetary Economics* 55 (2): 234–50.

Rodríguez-Clare, Andrés. 2007. "Clusters and Comparative Advantage: Implications for Industrial Policy." *Journal of Development Economics* 82 (1): 43–57.

Rodrik, Dani. 2012. "Unconditional Convergence in Manufacturing." *Quarterly Journal of Economics* 128 (1): 165–204.

Rodrik, Dani. 2014. "Are Services the New Manufactures?" Commentary, *Project Syndicate*, October 13. https://www.project-syndicate.org/commentary/are-services-the-new-manufactures-by-dani-rodrik-2014-10?barrier=accesspaylog.

Rodrik, Dani. 2016. "Premature Deindustrialization." *Journal of Economic Growth* 21 (1): 1–33.

Smith, Adam. 1776. *An Inquiry into the Nature and Causes of the Wealth of Nations.* London: W. Strahan and T. Cadell.

Söderbom, Måns, and Francis Teal. 2004. "Size and Efficiency in African Manufacturing Firms: Evidence from Firm-Level Panel Data." *Journal of Development Economics* 73 (1): 369–94.

Sorbe, Stéphane, Peter Gal, and Valentine Millot. 2018. "Can Productivity Still Grow in Service-Based Economies? Literature Overview and Preliminary Evidence from OECD Countries." Economics Department Working Paper 1531, Organisation for Economic Co-operation and Development, Paris.

Stiglitz, Joseph E. 2018. "From Manufacturing-Led Export Growth to a Twenty-First-Century Inclusive Growth Strategy: Explaining the Demise of a Successful Growth Model and What to Do about It." Working Paper 2018/176, United Nations World Institute for Development Economics Research (UNU-WIDER), Helsinki.

Szirmai, Adam. 2012. "Industrialisation as an Engine of Growth in Developing Countries, 1950–2005." *Structural Change and Economic Dynamics* 23 (4): 406–20.

Timmer, Marcel P., Gaaitzen J. de Vries, and Klaas de Vries. 2015. "Patterns of Structural Change in Developing Countries." In *Routledge Handbook of Industry and Development*, edited by John Weiss and Michael Tribe, 65–83. Abingdon, UK, and New York: Routledge.

UN (United Nations). 1993. *System of National Accounts 1993*. Brussels/Luxembourg, European Commission; Washington, DC: International Monetary Fund and World Bank; Paris: Organisation for Economic Co-operation and Development; and New York: UN. https://unstats.un.org/unsd/nationalaccount/docs/1993sna.pdf.

Verhoogen, Eric A. 2008. "Trade, Quality Upgrading, and Wage Inequality in the Mexican Manufacturing Sector." *Quarterly Journal of Economics* 123 (2): 489–530.

Wettstein, Steen, Antonella Liberatore, Joscelyn Magdeleine, and Andreas Maurer. 2019. "A Global Trade in Services Data Set by Sector and by Mode of Supply (TISMOS)." Methodological paper, World Trade Organization, Geneva.

World Bank. 2012. *World Development Report 2013: Jobs*. Washington, DC: World Bank.

World Bank. 2019. *World Development Report 2019: The Future of Work*. Washington, DC: World Bank.

World Bank. 2020. *World Development Report 2020: Trading for Development in the Age of Global Value Chains*. Washington, DC: World Bank.

WTO (World Trade Organization). 2019. *World Trade Report: The Future of Services Trade*. Geneva: WTO.

2 Productivity and Jobs in Services: Mind the Gaps

Introduction

If the services sector can no longer be dismissed as an important source of productivity growth and jobs—as the aggregate data now establish—policy makers need to better understand which subsectors and types of firms have the greatest potential for these twin gains as well as what drives the relationship between productivity growth and job creation.

Chapter 1 focused on comparisons between countries in their scope for services to help enable lower-income countries to catch up to the productivity of higher-income countries. To focus simply on the large productivity gaps between countries (regarding both services in aggregate and among services subsectors) could easily become an exercise in discouragement. Fortunately, however, the evidence shows that the growth in services is gradually helping many low- and middle-income countries (LMICs) to narrow this gap.

Exploring the Productivity-Jobs Relationship in Services

The aggregate data also point toward the potential *within* countries for catch-up through productivity growth, creating better jobs on the way. This chapter explores the within-country dynamics in more detail. It uses firm-level data to better understand how and where this productivity growth and expanded job creation could be achieved.

Given that the potential to achieve scale, innovation, and spillovers varies across the services subsector groups identified in chapter 1—global innovator services, low-skill tradable services, low-skill domestic services, and skill-intensive social services—this chapter compares these groups as well as firms and subsectors in these groups within countries.[1]

The microdata confirm that some service firms are extremely productive; the question is how to have more of them. To better understand how services firms contribute to productivity and jobs, this chapter analyzes a unique dataset on formal firms from 20 LMICs to establish a series of stylized facts. Services are compared not only with manufacturing but also with each other to explore the relative contributions across services subsectors, using the typology from chapter 1.

The data highlight that services firms are indeed far from monolithic. The services sector exhibits a large variation in the productivity of subsectors and firms. For example, across country income groups, one of the most productive subsectors, information and communication technology (ICT), is three to six times as productive as one of the least productive subsectors, hospitality services. But firm productivity also varies greatly *within* services subsectors, and in many countries this variance is higher than in manufacturing.

The channels highlighted in chapter 1 through which manufacturing has achieved productivity growth—scale, innovation, and spillovers—remain relevant for services but operate in slightly different ways:

- *The channel of scale* seems to be more muted. Services establishments tend to be smaller than manufacturers and their productivity less strongly related to size, suggesting more limited economies of scale at the establishment level. However, economies of scale can be achieved in other ways, such as through branching, franchising, or selling remotely.

- *The channel of innovation* is important, but the lower use of physical capital means that innovation will likely rely more on intangible forms of capital, including human capital. A lower need for physical capital also lowers barriers to entry, highlighting the potential for young firms to drive change in the sector.

- *The channel of spillovers* is particularly important for services because those services subsectors that are linked to other parts of the economy are among the most productive.

These productivity differences also have implications for jobs. Productivity is strongly related to wages and other aspects of job quality. In the formal sector, the top productivity decile of services firms pays average wages that are about 2.7–4.0 times higher than firms in the bottom productivity decile.

Consequently, the services sector varies greatly in the quality of jobs on offer. It provides some of the best-paid jobs in any economy, especially in global innovator services such as information technology (IT) and professional services. However, on the other end of the spectrum, less-productive sectors like small-scale retail, food services, and personal services see high degrees of informal employment, low wages, and few nonwage benefits. These subsectors are particularly large in LMICs. This matters from the perspective of economic inclusion. The important role of human capital in contributing to productivity also means that skill requirements can form a serious barrier for low-skilled workers to move into more-productive sectors.

This chapter is structured as follows:

- The next section presents new firm-level evidence from 20 countries to determine key stylized facts on patterns of productivity and jobs, taking advantage of the services subsector categories developed in chapter 1. The firm-level data corroborate that treating services as a monolith misses the important ways in which services subsectors perform very differently from each other.

- The chapter then discusses the implications of these facts in terms of the three channels of productivity growth identified in chapter 1: scale, innovation, and linkages.

- The implications for jobs are examined next. Job quality is strongly linked with productivity, both within and across sectors. Yet jobs are not distributed equally, with female workers often finding themselves on the lower end of the job quality spectrum. Building skills is crucial to facilitate movement to higher-productivity jobs, which tend to require higher skills. This means not just formal job training but also more informal methods such as on-the-job training.

- The conclusion summarizes the chapter's findings and connects them with the themes of subsequent chapters.

Services Firms and Their Productivity: Eight Stylized Facts

This section presents a set of stylized facts on services firms, focusing on these firms' size, productivity, capital use, and dynamic patterns. The productivity analysis centers on two measures of productivity: labor productivity and total factor productivity (TFP). Labor productivity is measured as value added per worker. TFP takes not only labor inputs but also the efficiency in the use of physical capital into account.

Both measures have important caveats: Even though labor productivity is easily calculated and tends to be readily available in official statistics, it inherently reflects not only the worker's contribution to productivity but also the amount of capital at the worker's disposal. TFP corrects for the use of physical capital. However (as highlighted in the "Spotlight" between this chapter and the next), estimating TFP correctly requires a more careful measurement of inputs, outputs, prices, and the production process, as well as additional assumptions on the nature of competition. Data limitations—such as the absence of data on intangible assets or sparse data on capital use and prices—mean that the TFP estimates presented in this chapter do not correct for intangible forms of capital and rely on a set of assumptions and imputations to allow for comparisons across sectors and countries.[2]

To better understand the productivity dynamics of firms in the services sector, this chapter analyzes a unique dataset of comprehensive firm-level data from 20 LMICs across all regions, taken from industrial censuses, representative surveys, business registers, and other administrative sources. This dataset covers formal enterprises and includes both establishment-level and firm-level data. Apart from excluding firms with no recorded employees, no minimum size thresholds have been applied. For 11 of these 20 countries, detailed panel data are available as well. (For an overview of the data sources, see annex 2A.) This dataset is supplemented with aggregated data from 46 middle- and high-income countries, compiled from the Organisation for Economic Co-operation and Development (OECD); the European Union's statistical office, Eurostat; and the US Census Bureau.

Although these data cover countries across all regions and income groups, there is still considerable room to improve data collection on firms in the services sector, in terms of both country coverage and the kinds of data collected. In several countries (such as Ethiopia and Morocco), key datasets on firms still exclude services establishments.[3] Even if the surveys include the services sector, more effort is needed to capture production inputs (particularly intangible capital), prices, or the quality of services, a difficult task given the lack of standardization or even durability of the output. (For more discussion of the data agenda, see also the "Spotlight" and chapter 6.)

Stylized Fact 1: Not All Services Are Equally (Un)Productive

These data confirm that the productivity of services firms varies substantially across the services subsector groups identified in chapter 1, with further variation *within* subsectors. Figure 2.1 shows the labor productivity and TFP of formal services firms relative to manufacturing firms in LMICs and high-income countries (HICs).

Global innovator services tend to have the highest productivity of all the services subsector groups, and they tend to have higher TFP than manufacturing. Among the global innovators, financial services see TFP levels that are 3.5 times higher than manufacturing in LMICs (and about 2.5 times in HICs). ICT services see TFP levels that are about 1.5 times higher in LMICs (and 1.3 times in HICs). Professional services see levels of labor productivity below that of manufacturing, but TFP levels—which correct for differences in physical capital—that are slightly above manufacturing (being 8 percent more productive than manufacturing in LMICs and 16 percent more productive in HICs).

Low-skill tradable and low-skill domestic services tend to have lower productivity than manufacturing, even when correcting for the use of physical capital. In low-skill tradable services, the lowest productivity occurs in hospitality: its TFP in LMICs is 34 percent of manufacturing TFP. Among low-skill domestic services, the lowest productivity is in "other services," which includes social, community, and personal services. Because these productivity estimates are based on formal firms only, they likely overestimate the productivity of sectors with high rates of informality—most notably, retail and personal services.

FIGURE 2.1 **Labor Productivity and TFP Vary across Services Subsectors, with Global Innovators Being the Most Productive**

Labor productivity and TFP of selected services subsectors relative to manufacturing, by country income group, latest available year, 2010–17

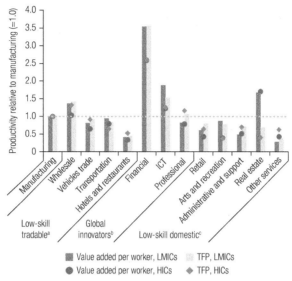

Source: Calculations based on administrative firm-level data, supplemented with aggregated data from the Organisation for Economic Co-operation and Development (OECD) and the European Union's statistical office, Eurostat.

Note: Data are from 56 countries, including 35 low- and middle-income LMICs, across all regions. Labor productivity (measured as value added per worker) and total factor productivity (TFP) cover formal services firms only and are reported compared with manufacturing in the same country. TFP corrects for physical capital and assumes a common production function between sectors. The data are reported as simple averages of country values (aggregated by income group). LMICs, by World Bank income group classifications, had 1994 gross national income (GNI) of less than US$8,955. "High-income countries" (HICs) had GNI exceeding US$8,955 in 1994. Sectors are classified using the ISIC Rev. 4 classification at the section level, except for wholesale, retail, and vehicles trade, which are reported at the (two-digit) division level. Services subsectors are grouped by sets of pro-development characteristics (defined in chapter 1), with skill-intensive social services excluded because of their limited coverage in firm-level data. ICT = information and communication technology. (For a full list of data sources and the periods covered in each dataset, see annex 2A.)

a. Low-skill domestic services employ mostly low-skilled workers and are less tradable internationally than other subsector groups.

b. Low-skill tradable services employ mostly low-skilled workers, are considered tradable in international markets, and may be amenable to offshoring.

c. Global innovator services employ mostly high-skilled workers, are highly traded internationally, and are the most amenable to offshoring.

When comparing services subsectors in more detail, productivity varies even more. Figure 2.2 further breaks down productivity at the industry level—as defined by the two-digit United Nations (UN) International Standard Industrial Classification of All Economic Activities (ISIC) Rev. 4 industrial classification. That breakdown shows, among other things, the following:

- *ICT services* exhibit high productivity among all its subsectors, with the highest levels in software programming and consulting as well as telecommunications. In telecommunications, labor productivity is especially high, reflecting the capital intensity of this subsector.

Within Services Subsectors, Productivity Is More Varied across More Narrowly Defined Industries

Labor productivity and TFP of selected service industries relative to manufacturing, by country income group, latest available year, 2010–17

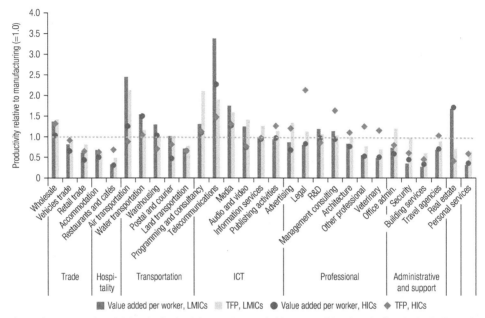

Source: Calculations using administrative firm-level data, supplemented with aggregated data from the Organisation for Economic Co-operation and Development (OECD) and the European Union's statistical office, Eurostat.

Note: Data are from 56 countries, including 35 low- and middle-income countries (LMICs) across all regions. Labor productivity (measured as value added per worker) and total factor productivity (TFP) cover formal services firms only and are reported relative to manufacturing firms in the same country. TFP corrects for physical capital and assumes a common production function between sectors. The data are reported as simple averages of country values (aggregated by income group). LMICs, by World Bank income group classifications, had 1994 gross national income (GNI) of less than US$8,955. High-income countries had GNI exceeding US$8,955 in 1994. Industries are classified using the International Standard Industrial Classification (ISIC) Rev. 4 industrial classification, at the section and the (two-digit) division levels. ICT = information and communication technology; R&D = research and development. For a full list of sources, by country, see annex 2A.

- *Transportation and storage services* show large differences between segments. Capital-intensive transportation services such as air and water transportation—which rely on a mix of high-skilled labor (such as captains and pilots) and lower-skilled labor (such as cabin crews)—have higher productivity than land transportation services. Warehousing shows productivity levels close to manufacturing.

- *Administrative and support services* exhibit the highest TFP in office administrative services and the lowest in building services, which includes cleaning activities.

The productivity of many services subsectors relative to manufacturing in the same country is quite similar across income groups. In fact, the relative productivity of most services subsectors is slightly *higher* in LMICs than in HICs. This in line with the finding highlighted in chapter 1 that the productivity gap between LMICs and HICs is not the same for all sectors but can also reflect the manufacturing sector's weak

At Your Service? The Promise of Services-Led Development

productivity performance in many lower-income countries (Hallward-Driemeier and Nayyar 2018).

The sectoral composition explains a large part of the observed labor productivity within a country. Figure 2.3 presents the shares of variation in labor productivity among firms in this book's firm-level dataset that are explained by sector, the use of capital, and other firm characteristics (such as firm size, age, and ownership). The analysis shows that close to half (45 percent) of observed variation in output per worker and more than a third (36 percent) of observed variation in value added per worker in the services sector can be explained by a firm's economic activity (that is, its industry). If we add firm characteristics and capital use to the equation, these combined factors account for 55 percent of the variation in output per worker and 41 percent of the variation in value added per worker. Nevertheless, the firm's industry remains the most important observable factor explaining productivity performance in the services sector.

Yet, at the same time, a large part of the variation remains unexplained by industry and observable firm characteristics—highlighting significant unexplained heterogeneity, even within industries and groups of firms. This heterogeneity has implications for the data agenda: clearly, additional dimensions of firm behavior could be captured, from better service-quality measures to management practices. Better understanding the characteristics of services firms and how they contribute to productivity is key.

FIGURE 2.3 **Industry and Firm Characteristics Explain about Half the Variation in Labor Productivity**

Shares of factors explaining labor productivity variation between firms, by two measures, in the services and manufacturing sectors of selected LMICs, latest available year, 2010–17

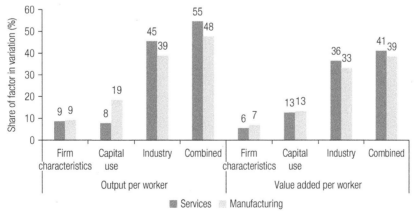

Source: Calculations based on administrative firm-level data and business censuses (see annex 2A).

Note: Data are from 13 low- and middle-income countries (LMICs) across all regions. Both measures of labor productivity (output per worker and value added per worker) are reported for formal services firms only. The explained shares are the R^2 of regressions of log output per worker or log value added per worker on year; industry dummies (either two-digit or four-digit for economic activity); log capital stock (where available); firm size, age, and (if available) ownership dummies (for firm characteristics); as well as all combined, averaged across countries. LMICs, by World Bank income group classifications, had 1994 gross national income of less than US$8,955.

In manufacturing, the role of scale and the importance of large firms for employment, productivity, and generating exports has been well documented (Bartelsman, Haltiwanger, and Scarpetta 2013; Di Giovanni, Levchenko, and Mejean 2017; Freund and Pierola 2015; Van Biesebroeck 2005). Comprehensive analysis of firm-level data from nine LMICs conducted by Ciani et al. (2020) confirms these findings for the countries studied, showing that in manufacturing, but not always in services, large firms account for most of the job creation and provide higher wages, are more productive, and are more likely to export than smaller-scale firms.

Even though—as highlighted later—some of the world's largest companies operate in the services sector, the average services firm is small. Statistics collected by Bento and Restuccia (2021), covering both formal and informal enterprises, highlight that services establishments tend to be significantly smaller than manufacturing establishments (figure 2.4). In LMICs, services establishments employ on average 3 workers—only

FIGURE 2.4 **Services Firms Are Smaller Than Manufacturing Firms across All Income Groups**

Average establishment size, by sector and country income level, average of latest available years, 2000–12

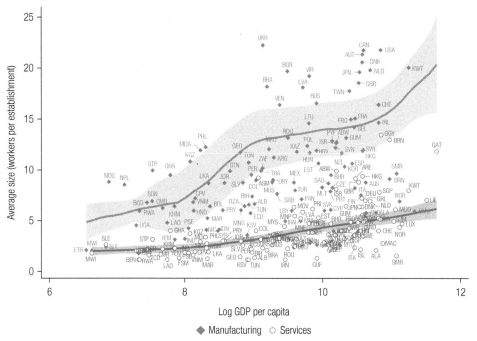

◆ Manufacturing ○ Services

Source: Calculations using data collected by Bento and Restuccia (2021).

Note: Data cover both formal and informal firms across all regions, based on 144 countries across all regions, and averages available data for the years 2000–12 (annual coverage varies across countries). Corrections have been applied to countries where data are reported on a firm level rather than on an establishment level. Countries are labeled using ISO alpha-3 codes. The shaded areas represent 95 percent confidence intervals.

about one-fourth of the average 11 workers in manufacturing establishments. In higher-income countries, services establishments are slightly larger (employing 5 workers on average), but the gap with manufacturing (employing on average 16 workers per establishment) remains.[4]

There are nevertheless establishment-size differences between sectors. Commerce (comprising wholesale and retail trade) and business services tend to be the smallest, while ICT services are closer in average size to manufacturing, although still smaller (figure 2.5).

Importance of Informal Firms

Even though most of the results highlighted in this chapter relate to the formal sector only, informal firms play an important role in services. In lower-income countries, many services firms are unregistered, particularly those in small-scale retail and personal services (box 2.1). Part of the observed gap in establishment size between lower- and higher-income countries (figure 2.4) can be explained by the presence of informality.

Many informal firms tend to be micro-size firms, with fewer than five employees. Moreover, informal firms tend to underperform formal enterprises in sales and productivity; are often run by managers with less education; rarely formalize over their lifetimes (La Porta and Shleifer 2014); and are often characterized by necessity entrepreneurship (Acs 2006). Even though some informal firms produce on a par

FIGURE 2.5 **Commerce and Business Establishments Are the Smallest, While the Average ICT and Manufacturing Establishments Are Close in Size**
Average establishment size in manufacturing and selected services subsectors, average of latest available years, 2000–12

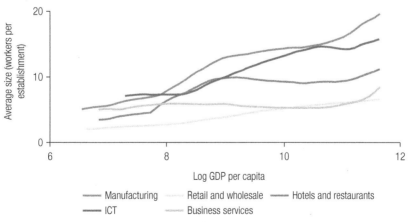

Source: Calculations using data collected by Bento and Restuccia (2021).

Note: Data cover both formal and informal firms in 144 countries across all regions and are averaged from the latest available data between 2000 and 2012 (annual coverage varies by country). Corrections have been applied to countries where data are reported on a firm level rather than on an establishment level. "Commerce" comprises retail and wholesale trade. ICT = information and communication technology.

BOX 2.1

Informality in the Services Sector

Many LMICs have a substantial informal sector—which (as chapter 1 highlighted) has accounted for much of the expansion of services in those economies. In line with the nature of informality, precise data on informal firms remain scarce in many countries. However, the available data suggest that low-skill service sectors, such as retail and personal services, form most of the informal sector. Recent World Bank Enterprise Surveys of unregistered firms in four countries show that more than 70 percent of these firms are in services, employing more than two-thirds of the informal workforce (figure B2.1.1).

Even though in manufacturing, informality is prevalent, especially when the share of unregistered firms (which, for example, in Brazil and Mexico is higher than for retail firms; Perry and Maloney 2007) is examined, a large part of employment and value added is still found in the formal sector. This is different for many services sectors, in which informality dominates employment and value added. For example, economic census data from Ghana show that even though the share of unregistered manufacturing firms is higher than in many services sectors, when employment and value added are examined, the share of unregistered businesses is higher than in manufacturing for several services subsectors, especially in retail, hospitality, and other services, the latter including social, community, and personal services (figure B2.1.2). The importance of informality in services sector employment is in line with the household survey data presented in chapter 1.

La Porta and Shleifer (2014) and Ulyssea (2020) discuss three commonly held views about informality and its potential for development:

FIGURE B2.1.1 **Most Informal Enterprises Operate in Retail Services**
Sectoral distribution of informal enterprises in four selected LMICs, 2018–19

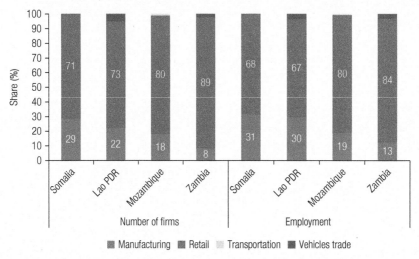

Source: World Bank Enterprise Surveys, 2018–19.

Note: Low- and middle-income countries (LMICs), by World Bank income group classifications, had 1994 gross national income of less than US$8,955.

Box continues on the following page

Informality in the Services Sector *(continued)*

FIGURE B2.1.2 **The Importance of Informality in Services Relative to Manufacturing Is Most Pronounced When Comparing Shares of Employment and Value Added**
Shares of value added and employment from unregistered businesses in Ghana, by sector, 2013

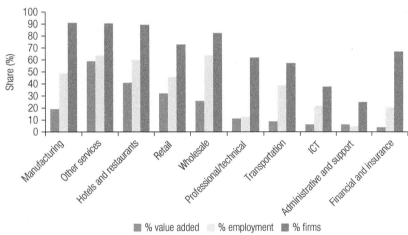

Source: Calculations using the 2013 Integrated Business Establishment Survey of the Ghana Statistical Service.
Note: The dataset includes only informal firms. Informality is determined by whether firms are registered at the Registrar General's Department. No minimum size threshold has been applied. ICT = information and communication technology.

- One view—commonly associated with De Soto (2000)—emphasizes the role of burdensome regulations in keeping firms informal and unproductive and asserts that removing barriers to formalization would encourage firm growth.
- A less favorable view of informality—as expressed by Farrell (2004) and Levy (2008)—emphasizes the benefits to informal firms of unfair competition and tax avoidance.
- A third view—as expressed by La Porta and Shleifer (2014)—contends that informality is a symptom of lacking capabilities and that informal and formal enterprises have very different characteristics.

Generally, the informal sector underperforms the formal sector in terms of revenue, profits, employment, and productivity (La Porta and Shleifer 2014), and many informal entrepreneurs likely operate their businesses out of necessity rather than opportunity (Acs 2006). In Sri Lanka, roughly two-thirds of informal entrepreneurs have characteristics more akin to wage workers than to formal entrepreneurs (De Mel, McKenzie, and Woodruff 2010). In Mozambique, 62.7 percent of informal entrepreneurs would prefer to have a wage job that provides a similar income (Aga et al. 2021).

These findings do not necessarily imply that informality is undesirable. From a social protection point of view, the informal sector is important in providing economic livelihoods to many who cannot find employment in the formal sector. Gulyani and Talukdar (2010) study informal enterprises in the slums of Nairobi and argue that—when factors explaining selection into entrepreneurship are controlled for—poverty is lower among

Box continues on the following page

Informality in the Services Sector *(continued)*

households with a microenterprise than those without. Operating in the informal sector can also have a few benefits over working in the formal sector, such as increased flexibility, control over hours, and independence (Perry and Maloney 2007, 66).

Another reason for some optimism is that informal firms exhibit considerable heterogeneity, and evidence suggests that certain informal firms could operate successfully in the formal sector—in line with either the "De Soto view" or the more pessimistic "parasite view" of Farrell (2004) and Levy (2008). The estimated share of such firms varies. Ulyssea (2018) estimates that, in Brazil, roughly half of informal firms could thrive in the formal sector, with roughly one out of five of these firms facing formalization costs that are prohibitive (in line with the "De Soto view"). In Mozambique, 7.6 percent of informal firms have characteristics and productivity levels similar to formal firms (Aga et al. 2021). In Sri Lanka, although most firms did not benefit from a formalization program, a small group of participants (5 percent) significantly increased their performance following registration (De Mel, McKenzie, and Woodruff 2010).

with formal micro firms and could have potential to grow—as examined by Ulyssea (2018) for Brazil and by Aga et al. (2021) for Mozambique—this potential tends to apply to only a small group of firms. Unfortunately, as highlighted in this book's "Spotlight," sources of comprehensive firm-level data on informal enterprises remain scarce.

Findings Specific to Formal Firms

When the analysis is restricted to formal firms, for which more data are available, the pattern of services firms being smaller than manufacturing persists and is visible across the services subsector groups identified in chapter 1 (figure 2.6). In both LMICs and HICs, the subsectors with the smallest average firm size are retail, vehicles trade, real estate, and professional services, all of which tend to be about four to five times smaller than a manufacturing firm in the same country. The sectors with the largest average firm size are transportation and storage; administrative and support services; and (in HICs) financial services.

These data, restricted to formal firms, show that in many sectors there are few differences between LMICs and HICs in average firm size. This is line with analysis from Latin America by Alfaro and Eslava (2020), who show that when including informal firms, small firms play a much larger role in LMICs than HICs, but when excluding these firms, the size gap between LMICs and HICs narrows. These narrowing gaps—at times, disappearing gaps—in firm size highlight the importance of informality in explaining firm-size differences between countries. Nevertheless, some subsectors continue to see a size gap between LMICs and HICs, most notably in the low-skill domestic services of retail and "other services" (including social, community, and personal services).

FIGURE 2.6 **When Data Are Restricted to Formal Firms, Services Firms Are Smaller Than Manufacturing Firms, on Average, in Both LMICs and HICs**

Average size of formal firms in manufacturing and selected services subsectors, by country income level, latest available year, 2010–17

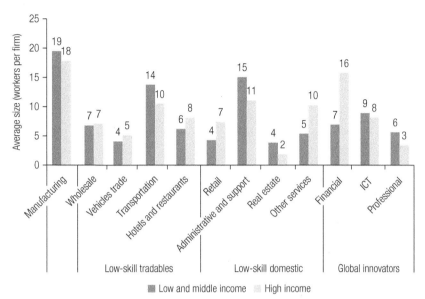

Sources: Calculations using administrative establishment-level and firm-level data, supplemented with aggregated data from the Organisation for Economic Co-operation and Development (OECD) and the European Union's statistical office, Eurostat.

Note: Data cover only formal firms from 54 countries, including 33 low- and middle-income countries (LMICs). No minimum size threshold has been applied. Establishment-level data are used where available. Services subsectors are grouped by sets of pro-development characteristics (defined in chapter 1), with skill-intensive social services excluded because of their limited coverage in firm-level data. LMICs, by World Bank income group classifications, had 1994 gross national income (GNI) of less than US$8,955. High-income countries (HICs) had GNI exceeding US$8,955 in 1994. ICT = information and communication technology. For a full list of sources, by country, see annex 2A.

Alternative measures of scale—for example, the share of employment or value added from smaller firms or the average number of coworkers that a worker has (the so-called coworker mean), as discussed in Gervais and Jensen (2013)—similarly show that, in many services subsectors, smaller firms play an important role. (For more about alternative measures of scale, see annex 2B.) Whereas in manufacturing, large firms (exceeding 250 employees) employ more than 40 percent of workers in that sector and produce more than half of value added, in many services subsectors, smaller firms account for most of the employment and value added (figure 2.7). For example, in retail, 44 percent of employment and 26 percent of value added in LMICs are contributed by firms with fewer than 10 employees. However, a few services subsectors look more like manufacturing in terms of large-firm contributions. These include administrative and support services, financial services, and transportation.

That services firms have a low average number of employees is not to say that large firms play no role at all. Of the world's 100 largest companies in the *Fortune* Global 500, 30 are firms operating predominantly in the services sector.[5] Large retail firms like

FIGURE 2.7 **In Services, Smaller Firms Contribute More to Employment and Value Added Than in Manufacturing, but Large Services Firms Still Contribute Significantly**

Firms' average contributions to employment and value added in selected sectors, by size and country income group, latest available year, 2010–17

a. Share of employment, by size class

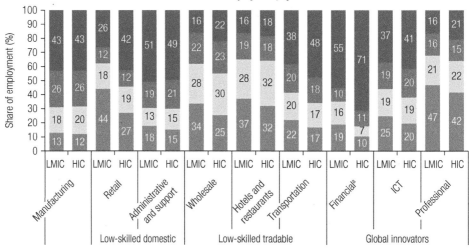

b. Share of value added, by size class

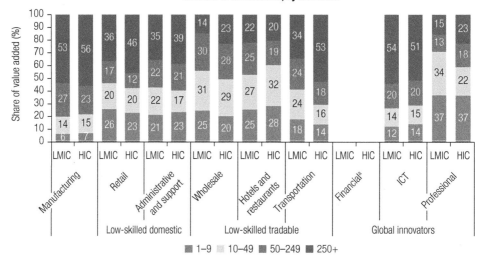

■ 1–9   ▨ 10–49   ■ 50–249   ■ 250+

Sources: Calculations using administrative firm-level data, supplemented with aggregated data from the Organisation for Economic Co-operation and Development (OECD) and the European Union's statistical office, Eurostat.

Note: The values are a simple average across 59 countries in the dataset, including 37 low- and middle-income countries (LMICs). The most recent year of data was used for each country. LMICs, by World Bank income group classifications, had 1994 gross national income (GNI) of less than US$8,955. High-income countries (HICs) had GNI exceeding US$8,955 in 1994. Industries are classified using the International Standard Industrial Classification (ISIC) Rev. 4 at the section and, for retail and wholesale, at the (two-digit) division levels. Services subsectors are grouped by sets of pro-development characteristics (defined in chapter 1), with skill-intensive social services excluded because of their limited coverage in firm-level data. ICT = information and communication technology. For a full list of sources, by country, see annex 2A.

a. Value added data for the financial sector are mostly missing and therefore not reported.

Walmart and Amazon employ close to 3 million people combined, although across multiple establishments in several countries. Large firms are present in every services subsector and contribute significantly to employment and value added (figure 2.7).

As discussed later in this chapter, establishment size is not the only relevant measure of scale. Firms can also scale up by setting up multiple branches or franchising. Digital technologies can also improve the opportunities to increase scale, as highlighted in chapter 3.

Stylized Fact 3: Size Matters Less for Productivity

Size has traditionally been associated with higher productivity for two main reasons. The first reason is that larger firms can seize efficiency gains resulting from scale economies (Bain 1954; Szirmai 2011). These gains can result from a variety of sources, such as an improved division of labor, the use of more specialized machines for tasks, and an improved bargaining position to reduce costs. The second reason relates to selection and resource reallocation. Under competitive conditions, more productive firms are more likely to grow than less productive ones, resulting in a positive relationship between size and productivity. Empirically this relationship has been well established, especially for manufacturing, as highlighted by Ciani et al. (2020) for nine LMICs, and Berlingieri, Calligaris, and Criscuolo (2018) for OECD countries.

Firm-level data show that the relationship between size and productivity is less strong for services than for manufacturing (figure 2.8, panel a). When looking at the gap in productivity between a micro firm (0–9 employees) and a large firm (with more than 250 employees), micro-size services firms can better match the labor productivity of large services firms, whereas micro-size manufacturing firms display a significant productivity gap relative to large manufacturing firms.

This difference is more pronounced in HICs. In Germany, a micro-size services firm's labor productivity is 96 percent that of a large services firm. Meanwhile, a micro-size manufacturing firm has labor productivity that is only 39 percent that of a large firm (figure 2.8, panel b). Many other HICs show similarly close productivity between micro and large services firms.

These results are in line with earlier findings on services firms—for example, the observation of Ciani et al. (2020) that only 15.4 percent of large services firms are among the top segment of productivity (compared with 60.8 percent of large manufacturing firms),[6] as well as a similar analysis of OECD countries highlighting a weaker productivity-size relationship for services (Berlingieri, Calligaris, and Criscuolo 2018). They are also in line with the finding that, in Chile, exporting (often closely related with productivity) is less dominated by large firms in the services sector than it is in manufacturing (Zahler, Iacovone, and Mattoo 2013).

FIGURE 2.8 **Especially in HICs, Small Services Firms Are Just as Productive as Large Ones**

Labor productivity of manufacturing and services firms relative to large firms (250 or more employees), latest available year, 2010–17

a. All firms, by size and country income group[a]

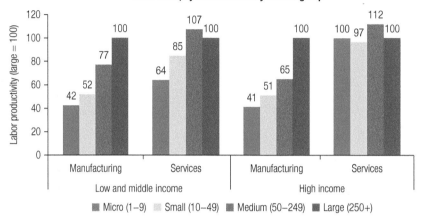

b. Firms with 0–9 employees, by country[b]

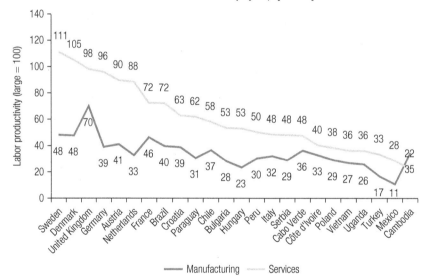

Sources: Calculations using administrative firm-level data, supplemented with aggregated data from the Organisation for Economic Co-operation and Development (OECD) and the European Union's statistical office, Eurostat.

Note: Labor productivity is measured as value added per worker. Data cover only formal firms in 51 countries, including 20 low- and middle-income countries (LMICs). Under World Bank income group classifications, LMICs had 1994 gross national income (GNI) of less than US$8,955. High-income countries (HICs) had GNI exceeding US$8,955 in 1994. For a full list of sources, with years of data, see annex 2A.

a. The values are a simple average across the 51 countries in the dataset.

b. Labor productivity is reported for micro firms (0–9 employees) relative to large firms (250 employees or more) in the same sector. The most recent year of data was used for each country.

At Your Service? The Promise of Services-Led Development

These findings are consistent with the traditional view that economies of scale matter less for services firms than for manufacturing. Part of the argument in Baumol (1967) on the relatively low productivity of services relied on his observation that much of the services sector is not characterized by scale. Some features of services could explain the lack of economies of scale. For example, the simultaneity of production and consumption often requires proximity to the consumer for a specific period of time, during which the provider cannot serve another customer (for example, in the case of customer services or personal services relying on contact). Services requiring high customization or coordination between provider and customer—such as professional services like architecture and engineering or business services like management consulting—could similarly lack opportunities to reduce the time spent on an assignment.

Yet the productivity gap between small and large services firms tends to be larger in LMICs. For example, among formal firms in Cambodia, Mexico, Turkey, Uganda, and Vietnam, large services firms remain three times as productive as micro-size firms. This could suggest that there is a larger gap in capabilities between micro-size firms and large firms in lower-income countries than in HICs, where micro-size firms achieve productivity similar to firms operating at larger scale. The wider gap in LMICs could also signify scale benefits that remain unseized and a scope for more large firms to operate in the services sector. For example, larger retail stores such as supermarkets—often part of global retail chains—tend to be less common in LMICs (Atkin, Faber, and Gonzalez-Navarro 2018) despite carrying large productivity benefits (Bronnenberg and Ellickson 2015; Lagakos 2016).[7]

On the subsector-specific level, the relationship between size and productivity is quite heterogeneous. In HICs, administrative and support services firms tend to be less productive with increasing size, whereas vehicles trade and ICT exhibit the strongest relationship between scaling-up and increased productivity (figure 2.9, panel a)—the result for ICT being driven mostly by its telecommunications subsector. For LMICs, the scale benefits seem to be the largest in ICT, retail, and hotels and restaurants (figure 2.9, panel b).

Stylized Fact 4: Physical Capital Plays a Small Role

In manufacturing, capital can play an important role in enabling firms to achieve economies of scale. In factory settings, for example, machines play a large role in producing large quantities efficiently. For the provision of services, however, physical capital usually plays a small role. In figure 2.10, most of the services subsectors are in the bottom-left quadrant, being both small and not capital intensive. This lack of capital intensity cuts across all the services subsector groups identified in chapter 1. For example, a low-skill domestic sector like retail has capital intensity

FIGURE 2.9 **In HICs, the Productivity Benefit of Scaling Up Is Smaller in Services Than in Manufacturing, but in LMICs, Some Services Subsectors Benefit More Than Manufacturing**

Productivity benefit of scaling up in manufacturing and selected services subsectors, by average firm size, latest available year, 2010–17

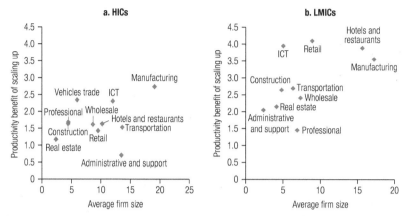

Sources: Calculations using administrative firm-level data, supplemented with aggregated data from the Organisation for Economic Co-operation and Development (OECD) and the European Union's statistical office, Eurostat.

Note: The "productivity benefit of scaling up" is defined as the productivity of a large firm (with more than 250 employees) divided by the productivity of a micro-size firm (with fewer than 9 employees). Data cover only formal firms in 21 low- and middle-income countries (LMICs) and 19 high-income countries (HICs). LMICs, by World Bank income group classifications, had 1994 gross national income (GNI) of less than US$8,955. HICs had GNI exceeding US$8,955 in 1994. ICT = information and communication technology. (For a full list of sources, by country, see annex 2A.)

similar to a high-skill global innovator like programming, and their average firm sizes are similar as well.

Nevertheless, a few service subsectors tend to be both capital intensive and to operate at a larger scale and are in this way similar to manufacturing: transportation (especially air and water transportation), telecommunications, warehousing, and R&D services. Some of these employ unskilled labor (such as transportation services and warehousing), but others likely rely more on skilled labor than unskilled labor (such as R&D services).

Stylized Fact 5: Productivity Dispersion Is Higher in Services Than in Manufacturing

The diversity in services sector productivity is seen not only between subsectors but also within subsectors. In 10 of the 13 countries with available data on dispersion, the dispersion in labor productivity is higher in services than in manufacturing (as measured by the ratio between the 10th and 90th percentiles). Figure 2.11 illustrates the labor productivity distribution for Kosovo and Sierra Leone. In Sierra Leone, a services firm in the 90th percentile appears to be almost 30 times as productive as a services firm in the 10th percentile.

FIGURE 2.10 **With Few Exceptions, Services Rely Less Than Industry on Physical Capital**

Capital per worker and average firm size in OECD countries, by industry, 2017 or earlier most recent available year

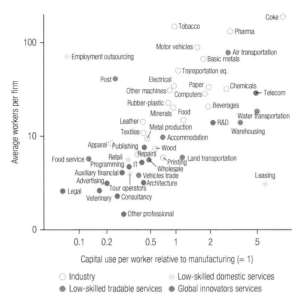

Sources: Calculations based on the Organisation for Economic Co-operation and Development (OECD) STructural ANalysis (STAN) and Structural Business Statistics databases.

Note: Average firm size is determined at the firm rather than establishment level. Data are averaged across 40 countries, including 21 low- and middle-income countries, from 2017 or the most recent earlier year. Capital use per worker is measured as net capital stock per employee, relative to the average of industry (equal to 1). "Industry" includes manufacturing, mining, construction, and utilities. Services subsectors are grouped by sets of pro-development characteristics (defined in chapter 1), with skill-intensive social services excluded because of their limited coverage in firm-level data. IT = information technology; R&D = research and development. For details on firm-level data sources, by country and year, see annex 2A.

These results are in line with results from other studies that highlight larger dispersion in services than in manufacturing, including Busso, Madrigal, and Pagés (2013) for several Latin American countries; De Vries (2014) for Brazil; Alfaro and Eslava (2020) for Colombia; Dias, Richmond, and Marques (2016) for Portugal; and Bartelsman and Wolf (2017) for the European Union.[8] Similarly, Sorbe, Gal, and Millot (2018), using the ORBIS database for OECD countries, find larger productivity gaps between frontier and laggard firms in the services sector than in manufacturing.

The higher degree of dispersion can signal distortions and resource misallocation. Compared with manufacturing, conclusive evidence on misallocation in the services sector remains scarce (Restuccia and Rogerson 2017). Hsieh and Klenow (2009) argue that the simultaneous presence of both very productive and less productive firms, which dispersion implies, is a sign that there is scope for productivity increases by reallocating production factors.

FIGURE 2.11 **Dispersion in Labor Productivity Is Higher in Services Than in Manufacturing**

Labor productivity dispersion in selected sectors, Sierra Leone and Kosovo

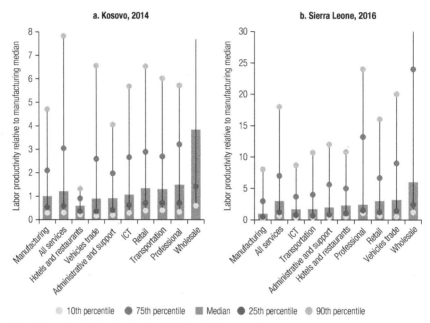

Source: Calculations using administrative firm-level data (detailed in annex 2A).

Note: Dispersion in labor productivity is measured as the ratio between the 10th and 90th percentiles (p10 and p90), relative to the manufacturing median. Wholesale sector results do not display p90 markers (or the p75 marker for Kosovo), those percentiles being outliers beyond the maximum values shown. ICT = information and communication technology.

In practice, many factors other than dispersion—including measurement issues—likely confound productivity dispersion, meaning that high dispersion cannot always be interpreted as higher misallocation. Some of these confounding factors might be even more important for services than for manufacturing.

Many of the potentially confounding factors result from using revenue-based productivity measures (such as value added per worker, or revenue total factor productivity [TFPR]) instead of quality-adjusted and quantity-based productivity measures (such as quantity total factor productivity [TFPQ]). As highlighted in this book's "Spotlight" on data, the heterogeneity and intangibility of services—as well as limited data coverage—create additional challenges in constructing quantity-based productivity measures. Revenue-based productivity measures reflect not only production but also prices. Such measures are particularly sensitive to the prices that firms charge, which in turn are determined by factors like quality and market power.

Differences in market power can lead to dispersion in revenue-based measures of productivity (De Loecker, Eeckhout, and Unger 2020). Firms with more market power can charge higher prices and will therefore likely appear more productive. An open question is whether services firms have higher market power than manufacturing firms. This likely depends on the subsector. Measures of competition restrictions, such as the OECD–World Bank Indicators of Product Market Regulation, suggest that restrictions can be high in certain services subsectors—for example, regulated occupations in professional services (Dauda and Drozd 2020; Sorbe, Gal, and Millot 2018). In Colombia and Ecuador, markups tend to be lower overall in services than in manufacturing, but services subsectors are considerably heterogeneous in this regard, with higher markups found in real estate, transportation, and ICT services (Alfaro and Eslava 2020).

These factors are in addition to other reasons why dispersion can arise, including differences in technology (David and Venkateswaran 2019) and adjustment costs (Asker, Collard-Wexler, and De Loecker 2014) as well as differences between average and marginal products (Bils, Klenow, and Ruane 2017). Risk and experimentation could be another source of dispersion. Investing in quality upgrading can be risky, and not all upgrading will be successful, which in turn can drive dispersion (Krishna, Levchenko, and Maloney 2020). This result could be particularly relevant to services, which tend to have lower start-up costs, which facilitates experimentation.

Dispersion matters, not only from the perspective of allocative efficiency but also in terms of economic inclusion. High productivity dispersion points toward the presence of a group of firms that are much less productive than the frontier firms. This dispersion is likely an underestimation and would be even larger if informal firms were included, since many informal enterprises operate at the lower end of the productivity distribution. Low-productivity firms are economically vulnerable (as low productivity usually also implies low earnings) and where economically more vulnerable groups (such as low-skilled workers or women) are disproportionally represented (see Aga et al. 2021 regarding Mozambique). Raising the productivity of these firms at the lower end of the productivity distribution, rather than just focusing on the better-performing upper end, would still raise aggregate productivity and, importantly for development, raise the earnings of the poor.

Stylized Fact 6: Services Firms' Employment Growth Is Lower Than in Manufacturing Firms

The next question concerns how firms contribute to jobs and productivity dynamics. Manufacturing firms exhibit a well-documented pattern of expanding their employment as they age—a sign that firms are investing in technology, markets, and product quality, hence enabling themselves to grow and hire more workers (Atkeson and Kehoe 2005). A firm's lack of employment growth could be a sign that distortions are creating a barrier against growth (Hsieh and Klenow 2014). However, the features of services themselves—for example, the simultaneity of production and consumption and the size of the local market—could be limiting the benefits of expanding in the same location.

Analysis from eight LMICs with suitable panel data confirms that services firms tend to have lower employment growth rates than manufacturing firms in their initial years (figure 2.12, panel a). Across these countries, a manufacturing firm expands employment by an average of 26 employees, tripling in size, while a retail firm on average added only 3 employees, only doubling in size (figure 2.12, panel b). Within the services sector, ICT, administrative and support, and transportation services tend to expand employment the most, while retail and wholesale services tend to expand employment the least.

Studies in other countries have shown similar patterns. In Brazil, the relationship between a firm's age and its employment size is weaker in services than in manufacturing (Brolhato de Oliveira et al. 2021). An analysis of new entrants in the Dutch services sector also showed little growth of services enterprises after they reached five employees (Audretsch, Klomp, and Thurik 1998). Services firms' relative lack of employment growth might well have to do with the sector's earlier-identified lower economies of scale in terms of establishment size. This would be in line with results from manufacturing firms, whose subsectors with lower scale economies also exhibit lower employment growth rates (Audretsch 1995).

This finding has implications for policy. Services firms' smaller size overall means that government programs likely would need to include more beneficiaries to cover the same amount of employment or economic activity as in manufacturing firms. In addition, focusing solely on firm employment growth as a policy outcome might make less sense for some services, since experiences from HICs have shown that a firm's employment growth by itself is not a necessary condition for achieving higher productivity (Berlingieri, Calligaris, and Criscuolo 2018).

Stylized Fact 7: But Firms Do Grow in Productivity over Their Life Cycles

Services firms' more limited employment growth and their weaker relationship between size and productivity raise the question of the importance of the traditional scale economies that emphasize establishment size. Yet such characteristics do not mean that firms are not growing in other respects. In fact, the firm-level data highlight that services firms in their initial years often show productivity growth like that of manufacturing firms (figure 2.13) despite not expanding employment as much.

Their growth in productivity—although employment growth is more stagnant—is an indication that services firms can expand their revenue throughout their life cycles. This implies that services firms have been able to either provide more services (expand the quantity of output) or charge a higher price. This higher price can reflect an increase in market power but can also reflect the increasing quality of the service.[9]

Quality is an important dimension for many services. The simultaneity of consumption and production as well as the importance of customization mean, for many

FIGURE 2.12 **Employment Growth during a Firm's Initial Years Tends to Be Lower in Services Than in Manufacturing**

Average number of employees in firms' first six years in selected LMICs, by sector or sector group, available years, 2003–17

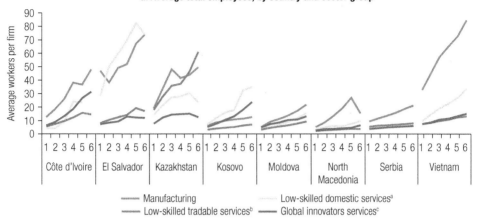

a. Average total employees, by country and sector group

Manufacturing
Low-skilled tradable services[b]
Low-skilled domestic services[a]
Global innovators services[c]

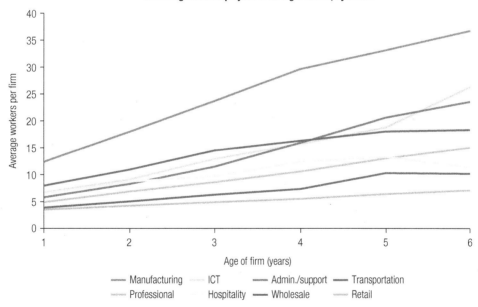

b. Average total employees in all eight LMICs, by sector

Manufacturing
Professional
ICT
Hospitality
Admin./support
Wholesale
Transportation
Retail

Source: Calculations using administrative firm-level data (detailed in annex 2A).

Note: Graphs illustrate a cohort analysis of firms in their first six years. Data cover 2003 through 2017, with annual coverage differing across countries. Services subsectors are grouped by sets of pro-development characteristics (defined in chapter 1), with skill-intensive social services excluded because of their limited coverage in firm-level data. Low- and middle-income countries (LMICs), by World Bank income group classifications, had 1994 gross national income of less than US$8,955. ICT = information and communication technology.

a. Low-skill domestic services include retail, administrative and support services, arts and recreation, real estate, and "other" services (the latter including varied social, community, and personal services).

b. Low-skill tradable services include wholesale, vehicles trade, transportation, and hospitality (hotels and restaurants).

c. Global innovator services include financial, professional, and ICT services.

FIGURE 2.13   Productivity Growth of Services Firms Is Similar to That of Manufacturing Firms

TFP growth of services and manufacturing firms in four LMICs, by sector or sector group, available years, 2003–17

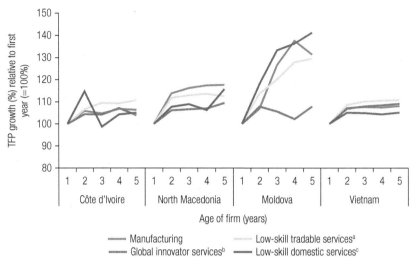

Source: Aterido et al. 2021, based on firm-level administrative data (see annex 2A).

Note: Data are for median total factor productivity (TFP) in four low- and middle-income countries (LMICs), which by World Bank income group classifications had 1994 gross national income of less than US$8,955. Data cover 2003–17, with annual coverage differing across countries. For full sources and data years, by country, see annex 2A.

a. Low-skill tradable services include wholesale, vehicles trade, transportation, and hotels and restaurants.

b. Global innovator services include financial, professional, and ICT services.

c. Low-skill domestic services include retail, administrative and support services, arts and recreation, real estate, and other services (the latter comprising social, community, and personal services).

services, that one service is not like another and that therefore product differentiation is high (Hoekman 2006; Markusen 1989). This differentiation is likely both vertical (with some firms providing higher-quality services, which clients value as such) and horizontal (with some clients having specific needs and preferences).[10]

This differentiation makes quality an important factor but, at the same time, one that is difficult to measure (and absent in the firm-level datasets studied for this chapter). Statistical agencies have applied a variety of approaches to improve measurements of quality—for example, by incorporating production costs or "hedonic" pricing models that attempt to value quality differences. The need to measure quality and the approaches used are discussed more extensively in this book's "Spotlight" on data.

Stylized Fact 8: Entry and Exit Play Much Bigger Roles in Job Creation and Destruction in Services Than in Manufacturing

In the services sector, firms' entry and exit play a larger role in explaining employment dynamics and productivity dynamics than in the manufacturing sector. From an employment perspective, workers in the services sector are much more likely than those in manufacturing to find themselves in a business that has either just been established or is about to wind down.

Employment Changes from Entry and Exit

For example, in Cambodia—where entry in the services sector brought larger job creation than in any of the countries analyzed—one in five workers in the services sector was in a business that was just established (figure 2.14, panel a). In Côte d'Ivoire, 6 percent of services workers found themselves in a business that was about to exit (figure 2.14, panel b). These results are in line with findings from the United States, where close to 20 percent of workers in services were employed in a firm younger than five years, compared with about 7 percent of workers in manufacturing (Decker et al. 2014).

Combining this finding with the earlier result highlighting a lack of growth among new entrants, services firms can be seen more as "churners" than as "growers" relative to manufacturing firms (figure 2.15). Despite some overlap between the services and manufacturing sectors, services subsectors are generally characterized by high rates of employment changes due to entry and exit but low rates of firm employment growth among new entrants. Meanwhile, manufacturing firms see more growth in their initial stages but less employment change due to entry and exit.

FIGURE 2.14 **Entry and Exit Play a Larger Role in Job Creation and Destruction in the Services Sector Than in Manufacturing**
Share of total employment in entrant and exiting firms in selected LMICs, by sector, latest available year, 2010–17

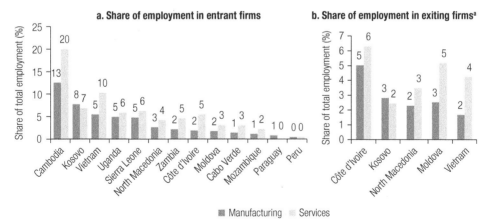

Source: Calculations using firm-level administrative data (see annex 2A).

Note: "Entrant" firms have existed for less than 12 months, and "exiting firms" have closed in the preceding 12 months. Low- and middle-income countries (LMICs), by World Bank income group classifications, had 1994 gross national income of less than US$8,955. For full sources and data years, by country, see annex 2A.

a. Countries are restricted to those with suitable panel data.

FIGURE 2.15 **Among Services Firms, Employment Changes Are Driven More by Entry and Exit Than by Firms' Growth**

Patterns of employment change in services relative to manufacturing during firms' first five years in six middle-income countries, latest available year, 2010–17

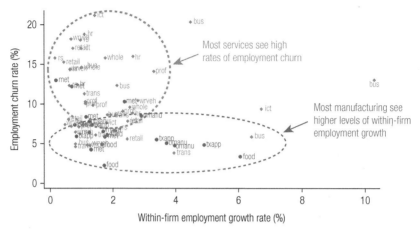

Source: Calculations using firm-level administrative data (see annex 2A) and Aterido et al. 2021.

Note: Datasets were obtained for six countries: Côte d'Ivoire, El Salvador, Kosovo, Moldova, North Macedonia, and Vietnam. Each point corresponds to a country-sector pair. Employment "churn" is defined as employment created by firm entry plus employment lost from firm exit divided by overall employment in that sector. Employment "growth" is defined as the size of a firm in its fifth year of existence relative to its first year. bus = business services; food = food services; hr = hotels and restaurants; ict = information and communication technology; met = metals and machinery; omanu = other manufacturing; prof = professional services; rs = real estate; retail = retail trade; trans = transportation and storage; txapp = textiles and apparel; whole = wholesale trade; wrveh = wholesale and retail of vehicles. Two outlying observations are not shown: textiles and apparel in El Salvador and Moldova.

Factors in Firm Entry and Exit

Among the drivers of the greater entry and exit in the services sector are its lower requirements for physical capital in setting up a business. Unlike many manufacturing subsectors that rely heavily on physical capital, services firms are generally less capital intensive and therefore need less start-up capital than manufacturing firms. In those subsectors that are less capital intensive, entry plays a larger role in driving job dynamics, particularly among global innovator services (figure 2.16). The relative ease of establishing a business in some services subsectors can also affect exit, since some firms will enter the market only to discover that the business opportunity is not there.

On the other hand, the establishment of new firms is limited by regulatory barriers to entry in certain services, such as in regulated professions, or in network industries like telecommunications or postal services. Reforms of product market regulations have generally eased firm entry (Bertrand and Kramarz 2002; Gal and Hijzen 2016; Schivardi and Viviano 2011). The importance of regulations in limiting entry and growth is discussed more extensively in chapter 5.

FIGURE 2.16 **In Industries with Lower Capital Intensity, Entry Plays a Larger Role in Job Creation**

Capital intensity in relation to employment among entrant firms, by industry, 2017 or most recent earlier available year

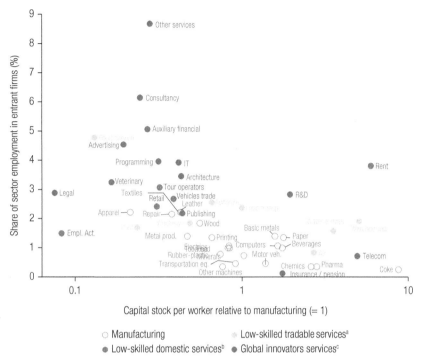

Source: Calculations, using the Organisation for Economic Co-operation and Development (OECD) STructural ANalysis (STAN) and Eurostat Business Demography databases.

Note: "Entrant" firms have existed for less than 12 months. Employment share is based on data for 34 European countries. "Capital stock per worker" (using data from 40 countries) is determined by the net capital stock per employee, relative to the average of manufacturing (equal to 1). "Industry" includes manufacturing, mining, construction, and utilities. Services subsectors are grouped by sets of pro-development characteristics (defined in chapter 1), with skill-intensive social services excluded because of their limited coverage in firm-level data. IT = information technology; R&D = research and development; Rent = rental and leasing activities; Empl. Act. = employment activities.

a. Low-skill tradable services employ mostly low-skilled workers, are considered tradable in international markets, and may be amenable to offshoring.

b. Low-skill domestic services employ mostly low-skilled workers and are less tradable internationally than other subsector groups.

c. Global innovator services employ mostly high-skilled workers, are highly traded internationally, and are the most amenable to offshoring.

Productivity Effects of Firm Entry and Exit

The prominence of entry and exit also matters for overall productivity dynamics. A common approach to quantify drivers of productivity growth is the "within-between" decomposition framework, introduced by Baily et al. (1992) and further refined by Olley and Pakes (1996); Foster, Haltiwanger, and Krizan (2001); and Melitz and Polanec (2015). In this framework, productivity is ascribed to three processes, which usually happen concurrently: (a) firm upgrading ("within-firm" growth); (b) improving allocative efficiency ("between-firm" growth); and (c) productive entry and exit. Even though not necessarily mutually exclusive, each of these can be linked to specific policies: firm upgrading is strongly associated with improving skills and firm capabilities, improving allocation with removing distortions in factor and product markets, and entry and exit with reducing barriers to entry and exit.

Quantifications of each component's contributions, using productivity decompositions, suggest that although it is difficult to draw strong conclusions on the relative importance of the "within" versus the "between" components, the "entry and exit" component tends to play a more prominent role in services. A Melitz and Polanec (2015) decomposition of productivity growth for five countries with suitable panel data shows substantial heterogeneity across countries and subsectors (figure 2.17, panel a).

One pattern that is common in most countries is that the joint contribution of entry and exit is larger in many of the services subsectors than in manufacturing, reflecting the more important role of entry and exit in services productivity (figure 2.17, panel b). In manufacturing, net entry effects contribute to 19–40 percent of the observed change in productivity, while in services subsectors this share is often more than 50 percent. Exit contributes positively, indicating that firms with less-than-average productivity are more likely to exit, while entry often contributes negatively, meaning that entrant firms are less productive on average than incumbent firms (figure 2.17, panel a). This could reflect not only the time that entrants might take to become more productive but also, potentially, that not all entry is necessarily productive. In other words, high levels of entry and exit do not necessarily imply creative destruction.

Implications for Productivity Growth

Chapter 1 identified three main channels through which services could achieve productivity growth—the first through increasing *scale* and the size of the market; the second through *innovation* and increased use of technology; and the third through *linkages* to other sectors. The question now becomes, what do the characteristics of services firms, as described in this chapter, mean in terms of the productivity contributions of each of these channels?

Scaling Up without Necessarily Sizing Up

The stylized facts presented in this chapter could seem to contend that scale is a less important productivity driver in services than in manufacturing. Indeed, the productivity patterns presented suggest that when measuring scale by the traditional metric of employees per establishment, there are fewer economies of scale to achieve in services than in manufacturing. This nevertheless does not rule out the importance of scale completely, for several reasons.

Correlation with labor productivity in LMICs. First (as figure 2.4 highlighted), services establishments are smaller in LMICs than in HICs, whereas (as figure 2.8

FIGURE 2.17 **Within-Firm, Between-Firm, and Entry and Exit Are Important Drivers of Productivity Growth in Both Services and Manufacturing**

Relative importance of productivity drivers in services and manufacturing in five middle-income countries, 2003–17

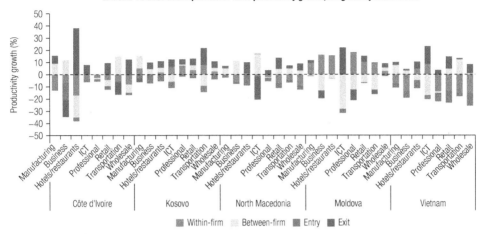

a. Melitz-Polanec decomposition of labor productivity growth, weighted by value added[a]

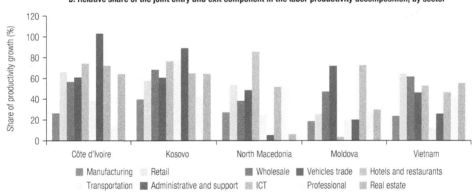

b. Relative share of the joint entry and exit component in the labor productivity decomposition, by sector[b]

Source: Calculations using administrative firm-level data (see annex 2A).

Note: Labor productivity is measured as value added per worker. The data include formal firms only. Productivity has been decomposed using the Melitz and Polanec (2015) decomposition.

a. In the decomposition framework, "within-firm" growth refers to firm upgrading (measured by simple average of productivity growth in surviving firms); "between-firm" growth to improving allocative efficiency (measured by changes in the correlation between value added and productivity); "entry" to the productivity growth contribution from entering firms; and "exit" to the productivity growth contribution from firm closures. ICT = information and communication technology.

b. The relative share of joint entry and exit is calculated by dividing the sum of the absolute values of the entry and exit component, divided by the sum of absolute values of all other components. bus = administrative and support services; hr = hotels and restaurants; ict = information and communication technology; manu = manufacturing; prof = professional services; rs = real estate; trans = transportation and storage; whole = wholesale; wrveh = wholesale/retail of vehicles.

highlighted) the correlation between size and labor productivity is larger in LMICs (although not as large as in manufacturing). This could be a sign of inefficiencies due to the smaller size of services firms in LMICs. Much of this difference in size nevertheless disappears when looking only at formal firms, suggesting that many of the inefficiencies are likely related to firms in the informal sector.

COVID-19's Impact on the Services Sector

The firm-level data analyzed in this chapter relate to the period before the COVID-19 pandemic, which has hit many services firms hard, particularly in sectors that are intensive in face-to-face interactions as well as in countries relying on tourism. High-frequency data on firms collected as part of the World Bank's Business Pulse Survey (BPS) initiative as well as Enterprise Survey follow-ups—jointly covering more than 60 countries—highlight that accommodation, food services, education, and transportation are among the hardest-hit sectors, showing average sales more than halving in 2020 (figure B2.2.1). Other services subsectors

FIGURE B2.2.1 **Firm Surveys Show That Accommodation, Food Services, and Education Have Been the Hardest-Hit Sectors during the COVID-19 Pandemic**
Average change in sales from 2019 to 2020, by sector

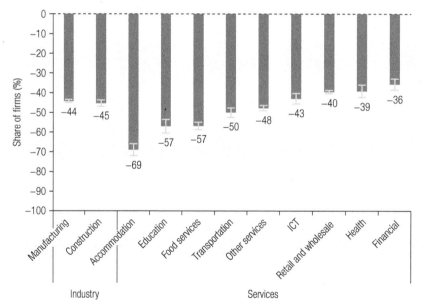

Source: Results from the first wave of the World Bank's COVID-19 Business Pulse Survey and Enterprise Surveys, conducted April–September 2020.

Note: The data for this figure cover more than 60 countries (primarily low- and middle-income countries) and more than 130,000 businesses. Figures are predicted average changes from a regression controlling for country, size, sector, and the number of weeks following the shock. The data have been reweighted so each country has an equal weight. Error bars indicate the 95 percent confidence intervals for each sector. For a description of the survey, see Apedo-Amah et al. (2020). "Other services" include various social, community, and personal services. ICT = information and communication technology.

Box continues on the following page

COVID-19's Impact on the Services Sector *(continued)*

(such as financial services, ICT, and retail and wholesale trade) have been less affected, even though firms in these subsectors also reported declines in sales.

In the short run, the impacts have already been severe—affecting the economic livelihoods of many in the services sector (figure B2.2.2) and disproportionally affecting small businesses and women. Household surveys conducted by the World Bank and partners indicate that in 37 out of 41 countries, female respondents were more likely than male respondents to have stopped working.[a] The BPS data similarly indicate that women-led enterprises were likelier than those led by men to be hit by the COVID-19 pandemic and its economic effects (Torres et al. 2021).

It will be hard to predict the long-term impacts of COVID-19, particularly on the most-affected services subsectors. The overall services sector's dynamism in terms of entry and exit might contribute to its resilience. For many services, the start-up costs of setting up a firm are lower than for manufacturing firms, which might make it easier for the sector to bounce back when demand returns. In addition, the pandemic might also accelerate trends toward greater digitalization and remote delivery of services. These trends are further explored in chapter 3 (box 3.1).

FIGURE B2.2.2 Household Surveys Show That, on Average, 38 Percent of Services Workers Stopped Working in 2020

Share of services workers who stopped working in 2020, selected countries

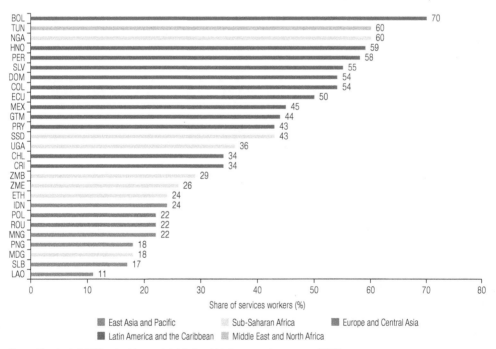

Source: Khamis et al. 2021, using labor market data from high-frequency phone surveys (HFPS).

Note: HFPS data were collected April–December 2020 in 21 countries across regions and income groups by the World Bank and partner agencies. Household weights have been applied to account for sampling. Countries are labeled using ISO alpha-3 codes.

a. Data from Khamis et al. (2021) and the World Bank's COVID-19 High-Frequency Monitoring Dashboard, an online dataset: https://www.worldbank.org/en/data/interactive/2020/11/11/covid-19-high-frequency-monitoring-dashboard.

Capacity to grow TFP. Second, services firms do grow in other respects, including TFP (figure 2.13). This growth can indicate firms' ability to expand their quantity of output. But it could also mean—since these measures of productivity are based on revenue—that firms have increased either the quality of their services or their market power, both of which could lead to higher prices.

Growth from branches or franchises. Third, the distinction between firms and establishments is important when assessing scale.[11] Proximity requirements might make it difficult to expand the size of one location, but services firms could scale up through multiple establishments. In the United States, the setting up of new establishments by large firms is an important source of firm growth (Haltiwanger, Jarmin, and Miranda 2013), particularly in the retail sector (Jarmin, Klimek, and Miranda 2009). The average US retail firm size increased from 19.3 to 22.8 employees between 1998 and 2012, about half of which came from an increase in the average number of establishments per retail firm (Hortaçsu and Syverson 2015).

However, branching remains a less common pattern in lower-income countries. For example, when the number of establishments per firm in Brazil and the United States is compared, retail firms in the United States tend to have more locations (on average, 1.7 establishments per firm) than in Brazil (1.1 per firm), as shown in figure 2.18.[12]

FIGURE 2.18 **In Commerce-Related Services, US Firms Have More Establishments per Firm Than Brazilian Firms**
Number of establishments per firm in Brazil and the United States, by sector, 2014–15

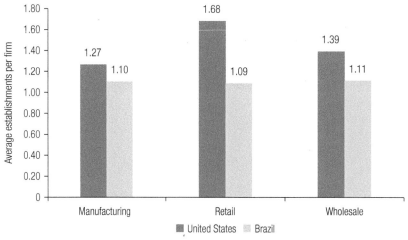

Source: Structural and Demographic Business Statistics (SDBS) database of the Organisation for Economic Co-operation and Development (OECD).
Note: Data for Brazil are from 2014, and US data are from 2015. "Commerce" comprises wholesale and retail trade.

At Your Service? The Promise of Services-Led Development

This type of expansion has been further facilitated by new technologies and increased trade in services. Information and communication technologies have made it easier for firms to reduce the marginal costs associated with the overhead of running a business across multiple establishments (Aghion et al. 2015). In the United States, top firms have expanded to new markets in small and mid-size cities with the aid of these new technologies, which reduce the marginal costs of setting up a new branch (Hsieh and Rossi-Hansberg 2020). Walmart has exemplified this expansion model, achieving scale by both having *large* establishments and having *many* of them.

Increased trade in services also has meant the establishment of more foreign affiliates through foreign direct investment (FDI). As chapter 1 (figure 1.7) highlighted, FDI is the most common mode of trade in services ("mode 3" under the General Agreement on Trade in Services [GATS] framework).

Moreover, scaling up does not always need to happen within the same firm. Franchising—whereby one firm buys the rights to operate a particular brand and business model—allows firms and entrepreneurs to scale up operations through different legal entities, sharing valuable intangible capital. Online platforms are another example of achieving scale without necessarily increasing the size of the firm but rather by relying on many individual providers.

Digital and remote delivery. E-commerce has also allowed firms to scale up without needing to be near the consumer. Companies like Amazon in the United States, Alibaba and JD.com in China, and Flipkart in India are among the largest companies in their home countries, but they have few physical retail establishments.[13] By reaching customers through their online platforms, they show how digital technologies enable firms to reach customers far beyond a limited geographical range. The role of e-commerce and digital technologies as ways to achieve scale are further explored in chapter 3.

Innovation from Intangible Rather Than Physical Capital

The limited role for physical capital in many services subsectors suggests that innovation is less likely represented by technology embedded in a machine than by more intangible forms—among them, digital technologies such as software. Such intangible capital plays an important role for the global innovator services (such as professional, financial, and ICT services), which employ ICT capital at much higher rates than manufacturing and other services (figure 2.19).

Other forms of intangible capital that are important for services include organizational know-how (including operating procedures and managerial practices), knowledge embedded in intellectual property, and brand value. These forms of "nontechnological" innovation are potentially more important in services than in manufacturing. In Chile, exporting services firms are about 7 percent more likely than

FIGURE 2.19 **Services Are More Likely Than Manufacturers to Be Intensive in ICT Capital**

Capital and ICT capital per worker in manufacturing and services subsectors, OECD countries, 2017

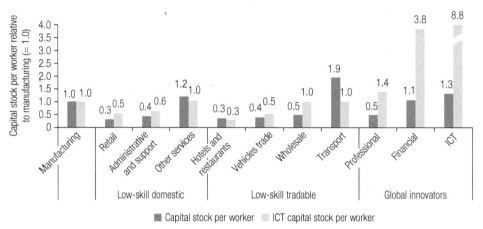

Source: Calculations, using the STructural ANalysis (STAN) database, Organisation for Economic Co-operation and Development (OECD).

Note: The value of the information and communication technology (ICT) capital stock per worker relative to manufacturing for ICT services is 8.8. Services subsectors are grouped by sets of pro-development characteristics (defined in chapter 1), with skill-intensive social services excluded because of their limited coverage in firm-level data.

exporting manufacturers to produce nontechnological innovations such as improvements in distribution, management, the working environment, and relationships with other firms (Zahler, Iacovone, and Mattoo 2014). The importance of intangibilities and digital technologies will be explored further in chapter 3.

The low physical capital requirements also help explain Stylized Fact 8 (regarding the large role of services firms' entries and exits in job creation and destruction). Having less need to invest in physical capital facilitates higher degrees of entry and exit because start-up costs are lower. This raises the potential for innovation through creative destruction by entrant firms that invent or adopt more-productive technologies.

Linkages to Other Sectors for More Productivity

Productivity analyses also suggest that intersectoral linkages play an important role in boosting productivity. Of the services sectors that tend to be more productive than manufacturing in OECD countries, most (other than insurance and pension services) are those that sell mainly to other firms rather than to final consumers (figure 2.20).

But not all services with high linkages are necessarily among the more productive ones. For example, sectors such as transportation and warehousing services are heavily

FIGURE 2.20 **More Productive Services Rely More on Linkages with Other Firms**
Relative TFP of services subsectors in relation to firm linkages, OECD countries, 2010–17

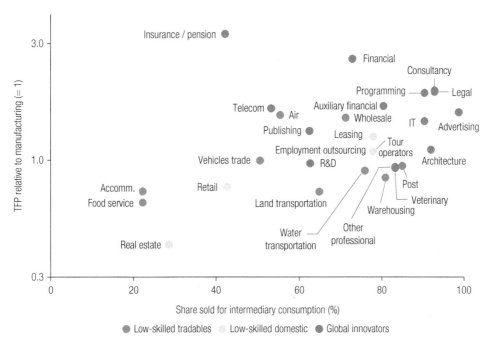

Source: Calculations using data from OECD.Stat (https://stats.oecd.org/) and the World Input-Output Tables.

Note: Total factor productivity (TFP) is calculated by assuming a Cobb-Douglas function with output elasticities of one-third for capital and two-thirds for labor and is averaged across Organisation for Economic Co-operation and Development (OECD) countries, based on data from 2010–17 (latest available year). "Share sold for intermediary consumption" is the share of consumption by domestic non-household entities, based on 2014 data. Services subsectors are grouped by sets of pro-development characteristics (defined in chapter 1), with skill-intensive social services excluded because of their limited coverage in firm-level data. IT = information technology; R&D = research and development.

linked to other sectors but are relatively less productive. This lower productivity is closely related to these sectors' reliance on more unskilled forms of labor.

Both manufacturing firms and services firms that rely on services as inputs tend to be more productive and can charge higher markups (Alfaro and Eslava 2020). The importance of services firms as "upstream" enablers is explored further in chapter 4.

Linkages can also affect other channels, such as by fostering innovation through knowledge sharing or spillovers or by enabling higher levels of scale. For example, one of the key reasons why productivity is so much higher in the wholesale sector than in the retail sector is the presence of scale economies among wholesalers due to their role as intermediaries (Kask, Kiernan, and Friedman 2002), in turn enabling these firms to achieve higher market shares and markups (Ganapati 2018).

On the other hand, the presence of scale economies in terms of firm size does not hold for all sectors with high linkages. Professional, technical, and IT services tend to sell services mostly to other firms but remain relatively small.

Implications for Job Creation

This chapter earlier presented a set of stylized facts on services firms, focusing on their size, productivity, capital use, and dynamic patterns. These facts highlighted that the channels through which manufacturing has achieved productivity growth—scale, innovation, and spillovers—are also relevant for services but operate differently than in manufacturing. The question is, what does this finding imply for employment? In particular, can services deliver on a promise similar to manufacturing—absorbing low-skilled labor and using this labor productively?

Chapter 1 already highlighted the varying skill needs across different services subsectors and the compositional shift toward global innovator services as countries' income levels rise. When looking at the relationship between productivity and employment, a similar picture emerges: in low-income countries, most of the services jobs are in lower-productivity subsectors (figure 2.21). Shifting the composition toward the more productive services will require both (a) changes in demand as incomes rise (for example, through increased linkages with other sectors) and businesses become more sophisticated; and (b) improvements in the quality of skills of those engaged in them.

These observations raise three important questions on job quality, gender equity, and the role of skills:

- *How does job quality vary across services subsectors?* Job quality is strongly correlated with productivity, both across and within sectors. The spectrum of job quality in the services sector is large, varying from low-wage jobs in the informal sector to some of the best-paid, highest-quality jobs.

- *How equitable is job quality in the presence of gender wage gaps?* As noted in chapter 1, women are less likely than men to be employed in higher-skill occupations, even within high-skill services.

- *What is the scope for improving skills—including through on-the-job learning—and moving into higher-skill occupations and services subsectors?*

Better Jobs from More Productive Sectors and Firms

In the aggregate, services seem to be providing lower-quality jobs than manufacturing. For both high- and low-skilled workers, wages in the services sector tend to be lower than in manufacturing. An International Monetary Fund (IMF) study finds that, in a sample of 20 high-income economies, the median difference in labor earnings between industry and services for high- and low-skilled workers is about 6 percentage points

FIGURE 2.21 **In Low-Income Countries, Most of the Services Jobs Are in Lower-Productivity Subsectors**

Prevalence of services jobs in LICs in relation to labor productivity, by subsector, latest available year, 2011–19

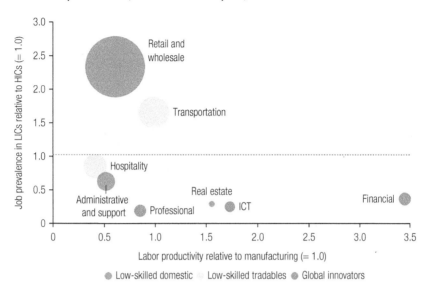

Source: Calculations using International Labour Organization (ILO) employment data from labor force surveys; administrative firm-level productivity data; and aggregated data from the Organisation for Economic Co-operation and Development (OECD) and the European Union's statistical office, Eurostat.

Note: Labor force survey data cover 32 low-income countries (LICs) and 21 high-income countries (HICs) from the latest available year (2011–19) and, depending on the underlying data source, include formal and informal employment. Dotted lines at 1.0 along both axes indicate the respective benchmarks of job prevalence and labor productivity in the manufacturing sector. Bubble size represents employment in a given sector in LICs. Labor productivity (using data from figure 2.1) is measured as value added per worker; reported relative to manufacturing in the same country (= 1.0); and covers formal firms only. A simple average was taken across countries. ICT = information and communication technology.

and 9 percentage points, respectively (IMF 2018). Similarly, in the United States, lower-wage workers in manufacturing earn about 11 percent more than their peers in other sectors, while high-wage manufacturing workers earn 4 percent more (Helper, Krueger, and Wial 2012).

But, again, heterogeneity in the services sector is large, and much of this is determined by productivity differences. Wages in higher-productivity subsectors such as financial and business services or transportation and communication services exceed those in commerce-related services (wholesale, retail, hotels, and restaurants) and manufacturing across 15 LMICs in Asia and Africa (Hovhannisyan et al. 2021). The wages of commerce-related services are about on a par with wages in manufacturing. Using data from India, Nayyar (2011) finds that similar workers earn more in business, finance, and telecommunications than they do in manufacturing, but those in wholesale and retail trade, hotels and restaurants, and community and personal services earn relatively less.

Productivity and wages are also closely related to the subsector's skill intensity. Those services identified as higher-skill in chapter 1—particularly those classified as global innovator services—are also more productive than lower-skill services. Also, at the firm level, skill is important in determining wage levels. Using detailed worker-firm panel data from Brazil, Artuç and Bastos (2020) find that the wage premium is higher in high-skill subsectors, whether in manufacturing or services.

Within subsectors, there is a strong relationship between firm-level productivity and the wages that these firms pay. Averaged across LMICs with suitable data, a firm in the top productivity decile pays a wage that is 1.9 to more than 4.3 times higher than a firm in the bottom decile (figure 2.22). This increasing pattern holds for both TFP (shown in the figure) and labor productivity. There are some indications that the returns to productivity are highest in wholesale and in global innovator services (ICT and professional services). Overall, these patterns imply that increasing job quality will have to rely on a combination of sectoral reallocation—that is, shifting employment to higher-productivity subsectors—and increasing firm-level productivity.

The differences in earnings across sectors also become clear when considering the wage distribution. Aggregating data from labor force surveys in 47 LMICs using the World Bank's International Income Distribution Dataset (I2D2), figure 2.23 highlights

FIGURE 2.22 **Just As in Manufacturing, Firm-Level Productivity in Services Is Closely Related to Wages**
Wage returns to firm-level productivity across selected LMICs, by sector and TFP decile, 2003–17

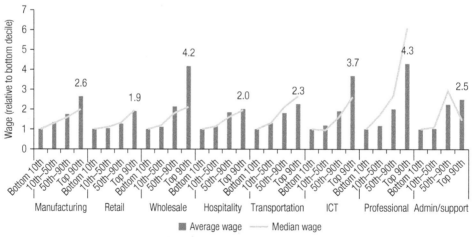

Source: Calculations using administrative firm-level data (see annex 2A).

Note: Data are averaged across nine low- and middle-income countries (LMICs) with available data on wages and total factor productivity (TFP): Cambodia, Côte d'Ivoire, Kosovo, Moldova, North Macedonia, Paraguay, Peru, Vietnam, and Zambia. LMICs, by World Bank income group classifications, had 1994 gross national income of less than US$8,955. ICT = information and communication technology. For full sources and data years, by country, see annex 2A.

FIGURE 2.23 **Commerce and Hospitality Workers in LMICs Are More Likely to Be in the Lowest Wage Quartile, While Half of Financial and Business Services Workers Are in the Highest Wage Quartile**

Share of workers, by manufacturing wage quartile, in selected services subsectors of LMICs, 2017 or most recent earlier year

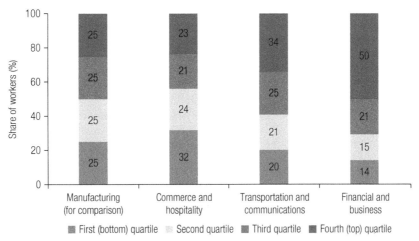

Source: Calculations from the World Bank's International Income Distribution Database (I2D2).

Note: Data are aggregated from labor force surveys in 47 LMICs (most recent year, 2017 or earlier). Wage quartiles are based on the manufacturing wage distribution. Earnings are determined by reported wages and are mostly only available for workers in wage employment. "Commerce and hospitality" includes the wholesale and retail trade as well as hotels and restaurants.

the services subsectors' shares of employment relative to the bottom and top quartiles of the manufacturing wage distribution. Workers in financial and business services, for example, are much more likely to be in the higher quartiles of the income distribution than in the lower quartiles. The commerce and hospitality subsectors show an opposite pattern, where workers are more likely to be in the lowest quartile of the manufacturing wage distribution.

At the lower end of the productivity spectrum (in commerce and hospitality), workers in LMICs (but not in HICs) are more likely to find themselves at the bottom of the wage distribution. A third of commerce and hospitality workers in LMICs see wages that fall in the bottom quartile, which means that a worker in this sector is close to 30 percent more likely than a worker in manufacturing to be in this quartile. These figures are based on wage employment only, and it is likely that if self-employment were included—often in the informal sector—the differences in earnings between sectors would be even starker.

The higher-productivity subsectors provide not only higher wages but also better jobs in other respects. Hovhannisyan et al. (2021) develop a job quality index based on nonwage benefits, job security, job satisfaction, and whether the wage income exceeds the US$1.90 international poverty line (measured in 2011 US$).[14] They find (based on household and labor force surveys from 27 LMICs) that job quality exceeds that of manufacturing in public administration, utilities, financial and business services, and transportation services (figure 2.24), while the job quality in commerce is similar to that in manufacturing. Brummund, Mann, and Rodríguez-Castelán (2018) find similar results in Latin America. Again, just as with wages, it is the higher-productivity services that also provide higher-quality jobs in terms of nonwage benefits.

There is also evidence that firms engaged in international trade—often among the more productive firms—offer better jobs. For example, in the United States, firms that export ICT and professional services pay higher wages than nonexporters, with the exporter wage premium being double that of manufacturing (Jensen 2011). In India and the Philippines, business process outsourcing (BPO) firms provide better-quality jobs than non-BPO firms in terms of wage and nonwage benefits (Messenger and Ghosheh 2010).

Gender Equity of High-Quality Jobs

The next question concerns gender equity in accessing higher-quality jobs. Chapter 1 noted that women have particularly benefited from the expansion of low-skill services

FIGURE 2.24 **In LMICs, Job Quality Is the Highest in Public Administration, Utilities, and Financial and Business Services**

Job quality index of sectors in 27 LMICs, latest available year, 2014–18

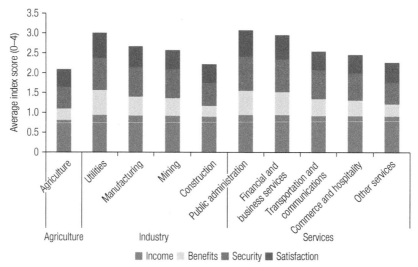

Source: Hovhannisyan et al. 2021.

Note: The index was compiled from household and labor force surveys covering wage employees in 27 low- and middle-income countries (LMICs): Bangladesh, Bolivia, Botswana, Brazil, Burkina Faso, Colombia, Costa Rica, the Dominican Republic, Ecuador, the Arab Republic of Egypt, Georgia, Honduras, Indonesia, Kenya, Mexico, Mozambique, Pakistan, Panama, Paraguay, Peru, the Philippines, Rwanda, Sri Lanka, Thailand, Togo, Turkey, and Uruguay. (LMICs, by World Bank income group classifications, had 1994 gross national income of less than US$8,955.) The index score (0–4) is the average of the presence of four components: (a) income above the international poverty line of US$1.90 in 2011 dollars; (b) nonwage benefits; (c) job security; and (d) job satisfaction. An individual with earnings below the poverty line has a 0 score in all categories. "Commerce and hospitality" includes the services subsectors of wholesale and retail trade as well as hotels and restaurants.

and, in some regions, from the expansion of global innovator services, even though men and women tend to work in different types of occupations.

Figure 2.25 highlights the occupational distribution across sectors. In transportation, women are in the minority, and those working in the sector are much less likely than men to be drivers or machine operators. In financial and business services, women are much more likely than men to perform clerical tasks. And even among occupations with similar shares of female and male employment, women's lower labor participation means that men continue to outnumber women in these roles.

Gender disparities also translate into job quality in terms of wages, where large gender gaps persist. Data from the United States suggest that these wage gaps might be the largest among the global innovator services. Women in financial services and professional services, respectively, earn 39 percent and 29 percent less than men (BLS 2019).

FIGURE 2.25   **Across Sectors in LMICs, the Occupational Distribution Differs between Men and Women**
Decomposition of occupational roles of females and males, by sector, latest available year, 2005–17

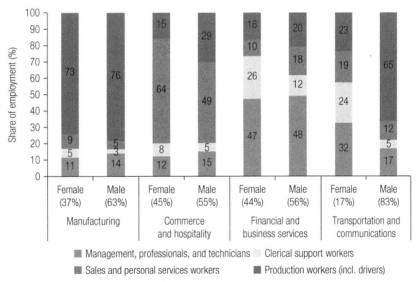

Source: Calculations based on World Bank's International Income Distribution Dataset (I2D2).

Note: The I2D2 is a global harmonized household survey database. The data cover 89 low- and middle-income countries (LMICs) across all regions for the latest available year between 2005 and 2017. (Under World Bank income group classifications, LMICs had 1994 gross national income of less than US$8,955.) Percentages in parentheses represent each gender's share in overall employment in that sector. Employment covers both paid and unpaid forms (for example, contributing family members). "Commerce and hospitality" includes the services subsectors of wholesale and retail trade as well as hotels and restaurants. Occupational groups are defined under the International Labour Organization's International Standard Classification of Occupations (ISCO), as follows: "Management, professionals, and technicians" covers ISCO major groups 1, 2, and 3. "Clerical support workers" covers major group 4. "Sales and personal services workers" covers major group 5. "Production workers (including drivers)" covers major groups 7, 8, and 9 (respectively craft workers, plant and machine operators, and elementary occupations). Within the transportation sector, "production workers" includes drivers. Major groups 6 (agricultural workers) and 10 (armed forces) are not reported but have values near 0 percent.

Gaps in low-skill services tend to be narrower; for example, in food services, women earn 15 percent less than men. Many LMICs see similar wage gaps (World Bank 2011).

Part, but not all, of the wage gap occurs because women tend to work in lower-skill occupations within higher-skill services. In the financial sector, for example, men are more likely to be in managerial positions while women are more likely to be bank tellers. In the United States, occupational differences within an industry explain roughly a third of the observed gender wage gap (Blau and Kahn 2017). Barrowman and Klasen (2020) document similar occupational gaps in LMICs, even though the gaps tend to be smaller in countries with larger services sectors.

Moreover, even when men and women have the same job in the same subsector, women's earnings are often still not equal. Data consistently show that "adjusted" wage gaps—measures that control for differences in education, occupation, and industry—remain present, although some of the gaps are narrowing (Blau and Kahn 2017; Olivetti and Petrongolo 2008, 2016; Oostendorp 2004). Analysis based on the World Bank's I2D2 labor force survey data suggest that when occupation is controlled for, women earn roughly 25 percent less than men.[15]

Chapter 1 highlighted similar gaps for women entrepreneurs, with female business owners being more likely than men to be in lower-skill services, especially retail, and more likely than men to run an informal business.

Skills for Productive Jobs

Human capital plays an important part in service delivery. Those services subsectors with the highest productivity, particularly the global innovator services, are also those with the highest needs for worker skills. Skill building is therefore crucial to allow for movements into the higher-productivity services and firms that offer high wages and higher-quality jobs.

A key question is, how much evidence is there for skills acquisition—and transferability of skills across sectors—in understanding the likely time it will take to expand jobs in more productive services? Some of these skills are obtained through formal education (the role of which will be further explored in chapter 5), but data show that more informal forms of training also play an important role in building skills.

Just as in manufacturing, some of the skills relevant to services are learned "on the job." Learning by working—broadly defined as human capital accumulation through experience in the labor market—is an important driver of rapid productivity growth. Variants of this process feature prominently in several leading theories of international trade and economic growth (Grossman and Helpman 1991; Krugman 1987; Lucas 1988; Redding 1999). Arguably, the movement of labor from farms to factories might have induced such learning by doing and boosted productivity growth during East Asia's growth miracle. Yet there is little direct empirical evidence on the extent to which learning opportunities differ systematically across sectors.

Some evidence suggests that the scope for on-the-job training is in fact larger in services than in manufacturing. Based on cross-sectional household survey data across 145 countries between 1990 and 2016, Islam at el. (2018) estimate that wages increase by 2.6 percent for each extra year of experience in the services sector compared with 2 percent in industry and 1.3 percent in agriculture.[16] In both HICs and LMICs, the returns to experience are higher in services than in industry and higher in industry than in agriculture.[17] The wage gap between services and nonservices sectors appears after only five years of experience and tends to widen over time. Furthermore, the returns to experience are higher in high-income economies than in low- and middle-income economies for all three sectors, and the sector with the highest returns in LMICs (services, at 2.4 percent) has lower returns than the sector with the lowest returns in HICs (agriculture, at 3.1 percent).

Looking across subsectors, the returns to experience in commerce (wholesale and retail); transportation and communications (the latter comprising post and telecommunications); finance; real estate; and business services exceed those in manufacturing in both HICs and LMICs. These subsector aggregates might conceal variations across constituent occupations. For example, evidence suggests that alongside agricultural workers, elementary service occupations (involving manual labor) have the lowest returns.

A more direct way to measure learning by doing is to measure returns to experience by following workers over time and across jobs. Yet most Mincer-type analyses of the relationship between age and wages do not fully capture learning by working in a particular sector because people may change jobs or sectors over their working lives. In a recent study based on 2003–15 longitudinal employer-employee panel data from the universe of formal sector workers and firms in Brazil, Artuç and Bastos (2020) circumvent this measurement challenge because they can track individual workers over time, as they move across firms and sectors. They show significant wage returns associated with experience, especially in global innovator services. Relative to all other subsectors (in manufacturing and services), the percentage wage change from one more year of experience was 2.2 percent in ICT services, compared with only 0.6 percent in accommodation and food services. The corresponding changes in apparel and automotive manufacturing, respectively, were 0.4 percent and 1.5 percent.[18]

In addition, learning by working might be more transferable in services than in manufacturing. In high-skill manufacturing industries, job experience only translates into higher wages when workers keep working in those industries, whereas in global innovator services, earnings associated with experience remain high even if workers move to a different industry (Artuç and Bastos 2020).[19] Relative to all other subsectors (in manufacturing and services), the percentage wage change from one more year of experience when the worker had changed industries was about 1.9 percent in global innovator services (figure 2.26). In manufacturing, the corresponding change in wages was negative.

FIGURE 2.26 **Global Innovator Services See the Highest Returns to Experience, Even When Workers Move to Other Sectors**

Wage returns from one more year of experience, by whether workers changed industries, Brazil, 2003–15

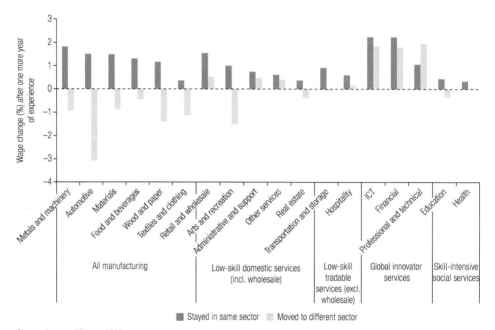

Stayed in same sector ■ Moved to different sector ■

Source: Artuç and Bastos 2020.

Note: Study used longitudinal employer-employee panel data from formal firms in all Brazilian sectors. The data show the percentage change in wages relative to all other sectors (manufacturing or services), according to whether a worker stayed within the same sector or moved to another sector. Services subsectors are grouped by sets of pro-development characteristics (defined in chapter 1), with wholesale grouped with retail under "low-skill domestic" rather than "low-skilled tradable." (No separate value for wholesale is available.) Sectors are classified using International Standard Industrial Classification (ISIC) Rev. 4. "Metals and machinery" also includes electronics. "Materials" includes petroleum, chemicals, and rubber. "Food and beverages" also includes tobacco. "Wood and paper" also includes furniture production. "Textiles and clothing" also includes footwear and leather. "Other services" includes personal services. ICT = information and communication technology.

As noted in chapter 1, LMICs see fewer people working in global innovator services than HICs. Increasing employment in higher-skill services not only creates benefits for workers—as highlighted in this section—but will also lead to higher productivity. Part of the productivity gap between LMICs and HICs is explained by a different composition of the services sector. A back-of-the-envelope calculation suggests that if the subsectoral composition of services in low-income countries were to match that in HICs, labor productivity could increase by about a third (figure 2.27). This is in addition to the labor productivity gains that are possible within sectors.[20]

This finding highlights the need for an ambitious policy agenda facilitating skill acquisition—through both formal and informal forms of training—and mobility across sectors. Digitalization trends might further change the skill needs. While some tasks require high-skilled work, automation can also allow lower-skilled workers

FIGURE 2.27 **The Services Sector's Composition Explains Part of the Productivity Gap between LMICs and HICs**

Labor productivity gain from sectoral reallocation to match services sector composition HICs, by LMIC income group

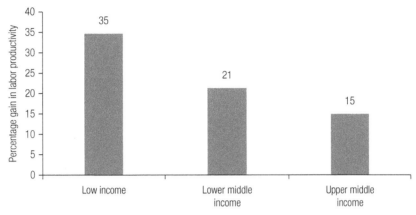

Source: Calculations using International Labour Organization (ILO) employment data and firm-level productivity data.

Note: The data cover 107 countries, using the most recent year for each country (between 2011 and 2019). The productivity gain is calculated as the gain in labor productivity (measured by value added per worker) that would result if low- and middle-income countries (LMICs) had the same employment shares as high-income countries (HICs) across services subsectors (defined at the "1-digit" ISIC Rev. 4 section level, separating retail, wholesale, and vehicles trade as separate sectors). LMICs, by World Bank income group classifications, had 1994 gross national income (GNI) of less than US$8,955. HICs had GNI exceeding US$8,955 in 1994.

(albeit with basic ICT skills) to provide more sophisticated services. This potential is explored further in chapter 3.

Conclusion

This chapter dived deeper into the patterns of productivity growth and job creation in the services sector, reinforcing the point made in chapter 1 that the services sector is far from monolithic. The data showed some encouraging signs that services have the potential to be productive and to contribute to productivity growth. Yet services firms differ from manufacturing firms in the roles of scale, capital, and entry and exit in creating productivity growth. These differences nevertheless do not preclude productivity growth in the services sector. In fact, cohort analyses showed that services firms—despite not necessarily sizing up—can still grow their productivity at rates similar to manufacturing firms.

At the same time, there is a tension that the most productive services subsectors are not where most of the jobs are, particularly in lower-income countries, and that these more-productive services have higher skill needs. This persistent tension raises big questions on how to shift the composition of services toward these higher-productivity activities (taking advantage of scale where possible) and how to raise the quality of services—ideally in ways that are inclusive of women and of less-skilled workers.

But potential exists even in some of the lower-productivity services. The existence of productivity gaps between low- and high-income countries in the productivity of low-skill services (highlighted in chapter 1) provides some hope that a productivity catch-up is possible.

The next chapters will look more deeply at the potential contribution of digital technologies to productivity and jobs and at the role of services firms as upstream enablers and downstream complements of the activities to which they are linked.

Finally, as chapters 3 and 4 will explore, the growing importance of digital technologies can increase opportunities for scale and innovation among low-skill services, while increased linkages of the global innovator services with other sectors can spread the productivity benefits more widely.

Annex 2A Data Sources

The firm-level analysis conducted in this chapter relies on firm-level data from 20 low- and middle-income countries (table 2A.1) as well as additional aggregated data from statistical sources—covering 56 countries in total across all income groups. Only in 11 countries were panel data available (of which two countries, South Africa and Turkey, allowed access to the data only in a secured data room).

TABLE 2A.1 Overview of Firm-Level Data

Country or territory	Year	Number of firms	Source	Description
Firm-level data sources				
Bangladesh	2013	3,336,726	Census	Establishment-level; includes informal enterprises; no capital information available
Cabo Verde	2014	9,185	Census	Establishment-level; no capital information available
Cambodia	2011	505,134	Census	Establishment-level; includes informal enterprises; no capital information available
Côte d'Ivoire	2003–12 (panel)	60,558	Census	Firm-level
El Salvador	2006–17 (panel)	150,406	Census	Establishment-level; no capital information available
Kazakhstan	2009–19 (panel)	72,689	Financial data	Establishment-level
Kosovo	2005–14 (panel)	177,736	Business registry	Firm-level; no capital information available
Moldova	2003–14 (panel)	288,188	Financial data	Establishment-level

Table continues on the following page

TABLE 2A.1   Overview of Firm-Level Data *(continued)*

Country or territory	Year	Number of firms	Source	Description
Mozambique	2016	42,884	Census	Firm-level; no capital information available
North Macedonia	2011–16 (panel)	311,143	Business registry	Firm-level
Paraguay	2014	3,210	Survey	Establishment-level; no capital information available
Peru	2007–12 (panel)	42,698	Survey	Establishment-level
Rwanda	2014	7,912	Census	Establishment level. No capital information available.
Sierra Leone	2016	15,777	Census	Firm-level; no capital information available
Serbia	2007–17 (panel)	73,019	Business registry	Firm-level
South Africa	2010–14 (panel)	112,247	Administrative data	Firm-level
Turkey	2007–16 (panel)	2,984,534	Administrative data	Firm-level
Uganda	2010	4,705	Survey	Firm-level; no capital information available
Vietnam	2009–14 (panel)	2,704,884	Census	Establishment-level
Zambia	2010	7,053	Survey	Establishment-level; no capital information available
Comparator data sources				
European Union (EU)	Varies	Varies	Structural Business Statistics survey (Eurostat and national statistical offices)	Only aggregated information available
Non-EU OECD countries	1995–17 (varies by country)	Varies	Surveys and censuses (OECD)	Only aggregated information available
United States	1998–17	3,653,746	US Census Bureau	Only aggregated information available

Note: OECD = Organisation for Economic Co-operation and Development.

All but two countries cover formal firms only; hence, for consistency, the results presented in this chapter focus on formal firms. Countries differ in the type of data available, and not all countries report the capital stock of firms or the use of intermediate inputs.

Annex 2B Alternative Measures of Scale

The main analysis in this chapter focused on the average number of employees as well as the distribution of employment among firms as a measure of scale. These are not the only

Alternative Measures of Scale Confirm That Scale Is Lower in Most Services Subsectors Than in Manufacturing, Except in Administrative and Support Services

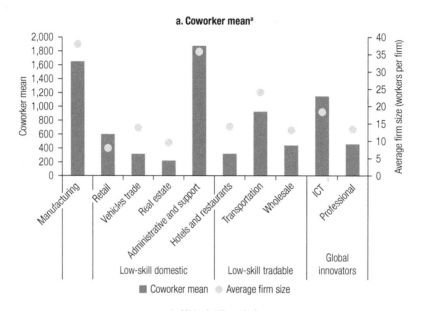

a. Coworker mean[a]

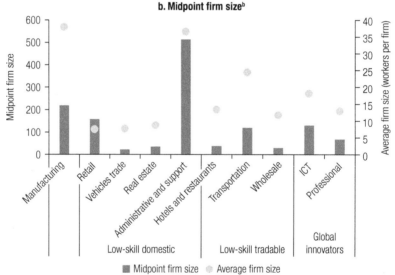

b. Midpoint firm size[b]

Source: Calculations using administrative firm-level data (see annex 2A).

Note: Sectors are classified using the International Standard Industrial Classification (ISIC) Rev. 4 at the section level, except for wholesale, retail, and vehicles trade, which are reported at the (two-digit) division level. Services subsectors are grouped by sets of pro-development characteristics (defined in chapter 1), with skill-intensive social services excluded because of their limited coverage in firm-level data. ICT = information and communication technology.

a. The "coworker mean" is the average number of coworkers that a worker in a particular subsector has. It is the employment-weighted average size of a firm.

b. The "midpoint firm size" is the smallest size of the largest firms accounting for 50 percent of subsector employment.

At Your Service? The Promise of Services-Led Development

relevant measures for employment-related scale. This annex explores two further measures: (a) coworker mean, and (b) mid-point firm size (as a measure for minimum efficient scale).

Coworker mean. The coworker mean is the average number of coworkers that a worker in a particular sector has. It is the employment-weighted average size of a firm and, as such, is a measure of concentration.

Gervais and Jensen (2013) show that in the United States, services firms are smaller, on average, than manufacturing firms (with employment averaging 45 in manufacturing and 13–18 in services). However, in business services, the coworker mean is higher (1,402 in business services, against 782 in manufacturing). In other services subsectors (commerce and personal services), the coworker mean in the United States is lower than in manufacturing.

The firm-level data analyzed for this book similarly show that the coworker mean is lower in many services than in manufacturing, except in administrative and support services—which are considered part of business services in the study by Gervais and Jensen (2013).

Minimum efficient scale. This second relevant measure, in an industrial organization, is the lowest scale at which a firm can produce such that its long-run average costs are minimized. Cost curves are difficult to measure, and therefore proxies are often used, including the Comanor and Wilson (1967) and Weiss (1963) proxies. The Weiss (1963) "midpoint firm size" calculates the smallest size of the largest firms that would account for half of an industry's employment or output—in other words, the firm size at which 50 percent of employment or output is in firms larger than this firm. In this dataset, the midpoint firm size for most services is lower than in manufacturing, except for—again—in administrative and support services.

Notes

1. The analysis in this chapter is mostly based on firm-level data from administrative sources or surveys covering the private sector. These data sources do not always comprehensively cover skill-intensive social services (health and education), because in many countries, many of these services are (at least partially) publicly provided. For this reason, much of the analysis in the chapter will focus on the other three services subsector groups.

2. One challenge for comparing TFP levels across sectors and countries is that TFP estimates depend on the output elasticities of production factors, which vary between sectors and likely across countries. Comparing the TFP values of two firms with different production functions leads to an "apples and oranges" problem, as coined by Bernard and Jones (1996). Two firms with the same TFP and capital and labor levels, but with different output elasticities, will likely see different output values. To get around this issue, the TFP estimates used for comparing sectors and country income groups (as in figures 2.1 and 2.2) rely on fixed output elasticities, set at two-thirds for employment and one-third for physical capital (following an approach similar to Bloom et al. 2020). Nevertheless, for analyses comparing TFP within a sector or looking at TFP growth rates (as in figures 2.13 and 2.22), where this "apples and oranges" problem is less pronounced, TFP estimates rely on output elasticities that vary across sectors.

3. The World Bank Enterprise Surveys have also extended their coverage of the services sector. They include retail and wholesale trade, hotels and restaurants, transportation, communication, and IT but exclude sectors such as professional services and administrative and business support services.

4. In LMICs, the average establishment size in services and manufacturing is 2.9 and 11.2 workers, respectively. In HICs, the corresponding figures are 5.4 and 16.5 workers. These figures are based on data collected by Bento and Restuccia (2021) from statistical sources on firms and establishments and cover both formal and informal establishments. Corrections have been applied to countries where data are reported at the firm level rather than at the establishment level.

5. These 30 large services companies are Walmart, Costco, Carrefour (retail), Amazon (retail and cloud services), Itochu (trading), CVS Health, Walgreens-Boots, Anthem (health), Ping An Insurance, AT&T, Verizon, Nippon, Deutsche Telekom, ICBC (banking), Fannie Mae, Bank of America, Crédit Agricole, Wells Fargo, Citigroup, HSBC (banking), Banco Santander, SoftBank, BNP Paribas (banking), China Post (postal and shipping), Allianz, Prudential (financial and insurance), Legal & General (financial and insurance), Aviva (insurance), Alphabet/Google, and Microsoft (IT). Note that this number excludes firms registered under a different economic activity. For example, Apple is registered as a computer equipment firm despite being an important provider of software and cloud services as well.

6. Ciani et al. (2020) use the following method to determine overlap between size and productivity: they count the number of firms with more than 100 employees in each sector and country and then look at the overlap of these firms with the same number of most-productive firms in their respective sectors and countries.

7. Some of the lack of large retail stores can reflect differences in policy regimes. Several countries restrict larger retail chains, or big-box stores, from entering. For example, in India, foreign ownership in multibrand retail stores (those selling more than just one brand, such as department stores) is capped at 51 percent and subject to (a) a minimum of US$100 million in foreign direct investment (FDI); (b) investment of 50 percent of the total foreign investment in back-end infrastructure; and (c) restriction of multibrand retail stores to cities with more than 1 million in population. See also box 5.1 for a further discussion of scale and FDI in retail.

8. Bartelsman and Wolf (2018) analyze TFP dispersion in 21 European countries. The interquartile range of TFP in services is higher than that in manufacturing in 20 of the countries included.

9. As discussed more extensively by Cusolito and Maloney (2018), whether quality is also reflected in the price depends on demand-side factors such as consumers' willingness to pay as well as the information available. In addition, given that the quality of services might be hard to establish or contract on, inefficiencies related to information asymmetries are likely to occur, meaning that factors such as reputation play an important role in the pricing of services (see, for example, Shapiro 1983). Improving information on quality shows that there is a premium for higher-quality services, as shown by the examples of hygiene grade cards for restaurants (Jin and Leslie 2003) or reputation ratings of sellers on online marketplaces (Tadelis 2016).

10. An example of horizontal and vertical product differentiation in the hotel industry is given by Becerra, Santaló, and Silva (2013), who show that both hotels with more stars (an example of vertical differentiation, as stars tend to indicate higher quality) and branded hotels that target a particular customer base (an example of horizontal differentiation) are charging higher prices. Other examples of horizontal product differentiation include different insurance products for consumers with different risk factors (see, for example, Spence 1978) and consulting firms that specialize in particular sectors (McKenna 2006).

11. Data reporting on firms versus establishments differs across countries, with many OECD countries reporting national statistics on firms at the level of the firm rather than the establishment. Unfortunately, few countries report both firms and establishments. The dataset of Bento and Restuccia (2021) derived from statistical accounts, used in figures 2.4 and 2.5, corrects for these differences.

12. Few countries report data on both the number of firms and the number of establishments. In their analysis of statistical sources on manufacturing firms, Bento and Restuccia (2017) highlight that 83 countries report their data at the level of the establishment, 67 at the level of the firm, and only 16 countries at the level of both the establishment and the firm (and only 4 countries with below-median incomes).

13. Flipkart in India is now majority-owned by US-based Walmart.

14. The job quality index takes the average of four components: (a) income above the international poverty line of US$1.90 in 2011 dollars; (b) nonwage benefits including social security leave, overtime pay, and nonfood in-kind benefits such as housing and transportation; (c) job security as measured by contracts, tenure, and formality; and (d) job satisfaction reflected in whether an individual has a second paid job and whether weekly working hours are excessive. A job that fulfills the conditions of each category and pays above the poverty line has a maximum score of 4, while the lowest possible score is 0. Except for the job satisfaction component, an individual must only fulfill one of the subcomponents for their job to be considered as exhibiting that particular job quality component.

15. This finding is based on analysis of the World Bank's I2D2 dataset covering 36 LMICs with suitable wage data. Among these countries, the median of the gender wage gap (defined as the percentage difference between a country's male wage and female wage), with occupation controlled for, is 28 percent for manufacturing, 26 for commerce, 8 percent for transportation and communications, and 27 percent for financial and business services.

16. The wage-increase percentages are population-weighted averages.

17. HICs here are those so classified by the World Bank circa 2016.

18. In estimating these earnings profiles, observable measures of ability, experience acquired in other sectors, and worker and location fixed effects are accounted for.

19. These results are robust to accounting for firm size and average education. Learning effects vary with worker education but are relatively similar for males and females.

20. Figure 1.18 highlighted the productivity gaps between countries within the same sector, indicating the scope of potential within-sector productivity gains.

References

Acs, Zoltan. 2006. "How Is Entrepreneurship Good for Economic Growth?" *Innovations: Technology, Governance, Globalization* 1 (1): 97–107.

Aga, Gemechu, Francisco Campos, Adriana Conconi, Elwyn Davies, and Carolin Geginat. 2021. "Informal Firms in Mozambique: Status and Potential." Policy Research Working Paper 9712, World Bank, Washington, DC.

Aghion, Philippe, Jing Cai, Mathias Dewatripont, Luosha Du, Ann Harrison, and Patrick Legros. 2015. "Industrial Policy and Competition." *American Economic Journal: Macroeconomics* 7 (4): 1–32. doi:10.1257/mac.20120103.

Alfaro, Laura, and Marcela Eslava. 2020. "Development and the Comparative Advantage of Services." Unpublished manuscript, Harvard Business School and University of the Andes (Uniandes), Bogotá, Colombia.

Apedo-Amah, Marie Christine, Besart Avdiu, Xavier Cirera, Marcio Cruz, Elwyn Davies, Arti Grover, Leonardo Iacovone, et al. 2020. "Unmasking the Impact of COVID-19 on Businesses: Firm-Level Evidence from across the World." Policy Research Working Paper 9434, World Bank, Washington, DC.

Artuç, Erhan and Paulo Bastos. 2021. "Learning by Working in High-Skill Industries: Manufacturing versus Services in Brazil." Unpublished manuscript, World Bank, Washington, DC.

Asker, John, Allan Collard-Wexler, and Jan De Loecker. 2014. "Dynamic Inputs and Resource (Mis) Allocation." *Journal of Political Economy* 122 (5): 1013–63.

Aterido, Reyes, Elwyn Davies, Mary Hallward-Driemeier, and Gaurav Nayyar. 2021. "Revisiting the Size-Production Relationship in Services." Unpublished manuscript, World Bank, Washington, DC.

Atkeson, Andrew, and Patrick J. Kehoe. 2005. "Modeling and Measuring Organization Capital." *Journal of Political Economy* 113 (5): 1026–53. doi:10.1086/431289.

Atkin, David, Benjamin Faber, and Marco Gonzalez-Navarro. 2018. "Retail Globalization and Household Welfare: Evidence from Mexico." *Journal of Political Economy* 126 (1): 1–73.

Audretsch, David B. 1995. "Innovation, Growth and Survival." *International Journal of Industrial Organization* 13 (4): 441–57. doi:10.1016/0167-7187(95)00499-8.

Audretsch, David B., Luuk Klomp, and Roy Thurik. 1998. "Do Services Differ from Manufacturing? The Post-Entry Performance of Firms in Dutch Services." Discussion Paper 98-012/3, Tinbergen Institute, Amsterdam.

Baily, Martin Neil, Charles Hulten, and David Campbell, Timothy Bresnahan, and Richard E. Caves. 1992. "Productivity Dynamics in Manufacturing Plants." *Brookings Papers on Economic Activity: Microeconomics* 23: 187–267. doi:10.2307/2534764.

Bain, Joe S. 1954. "Economies of Scale, Concentration, and the Condition of Entry in Twenty Manufacturing Industries." *American Economic Review* 44 (1): 15–39.

Bartelsman, Eric, John Haltiwanger, and Stefano Scarpetta. 2013. "Cross-Country Differences in Productivity: The Role of Allocation and Selection." *American Economic Review* 103 (1): 305–34. doi:10.1257/aer.103.1.305.

Bartelsman, Eric J., and Zoltan Wolf. 2018. "Measuring Productivity Dispersion." In *The Oxford Handbook of Productivity Analysis*, edited by Emili Grifell-Tatjé, C. A. Knox Lovell, and Robin C. Sickles, 593–624. New York: Oxford University Press.

Baumol, William J. 1967. "Macroeconomics of Unbalanced Growth: The Anatomy of Urban Crisis." *American Economic Review* 57 (3): 415–26.

Becerra, Manuel, Juan Santaló, and Rosario Silva. 2013. "Being Better vs. Being Different: Differentiation, Competition, and Pricing Strategies in the Spanish Hotel Industry." *Tourism Management* 34: 71–79.

Bento, Pedro, and Diego Restuccia. 2017. "Misallocation, Establishment Size, and Productivity." *American Economic Journal: Macroeconomics* 9 (3): 267–303.

Bento, Pedro, and Diego Restuccia. 2021. "On Average Establishment Size across Sectors and Countries." *Journal of Monetary Economics* 117: 220–42. doi:10.1016/j.jmoneco.2020.01.001.

Berlingieri, Giuseppe, Sara Calligaris, and Chiara Criscuolo. 2018. "The Productivity-Wage Premium: Does Size Still Matter in a Service Economy?" *AEA Papers and Proceedings* 108: 328–33. doi:10.1257/pandp.20181068.

Bernard, Andrew B., and Charles I. Jones. 1996. "Comparing Apples to Oranges: Productivity Convergence and Measurement across Industries and Countries." *American Economic Review* 86 (5): 1216–38. doi:10.1257/aer.91.4.1160.

Bertrand, Marianne, and Francis Kramarz. 2002. "Does Entry Regulation Hinder Job Creation? Evidence from the French Retail Industry." *Quarterly Journal of Economics* 117 (4): 1369–1413.

Bils, Mark, Peter J. Klenow, and Cian Ruane. 2017. "Misallocation or Mismeasurement?" Working Paper 599, Stanford Center for International Development, Stanford, CA.

Blau, Francine D., and Lawrence M. Kahn. 2017. "The Gender Wage Gap: Extent, Trends, and Explanations." *Journal of Economic Literature* 55 (3): 789–865. doi:10.2307/j.ctt1tm7gsm.15.

Bloom, Nicholas, Philip Bunn, Paul Mizen, Pawel Smietanka, and Gregory Thwaites. 2020. "The Impact of Covid-19 on Productivity." Working Paper 28233, National Bureau of Economic Research, Cambridge, MA.

BLS (US Bureau of Labor Statistics). 2019. "Women in the Labor Force: A Databook." *BLS Reports* 1084.

Borrowman, Mary, and Stephan Klasen. 2020. "Drivers of Gendered Sectoral and Occupational Segregation in Developing Countries." *Feminist Economics* 26 (2): 62–94. doi:10.1080/13545701 .2019.1649708.

Brolhato de Oliveira, Sara, Xavier Cirera, Ana P. Cusolito, and Eric Jardim. 2021. "Business Dynamism Across Sectors: Evidence Using Employer-Employee Data in Brazil." Unpublished manuscript, World Bank, Washington, DC.

Bronnenberg, Bart J., and Paul B. Ellickson. 2015. "Adolescence and the Path to Maturity in Global Retail." *Journal of Economic Perspectives* 29 (4): 113–34.

Brummund, Peter, Christopher Mann, and Carlos Rodríguez-Castelán. 2018. "Job Quality and Poverty in Latin America." *Review of Development Economics* 22 (4): 1682–1708. doi:10.1111 /rode.12512.

Busso, Matias, Lucia Madrigal, and Carmen Pagés. 2013. "Productivity and Resource Misallocation in Latin America." *B.E. Journal of Macroeconomics* 13 (1): 903–32.

Ciani, Andrea, Marie Caitriona Hyland, Nona Karalashvili, Jennifer L. Keller, Alexandros Ragoussis, and Trang Thu Tran. 2020. *Making It Big: Why Developing Countries Need More Large Firms.* Washington, DC: World Bank.

Comanor, William S., and Thomas A. Wilson. 1967. "Advertising Market Structure and Performance." *Review of Economics and Statistics* 49 (4): 423–40.

Cusolito, Ana Paula, and William F. Maloney. 2018. *Productivity Revisited: Shifting Paradigms in Analysis and Policy.* Washington, DC: World Bank.

Dauda, Seidu, and Maciej Drozd. 2020. "Barriers to Competition in Product Market Regulation: New Insights on Emerging Market and Developing Economies." Finance in Focus note, World Bank, Washington, DC.

David, Joel M., and Venky Venkateswaran. 2019. "The Sources of Capital Misallocation." *American Economic Review* 109 (7): 2531–67. doi:10.1257/aer.20180336.

Decker, Ryan, John Haltiwanger, Ron Jarmin, and Javier Miranda. 2014. "The Role of Entrepreneurship in US Job Creation and Economic Dynamism." *Journal of Economic Perspectives* 28 (3): 3–24. doi:10.1257/jep.28.3.3.

De Loecker, Jan, Jan Eeckhout, and Gabriel Unger. 2020. "The Rise of Market Power and the Macroeconomic Implications." *Quarterly Journal of Economics* 135 (2): 561–644. doi:10.1093 /qje/qjz041.

De Mel, Suresh, David McKenzie, and Christopher Woodruff. 2010. "Who Are the Microenterprise Owners? Evidence from Sri Lanka on Tokman versus De Soto." In *International Differences in Entrepreneurship,* edited by Josh Lerner and Antoinette Schoar, 63–88. Chicago: University of Chicago Press. doi:10.7208/chicago/9780226473109.003.0003.

De Soto, Hernando. 2000. *The Mystery of Capital: Why Capitalism Triumphs in the West and Fails Everywhere Else.* New York: Basic Books.

De Vries, Gaaitzen J. 2014. "Productivity in a Distorted Market: The Case of Brazil's Retail Sector." *Review of Income and Wealth* 60 (3): 499–524. doi:10.1111/roiw.12017.

Dias, Daniel A., Christine J. Richmond, and Carlos Robalo Marques. 2016. "A Tale of Two Sectors: Why Is Misallocation Higher in Services Than in Manufacturing?" Working Paper 16/220, International Monetary Fund, Washington, DC.

Di Giovanni, Julian, Andrei A. Levchenko, and Isabelle Mejean. 2017. "Large Firms and International Business Cycle Comovement." *American Economic Review* 107 (5): 598–602. doi:10.1257/aer.p20171006.

Farrell, Diana. 2004. "The Hidden Dangers of the Informal Economy." *McKinsey Quarterly* 3: 26–37.

Foster, Lucia, John C. Haltiwanger, and C. J. Krizan. 2001. "Aggregate Productivity Growth: Lessons from Microeconomic Evidence." In *New Developments in Productivity Analysis*, edited by Charles R. Hulten, Edwin R. Dean, and Michael J. Harper, 303–72. Chicago: University of Chicago Press.

Freund, Caroline, and Martha Denisse Pierola. 2015. "Export Superstars." *Review of Economics and Statistics* 97 (5): 1023–32. doi:10.1162/REST_a_00511.

Gal, Peter N., and Alexander Hijzen. 2016. "The Short-Term Impact of Product Market Reforms: A Cross-Country Firm-Level Analysis." Working Paper 16-116, International Monetary Fund, Washington, DC.

Ganapati, Sharat. 2018. "The Modern Wholesaler: Global Sourcing, Domestic Distribution, and Scale Economies." Working Paper CES-18-49, Center for Economic Studies, US Census Bureau, Washington, DC.

Gervais, Antoine, and J. Bradford Jensen. 2013. "The Tradability of Services: Geographic Concentration and Trade Costs." Working Paper 19759, National Bureau of Economic Research, Cambridge, MA.

Grossman, Gene M., and Elhanan Helpman. 1991. *Innovation and Growth in the Global Economy.* Cambridge, MA: MIT Press.

Gulyani, Sumila, and Debabrata Talukdar. 2010. "Inside Informality: The Links between Poverty, Microenterprises, and Living Conditions in Nairobi's Slums." *World Development* 38 (12): 1710–26. doi:10.1016/j.worlddev.2010.06.013.

Hallward-Driemeier, Mary, and Gaurav Nayyar. 2018. *Trouble in the Making? The Future of Manufacturing-Led Development.* Washington, DC: World Bank.

Haltiwanger, John, Ron S. Jarmin, and Javier Miranda. 2013. "Who Creates Jobs? Small versus Large versus Young." *Review of Economics and Statistics* 95 (2): 347–61. doi:10.1162/REST_a_00288.

Helper, Susan, Timothy Krueger, and Howard Wial. 2012. "Why Does Manufacturing Matter? Which Manufacturing Matters? A Policy Framework." Paper, Metropolitan Policy Program at Brookings, Washington, DC.

Hoekman, Bernard. 2006. "Liberalizing Trade in Services: A Survey." Policy Research Working Paper 4030, World Bank, Washington, DC.

Hovhannisyan, Shoghik, Veronica Montalva-Talledo, Tyler Remick, Carlos Rodríguez-Castelán, and Kersten Stamm. 2021. "A Global Job Quality Index." Unpublished manuscript, World Bank, Washington, DC.

Hortaçsu, Ali, and Chad Syverson. 2015. "The Ongoing Evolution of US Retail: A Format Tug-of-War." *Journal of Economic Perspectives* 29 (4): 89–112. doi:10.1257/jep.29.4.89.

Hsieh, Chang-Tai, and Peter J. Klenow. 2009. "Misallocation and Manufacturing TFP in China and India." *Quarterly Journal of Economics* 124 (4): 1403–48.

Hsieh, Chang-Tai, and Peter J. Klenow. 2014. "The Life Cycle of Plants in India and Mexico." *Quarterly Journal of Economics* 129 (3): 1035–84. doi:10.1093/qje/qju014.

Hsieh, Chang-Tai, and Esteban Rossi-Hansberg. 2019. "The Industrial Revolution in Services." Working Paper 2019-87, Becker Friedman Institute for Economics, University of Chicago. doi:10.2139/ssrn.3404309.

IMF (International Monetary Fund). 2018. "Manufacturing Jobs: Implications for Productivity and Inequality." In *World Economic Outlook, April 2018: Cyclical Upswing, Structural Change*, 129–171. Washington, DC: IMF.

Islam, Asif, Remi Jedwab, Paul Romer, and Daniel Pereira. 2018. "Returns to Experience and the Misallocation of Labor." Background paper for *World Development Report 2019: The Changing Nature of Work*. Washington, DC: World Bank.

Jarmin, Ronald S., Shawn D. Klimek, and Javier Miranda. 2009. "The Role of Retail Chains: National, Regional, and Industry Results." In *Producer Dynamics: New Evidence from Micro Data*, edited by Timothy Dunne, J. Bradford Jensen, and Mark J. Roberts, 237–62. Chicago: University of Chicago Press.

Jensen, J. Bradford. 2011. *Global Trade in Services: Fear, Facts, and Offshoring.* Washington, DC: Peterson Institute for International Economics.

Jin, Ginger Zhe, and Phillip Leslie. 2003. "The Effect of Information on Product Quality: Evidence from Restaurant Hygiene Grade Cards." *Quarterly Journal of Economics* 118 (2): 409–51.

Kask, Christopher, David Kiernan, and Brian Friedman. 2002. "Labor Productivity Growth in Wholesale Trade, 1990–2000." *Monthly Labor Review* 125 (12): 3–14.

Khamis, Melanie, Daniel Prinz, David Newhouse, Amparo Palacios-Lopez, Utz Pape, and Michael Weber. 2021. "The Early Labor Market Impacts of COVID-19 in Developing Countries: Evidence from High-Frequency Phone Surveys." Policy Research Working Paper 9510, World Bank, Washington, DC.

Krishna, Pravin, Andrei A. Levchenko, and William F. Maloney. 2020. "Growth and Risk: A View from International Trade." Policy Research Working Paper 9296, World Bank, Washington, DC. doi:10.1596/1813-9450-9296.

Krugman, Paul. 1987. "The Narrow Moving Band, the Dutch Disease, and the Competitive Consequences of Mrs. Thatcher: Notes on Trade in the Presence of Dynamic Scale Economies." *Journal of Development Economics* 27 (1–2): 41–55. doi:10.1016/0304-3878(87)90005-8.

Lagakos, David. 2016. "Explaining Cross-Country Productivity Differences in Retail Trade." *Journal of Political Economy* 124 (2): 579–620.

La Porta, Rafael, and Andrei Shleifer. 2014. "Informality and Development." *Journal of Economic Perspectives* 28 (3): 109–26.

Levy, Santiago. 2008. *Good Intentions, Bad Outcomes: Social Policy, Informality, and Economic Growth in Mexico.* Washington, DC: Brookings Institution Press.

Lucas, Robert E. Jr. 1988. "On the Mechanics of Economic Development." *Journal of Monetary Economics* 22 (1): 3–42.

Markusen, James R. 1989. "Trade in Producer Services and in Other Specialized Intermediate Inputs." *American Economic Review* 79 (1): 85–95.

McKenna, Christopher D. 2006. *The World's Newest Profession: Management Consulting in the Twentieth Century.* Cambridge: Cambridge University Press.

Melitz, Marc J., and Sašo Polanec. 2015. "Dynamic Olley-Pakes Productivity Decomposition with Entry and Exit." *RAND Journal of Economics* 46 (2): 362–75. doi:10.1111/1756-2171.12088.

Messenger, Jon C., and Naj Ghosheh, eds. 2010. *Offshoring and Working Conditions in Remote Work.* Basingstoke, UK: Palgrave Macmillan UK.

Nayyar, Gaurav. 2011. "The Quality of Employment in India's Services Sector: Exploring the Heterogeneity." *Applied Economics* 44 (36): 4701–19.

Olivetti, Claudia, and Barbara Petrongolo. 2008. "Unequal Pay or Unequal Employment? A Cross-Country Analysis of Gender Gaps." *Journal of Labor Economics* 26 (4): 621–54.

Olivetti, Claudia, and Barbara Petrongolo. 2016. "The Evolution of Gender Gaps in Industrialized Countries." *Annual Review of Economics* 8 (1): 405–34.

Olley, G. Steven, and Ariel Pakes. 1996. "The Dynamics of Productivity in the Telecommunications Equipment Industry." *Econometrica* 64 (6): 1263–97.

Oostendorp, Remco H. 2004. "Globalization and the Gender Wage Gap." Policy Research Working Paper 3256, World Bank, Washington, DC.

Perry, Guillermo E., and William F. Maloney. 2007. "Overview." In *Informality: Exit and Exclusion.* Washington, DC: World Bank.

Redding, Stephen. 1999. "Dynamic Comparative Advantage and the Welfare Effects of Trade." *Oxford Economic Papers* 51 (1): 15–39. doi:10.1093/oep/51.1.15.

Restuccia, Diego, and Richard Rogerson. 2017. "The Causes and Costs of Misallocation." *Journal of Economic Perspectives* 31 (3): 151–74.

Schivardi, Fabiano, and Eliana Viviano, 2011. "Entry Barriers in Retail Trade." *Economic Journal* 121 (551): 145–70.

Shapiro, Carl. 1983. "Premiums for High Quality Products as Returns to Reputations." *Quarterly Journal of Economics* 98 (4): 659–80.

Sorbe, Stéphane, Peter Gal, and Valentine Millot. 2018. "Can Productivity Still Grow in Service-Based Economies? Literature Overview and Preliminary Evidence from OECD Countries." Economics Department Working Paper 1531, Organisation for Economic Co-operation and Development, Paris.

Spence, Michael. 1978. "Product Differentiation and Performance in Insurance Markets." *Journal of Public Economics* 10 (3): 427–47. doi:10.1016/0047-2727(78)90055-5.

Szirmai, Adam. 2011. "Manufacturing and Economic Development." Working Paper 2011/75, United Nations World Institute for Development Economics Research (UNU-WIDER), Helsinki.

Tadelis, Steven. 2016. "Reputation and Feedback Systems in Online Platform Markets." *Annual Review of Economics* 8 (1): 321–40. doi:10.1146/annurev-economics-080315-015325.

Torres, Jesica, Franklin Maduko, Isis Gaddis, Leonardo Iacovone, and Kathleen Beegle. 2021. "The Impact of the COVID-19 Pandemic on Women-Led Businesses." Working paper, World Bank, Washington, DC.

Ulyssea, Gabriel. 2018. "Firms, Informality, and Development: Theory and Evidence from Brazil." *American Economic Review* 108 (8): 2015–47.

Ulyssea, Gabriel. 2020. "Informality: Causes and Consequences for Development." *Annual Review of Economics* 12 (1): 525–46.

Van Biesebroeck, Johannes. 2005. "Firm Size Matters: Growth and Productivity Growth in African Manufacturing." *Economic Development and Cultural Change* 53 (3): 545–83. doi:10.1086/426407.

Weiss, Leonard W. 1963. "Factors in Changing Concentration." *Review of Economics and Statistics* 45 (1): 70–77.

World Bank. 2011. *World Development Report 2012: Gender Equality and Development.* Washington, DC: World Bank.

Zahler, Andrés, Leonardo Iacovone, and Aaditya Mattoo. 2014. "Trade and Innovation in Services: Evidence from a Developing Economy." *World Economy* 37 (7): 953–79. doi:10.1111/twec.12117.

Bringing Services to the Surface: The Measurement Challenge

Introduction

Discussing services is not possible without discussing data—or all too often, the lack thereof. Fewer economic statistics have been collected about firms in the services sector than firms in the manufacturing sector.

This gap has its antecedents in history. For classical economists such as Adam Smith, services were products of labor that perish the moment the labor is performed, seldom leave any trace or value behind, and thus amount to unproductive economic activities.[1] Similarly, on the other end of the ideological spectrum, the Material Product System (MPS) of accounting, based on the Marxist-Leninist theory of social production, distinguished between "material" and "nonmaterial" production—the former representing productive economic activities and the latter, unproductive economic activities (Nayyar 2012).[2] Reflecting on US economic statistics in the 1990s, Griliches (1994) dubbed many services sectors as "unmeasurable" in practice, under the data collection practices at that time, concluding that their "productivity effects, which are likely to be quite real, are largely invisible in the data." What was less measured was therefore also less studied.

Only in recent decades has much progress been made to better capture the outputs, inputs, prices, productivity, and trade patterns of the services sector (see, for example, Grassano and Savona 2014; Triplett and Bosworth 2003). These more-refined methodologies (see OECD and Eurostat 2014) have been adopted more widely, especially in higher-income countries, leading to the availability of more-detailed data on services, even though important gaps remain. Nevertheless, for lower-income countries, statistics on the services sector tend to be even more scarce.

However, simply applying the approaches used by firm censuses and surveys in the manufacturing sector to improve data collection and analysis in the services sector does not always work. The manufacturing sector often allows for a clear definition of a production process—tangible raw materials that are transformed by people and machines into a tangible product—but, for the services sector, defining the production process and quantifying inputs and outputs is often more challenging. Similar measurement issues affect estimations of trade in services because there are many forms through which services trade can take place. As a result, there are difficulties in estimating value added, productivity, and participation in international trade.

This "Spotlight" reflects further on these measurement issues surrounding services and what could be done to mitigate some of these challenges.

Measuring Outputs

Capturing the outputs of the services sector—sales, value added, or quantity produced—is key for the compilation of gross domestic product (GDP) figures as well as to calculate productivity. These processes require good data on both outputs and prices. Unfortunately, both are difficult to measure, and even more so for services.

Challenges with Revenue-Based Measures

Measuring the quantity of output is challenging for services because there is no physical good that can be easily verified and priced, and services are often nonstandardized and highly customized to the client. Some quantification might be possible (for example, by counting meals in a restaurant or beds occupied by hotel guests). However, services are often multifaceted—a restaurant customer receives not only a meal but also service from a waiter and an ambience to enjoy, and no two customers necessarily have the same combination of items in their meals—and heterogeneous in quality. For these reasons, revenue is typically used to measure output.

Biases from Unadjusted Revenue
The use of revenue-based measures means that the measured output no longer reflects only the quantity produced; it also reflects the price at which it is sold. This revenue-based measurement introduces new biases.

First, the presence of market power can upward-bias the prices of firms with price-setting power. These firms can charge higher prices and, unless an adjustment is made for this, the captured output will be higher. This might matter more for services in which the need for physical proximity between producers and consumers means that geographically limited markets potentially reduce competition between suppliers.

Second, prices also reflect quality differences that can be hard to objectively verify. The quality of many services is tailored to the needs of the client (for example, in the case of professional and technical services). This could be related to differences in tastes (for example, for accommodation and food or for entertainment services) as well as varying business needs (such as for information technology [IT] support). Unless an adjustment for quality is made, the output of firms that produce high-quality services risks being downward-biased.

Using Price Deflators for Price and Quality Adjustments

When using revenue-based measures of outputs, using the right price deflators is key. Prices are hard to measure and can vary within the same firm for different customers or combinations of outputs. Nevertheless, there is scope for improvement here, by collecting more accurate deflators at the level of the firm.

Currently, many analyses rely on producer price indexes (PPIs) or consumer price indexes (CPIs) to deflate output for services. These indexes are aggregated at the level of the sector or economy. Analysis conducted on firms engaged predominantly in manufacturing suggests that applying more accurate price deflators led to substantial revisions in productivity estimations (Cusolito and Maloney 2018). Applying a similar approach can be challenging for services because there is not always an obvious "unit" to be priced, so alternatives might need to be sought. For example, for management consultancy services, one could use the hourly fee as a price. Although such a method would result in deflators that are firm-specific, it stills ignores differences in quality. The customized nature of services could mean that these differences are large.

It would be even better if a deflator reflects both the type of service and its quality. A variety of approaches could be used. They include, for example, using firm-specific production costs as a proxy or "hedonic" pricing models that attempt to price quality differences between services using a statistical model (for example, based on a regression). In the context of management consultancy, for instance, this would be a deflator based on contract-specific terms between the consultant and the client.

The collection of firm-specific price data and adjusting for quality is a time- and knowledge-intensive process because it requires a deep understanding of a particular sector and, often, various assumptions too. Firms might also charge customers different prices for the same service or different prices depending on how services are bundled (price discrimination). Statistical agencies in high-income countries have made significant progress in developing methodologies to capture quality in price deflators for services firms (see, for example, Eurostat 2016).

Table S.1 provides examples of deflation methods for capturing firm-level prices and quality. Nevertheless, in practice, statistical agencies often rely on deflation methods that are less than perfect, particularly in the services sector (Inklaar, Timmer, and Van Ark 2008).[3]

Sector-Specific Challenges in Measuring Output

In addition, measuring output is particularly difficult in certain groups of services subsectors, including the several described below.

Nonmarket public sector services. A first group of services subsectors where output can be hard to measure consists of nonmarket services, which mainly operate in the public sector (such as government services, social services, and many education and

TABLE S.1   Examples of More Careful Price Measurement for Services

Subsector	Least preferred price deflator	Example of more firm-specific price deflator	Example of adjustment for quality
Restaurant	PPI or CPI	Price of a meal	Incorporating the quality of the meal
Hotel	PPI or CPI	Price of a room	Incorporating the comfort and amenities of the room
Management consultancy	PPI or CPI	Hourly fee of consultant	Incorporating contract-specific terms
Advertising	PPI or CPI	Price of a printed ad or of 1 minute of television advertising	Accounting for the number of viewers seeing the advertisement

Source: Elaboration from Eurostat 2016.

Note: CPI = consumer price index; PPI = producer price index.

health services). These services, by definition, do not carry a market price and are usually excluded from firm-level analyses.

Financial services. A second group comprises financial services, whose sales or output can be difficult to define. Customer fees alone do not capture a bank's full income from borrowers or account holders, especially given that many financial service providers charge low fees or none at all. To get around this issue, national accounts statistics attempt to measure output by looking at spreads between interest rates that banks face (measured by reference rates) and that banks provide to deposit account holders or charge to their borrowers.[4] Constructing such measures gets especially complicated with more-complex financial products involving different currencies or risk profiles. Because of the complications around measurement, financial sector firms are usually excluded from firm-level data analysis or treated separately.

Services delivered for free. Radio, television, and digital services that are delivered for free pose additional challenges for measuring output. Advertising revenue could provide some indication of value, but this value does not always reflect the full value that consumers obtain from these services. This underestimation of the value of free services is particularly relevant for many digital services, as discussed more extensively later in this Spotlight.

Measuring Inputs

Quantifying inputs such as labor, capital, and other intermediate goods and services can similarly be more challenging for services than for manufacturing.

Labor. First, the quality of labor is hard to measure. As chapter 1 highlighted, services subsectors vary greatly in their use of skilled labor. Even though productivity measures rarely adjust for the skill content of labor, a differentiation between unskilled and skilled labor can be useful to better understand variations in productivity across sectors.

The question is how to measure the skill content of labor. One approach is to use wages as a measure of quality-adjusted labor input, but wages often reflect not only the contribution of labor to production but also the competitiveness of the labor market. Alternative measures of human capital—such as educational attainment or work experience—are often not available and require datasets covering both employees and employers. One such dataset is the matched employer-employee dataset (the Annual Social Information Report, RAIS) in Brazil.

Capital. Second, many services tend to rely more on intangible forms of capital than on physical capital, and these are harder to measure. Intangible capital covers a wide range of assets, such as software, research and development (R&D), organizational culture, brand value, and relationships with clients and suppliers.

The value of these assets is often difficult to measure, especially when they are developed in house rather than purchased externally. Brynjolfsson, Rock, and Syverson (2021) argue that unmeasured intangible capital can lead to underestimations of productivity at early stages of a firm's life cycle (because physical capital and labor are used to produce unmeasured intangible capital that provides few returns to begin with) but can lead to overestimations of productivity later (when the intangible capital has generated benefits as a productive, albeit unmeasured, input).

Nevertheless, some progress has been made to improve the measurement of some forms of intangible capital, especially of information and communication technology (ICT) capital. Unfortunately, such measurements often tend to be available only in high-income countries. In some cases, indirect measures of intangible capital could be used, such as the market valuation of a firm (as discussed, for example, in Hall 2001).

Intermediate inputs. Third, services often rely on other services as intermediate inputs, meaning that all the issues related to measuring the output of services—discussed in the previous section—will also affect the measurement of inputs. Griliches (1994) argued that productivity measurements of the IT sector in the United States should be interpreted with care because, among other reasons, many of the intermediate inputs were not appropriately deflated. A better measurement of services outputs will therefore also improve the measurement of the inputs in this sector.

Transaction-level data—for example, from tax records or digitally collected through electronic fiscal devices (EFDs) or electronic invoices (EIs)—can especially help to disentangle links between firms. Such datasets are now increasingly available and are used by researchers to better understand how linkages matter for firm performance, including those between manufacturing and services firms (Avdiu et al. 2021).[5]

In addition, many of the challenges present in manufacturing—such as difficulties in constructing measures of capital stock (even though services tend to use less physical capital) or determining the factor elasticities of inputs—are likely also present for services. Factor markets are also rarely fully competitive, meaning that value-based approaches to measuring inputs (as used for measuring capital, for example) are prone to capture not only quality but also market power.

Subsectors that are particularly challenging for measuring production inputs are those involved in the leasing or outsourcing of these inputs—for example, employment outsourcing firms, real estate rental agencies, and machine leasing firms. In most datasets, the inputs would appear on the balance sheet of the outsourcing or leasing firm, but the production benefits are realized in the host firm where production takes place. This could lead to an underestimation of these inputs for the host firm (since they are not counted as being part of the host firm) and therefore an overestimation of productivity. For the outsourcing firm, productivity is likely underestimated, since output is determined by the fees paid by the host firm and not the actual production that the workers or capital are contributing to.

Estimating Productivity

These challenges of measuring outputs and inputs also affect the estimation of productivity since productivity, in its essence, is a ratio between outputs and inputs. The potential for mismeasurement has long worried economists regarding whether productivity in the services sector, particularly in digitally enabled services, had been underestimated.

One of the big productivity puzzles of recent years is understanding the marked slowdown in measured productivity since 2000, all at a time when digital technologies have made tremendous gains. The advances in the data economy appear everywhere but in productivity data (see, for example, Brynjolfsson and MacAfee 2014; Feldstein 2017). Even though the extent to which mismeasurement fully explains the observed lower productivity growth rates has been questioned (for example, in Syverson 2017), mismeasurement remains a concern and highlights the need for better data collection.

Metrics of Productivity

In its simplest form, productivity can be measured as labor productivity by calculating the ratio of outputs or value added to employment (for example, value added per worker). This approach has the advantage that it can often be easily calculated using readily available data and can also be easily compared between sectors and countries (even as this comparison can be misleading for all the reasons discussed here).

Value added is often preferable to revenue as a measure of output, especially for sectors relying significantly on physical inputs, such as the retail and food sectors. The disadvantage of this measure is that it does not correct for the use of capital: capital-intensive firms will appear to be productive even if they do not use their capital productively. Even though services firms tend to be less intensive in physical capital than manufacturing, there are some exceptions (such as air transportation, water transportation, and telecommunications), meaning that labor productivity comparisons with these sectors can potentially be misleading. Labor productivity also does not correct for the use of intangible capital, which can be highly important as well.

Total factor productivity (TFP) gives a more complete account of the technical efficiency of how capital, labor, and intermediate inputs are jointly used in the production process and therefore is often a preferred metric. The challenge is that TFP is not directly observed but instead is estimated using either a production function or a cost function approach. This introduces a further need for assumptions, including on how inputs are combined in the production process. In addition, since TFP corrects for capital use, any mismeasurement of capital will affect the estimated productivity level. The likely underreporting of intangible capital in services provision will therefore also affect TFP estimations.

Separating Prices and Quantities

The importance of separating prices and quantities was already highlighted in the earlier section on measuring outputs, but for productivity analyses that compare firms, this is especially important. Prices can reflect both market power and quality, meaning that value-based productivity measures become intertwined with both (see, for example, Cusolito and Maloney 2018; De Loecker, Eeckhout, and Unger 2020; Hsieh and Klenow 2009). Firms that appear to be productive may in fact simply face limited competition. Higher prices can reflect higher quality, but they do not necessarily. With technological innovations, it may be possible to lower prices while producing outputs at the same or even higher quality. The larger heterogeneity in quality as well as potential competition concerns in certain sectors mean that the scope is larger for market power and quality differences to play a role.

For most analyses, the preference is therefore to use quantity-based measures of productivity (such as quantity TFP, abbreviated TFPQ) instead of value-based measures of productivity (such as revenue TFP, abbreviated TFPR) and ideally to also control for quality differences. A variety of methods have been adopted to correct the influence of prices in productivity measurements by applying some correction derived from economic theory. This usually requires making assumptions, such as what demand looks like (for example, Hsieh and Klenow 2009) or that firms are choosing inputs such that costs are minimized (for example, De Loecker and Warzynski 2012). The appropriateness of such corrections is still a subject of debate, but no standard approach has yet emerged (Syverson 2020).

Estimation Challenges: Simultaneity, Selection, and Heterogeneity

In addition to the issues involved in measuring outputs and inputs and the difficulties in incorporating market power and quality, there are other challenges in estimating TFP that may be more problematic for services than for manufacturing. There are the usual concerns about the simultaneity bias between productivity and input choices, as well as selection biases that can make it difficult to interpret econometric estimates. The heterogeneity of the services sector might also be greater.

Simultaneity bias. The simultaneity bias relates to how to disentangle whether it is that the increased use of inputs raises outputs or that managers have firm-specific knowledge about their potential to raise output or prices that leads them to increase their inputs. With services relying less on fixed inputs that cannot be increased or decreased easily (for example, capital) and more on variable inputs that can be adjusted in a shorter amount of time (for example, labor), the simultaneity bias is likely different for services firms than for manufacturing firms.

Selection bias. The selection bias relates to firm exit often being correlated with productivity, with less-productive firms being more likely to exit than more-productive firms, such that productivity measures appear to be higher. Given that rates of firm churn are much higher in services, this is a relatively bigger concern for estimating TFP in services than in manufacturing.

Observed heterogeneity. Another concern is the assumption of a common production function across firms in a sector. While not unique to services, the greater observed heterogeneity in value added per worker in services is consistent with quality differences being more varied. If inputs and outputs cannot be adjusted well for quality, assuming a common production function may lead to misleading results.

Corrections can be applied to reduce the influence of some of these biases. For example, common methods to correct for simultaneity bias and selection bias include those by Ackerberg, Caves, and Frazer (2015), Levinsohn and Petrin (2003), and Olley and Pakes (1996). Nevertheless, some of the wider challenges around market power and quality will be harder to address, unless better and more detailed data are available.

Measuring Trade

Many of these challenges related to measuring outputs and inputs also apply to measuring trade in services. Although goods trade can be measured by tracking customs records, many services—unless they are either embodied in goods (such as film on a Blu-ray disc or software on a DVD)[6] or result in the movement of goods (such as transportation services)—will not be passing through customs. In some cases, it is not the service itself that crosses a border but rather either the provider (such as through temporary migration or setting up a subsidiary firm) or the consumer (as through tourism). Capturing each form of services trade might require different measurement approaches.

The key data sources for trade in services are balance of payment (BoP) statistics. As part of these statistics, countries report services transactions between resident and nonresident firms and persons (see IMF 2009). Residence is generally determined by the so-called center of economic interest. For firms, this is usually their location of incorporation; for natural persons, this is usually determined by the length of their stay (persons present in a country for more than a year are considered residents). Overall, BoP statistics capture three out of the four modes of trade in services identified under the General Agreement on Trade in Services (GATS) (table S.2).

Commercial presence (mode 3) is generally not captured by BoP statistics because subsidiaries of foreign enterprises are considered resident firms in BoP statistics.[7] Instead, additional statistics—such as the Foreign Affiliate Statistics (FATS) and the Activity of Multinational Enterprises (AMNE) database of the Organisation of Economic Co-operation and Development (OECD)—are used to capture this particular mode of trade.

Both BoP statistics and FATS rely on a wide range of data sources, including firm surveys, tourism surveys, bank records of international transactions, migration

TABLE S.2   Ways to Measure the GATS Modes of Trade in Services

Mode	Description	Data sources
1: Cross-border supply	Providing a service to a client abroad, without the movement of natural persons *Example:* services delivered digitally	Included in balance of payment (BoP) statistics; often based on firm surveys and transaction data
2: Consumption abroad	A foreign visitor consuming a service in another country *Examples:* tourism, health tourism, studying abroad	Included in BoP statistics; often based on tourism surveys
3: Commercial presence	Providing a service to a client abroad through a subsidiary firm (that is, as foreign direct investment [FDI])	Usually not included in BoP statistics but included in Foreign Affiliates Statistics (FATS) and the OECD Activity of Multinational Enterprises (AMNE) database, often based on FDI surveys or business statistics
4: Presence of natural persons	A natural person travels to another country to provide a service to a client there	Included in BoP statistics; also covered through statistics on migration, even though a narrow definition is often used
		Might overlap with mode 3 when natural persons travel to deliver services to firms through a subsidiary

Source: Adapted from WTO 2010.

Note: GATS = General Agreement on Trade in Services (of the World Trade Organization); OECD = Organisation for Economic Co-operation and Development. For a further discussion of the four modes of trade in services, see box 1.1.

statistics, foreign direct investment (FDI) surveys, and administrative records.[8] Comprehensively capturing trade in services requires sophisticated and detailed data, which can be challenging to collect, especially in lower-income settings. For example, firms might not always know whether their customers are foreign residents. Digital services that are provided free to visitors from abroad (for example, websites, social networks, and apps) also are usually not recorded in trade statistics.[9] For some sectors, trade in services overlaps significantly with trade in goods. Exports by firms in distribution and transportation services are linked, in large part, to the movement of goods and therefore are accounted for in trade in goods statistics.[10]

The variety of approaches to measuring trade in services often leads to asymmetries between reported imports and exports of services. Even though efforts have been made to standardize the compilation of trade in services, countries differ in the availability of certain data (for example, international bank transactions) and how BoP statistics are compiled using these data. The difficulties of measuring trade values mean that these asymmetries can be larger for services than for merchandise trade (Fortanier et al. 2017). The OECD and the World Trade Organization (WTO) have sought to create balanced statistics on trade in services, through the Balanced Trade in Services (BaTIS) database, by attempting to reconcile reported values by importers and exporters. Discrepancies nevertheless remain.

Measuring Value by Mode of Trade and Firm Characteristics

Another challenge is the inability to distinguish between modes of trade. Since BoP statistics record transactions between residents and nonresidents, regardless of where these residents are located, they do not allow for attributing trade to particular modes. Newer datasets, such as the experimental WTO Trade in Services data by Mode of Supply (TiSMoS) dataset (which chapter 1 used to highlight the importance of FDI as a mode of supply) try to bridge this gap (Wettstein et al. 2019). Nevertheless, with a few exceptions, most countries do not distinguish between different modes in their official statistics, and TiSMoS therefore partly relies on a set of assumptions to allocate trade to modes.

Besides the lack of data, there are other reasons why distinguishing between modes can be challenging. Modes can overlap, for example. A service provider traveling to provide a service would be counted under mode 4 (movement of natural persons), but if that provider does so through a subsidiary firm, it would be counted under mode 3 (commercial presence).

Current trade in services statistics usually follow the GATS definitions, which might not capture all forms of services trade under broader definitions. For example, in the case of mode 4 trade (movement of natural persons), the GATS definitions exclude migration to seek employment from its scope, and consequently trade statistics usually exclude this as well. In other words, a person traveling to another country to be employed (or seeking to be employed) by a foreign firm would not be counted under mode 4 trade, but a self-employed worker fulfilling a contract abroad *would* be counted under mode 4 trade. Also, as will be discussed in the next section, services embodied in goods are usually captured as goods rather than services trade.

More comprehensive data on trade in services are needed. In addition to the lack of more detailed data on different modes, a particular gap is the general unavailability of data that link services trade to firm-level characteristics. Most data sources that link firms with trade data focus solely on trade in goods—for example, the OECD/Eurostat Trade by Enterprise Characteristics (TEC) and the World Bank's Exporter Dynamics Database (EDD), which matches firm-level data with customs records.

Some progress has been made to capture services trade in firm-level data collection. For example, Eurostat has started publishing experimental statistics on Services Trade by Enterprise Characteristics (STEC) for 15 EU countries based on data published by national agencies, but these data remain absent for many lower-income countries.[11]

A Fading Border between Manufacturing and Services

The larger scale of production and the application of new technologies typically made it more profitable for manufacturing firms to "contract out" service activities to specialist providers than to produce them in house—a process that Bhagwati (1984) refers to as "splintering." However, chapter 4 documents the more recent trend of "servicification," whereby manufacturing firms are increasingly selling services. For one thing, many traditional manufacturing firms have offshored production jobs to lower-cost locations while retaining their R&D, design, and branding services. (Apple, for instance, is registered as a computer manufacturing firm despite being one of the largest software developers in the world.) For another, many manufacturers of consumer durables increasingly bundle after-sales services with manufactured goods to exploit complementarities between the two.

With multiactivity firms providing both goods and services, the line between the manufacturing and services sectors has therefore become increasingly blurred. This creates a measurement challenge in that not all services activities are provided by firms whose primary economic activity is in the services sector. The increased service intensity of manufacturers, as it takes place within firm boundaries, is likely to underestimate the role of the services sector in generating growth and productivity. To the extent that manufacturing firms are providing more services in house, activities that had been provided externally in the past and thus were classified as services value added may now be considered manufacturing value added.

The latter holds true for tech companies such as Apple and Microsoft (which started out as manufacturers of computing equipment) as well as for producers of consumer durables. The same issue plays a role in trade statistics, wherein services embodied in goods (sometimes dubbed "mode 5" trade) are usually reported under trade in goods rather than trade in services. On the flip side, many services firms now produce goods, such as Google in the tablet market and Amazon with its Kindle e-reader (Lopez-Bassols and Millot 2013). Unless this activity is identified separately in the data, this manufacturing activity risks being counted as services value added.[12]

More detailed data are crucial to understand the trends regarding the myriad goods and services that firms are offering and how their distribution of production and services workers is changing. Several high-income countries and some large emerging markets have already been collecting and reporting firm-level data that separate the sale of goods from the sale of services among firms that produce both. For example, the Prowess database in India tracks the product mix that firms reported in their annual reports. This product-level information that distinguishes between goods and services as revenue streams is available for 85 percent of Indian manufacturing firms, collectively accounting for more than 90 percent of the manufacturing output and exports of firms included in the database (Grover and Mattoo 2020). Similarly, in some cases, employer-employee administrative data (available in Brazil and Turkey, for example) including worker occupations can shine a light on workers being employed in services-related activities.

Measurement of Digital Services

Digital services pose additional measurement challenges. The increased "servicification" of nonservices sectors discussed earlier is attributable, at least in part, to the growing importance of digital technologies in many firms whose primary activities are not IT-related. This means that the measurement challenges associated with digital services are no longer restricted to IT sector firms but have ramifications for a larger set of economic activities.

Many digital services are delivered for free or at a low cost and therefore lack easily measured market prices. Such services include search engines, social networks, media websites, and other services such as messaging apps or email. Currently, the value of these services either remains unmeasured or is measured through the value of advertising, which usually provides the vast share of revenue. Nevertheless, advertising revenue does not necessarily capture the full benefits to the consumer from these services.

Several approaches have been made to better quantify these gains by attempting to measure consumer surplus (technically defined as the difference between willingness to pay and the price paid for a product of service) more accurately. For example, using time spent on internet services as a measure of consumer welfare, Brynjolfsson and Oh (2012) estimate that free internet services in the United States represent an annual value of more than US$100 billion.[13] Another approach is to measure "willingness to pay" more directly. For example, Brynjolfsson, Collis, and Eggers (2019) conduct an online lab experiment in which they ask respondents how much they are willing to pay to avoid losing access to an online service.[14] Each of these approaches suggests that the value of consumer surplus is much larger than the value that is measured through traditional means, such as advertising revenue.

Many digital services are also difficult to measure because they rely largely on intangible capital and assets. The use of digital services as well as the underlying data and data analytics has become an important driver of many enterprises' business models, but it remains difficult to value these data properly. In the *System of National Accounts 2008* (UN et al. 2009), the value of data is established by calculating the sum of the costs to prepare a dataset, but in fact, the value of data to a firm is likely much higher than that (Ker and Mazzini 2020; World Bank 2021).

Analyzing the use and value of data often requires a tailored approach, specific to the firm and type of data. Examples of such approaches to measure the use and value of data include capturing firms' expenditure on digital storage devices, measuring the price of commercial databases that firms sell, and considering the market valuation of firms that are heavily reliant on data (Nguyen and Paczos 2020).

Similar issues also occur when measuring digital trade. Data flows—which can be considered a "mode 1" (cross-border supply) trade in services—are usually not captured in customs records but can nevertheless carry economic value. Even though financial transactions associated with these data flows can provide some information on its value, cross-border services that are provided free of charge cause similar measurement issues for trade as they do for measuring output. One of the recommendations made in the *Handbook of Measuring Digital Trade* (OECD, WTO, and IMF 2020) is that firm-level surveys include more specific questions on digitally delivered services, particularly those crossing borders.

Data Coverage and Access

Further gaps in the coverage and reporting of data create additional challenges in comprehensively assessing the output and performance of the services sector.

Inadequate Coverage of Informal Firms

Chapter 2 already discussed the broader implications of the prevalence of informality, but the presence of informality has significant implications for data collection and firm-level analyses. Many of these analyses use administrative data sources like tax records or business registers for their analysis or as a sampling frame for a survey. Informal firms are, by definition, excluded from such records, even though (as noted in chapter 2) they provide for a large share of employment and output in many low- and middle-income countries (LMICs). This means that such analyses miss out on an important part of the economy.

Capturing informal firms is difficult. To achieve representativeness, it often requires an extensive data collection effort that comprehensively enumerates large areas or even entire countries—as is done, for example, in economic censuses or labor force surveys. Nevertheless, certain data methods could provide some relief. For example, the World Bank Enterprise Surveys use an adaptive cluster sampling approach (Thompson 1990) that allows for achieving a representative sample by only enumerating a randomly selected small subset of areas, without needing a full enumeration.

A Need for Panel Data to Follow Firms over Time

The absence of good and comprehensive firm-level data in many settings, especially in a panel format, poses further difficulties. Several of the techniques used to improve estimates of technical efficiency or TFP rely on panel data. Following the same firms over time also allows for some of the characteristics of firms that remain constant to be factored out in explaining why performance might be changing over time. Understanding the dynamics of productivity and jobs also requires an understanding of how firms adjust to various shocks.

Currently, few countries collect panel data, and when they do, it is more often done for firms in the manufacturing sector. The analysis in this book is based on panel data of services firms in 10 LMICs, many of them smaller economies. Having more and larger LMICs collecting this type of data would both help inform policy making in these countries and contribute to global knowledge on the drivers of productivity, job dynamics, and the efficacy of various policy choices.

Access to Disaggregated Data

Access to disaggregated data is a further challenge. Given the heterogeneity of the services sector, it is important to collect statistics beyond the broad aggregates reported in macro-level data (often covering four to eight subsectors). Having more-granular data—for example, at the International Standard Industrial Classification (ISIC) two-digit sector-level (which has 45 subsectors)—would be an improvement, but nevertheless significant heterogeneity within narrowly defined subsectors remains.

Firm-level microdata are crucial to better understand the performance of services firms. However, giving researchers access to such data is often a challenge, given potential sensitivity about the commercial value of access to the data, especially of larger firms or potential market competitors. This issue is not unique to services data, but the role of intangible capital may make it more sensitive. Nevertheless, for publicly listed firms, many of the data have to be available in any case. Also, for most research, the interest is not in the identity of individual firms but rather in the dynamics of groups of firms.

Anonymizing the data could be one solution—or providing access on secure servers with limitations on reporting any results for individual or small sets of firms (that is, requiring that any reported statistic be based on at least 5 or 10 firms). Alternatively, information on the structure of the data could be shared, with researchers writing code to conduct the analysis of interest, which is then run by in-house analysts.

The Way Forward

In sum, measuring outputs, inputs, and engagement in international trade for firms in the services sector remains prone to errors and biases, despite significant improvements in both methodologies and data collection. This is largely because of the nature of services and (often) the lack of tangible products that can be independently verified for quantity and quality. Sector-specific challenges, the importance of informality, and the blurring lines between manufacturing and services create additional difficulties.

Better data are crucial to fully grasp the contribution of the services sector to productivity growth and international trade. The conclusion of this book (chapter 6) formulates a number of recommendations—calling for more disaggregated data, better coverage of services firms, and more detailed firm-level data collection to help close important knowledge gaps.

Notes

1. Smith's conception of "unproductive labor" included servants of wealthy individuals, government employees, the military, the clergy, lawyers, doctors, writers, and musicians (Smith 1776).

2. The national accounts statistics of centrally planned economies considered all services that catered to people's social and personal needs as part of nonmaterial production and hence unproductive. The only exceptions were trade and transportation that contributed directly to material production (Lequiller and Blades 2014).

3. Methods that adjust for the quality of services are considered by Eurostat (2016) as "A-methods," while those capturing only firm-level prices are usually considered less preferred "B-methods." Using an industrywide PPI or countrywide CPI is in many sectors considered as a "C-method," the least preferred, and should be avoided. In the context of management consultancy, a less perfect deflating method would use firm-level prices (hourly fees or charged rates) or use data from closely related sectors. In practice, many analyses—and especially those conducted in low- and middle-income countries (LMICs)—rely on "C-methods," often countrywide or industrywide price indexes such as the CPI or PPI.

4. In the System of National Accounts (SNA), the United Nations (UN) standard for national accounting, this approach is called financial intermediation services indirectly measured (FISIM).

5. Examples of countries with such analyses include Turkey (Avdiu et al. 2021); Costa Rica (Alfaro-Ureña, Manelici, and Vasquez 2021); Ecuador (Brugués 2020); and Chile (Huneeus 2018).

6. Noncustomized software sold on a physical carrier is generally recorded as trade in goods, but customized software is recorded as trade in services under mode 1 (cross-border supply), even when traded on a physical carrier (UN 2011, 15; UN et al. 2011, 68). The trade of goods with services embodied in them is sometimes designated as "mode 5" trade in services.

7. Short-term commercial presence (under mode 3), such as a firm having a temporary local office that does not qualify as a resident establishment, would still be included in BoP statistics. This is particularly relevant for construction services.

8. The *Manual on Statistics of International Trade in Services Compiler's Guide 2010* (UN et al. 2016) provides an overview of data sources used for compiling BoP and trade in services statistics, including best practices.

9. The value of these services could be measured through advertising, but as noted earlier, this does not always capture the full consumer value of the service provided. In addition, the advertiser is not necessarily located in the same country as the web-page visitor.

10. In the BoP statistics (IMF 2009), imports and exports by distribution services firms (retailers and wholesalers) are generally included in the goods account. Countries publishing more detailed BoP statistics under the Extended Balance of Payments Services (EBOPS) classification framework can choose to report the services trade by distribution services firms under "total trade-related transactions."

11. Studies that analyze characteristics of service exporters, based on data from the United Kingdom and European Union countries, include Ariu et al. (2019), Breinlich and Criscuolo (2011), and Haller et al. (2014).

12. The UN System of National Accounts recommends that the production of enterprises with multiple activities—to the extent possible—be broken down by activity for the purposes of constructing national accounts (UN et al. 2009). Nevertheless, practices vary among countries. Datasets focusing on enterprises generally classify enterprises on the basis of their primary activity (for example, Eurostat's Structural Business Statistics, https://ec.europa.eu/eurostat/web/structural-business-statistics).

13. This estimate is based on the time-valuation method of Goolsbee and Klenow (2006).

14. Directly asking for willingness to pay can lead participants to understate the benefit they receive from such a service to avoid paying that amount. The online experiment of Brynjolfsson, Collis, and Eggers (2019) implements a method that leads to a truthful revelation of their willingness to pay, by asking participants the amount of compensation they need for losing access to a website and then paying this compensation to those participants who refrain from visiting that website during the study period.

References

Ackerberg, Daniel A., Kevin Caves, and Garth Frazer. 2015. "Identification Properties of Recent Production Function Estimators." *Econometrica* 83 (6): 2411–51. doi:10.3982/ECTA13408.

Alfaro-Ureña, Alonso, Isabela Manelici, and Jose P. Vasquez Carvajal. 2021. "The Effects of Joining Multinational Supply Chains: New Evidence from Firm-to-Firm Linkages." Working paper for the Private Enterprise in Low-Income Countries (PEDL) initiative, Centre for Economic Policy Research (CEPR), London.

Ariu, Andrea, Elena Biewen, Sven Blank, Guillaume Gaulier, María Jesus González, Philipp Meinen, Daniel Mirza, Cesar Martín, and Patry Tello. 2019. "Firm Heterogeneity and Aggregate Business Services Exports: Micro Evidence from Belgium, France, Germany and Spain." *World Economy* 42 (2): 564–89. doi:10.1111/twec.12707.

Avdiu, Besart, Banu Demir, Umut Kilinc, and Gaurav Nayyar. 2021. "Does the Services Sector Benefit from a Manufacturing Core? Firm-Level Evidence from Turkey." Unpublished manuscript, World Bank, Washington, DC.

Bhagwati, Jagdish N. 1984. "Splintering and Disembodiment of Services and Developing Nations." *World Economy* 7 (2): 133–44.

Breinlich, Holger, and Chiara Criscuolo. 2011. "International Trade in Services: A Portrait of Importers and Exporters." *Journal of International Economics* 84 (2): 188–206. doi:10.1016/j.jinteco.2011.03.006.

Brugués, Felipe. 2020. "Take the Goods and Run: Contracting Frictions and Market Power in Supply Chains." Job Market Paper 1, Department of Economics, Brown University, Providence, RI.

Brynjolfsson, Erik, Avinash Collis, and Felix Eggers. 2019. "Using Massive Online Choice Experiments to Measure Changes in Well-Being." *PNAS* 116 (15): 7250–55. doi:10.1073/pnas.1815663116.

Brynjolfsson, Erik, and Andrew McAfee. 2014. *The Second Machine Age: Work, Progress, and Prosperity in a Time of Brilliant Technologies.* New York: W. W. Norton & Company.

Brynjolfsson, Erik, and Joo Hee Oh. 2012. "The Attention Economy: Measuring the Value of Free Digital Services on the Internet." *International Conference on Information Systems (ICIS) 2012 Proceedings* 4: 3243–61.

Brynjolfsson, Erik, Daniel Rock, and Chad Syverson. 2021. "The Productivity J-Curve: How Intangibles Complement General Purpose Technologies." *American Economic Journal: Macroeconomics* 13 (1): 333–72. doi:10.1257/mac.20180386.

Cusolito, Ana Paula, and William F. Maloney. 2018. *Productivity Revisited: Shifting Paradigms in Analysis and Policy.* Washington, DC: World Bank.

De Loecker, Jan, Jan Eeckhout, and Gabriel Unger. 2020. "The Rise of Market Power and the Macroeconomic Implications." *Quarterly Journal of Economics* 135 (2): 561–644. doi:10.1093/qje/qjz041.

De Loecker, Jan, and Frederic Warzynski. 2012. "Markups and Firm-Level Export Status." *American Economic Review* 102 (6): 2437–71. doi:10.1257/aer.102.6.2437.

Eurostat. 2016. *Handbook on Prices and Volume Measures in National Accounts.* Luxembourg: European Union.

Feldstein, Martin. 2017. "Underestimating the Real Growth of GDP, Personal Income, and Productivity." *Journal of Economic Perspectives* 31 (2): 145–64. doi:10.1257/jep.31.2.145.

Fortanier, Fabienne, Antonella Liberatore, Andreas Maurer, Graham Pilgrim, and Laura Thomson. 2017. "The OECD-WTO Balanced Trade in Services Database." Methodology paper for the first edition of the BaTIS dataset, Organisation for Economic Co-operation and Development (OECD), Paris; and World Trade Organization (WTO), Geneva.

Goolsbee, Austan, and Peter J. Klenow. 2006. "Valuing Consumer Products by the Time Spent Using Them: An Application to the Internet." *American Economic Review* 96 (2): 108–13. doi:10.1257/000282806777212521.

Grassano, Nicola, and Maria Savona. 2014. "Productivity in Services Twenty Years On: A Review of Conceptual and Measurement Issues and a Way Forward." Working Paper Series 2014-01, Science Policy Research Unit (SPRU), University of Sussex, UK.

Griliches, Zvi. 1994. "Productivity, R&D, and the Data Constraint." *American Economic Review* 84 (1): 1–23.

Grover, Arti, and Aaditya Mattoo. 2020. "Why Do Manufacturing Firms Sell Services? Evidence from India." Unpublished paper, World Bank, Washington, DC.

Hall, Robert E. 2001. "The Stock Market and Capital Accumulation." *American Economic Review* 91 (5): 1185–1202. doi:10.1257/aer.91.5.1185.

Haller, Stefanie A., Jože Damijan, Ville Kaitila, Črt Kostevc, Mika Maliranta, Emmanuel Milet, Daniel Mirza, and Matija Rojec. 2014. "Trading Firms in the Services Sectors: Comparable Evidence from Four EU Countries." *Review of World Economics* 150 (3): 471–505. doi:10.1007/s10290-014-0190-9.

Hsieh, Chang-Tai, and Peter J. Klenow. 2009. "Misallocation and Manufacturing TFP in China and India." *Quarterly Journal of Economics* 124 (4): 1403–48.

Huneeus, Federico. 2018. "Production Network Dynamics and the Propagation of Shocks." Job Market Paper, Princeton University, Princeton, NJ.

IMF (International Monetary Fund). 2009. *Balance of Payments and International Investment Position Manual (BPM6)*. 6th ed. Washington, DC: IMF.

Inklaar, Robert, Marcel P. Timmer, and Bart van Ark. 2008. "Data for Productivity Measurement in Market Services: An International Comparison." *International Productivity Monitor* 16: 72–81.

Ker, Daniel, and Emanuele Mazzini. 2020. "Perspectives on the Value of Data and Data Flows." Digital Economy Paper 299, Organisation for Economic Co-operation and Development (OECD), Paris.

Lequiller, François, and Derek W. Blades. 2014. *Understanding National Accounts*. Paris: Organisation for Economic Co-operation and Development.

Levinsohn, James, and Amil Petrin. 2003. "Estimating Production Functions Using Inputs to Control for Unobservables." *Review of Economic Studies* 70 (2): 317–41.

Lopez-Bassols, Vladimir, and Valentine Millot. 2013. "Measuring R&D and Innovation in Services: Key Findings from the OECD INNOSERV project." Paper prepared for the Working Party of National Experts on Science and Technology Indicators (NESTI) and the Working Party on Innovation and Technology Policy (TIP), Organisation for Economic Co-operation and Development (OECD), Paris.

Nayyar, Gaurav. 2012. *The Service Sector in India's Development*. New York: Cambridge University Press.

Nguyen, David, and Marta Paczos. 2020. "Measuring the Economic Value of Data and Cross-Border Data Flows." Digital Economy Paper 297, Organisation for Economic Co-operation and Development (OECD), Paris.

OECD (Organisation for Economic Co-operation and Development) and Eurostat. 2014. *Eurostat-OECD Methodological Guide for Developing Producer Price Indices for Services*. 2nd ed. Paris: OECD Publishing. doi:10.1787/9789264220676-en.

OECD, WTO, and IMF (Organisation for Economic Co-operation and Development, World Trade Organisation, and International Monetary Fund). 2020. *Handbook on Measuring Digital Trade. Version 1*. Paris: OECD.

Olley, G. Steven, and Ariel Pakes. 1996. "The Dynamics of Productivity in the Telecommunications Equipment Industry." *Econometrica* 64 (6): 1263–97.

Smith, Adam. 1776. *An Inquiry into the Nature and Causes of the Wealth of Nations*. London: W. Strahan and T. Cadell.

Syverson, Chad. 2017. "Challenges to Mismeasurement Explanations for the US Productivity Slowdown." *Journal of Economic Perspectives* 31 (2): 165–86.

Syverson, Chad. 2020. "Measuring Productivity in Services?" Unpublished manuscript, Booth School of Business, University of Chicago.

Thompson, Steven K. 1990. "Adaptive Cluster Sampling." *Journal of the American Statistical Association* 85 (412): 1050–59.

Triplett, Jack E., and Barry P. Bosworth. 2003. "Productivity Measurement Issues in Services Industries: Baumol's Disease Has Been Cured." *Economic Policy Review* 9 (3): 23–33.

UN (United Nations). 2011. *International Merchandise Trade Statistics: Concepts and Definitions 2010*. New York: UN.

UN, Eurostat, IMF, OECD, UNCTAD, UNWTO, and WTO (United Nations, Eurostat, International Monetary Fund, Organisation for Economic Co-operation and Development, UN Conference on Trade and Development, UN World Tourism Organization, and World Trade Organization). 2016. *Manual on Statistics of International Trade in Services Compiler's Guide 2010*. New York: UN.

UN, IMF, OECD, Eurostat, UNCTAD, UNWTO, and WTO (United Nations, International Monetary Fund, Organisation for Economic Co-operation and Development, UN Conference on Trade and Development, World Tourism Organization, and World Trade Organization). 2011. *Manual on Statistics of International Trade in Services 2010.* New York: UN.

Wettstein, Steen, Antonella Liberatore, Joscelyn Magdeleine, and Andreas Maurer. 2019. "A Global Trade in Services Data Set by Sector and by Mode of Supply (TISMOS)." Methodological paper, World Trade Organization, Geneva.

World Bank. 2021. *World Development Report 2021: Data for Better Lives.* Washington, DC: World Bank.

WTO (World Trade Organization). 2010. "Measuring Trade in Services." Training module, WTO, Geneva.

3 Will Technology Make the Twain Meet? A Changing Productivity-Jobs Dichotomy in Services

Introduction

The manufacturing sector has typically absorbed a substantial part of the economy's unskilled labor and placed that labor on a productivity path that rises up to the global frontier. For services, however, the twin gains of productivity growth and job creation are less prevalent within the same subsector group, as illustrated in chapter 2. High-skill "global innovator services" (comprising finance, information and communication technology [ICT] and business services), which have contributed to productivity growth and high-quality jobs across low- and middle-income countries (LMICs), have been intensive in skilled labor. On the other hand, "low-skill domestic services" have absorbed labor but shown little productivity growth. At the same time, as chapter 1 showed, low-skill tradable services, including transportation, wholesale trade, and accommodation and food services, combine the absorption of low-skilled labor with trade in international markets and linkages with other sectors.

This chapter examines whether technological change is likely to accentuate or diminish this dichotomy between productivity growth and job creation across the services sector in the future. Chapter 1 outlined the defining characteristics of the services sector—such as simultaneity in production and consumption and the inherent role of labor—that constrain its potential for scale and innovation relative to manufacturing. The digital revolution that spawned the spread of computerization and the internet in the 1990s enabled the separation of production and consumption in some services and enhanced the sector's ability to leverage labor with technology and (often intangible) capital. The diffusion and wider application of these information and communication technologies, such as through software applications and digital platforms, as well as the emergence of artificial intelligence (AI) as a new general purpose technology (GPT) over the past three decades, has made the services sector (a) less dependent on physical proximity between buyers and sellers; (b) more subject to automation; and (c) increasingly characterized by intangible capital.

In one of these transformative trends, the rapid expansion of bandwidth and new collaborative digital platforms has reduced the importance of the physical proximity between service providers and consumers. The variety of online markets is also increasing more than ever across a range of sectors matching workers and firms, investors and entrepreneurs, vacant rooms and travelers, and so on. Examples include ICT and professional services (such as Upwork and Freelancer); transportation services (such as Uber, Lyft, BlaBlaCar, and DiDi); accommodation (such as Airbnb, KOZAZA, and Couchsurfing); and household services (such as TaskRabbit and Care). These new possibilities for matching demand and supply and remote delivery—including across international markets—increase the services sector's potential to achieve scale economies.

Digital technologies are also expanding the scope for innovation in the services sector in two ways. First, many services are more automatable than before. This trend challenges the assumed inherent role of labor in services as apps, software, and digital interfaces increasingly automate business processes, thereby replacing labor in certain tasks while also expanding employment opportunities by creating new tasks. Furthermore, although Industry 4.0, particularly robotization, has focused on industrial automation in the manufacturing sector, AI-enabled machine learning (ML) is fundamentally altering the possibilities associated with computational power—whereby the uptake of image recognition, voice recognition, and machine translation is increasingly relevant for the services sector. This is especially noteworthy because, during the previous ICT wave in the 1990s, only a relatively narrow range of routine manual tasks were suitable for automation.

Second, digital technologies have expanded the potential for trends in intangible capital to accelerate innovation by augmenting labor. Although intangible capital—such as branding, management practices, and business processes—has traditionally complemented labor, the diffusion of computer-related software and data can enhance the accumulation of this intangible capital. The greater use of intangible capital will cause some disruptions and shift some of the skills needed for managers and workers, but distinguishing between firms as creators and users of the underlying technology is important. Advanced skills are needed to create innovative properties such as research and development (R&D) and design, but not so for using standardized software to inform menu selections and meal preparation in restaurants, to manage the efficiency of transportation networks, or to access talent across hospitals.

Notably, the match between different types of digital technologies and any of these three trends—reduced proximity, greater automatability, and rising intangible capital intensity—is not always mutually exclusive. For example, making travel reservations through digital platforms reduces the importance of physical *proximity* between producers and consumers. At the same time, it *automates* tasks previously done by travel agency employees and raises the level of *intangible capital* in incumbent services providers, such as airline companies, by emphasizing data analytics to improve their marketing. Similarly, investment in ML algorithms makes some services tasks more *automatable* but may also drive investment in *intangible capital* such as R&D, design, and managerial skills while reducing the need for (language) *proximity* between producers and consumers through machine translation. In sum, the technology categories can overlap, but the focus here is on their impacts on the dynamics of remote delivery, automation, and labor-augmenting intangible capital.

A Shifting Productivity-Jobs Dichotomy

These three trends of remote delivery, greater automation, and increased role for intangible capital all present new opportunities to raise productivity by increasing the potential to achieve scale and innovation in the services sector. As for job creation, the reduced importance of proximity can shape where the jobs might be created, automation can replace labor in certain tasks, and intangible capital might emphasize skilled labor.

The importance of these trends and how they shape opportunities for productivity growth and job creation will vary across services subsectors. For instance, the intensity of face-to-face interactions might be so innate for some services that digital technologies can do little to reduce the importance of physical proximity. Similarly, while some low-skill services are increasingly subject to automated business processes, other skill-intensive services are increasingly suitable for automation through machine learning. Further, the rise of intangible capital might be higher in services where the diffusion of digital technologies is greater.

The remainder of the chapter first outlines whether and how technological change is (a) reducing the importance of physical proximity between producers and consumers; (b) reducing the inherent role of labor in making some services more subject to automation; and (c) increasing the accumulation of intangible capital. It then explores the potential implications of these changes for productivity growth and job creation. In doing so, it will distinguish between the four categories of services (as identified in chapter 1) to look at changing opportunities for trade, innovation, and entrepreneurship.

Reduced Dependence on Physical Proximity

Blinder (2009) assessed the offshorability of different tasks by measuring the importance of face-to-face interactions with consumers based on the extent to which an occupation involves (a) establishing and maintaining personal relationships; (b) assisting and caring for others; (c) performing for or working directly with the public; and (d) selling to or influencing others.

Such face-to-face interactions are least important among the group of global innovator services identified in chapter 1. As a result, the ICT revolution enabled the offshoring of these services to lower-cost destinations with the relevant language skills (as further discussed in chapter 4).

It is therefore not surprising that these ICT and professional, scientific, and technical services that require little face-to-face interaction with consumers are also the most amenable to remote delivery. The latter can be measured by whether a job can be done from home on the basis of its inclusion of at least one of 15 tasks, such as "daily work outdoors" or the "operation of vehicles, mechanized devices, or equipment" (Dingel and Neiman 2020).[1] This measure of home-based work suggests that more than three-fourths of US jobs in ICT and professional services can be done remotely and are therefore among the most tradable services (figure 3.1).

There are services in which remote delivery is possible despite the intensity of face-to-face interactions with consumers. Financial and education services stand out in this regard; although they are intensive in face-to-face interactions, they are suitable for remote delivery because more than three-fourths of these jobs in the United States can be done from home (figure 3.1). In financial services, for example, branch managers and investment advisers can communicate in real time with clients through online and telephone banking. In education, high school teachers and university professors can deliver lectures digitally through web-based applications. This is consistent with evidence which shows that firms are more likely to enter export markets in services subsectors where the importance of face-to-face communication with customers (interactive tasks) has become less binding (Ariu and Mion 2016).

There remains a set of services that are the among the most intensive in face-to-face interactions but are *not* amenable to remote delivery. These include accommodation and food services and retail trade, where less than 20 percent of jobs can be done from home in the United States. The same holds true for transportation services, despite not being intensive in face-to-face interactions with consumers.

Global Innovator Services and the Online Gig Economy

The rapid expansion of bandwidth and new collaborative digital platforms such as Skype for Business, Slack, Trello, and Basecamp have enhanced the remote (digital) delivery of global innovator services. The wider deployment of the fifth-generation technology standard (5G) for broadband cellular networks is expected to further increase the quality and reliability of videoconferencing by increasing internet capacity and improving data streaming (ITU 2018).

For a range of global innovator services, digital platforms have given rise to online marketplaces that match buyers and suppliers, hence reducing search costs—costs that

FIGURE 3.1 **While Remote Delivery and Face-to-Face Interactions Expectedly Go Hand-in-Hand, the Two Measures Diverge in Some Industries**

Share of jobs amenable to home-based work in relation to intensity of face-to-face interactions with consumers, by industry, 2018

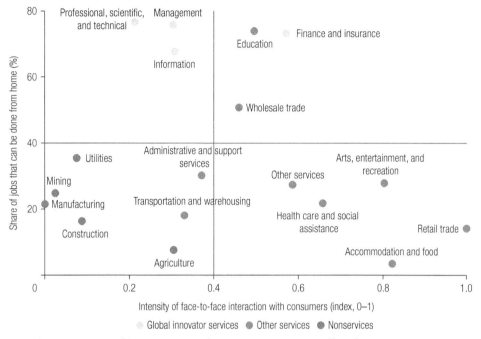

Source: Calculations using the US Department of Labor's Occupational Information Network (O*NET) database and US Bureau of Labor Statistics (BLS) data.

Note: Red lines indicate average values across industries. "Other services" refers to other social, community, and personal services. Dingel and Neiman (2020) estimate whether a job can be done from home based on whether it comprises at least one of 15 tasks, such as "daily work outdoors" or the "operation of vehicles, mechanized devices, or equipment." The index of face-to-face interactions with consumers, developed by Avdiu and Nayyar (2020), measures the extent to which an occupation involves (a) establishing and maintaining personal relationships; (b) assisting and caring for others; (c) performing for or working directly with the public; and (d) selling to or influencing others. Both indexes are scored at the occupation level using surveys—updated periodically, with the last major update in 2014—from the US Department of Labor's Occupational Information Network (O*NET) and then merged with the prevalence of each occupation across industries in 2018 from US Bureau of Labor Statistics data.

are likely to be even higher when the potential trade opportunity is cross-border (Jullien 2012). The emergence of digital platforms is associated with a new form of online outsourcing for computer programming and other professional services, whereby low search costs enable clients to contract third-party individuals as freelancers.

These digital platforms help match buyers and sellers, just as traditional e-commerce does for goods trade. In 2016, the market size for online freelancing was estimated at US$4.4 billion (Kuek et al. 2015). Compared with traditional outsourcing, hiring remote foreign freelancers also casts a wider net of workers, time zones, and nontraditional schedules as well as flexibility regarding hiring and firing regulations. Upwork, the world's largest such platform, had over 12 million registered freelancers from over 100 countries in 2017 and processes more than US$1 billion worth of work annually.

Based on data from five such platforms that represent at least 60 percent of the global market for English-language online outsourcing, the Oxford Internet Institute's iLabour research project finds that software development services is the top category, with the estimated number of online gig workers increasing fourfold, from 10 million in 2017 to 40 million in 2020. The next biggest category, creative and multimedia services, increased from 10 million in 2017 to 30 million in 2020. Among global innovator services, professional services such as accounting, business consulting, and legal advice grew little over this period, representing less than 5 percent of the overall online gig economy (figure 3.2).[2]

Low-Skill Services and Digital Platforms

It is not that digital platforms are not relevant in low-skill services subsectors. In fact, they have become integral to many low-skill tradable services. Travel-related transportation and accommodation services are especially reliant on the customer convenience of online platforms. Booking.com offers 29 million accommodation listings in

FIGURE 3.2 **Software Development Services Have Experienced the Largest Increase in the Number of Online Freelancers**
Workers in platform-based online freelancing, by occupational type, June 2017–October 2020

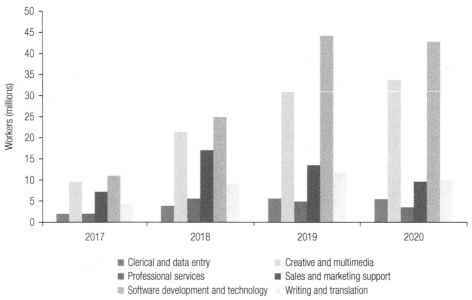

Source: Online Labor Index Worker Supplement of the iLabour Project, Oxford Internet Institute, University of Oxford, https://ilabour.oii .ox.ac.uk/online-labour-index/.

At Your Service? The Promise of Services-Led Development

154,000 destinations worldwide and operates in 190 countries. Similarly, Tripadvisor reports 8.4 accommodation listings in 156,000 destinations spread across 49 markets (Lopez-Cordova 2020). Tourism service providers' use of these digital platforms is growing, both across traditional (hotels) and nontraditional ("bed and breakfast") accommodation establishments in LMICs.

At the same time, foreign travelers increasingly rely on digital platforms to make their travel plans. In 2014, an estimated 59 percent of European Union (EU) residents traveling internationally relied on digital tools to book accommodation, and 67 percent used them to book flights (Lopez-Cordova 2020). This increased use of digital tools by travelers and firms providing accommodation and transportation services reflects the reduced importance of proximity in gathering information on travel costs (airfares, hotel room rates, and so on) and facilitating market transactions.[3]

Digital platforms have had a similar, albeit smaller, impact on low-skill domestic services. In 2014, the share of online retailing in overall retail trade services was only 6.4 percent in the United States (Hortaçsu and Syverson 2015) and averaged only 4 percent across LMICs, but this conceals differences across industries. For example, the share of online retail for apparel, footwear, electronics, and appliances—durable goods often sold online—increased from close to zero in 2009 to 31 percent in 2014 in China and from 5 percent to 23 percent in the United States (Bronnenberg and Ellickson 2015). There are further signs of change. The share of online retail in overall retail sales was 14 percent in the last quarter of 2020 in the United States, and this increase was attributable, at least in part, to the COVID-19 pandemic.[4]

Among low-skill domestic services, digital platforms such as TaskRabbit and Care.com that match suppliers with buyers are also increasingly applicable to a range of personal household services, including home repair, plumbing, and cleaning. In Ecuador, Kunpa connects customers with verified providers for household services such as plumbing, gardening, hairdressing, and the like and features a rating system to guide consumers' choices.[5] BabaJob, established in 2007, is one of India's leading job-matching websites and also matches workers to potential employers in low-skill-intensive informal services. In 2015, for example, BabaJob's total job listings for sales and service workers exceeded the total for managers and professionals (Nomura et al. 2017).

Yet, beyond working as "online tools" to match market demand and supply, digital platforms do not enable the remote provision of these low-skill services whose delivery remains tied to the physical proximity between producers and consumers.

Increased Role of Automation

Unlike for manufactured goods, digital technologies are likely to have a big downward effect on the cost of trading services but an insignificant impact on the labor-cost shares in services (Baldwin and Forslid 2020). This is consistent with a well-established framework that estimates which jobs are at risk of automation based on which tasks computers can execute reliably (Autor, Levy, and Murnane 2003). These tasks are procedural, rule-based activities that primarily involve the organization, storage, retrieval, and manipulation of information that can be entirely codified as a series of precise instructions to be executed by a computer. A large body of evidence, based on data from the United States and other high-income countries, shows that the computerization of such "routine" (or "codifiable") tasks resulted in job polarization—meaning that high- and low-skill jobs have grown at the expense of many more-automatable middle-skill jobs such as bookkeeping, clerical work, and repetitive production (Autor and Dorn 2013; Autor, Katz, and Kearney 2006, 2008; Goos and Manning 2003).

At both ends of the skill spectrum, services tasks have been more challenging to automate. Among these are cognitive tasks, characteristic of many professional, technical, and managerial services that employ highly skilled workers and emphasize problem-solving capabilities, intuition, creativity, and persuasion. Also difficult to automate are the manual tasks, characteristic of health care, food preparation and serving jobs, cleaning work, and numerous jobs in the personal services sector that are not skill intensive but emphasize situational adaptability, visual and language recognition, and in-person interactions (Autor, Levy, and Murnane 2003).

Yet the prevalence of routine tasks, especially across low-skill services subsectors, means that more than two-thirds of jobs in the accommodation and food services and retail trade subsectors, for instance, are suitable for greater computerization.[6] Furthermore, recent evidence is indicative of more widespread ICT adoption across services subsectors, although this is more uneven in LMICs.[7]

Catch-Up in ICT Use among Low-Skill Services in Higher-Income Countries

The average share of ICT and finance firms with a broadband connection across Organisation for Economic Co-operation and Development (OECD) countries already exceeded 95 percent in 2010. Meanwhile, the average share of retail firms with a broadband connection increased from about 84 percent in 2010 to about 95 percent in 2017, and the corresponding share in accommodation and food services rose from 76 percent to 94 percent over the same period (figure 3.3, panel a).

Similarly, the share of ICT services and finance firms whose employees regularly use a computer in their work already averaged more than 90 percent in 2010. The same

FIGURE 3.3 **The Share of Firms and Workers in Low-Skill Services That Use ICT Has Increased, on Average, in OECD Countries**

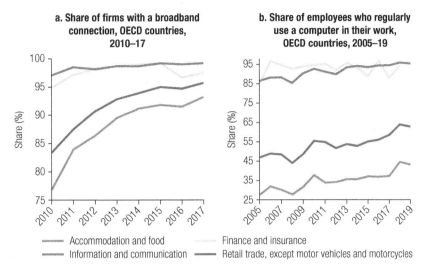

a. Share of firms with a broadband connection, OECD countries, 2010–17

b. Share of employees who regularly use a computer in their work, OECD countries, 2005–19

—— Accommodation and food   ⋯⋯ Finance and insurance
—— Information and communication   ▬▬ Retail trade, except motor vehicles and motorcycles

Source: OECD ICT Access and Usage by Businesses database.

Note: Dataset covers all Organisation for Economic Co-operation and Development (OECD) member countries. Broadband connections may be either fixed or mobile.

share among accommodation and food services workers increased from 25 percent in 2005 to 45 percent in 2019 and among retail workers from 45 percent to 65 percent (figure 3.3, panel b).

There is also evidence of catch-up in ICT adoption across OECD countries in service subsectors that are intensive in low-skilled labor. In accommodation and food services, for example, countries with a smaller share of firms with a broadband connection in 2010 experienced a larger percentage point change in the share of firms with a broadband connection between 2010 and 2017 (figure 3.4, panel a). The same pattern of convergence also holds in the retail trade subsector (figure 3.4, panel b).

Slower Progress among Low-Skill Services in LMICs

This more widespread adoption of ICT across low-skill-intensive services is less visible among LMICs, which highlights widespread differences between and within countries. For instance, the share of firms in retail services and hotels and restaurants that used email in their business was less than 50 percent across most African countries, compared with 80 percent or more in China and across Latin America (map 3.1, panel a).

Firms in these services still rely mostly on manual processes for a range of business functions. In Senegal, 60 percent use manual costing as the most frequent technology for pricing, 80 percent use manual selection as the most frequent technology for merchandising, and 62 percent use handwritten records for inventory management

FIGURE 3.4 **There Is Evidence of Catch-Up in Broadband Connectivity among Low-Skill Services Firms across OECD Countries**

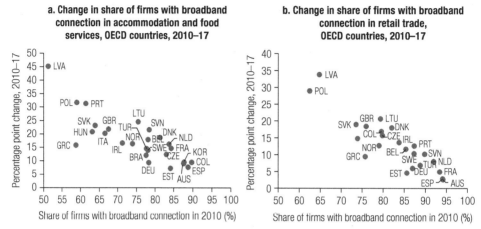

a. Change in share of firms with broadband connection in accommodation and food services, OECD countries, 2010–17

b. Change in share of firms with broadband connection in retail trade, OECD countries, 2010–17

Source: Calculations based on OECD ICT Access and Usage in Businesses database.

Note: Graphs show countries' percentage of firms with a broadband connection in 2010 (x-axis) in relation to those countries' percentage point change in firms with a broadband connection between 2010 and 2017 (y-axis). Countries are labeled using ISO alpha-3 codes. OECD = Organisation for Economic Co-operation and Development.

(Cirera et al. 2020a). Micro-size informal enterprises in Senegal lag considerably in the adoption of digital technologies, and almost 60 of these firms are in the retail trade subsector (Atiyas and Dutz 2021).

However, the slow pace of technology diffusion among firms in low-skill services is not that different from those in manufacturing. For instance, the share of firms in retail and hotels and restaurants that use websites for business across African countries is not substantially lower than the corresponding share of manufacturing firms (map 3.1, panels b and c).

Furthermore, data from the World Bank's Firm-Level Adoption of Technology (FAT) survey in Senegal and Vietnam show that firms in retail trade and firms in apparel manufacturing have similar scores regarding the sophistication of their most widely used technologies across a range of business functions, including business administration, marketing, and inventory management (figure 3.5).[8]

Effects of Big Data and Machine Learning

The recent progress of big data and machine learning (ML) has dramatically increased predictive power in many areas such as cognition, problem solving, speech recognition, and image recognition. Unlike the last generation of information technology (IT), which required humans to codify tasks explicitly, ML is designed to learn the patterns automatically from examples (Brynjolfsson and Mitchell 2017). Rapid progress in ML over the past six to eight years is due in large part to the sheer volume of

MAP 3.1 **Firms' Adoption of ICT across Low-Skill Services Is Less Widespread among Lower-Income Countries, but These Adoption Rates Are Similarly Low in the Manufacturing Sector**

a. Share of firms using email in the retail and hotels and restaurants subsectors

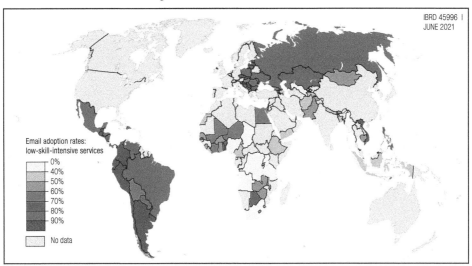

b. Share of firms having a website in the retail and hotels and restaurants subsectors

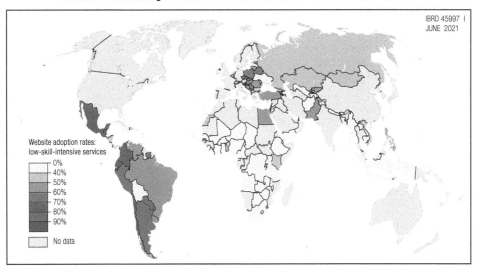

Map continues on the following page

MAP 3.1

Firms' Adoption of ICT across Low-Skill Services Is Less Widespread among Lower-Income Countries, but These Adoption Rates Are Similarly Low in the Manufacturing Sector *(continued)*

c. Share of firms having a website in the manufacturing sector

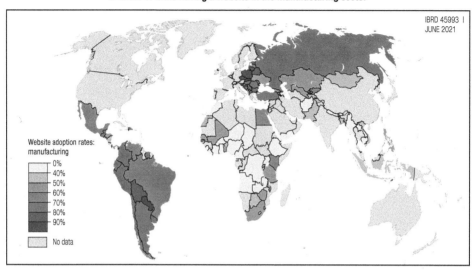

Source: Cusolito and Peña 2020, based on World Bank Enterprise Survey Data. ©World Bank. Further permission required for reuse.
Note: Data are from latest available year per country.

FIGURE 3.5 **The Most Widely Used Digital Technologies in Some LMICs Are Similar in Sophistication across Firms in Retail Trade and Apparel Manufacturing**

a. Technology adoption index in retail versus apparel manufacturing firms in Senegal, by business function, 2020

b. Technology adoption index in retail versus apparel manufacturing firms in Vietnam, by business function, 2020

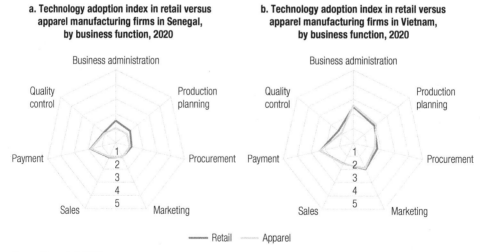

Source: Cirera at al. 2020b.

Note: The radar diagrams illustrate the relative sophistication of firms' most widely used technology in each of seven business functions. Index values are ranked from 1 (least sophisticated) to 5 (most sophisticated). Data are from the World Bank's 2020 Firm-Level Adoption of Technology (FAT) survey, conducted in Senegal and Vietnam.

training data available,[9] which can help capture highly valuable and previously unnoticed regularities—perhaps impossibly large for a person to examine or comprehend. This is particularly noteworthy because pre-ML automation mainly affected a relatively narrow range of routine tasks, but ML systems will increasingly be able to replace cognitive tasks. This implies that a larger number of activities and industries in the services sector might be increasingly automatable.

In fact, based on data from the United States, global innovator services (such as ICT; professional, scientific, and technical services; and financial services) have the lowest incidence of routine manual tasks but are among the industries that are most "suitable for machine learning" (figure 3.6). In applying this established rubric for estimating the suitability for machine learning (SML) (Brynjolfsson, Mitchell, and Rock 2018) to data

FIGURE 3.6 **Global Innovator Services Have the Lowest Incidence of Routine Manual Tasks but May Be Increasingly Subject to Automation through Machine Learning**

Routine Manual Tasks Index and SML Index scores, by industry, United States, 2018

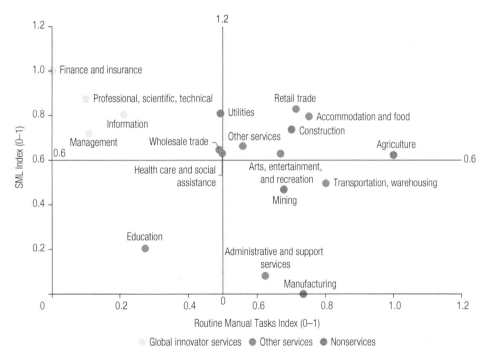

Source: Calculations using the US Department of Labor's Occupational Information Network (O*NET) database and US Bureau of Labor Statistics (BLS) data.

Note: The Routine Manual Tasks Index (0–1 scale), developed by Oldenski (2012), represents the importance of tasks related to (a) "handling objects," (b) "operating machines other than vehicles," and (c) "general physical activities." The Suitability for Machine Learning (SML) index (0–1 scale), developed by Brynjolfsson, Mitchell, and Rock (2018), represents the evaluation of 23 distinct task properties on a 5-point scale varying from "strongly disagree" to "strongly agree." The two indexes are scored at the occupation level using surveys—updated periodically, with the last major update in 2014—from the Occupational Information Network (O*NET) and then merged with the prevalence of each occupation across industries in 2018 from the US Bureau of Labor Statistics. Red lines designate average value across industries. "Other services" refers to other social, community, and personal services.

from India, Bhatia and Mani (2020) similarly find that ICT services—computer programming, consultancy, and related activities; data processing, hosting, and related activities; and other information service activities—are higher than the 75th percentile SML score, on average, across all industries.

Beyond the suitability for machine learning, robotic process automation (RPA) software is already increasingly commonplace in global innovator services. For example, the share of European firms that use customer relationship management (CRM) software is highest in the ICT services sector, followed by professional, scientific, and technical services (Hallward-Driemeier et al. 2020). The use of AI and ML is also most prevalent in global innovator services, and this has increased in recent years. Globally, a disproportionately large number of firms that use AI or ML software are in the computer software industry, although skill-intensive social services such as higher education and health care are also among the most automated (figure 3.7). The penetration of AI skills is also most widespread in the computer software and IT services industries and increased significantly between 2016 and 2018 (figure 3.8).

FIGURE 3.7 **The Use of AI or ML Software Is Most Prevalent among Global Innovator Services and Skill-Intensive Social Services**

Number of firms that purchased AI or ML software worldwide, by industry, 2018

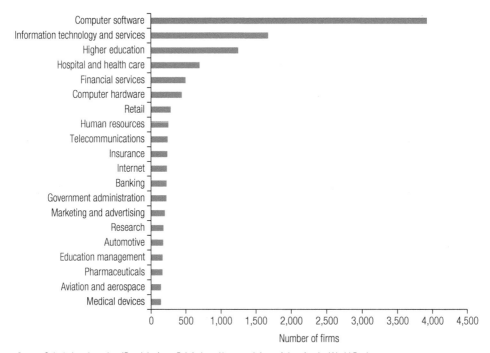

Source: Calculations based on iDatalabs (now Enlyft, http://www.enlyft.com) data for the World Bank.

Note: The dataset is generated using web scraping. It covers 17,000 formal firms in 107 countries across regions and income levels. AI = artificial intelligence; ML = machine learning.

FIGURE 3.8 **The Penetration of AI-Related Skills in Global Innovator Services Increased Considerably between 2016 and 2018**

AI-related skills penetration, by industry, 2016–18

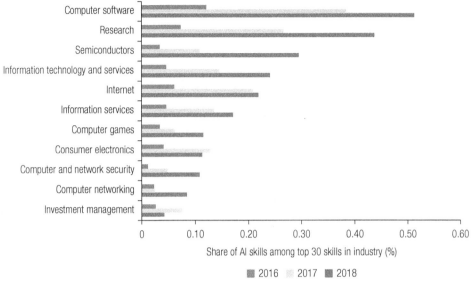

Source: "Digital Data for Development" collaboration of the World Bank Group and LinkedIn Corp., (https://linkedindata.worldbank .org/data), available under Creative Commons license (CC BY 3.0).

Note: Dataset covers self-reported LinkedIn profiles of users across more than 100 countries across all regions and income levels. "Skill penetration" looks at how many skills from each of LinkedIn's 249 skill groups appear among the top 30 skills for each occupation in an industry. For example, if 3 of 30 skills for data scientists in the information services industry fall into the artificial intelligence (AI) skill group, then AI skills have a 10 percent penetration among data scientists in information services. These penetration rates are then averaged across occupations to derive the industry averages reported in the figure. The metrics included here are limited to the six knowledge-intensive industries—financial services, professional services, information and communication technology (ICT), the arts and creative industries, manufacturing, and mining/quarrying—for which LinkedIn data can provide a more representative global picture.

However, the technical suitability for machine learning does not necessarily mean that these services tasks will be automated, owing to commercial viability considerations and capacity constraints, particularly in LMICs. For instance, the number of firms in India that use ML algorithms is one-tenth that in the United States (figure 3.9).

The trajectory of industrial automation along assembly lines is similar. For example, the use of industrial robots in low- and middle-income economies relative to high-income economies is negligible except in China, which is robotizing rapidly (Hallward-Driemeier and Nayyar 2018). Furthermore, despite some early signs such as the relative decline in the machine operator category in Brazil, Indonesia, and Mexico, the evidence of labor market polarization in LMICs is limited so far (Maloney and Molina 2016). The lower magnitude of automation in these economies might be explained, in large part, by lower labor costs. Automation might also be slow because of constraints that hinder the adoption of any technology: constraints on absorptive capacity, workforce

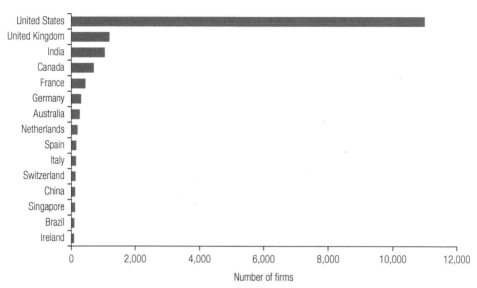

FIGURE 3.9 **AI or ML Software Is Used More Widely in High-Income Countries**
Number of firms that purchased AI or ML software, top 15 countries, 2018

Source: Calculations based on iDatalabs (now Enlyft, http://www.enlyft.com) data for the World Bank.
Note: The dataset is generated using web scraping. It covers 17,000 formal firms in 107 countries across regions and income levels. AI = artificial intelligence; ML = machine learning.

skills, changes in organizational design and business models, legal constraints, and even cultural expectations (Brynjolfsson and Mitchell 2017).

The Rise of Intangible Capital

Chapter 2 showed that except in transportation, warehousing, and telecommunications, physical capital has typically played a much smaller role in the production process among services firms than among manufacturing firms. The physical capital per worker for *low-skill services* sectors such as retail or accommodation and food services is a third of that in manufacturing, and it was also lower in many *global innovator services* such as programming and IT.

The question is the extent to which the steady rise of firms' investment in intangible capital over the past 20 years—often even exceeding growth in tangible capital (Corrado et al. 2018)—will affect the services sector. Evidence from high-income economies suggests that for every £1 of investment in tangible capital such as buildings or machinery, firms spent £1.10 on intangible capital in 2013 (Haskel and Westlake 2018).

Intangible capital can be classified into three broad categories: (a) computer-related software and data; (b) properties of innovation such as R&D, design, and artistic originals; and (c) company competencies such as marketing and branding,

At Your Service? The Promise of Services-Led Development

firm-specific training, and business process engineering (Corrado, Hulten, and Sichel 2005). Investments in these intangible assets complement each other. For instance, the impact of R&D investment depends on the firm's ability to invest in other intangibles such as managerial skills, network building, or organizational practices (Andrews, Nicoletti, and Timiliotis 2018; Bloom, Sadun, and Van Reenen 2012; McAfee and Brynjolfsson 2012). The success of the tech giant Apple illustrates how R&D and design in the iPhone, combined with the organizational design of the App Store as well as Apple's branding, have created one of the world's most profitable products.

The increase in intangible capital has been associated with the diffusion of information and communication technologies because realizing the potential of investment in computers and the internet also requires firms to create new business processes, develop managerial skills, train workers, patch software, and build a strong company brand (Basu, Fernald, and Kimball 2004; Bresnahan 2010; Bresnahan and Trajtenberg 1995). And the importance of intangible capital is only likely to increase as ICT becomes more sophisticated, such as with the advance of cloud computing and big-data analytics. In fact, the advent of AI and ML represents a new GPT that is likely to spawn complementary investments in intangible capital as it improves over time (Brynjolfsson, Rock, and Syverson 2021).

Investments in intangible capital are not readily measured in firms' balance sheets, and therefore there is little traceable data in a standard accounting sense. Yet, available evidence from high-income economies suggests that the services sector accounts for 64 percent of total investment in intangible capital in the United States and for 61 percent in the EU-14.[10] Services are also more intensive in the use of intangible capital relative to tangible capital. This higher propensity for investing in intangible capital in the services sector relative to manufacturing is seen in both the United States (1.25 versus 1.03) and the EU-14 countries (0.85 versus 0.79) (Corrado et al. 2018).

Investment in innovation. R&D intensity as an indicator of innovation was the highest in the manufacturing sector, on average, across OECD economies in 2017.[11] Among services subsectors, firms in professional, scientific, and technical services; ICT services; and education services had the highest R&D intensities in 2017 (figure 3.10). These data reinforce evidence from US-listed firms, where, between 1990 and 2006, knowledge-based intangible assets in the services sector were sizable only in these *global innovator services* (Demmou, Stefanescu, and Arquié 2019).

Services firms tend to innovate less than manufacturing firms in LMICs too, even when innovation is defined more broadly to include the introduction of a new or significantly improved product or production method. Among services subsectors, the share of firms that engage in such product and process innovation is the highest in professional services (50 percent) and lowest in retail services (25 percent) (Cirera and Maloney 2017).

Investment in computer software and data. Innovation in much of the services sector relates less to formal R&D and technological (product and process) innovation than to

FIGURE 3.10 **The Intensity of Investments in Software and Data Is the Highest among Firms in Global Innovator Services**

Expenditure on software and R&D per worker in OECD countries, by sector, 2017

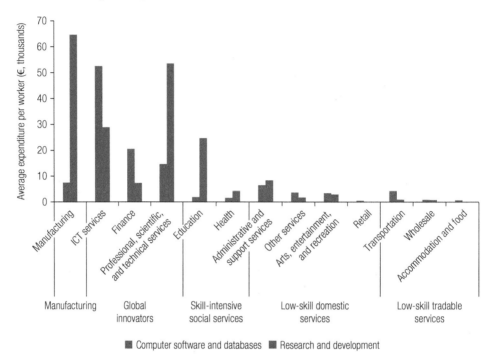

■ Computer software and databases   ■ Research and development

Source: OECD STructural ANalysis (STAN) Database.

Note: Dataset covers 23 Organisation for Economic Co-operation and Development countries, including Canada, the Republic of Korea, and European countries. "Other services" refers to other social, community, and personal services. OECD = Organisation for Economic Co-operation and Development; R&D = research and development.

investments in ICT adoption (OECD 2010; Polder et al. 2010). Among OECD economies in 2017, expenditure per worker on computer software and databases was higher across several services subsectors, on average, than in the manufacturing sector. It was the highest across the *global innovator services*—ICT, finance, and professional services (figure 3.10).

The trends over time are similar. For instance, the intensity in the expenditure per worker on computer software and databases from 2000 to 2017 increased the most discernibly in global innovator services (figure 3.11).

Investment in company competencies. Intangible assets that relate to company competencies based on either marketing or organizational innovation are much more widespread than technological innovation across the services sector. "Organizational innovation" refers to the implementation of a new organizational method in the firm's business practices, workplace organization, or external relations. "Marketing innovation" refers to the implementation of a new marketing method involving significant

FIGURE 3.11 **The Intensity of Investments in Software and Data Experienced the Most Discernible Increase among Firms in Global Innovator Services**

Expenditure on computer software and databases per worker in OECD countries, by sector, 2008–17

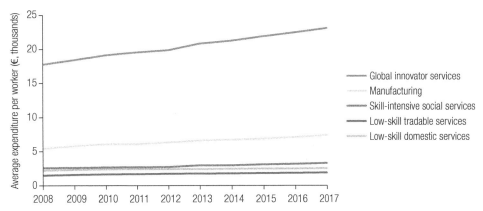

Source: OECD STructural ANalysis (STAN) Database.

Note: Dataset covers 23 Organisation for Economic Co-operation and Development countries, including Canada, the Republic of Korea, and European countries. "Other services" refers to other social, community, and personal services. OECD = Organisation for Economic Co-operation and Development.

changes in product design or packaging, product placement, product promotion, or pricing (OECD and Eurostat 2005).

Among OECD economies in 2018, for example, the share of firms that introduced new methods for product placement or new methods of organizing external relations were higher among most services subsectors than in manufacturing and not very different from each other (figure 3.12). This reinforces evidence from the United States that organizational capital dominates intangible assets in low-skill services such as wholesale and retail trade (Demmou, Stefanescu and Arquié 2019).

Implications for Productivity Growth and Job Creation

The three technology-driven trends described above—less dependence on physical proximity, increased automation, and rising investments in intangible capital—all have the potential to raise productivity in the services sector in several ways. First, increased possibilities to deliver services remotely (including internationally), enabled by the diffusion of new digital platforms, bring the productivity benefits associated with scale economies.

Second, automating business processes through the wider application of ICT, ML algorithms, and other AI-driven technologies can drive innovation in services even when the inherent role of labor remains important; some tasks may be automated, but not the whole service. However, much like in export-led manufacturing, automation in high-income countries can also negatively affect productivity growth in LMICs to the

FIGURE 3.12

Investment in Marketing and Organizational Innovation Is More Widespread across Most Services Subsectors Than in the Manufacturing Sector

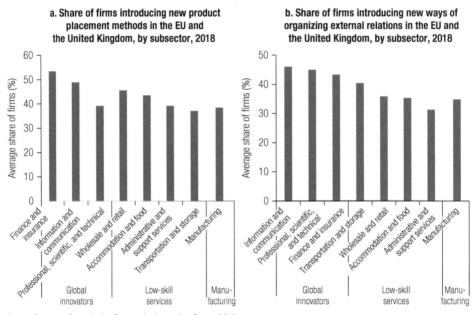

a. Share of firms introducing new product placement methods in the EU and the United Kingdom, by subsector, 2018

b. Share of firms introducing new ways of organizing external relations in the EU and the United Kingdom, by subsector, 2018

Source: European Commission Community Innovation Survey 2018.
Note: Survey covers all current EU member states and the United Kingdom.

extent that it disrupts traditional patterns of comparative advantage and reduces exporting opportunities for LMICs in the services sector.

Third, the potential for innovation is also enhanced by intangible investments in marketing, information, or training that are associated with sunk costs and therefore facilitate scale and replication. In fact, firms can scale up operations through intangible capital enhanced by data and software more readily than through physical capital. For example, Uber can serve more customers with its existing software, while the local taxi firm has to buy more cars.[12] These new opportunities for scale and innovation in the services sector will likely grow as technological change enables the dematerialization of consumption, shifting demand away from goods and toward services (box 3.1).

These three trends also matter for job creation. The reduced importance of physical proximity between producers and consumers expands *where* services jobs can be done, including across international boundaries. This reflects the promise of many new jobs in the gig economy enabled by digital platforms. At the same time, the advent of AI and ML algorithms can increasingly automate jobs in the services sector. And although concerns about direct automation might be less relevant in LMICs with low-cost labor, such automation in high-income countries can reduce services jobs in LMICs to the extent that it results in reshoring or reduces the offshoring of such jobs in the future.

Technological Change and the Rising Demand for Services

The dematerialization of consumption, enabled by the sharing economy and concerns about climate change, has boosted the demand for some services at the expense of manufactured goods. The sharing of large durable items, such as cars, is one trend that is already starting. The growing expectation is that ridesharing is boosting the demand for transportation services at the expense of car ownership (Araya 2019). For example, according to one YouGov survey, 43 percent of Londoners believe that services like Uber are a genuine alternative to owning a car (Shead 2017).

Similarly, consumer demand has shifted from physical music and video recordings, such as CDs and DVDs, to digital downloads through online streaming services. Goldman Sachs (2019) predicts that there will be 1.15 billion paying streaming subscribers for entertainment services globally in 2030 and that 68 percent of those subscribers will come from emerging markets.

These trends are likely to only strengthen given the demographic trends. In a global survey by Nielsen (2014), 42 percent of millennial and Generation Z respondents (born 1981–96 and 1997–2012, respectively) said they are likely to rent services in shared communities, in contrast with only 17 percent of Generation X respondents (born 1965–80) and 7 percent of baby boomers (born 1945–64). Millennials and Generation Z also constitute more than half the users of major social media platforms (GlobalWebIndex 2018).

The diffusion of technologies might also emphasize the move toward certain services, potentially at the expense of others. For example, 3-D printing reduces the need to move manufactured goods over long distances and instead puts the premium on trade in data flows as part of the manufacturing process. For example, designs, data, and other information from a product designer or producer in an exporting country are delivered digitally for printing in a target market (Arvis et al. 2017). This increases the demand for ICT and professional, scientific, and technical services, while reducing the demand for transportation services.

Intangible capital places a premium on skills, but mainly for the creators of digital technologies and platforms. The diffusion of software might even be low-skill-biased to the extent that apps substitute for the lack of numeracy or language skills.

Based on the degree of technology diffusion and potential for offshorability, the implications of the reduced importance of proximity, greater automation, and increased intangible capital for productivity growth and job creation in services will vary by services subsector group. All three trends matter for *global innovator services*. They matter the least for *low-skill domestic services*. And their significance varies across subsectors among *low-skill tradable services* and *skill-intensive social services* (figure 3.13). The rest of this section discusses the implications for each of the four subsector groups in turn.

Global Innovator Services

Greater Exporting Opportunities through Online Outsourcing

The emergence of online outsourcing through digital platforms has created new exporting opportunities in ICT and professional, scientific, and technical services—subsectors characterized by the highest shares of jobs that can be done remotely.

FIGURE 3.13 **All Three Trends—Reduced Proximity, Increased Potential for Automation, and Increased Intangible Capital—Matter Most for Global Innovator Services**

Share of jobs amenable to home-based work, suitability for ML, and expenditure on R&D and software per worker across services subsectors, 2017–18

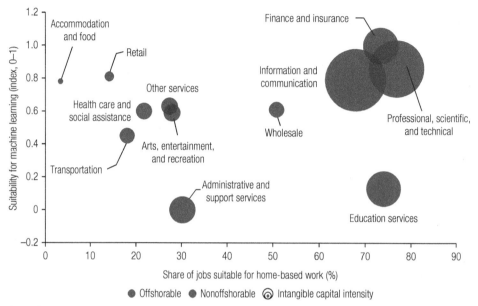

Source: Calculations using data from Blinder and Krueger 2013; Brynjolfsson, Mitchell, and Rock 2018; Dingel and Neiman 2020; OECD STructural ANalysis (STAN) Database; and International Labour Organization.

Note: Figure uses 2018 US data for home-based work and suitability for machine learning (SML) and 2017 Organisation for Economic Co-operation and Development (OECD) data for expenditure on intangible capital. Bubble size indicates the expenditure on intangible capital (R&D and software) normalized by the number of workers employed. Red bubbles indicate sectors that can be easily offshored, and blue bubbles, those whose jobs are not offshorable (see figure 1.6). "Other services" refers to other social, community, and personal services.

Global supply and demand patterns. Much of global demand for English-language online outsourcing services comes from just four high-income countries: Australia, Canada, the United Kingdom, and the United States. For example, 75 percent of all demand on Upwork came from those four countries (Kuek et al. 2015).[13] At the same time, the Oxford Internet Institute's iLabour Project estimates that 68 percent of all online freelancers who completed projects on five of the largest English-language online outsourcing platforms between June 2017 and October 2020 were located in LMICs.[14] In fact, an estimated one-fourth of such freelancers are based in India, another one-fourth in Bangladesh and Pakistan, and another one-eighth in the United Kingdom and the United States (figure 3.14). Other big emerging market suppliers include (in order of total freelancers) the Philippines, China, Ukraine, the Russian Federation, the Arab Republic of Egypt, Sri Lanka, Kenya, Indonesia, Nigeria, Vietnam, and Romania.

FIGURE 3.14 **About Two-Thirds of All Online Freelancers Who Completed Projects on Five of the Largest English-Language Online Freelancing Platforms Live in LMICs**

Supply of online freelancers, top 20 countries, June 2017–October 2020

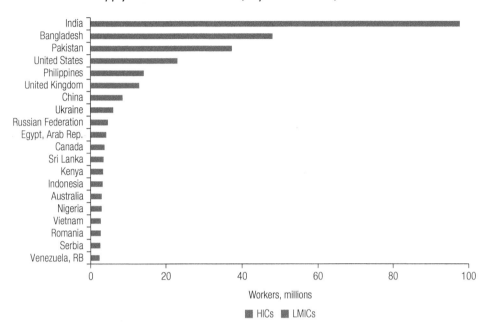

Source: Online Labor Index Worker Supplement of the iLabor Project, Oxford Internet Institute at the University of Oxford, https://ilabour.oii.ox.ac.uk/online-labour-index/.

Note: Low- and middle-income countries (LMICs), by World Bank income group classifications, had 1994 gross national income (GNI) of less than US$8,955. High-income countries (HICs) had GNI exceeding US$8,955 in 1994.

Another study of online freelancing contracts on Upwork—the largest online freelancing platform in 2016—found that the largest buyers were (in this order) the United States, Australia, and the United Kingdom, while the largest suppliers were the Philippines, India, and Bangladesh (Horton, Kerr, and Stanton 2017). The online gig economy is therefore associated with the productivity benefits that result from offshoring services tasks to lower-cost locations.

Fewer language constraints, bigger pool of online freelancers. These patterns reflect the importance of language considerations: much of the demand for English-language online outsourcing from high-income countries is met by suppliers in South Asia, where English is the preferred language for business transactions. This importance of the English language, however, diminishes with the diffusion of AI-enabled machine translation.

Brynjolfsson, Hui, and Liu (2019) studied the effects of eBay's machine translation system, eMT, on exports.[15] They find that US exports to Spanish-speaking Latin American countries increased by 17.5–20.9 percent on eBay after adoption of eMT.[16]

Similarly, eBay's introduction of eMT was associated with an increase in exports from the United Kingdom to France, Italy, and Spain by about 13 percent combined.[17] This suggests that buyers with higher translation-related search costs benefit more from eMT and therefore respond with a larger increase in trade.

Moreover, the magnitude of eMT's effect on exports is greater than the estimated effect of reduced physical distance between countries, suggesting that the capability of ML to cut language barrier frictions is of first-order importance in increasing connectivity (Brynjolfsson, Hui, and Liu 2019). This advent of machine translation could similarly expand the global supply of online freelancers in LMICs where computer programmers or accountants earn a fraction of their counterparts in the United States but where English is not the preferred language for business transactions (Baldwin 2019).

AI-Related Automation and the Reshoring Challenge

The AI-enabled automation that increasingly pervades global innovator services is increasingly associated with productivity growth. Although the technology is still nascent and in the process of diffusing, recent evidence from all current EU member states, the United Kingdom, and the United States indicate that the partial or full implementation of big-data analytics and AI software is positively associated with firm-level labor productivity (Cathles, Nayyar, and Rückert 2020).

Examples abound: Google's DeepMind team has used ML systems to improve the cooling efficiency of data centers by more than 15 percent (Brynjolfsson and McAfee 2017). The use of vast amounts of data from résumés and social media profiles has improved the productivity of firms such as Gild and Entelo in their recruiting tasks (Schulte 2019). And dozens of investment companies are using ML to decide which trades to execute on Wall Street.

Implications for LMICs: The Offshore Services Equation

Big-data- and AI-related automation has fewer implications for productivity growth in LMICs given its minimal diffusion. However, there could also be fewer exporting opportunities to the extent that ML software adoption in high-income countries affects the export competitiveness of LMICs in the market for global innovator services by making labor a smaller share of overall costs. Additional "potential exports" could be lost by never being created if these services are offshored less in the future. These concerns mirror the speculation and early evidence of how industrial automation might result in the reshoring of manufacturing activity to high-wage countries.

RPA software and routine back-office tasks. "Software robots" can reduce the importance of low labor costs in back-office processes commonly found in finance, accounting, supply chain management, customer service, and human resources.

The Institute for Robotic Process Automation and AI (IRPA/AI) estimates that an RPA software robot costs as little as one-fifth the price of full-time local workers in the United States and one-third the price of full-time offshore workers located in, say, India.[18] According to Genfour (acquired by Accenture in 2017), an onshore full-time equivalent (FTE) worker costing US$50,000 can be replaced by an offshore FTE worker for US$20,000, but a digital worker can perform the same function for US$5,000 or less, without the drawbacks of managing and training offshore labor (Baldwin 2019).[19] Similarly, Sutherland Global Services, an outsourcing company in Rochester, New York, says it can reduce costs for its clients by 20–40 percent by shifting IT work to a low- or middle-income economy, but it can reduce costs by up to 70 percent if it couples automation software with its US-based employees to complete tasks involving high volumes of structured data (Lewis 2014).

Beyond these anecdotes, however, there is a paucity of evidence on whether using RPA for "knowledge assembly-line" tasks will affect the offshore services equation.

ML algorithms and cognitive tasks. The use of ML in cognition and problem-solving-related tasks can similarly reduce the labor cost advantage of LMICs in exporting a range of professional, scientific, and technical services. Until recently, for instance, creating a new computer program involved a labor-intensive process of manual coding. But this expensive process is increasingly being automated by running an existing ML algorithm on appropriate training data (Brynjolfsson and Mitchell 2017). Cybersecurity companies (such as Deep Instinct) are also increasingly using ML to detect malware, while financial services providers (such as PayPal) are doing so to prevent money laundering (Brynjolfsson and Mitchell 2017). Similarly, sophisticated ML algorithms embedded in legal analytics platforms, such as Lex Machina and Ravel Law, function as "robo-lawyers" that can plow through information and suggest legal strategies (Baldwin 2019).

ML-enabled voice recognition and perception-related tasks. The use of ML in perception-related tasks through voice recognition can similarly affect the labor cost advantage of LMICs in exporting call center and other back-office services related to customer interaction. Some of the most practical ML advances have been made in voice recognition, with millions of people now using digital assistants such as Siri, Alexa, and Google Assistant. A study by the Stanford computer scientist James Landay and colleagues found that voice recognition is now about three times as fast, on average, as typing on a cell phone—and that the error rate, once 8.5 percent, has dropped to 4.9 percent (Brynjolfsson and McAfee 2017).[20]

Sales and customer interaction, such as through call centers, are potentially a good fit for automation through voice recognition ML software. Further, transcripts from online chats between sales representatives and customers can be used as training data for a simple chatbot to recognize answers to common queries (Brynjolfsson and McAfee 2017).

There are early indications that the use of AI and ML in high-income countries might adversely affect the export competitiveness of IT and IT-enabled services in LMICs. For example, in a survey of senior executives across 300 firms in India's ICT services sector, 84 percent of respondents indicated that increased use of AI and ML technologies by foreign competitors was a constraint on their performance. Of these, more than 90 percent were exporters (Sáez et al. 2019). Similarly, in the Philippines, data from online recruitment portal Jobstreet.com show that available business process outsourcing (BPO) jobs for fresh graduates declined by one-third between 2016 and 2017, with AI seen as a contributing factor (Muñiz 2018).

Yet there is little systematic evidence on whether automation in high-income countries is causing firms to reshore global innovator services from LMICs. In fact, the increased intensity of ML-related capabilities in the United Kingdom between 2012 and 2018 did not reduce but increased the country's offshoring of ICT-related business and professional services to LMICs (Stapleton and O'Kane 2021). The evidence shows that India has been by far the biggest beneficiary of this increased offshoring from firms in the United Kingdom.

This result is consistent with the "income" effect of automation outweighing the "substitution" effect. On the one hand, AI algorithms make it economically profitable to reshore some tasks to high-income economies. On the other hand, efficiency gains resulting from the use of AI algorithms leads to an expansion in the scale of production, which results in greater offshoring to LMICs.

Scaling Up through Network Effects and Intangible Capital

The rise of intangible capital has also enabled firms in global innovator services to scale up in an unprecedented way. This is supported by the examples of tech firms such as Apple, Facebook, and Microsoft that own complexes of valuable intangible assets such as software, advertising space, and branding that derive from strong network effects and access to data.

Take, for example, the two most common, competing operating systems for mobile devices: Apple's iOS versus Google's Android. Network effects make it less desirable for users to switch to another platform once they have invested in a preferred or favorite platform. Similarly, massive amounts of accumulated user data can enable platform companies to steer users to their own advantage via filtering, framing, ordering results, advertisements, nudging, and so on (Hallward-Driemeier et al. 2020).

Scaling up operations based on these intangible assets and the low additional costs of supplying additional consumers is reflected in the productivity and profit margins of the leading platform firms among the global innovator services. The combined market capitalization of the five largest tech companies in the S&P 500

Index—Alphabet (Google), Amazon, Apple, Facebook, and Microsoft—amounted to about US$4 trillion in 2019, which is larger than the sum of the market capitalizations of the 250 smallest companies in the same index. Furthermore, these tech companies generate well over US$1 million in revenues per employee per year, which exceeds the corresponding ratio for many traditional manufacturing companies by a factor of 4 to 10 (Fraunhofer Institute 2019).

Although such scale economies bring productivity benefits, they can also endanger market competition. If leading tech firms can pull away from their competition by scaling up over their intangible assets, combining intangibles in a way that others cannot, and further assimilating intangible capital from rivals by acquiring them, this can have negative implications for productivity growth in the medium to long term.

The productivity benefits of intangible capital that is highest among global innovator services are also prone to mismeasurement. Brynjolfsson, Rock, and Syverson (2021) refer to this phenomenon as the "productivity J-curve." As firms adopt a new GPT, total factor productivity (TFP) growth is initially underestimated because the investment rate in intangible capital is higher than in other types of capital, but TFP subsequently rises as growing intangible stocks begin to contribute to measurable output. Such mismeasurement might be particularly problematic because the advent of AI, which is most significant in global innovator services, has initiated the early stage of complementary investment in intangible capital.

Implications for Inclusion

The increased possibilities for remote delivery of global innovator services mean that more jobs can be offshored to lower-wage countries. The Oxford Internet Institute's iLabour Project estimates that 333 million gig-economy workers completed projects on the five largest English-language online labor platforms—representing at least 60 percent of the market—between June 2017 and October 2020, and most of these workers were in LMICs. No evidence yet suggests that the diffusion of ML algorithms in high-income countries has either reshored these services or reduced offshoring them to firms in lower-wage countries. And full-time international freelancers in LMICs make more than their peers who have traditional jobs (Baldwin 2019). They also benefit from flexibility in hours and schedules, but there are some disadvantages: uncertainty in contractual arrangements; irregular working hours due to time differences with client countries; and the absence of nonwage benefits such as health insurance, pension contributions, and leave days (Heeks 2017).

Furthermore, as technology creates new occupations largely in the nonroutine cognitive category, much of these reside in global innovator services. A detailed cross-country analysis of 2,000-plus work activities across more than 800 occupations finds that the categories with the highest percentage job growth net of automation include

IT professionals and other technology specialists as well as those involved in IT-enabled professional services: engineers, scientists, accountants, and analysts (Manyika et al. 2017). Another study—following the Autor (2014) classification of occupation groups by skill level—finds that two-thirds of new occupations in India and 85 percent in Vietnam are in professional service sectors (Khatiwada and Maceda Veloso 2019).[21] Most of these new skill-biased job titles are ICT-related: data analysts, software engineers, system programmers, database design analysts, computer system hardware analysts, and computer quality assurance analysts.

This job creation is all good news for inclusion, but there are risks of increased inequality too, given the premium on advanced digital skills. In fact, data from the online business and employment networking service LinkedIn show that value creation from transformative GPTs such as AI and ML stems from IT-related intangible capital and digital skills (Brynjolfsson, Rock, and Syverson 2021). This finding suggests that the key to unlocking broader benefits from the advent of AI-related automation among global innovator services is complementary investment in new skills (Brynjolfsson and Hitt 2000; Brynjolfsson, Hitt, and Yang 2002) (box 3.2).

BOX 3.2

AI, Jobs, and the Demand for Skills in India's ICT Services Sector

The potential displacement of labor by the diffusion of AI is not widespread, according to a 2019 World Bank survey of senior executives across 300 firms in India's IT and IT-enabled services spanning application software, data processing, and outsourcing services, IT consulting, and system software. About 46 percent of the respondents do not expect any redundancy in their workforce over the next three years, 19 percent expect less than 20 percent of their workforce to become redundant, and a little over 10 percent expect more than 50 percent of their workforce to become redundant (Sáez et al. 2019).

About two-thirds of the respondents indicated that AI would increase total employment in their firms, despite some layoffs. This is consistent with the widespread expectation that although AI and ML may substitute for labor in certain tasks, productivity growth resulting from automation will increase the scale of the business and therefore increase the demand for labor in nonautomated tasks.[a]

These new tasks are likely to be skill intensive. In the 2019 World Bank survey, most firms predict an increase in employment of individuals with AI work experience (affirmed by 67 percent of respondents), an engineering degree (67 percent), or postgraduate education (62 percent), as shown in figure B3.2.1. Further, respondent firms expect a wide variety of technical talent—ranging from software developers and cloud computing specialists to data management specialists and AI and ML specialists—to become increasingly important. Yet nearly 75 percent of respondents mentioned that the shortage of employees with the relevant AI and ML skills will constrain their international competitiveness.

Investments in skill development are therefore the need of the hour. About 69 percent of respondents expect that their workforce will require significant retraining, with the median firm expecting 22 percent of its workforce to be retrained. Investments in reskilling the workforce to equip them with skills required to

Box continues on the following page

AI, Jobs, and the Demand for Skills in India's ICT Services Sector *(continued)*

FIGURE B3.2.1 **Most ICT Firms Predict an Increase in Employment for Highly Skilled Individuals, Including Those with Prior AI Work Experience**

Perceived impact of AI on ICT firms' total employment in India, by employee education level, 2019

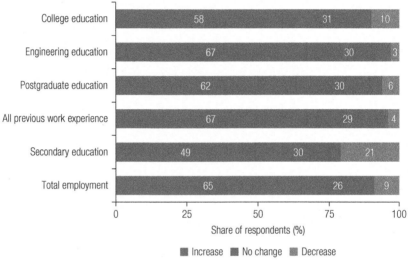

Source: Sáez et al. 2019.

Note: The figure represents results from a 2019 World Bank survey of senior executives across 300 firms in India's information and communication technology (ICT) services sector. AI = artificial intelligence.

work with AI constitute a relatively substantial share of training investments. On average, 36 percent of firms' training investments are focused on this reskilling.[b]

Most of the respondents expect these training investments to increase either significantly (38 percent) or moderately (43 percent) between 2020 and 2022.

Source: Sáez et al. 2019.

a. The survey results reinforce other research in this area. For example, the first comprehensive research study on the future of jobs in India predicts that, by 2022, about 46 percent of the workforce in India's ICT sector will be engaged in new jobs that did not exist in 2017 or will require radically changed skill sets (EY, FICCI, and NASSCOM 2017).

b. These results are also borne out by a 2018 LinkedIn study, which finds that AI skills are among the fastest-growing skills on LinkedIn members' profiles, reflecting a 190 percent increase from 2015 to 2017 (LinkedIn 2018).

Gains and Limitations of the Reduced Proximity Burden

Digital technologies have reduced the importance of physical proximity in market transactions by, among other things, reducing the costs of searching for, matching, tracking, and verifying information (Goldfarb and Tucker 2019). Low-skill services, which have fewer barriers to entry for workers and entrepreneurs, are no exception to this norm. Uber, for example, allows drivers to observe which customers across a vast geographical area have the most attractive pickup and drop-off locations (Wu, Wang, and Zhu 2016). Similarly, Booking.com helped its clients gain an average of 7 percent more revenue by helping them identify consumers across the world whose data indicate they would be willing to pay more (Li, Nirei, and Yamana 2019).

The efficiency gains are visible. Based on firm-level data from 10 OECD countries[22] across four industries—hotels, restaurants, taxis, and retail trade—Rivares et al. (2019) find that the average service provider saw bigger total factor productivity increases between 2011 and 2017 in countries with high online platform development[23] than in countries with low online platform development.[24] In China, the participation of a Chinese fast-food restaurant chain across four food delivery (aggregator) platforms (Baidu, Meituan, Ele.me, and Koubei) between 2013 and 2015 increased total sales in the long run to the tune of 34 percent (Zhang, Pauwels, and Peng 2019).[25] Similarly, based on a survey of firms, Mohamed et al. (2009) found that e-commerce improved firm performance in Malaysia's tourism sector (hotels, resorts, and health tourism hospitals).

Digital platforms have made low-skill tradable services more internationally tradable too. There is evidence that e-commerce platforms have enabled retail firms to access international markets by reducing the costs of matching buyers and sellers all over the world. For example, the impact of distance on cross-border trade flows across 61 countries and 40 product categories is about 65 percent smaller for eBay transactions relative to total international trade (Lendle et al. 2016).

Digital platforms are also increasingly used by travelers and businesses in tourism-related accommodation and transportation services. The expectation is that less-traditional destinations may overcome the lack of information, and abate travel costs, through digital tools, thereby attracting more visitors. Analyzing populationwide internet use in origin countries and business-to-consumer internet use in destination countries, Lopez-Cordova (2020) finds that digital platforms have boosted the demand for international tourism services in Africa.[26] Similarly, Ollivaud and Haxton (2019) find that digital platforms that connect customers with hotels, restaurants, or taxis have improved the competitiveness of Indonesia's tourism industry.

Yet, beyond matching supply and demand by reducing information asymmetries, these digital tools do little for the remote provision of these low-skill tradable services because, for many of them, in-person delivery remains necessary. This was best illustrated by the COVID-19 pandemic, which resulted in a larger contraction in services than in manufacturing, with accommodation and food services and passenger transportation particularly affected. Being intensive in face-to-face interactions with consumers, these services have been adversely affected by continued social-distancing precautions (Avdiu and Nayyar 2020). This has, at least in the short run, negative implications for the export of tourism-related accommodation and food and transportation services (box 3.3).

The simultaneity of production and consumption has also become less important in some low-skill domestic services. For example, some administrative support services are increasingly delivered remotely through online freelancing platforms. Based on data from five such platforms, sales and marketing services, writing and translation services, and clerical and data entry services, respectively, accounted for about 10 million, 10 million, and 5 million workers in 2020 (figure 3.2).[27]

There are similar possibilities to achieve scale in arts, entertainment, and recreation services. Extending the Baumol (1967) string quartet example (discussed in chapter 1), today's video recordings of live performances that can then be replayed through digital platforms vastly expand the available audience for (and potential revenue from) each performance. Streaming platforms such as Netflix and YouTube have a wide global reach and are fast enabling artists from LMICs to export their creative content to international markets at low cost. Moreover, COVID-19 has inspired performing artists to envision new ways of sharing their talents with audiences virtually.

Blunted Effects of AI-Based Automation in LMICs

A much larger set of occupations and industries are suitable for automation through ML, and this includes even low-skill domestic services. Retailers, for instance, can use AI to monitor consumer behavior on the demand side and optimize inventories on the supply side (Shankar 2018). L'Occitane, for example, increased its mobile sales by 15 percent by using AI to identify "pain points" in the shopping experience and adjusted its mobile shopping app accordingly. Similarly, Amazon employs ML to optimize inventory management and improve product recommendations to customers (Brynjolfsson and McAfee 2017).

Similar examples come from accommodation and food services. Starbucks introduced an AI-enabled personalized app, which accounted for 20 percent of sales within a year. A restaurant chain, TGIF (Thank God It's Friday), reported increasing sales by US$150 million in a little over a year by using AI to tailor its marketing via the company app and the use of a bot to offer customers personal deals by text message (Shankar 2018).

Among low-skill tradable services, the transportation sector might also be increasingly subject to AI-related automation. At ports, autonomous vehicles might unload, stack, and reload containers faster and with fewer errors. Similarly, automation through the Internet of Things (IoT) has the potential to increase the efficiency of delivery

Impact of COVID-19 on Digitalization and Remote Delivery

The COVID-19 pandemic is accelerating trends of digitalization. The World Bank's Business Pulse Survey (BPS) data show an increased reliance on digital technologies and remote work during the COVID-19 pandemic (figure B3.3.1). These increases have been the highest in high-skill services like ICT, financial services, and education, which suggests that much of the work in these sectors that has long been conducted in person is now increasingly being delivered digitally and remotely. Digitalization is also occurring in some of the low-skill services subsectors; for example, roughly a third of the retail firms surveyed report that they have started or increased the use of digital platforms to execute transactions.

Yet the actual delivery of services, such as accommodation and food as well as passenger transportation, remain intensive in face-to-face interactions with consumers and will likely be slower to recover as people continue to exercise social-distancing precautions. In the United States, for example, most of the fall in restaurant reservations occurred before the imposition of any government-mandated closures (Maloney and Taskin 2020). Manufacturing and construction, in contrast, are likely to see workers return to their jobs more easily as lockdown restrictions ease, given the low face-to-face interactions with consumers.

FIGURE B3.3.1 **COVID-19 Has Accelerated the Use of Digital Technologies and Home-Based Work Most among Firms in Global Innovator Services**

Firms' adoption of digital platforms and home-based work during the COVID-19 pandemic, by sector, 2020

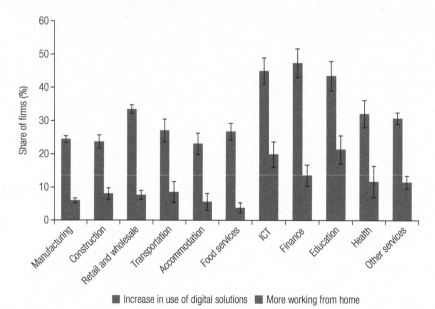

■ Increase in use of digital solutions ■ More working from home

Source: World Bank COVID-19 Business Pulse Survey (BPS) and Enterprise Surveys (ES), conducted April–September 2020.

Note: The data cover more than 130,000 businesses in 60 countries, primarily low- and middle-income countries (LMICs). The graph displays the predicted average changes from a regression controlling for country, size, sector, and the number of weeks following the shock. The data have been reweighted so each country has an equal weight. Error bars indicate 95 percent confidence intervals. LMICs, by World Bank income group classifications, had 1994 gross national income (GNI) of less than US$8,955. "Other services" includes other social, community, and personal services. ICT = information and communication technology. For a full description of the survey, see Apedo-Amah et al. (2020).

services by tracking shipments in real time, while improved and expanded navigation systems may help route trucks based on current road and traffic conditions (World Bank 2020).

These revenue and productivity gains from AI-related automation are unlikely to be substantial in LMICs, owing to low adoption rates. Furthermore, the potential for AI- and ML-related automation in high-income countries to challenge traditional patterns of offshoring is less relevant for these low-skill tradable services where geographic proximity between producers and consumers remains important. The export of accommodation and food services and passenger transportation services linked to tourism, for example, is tied to the exporting country's location.

Widespread Productivity Gains from ICT-Based Automation

The lack of technology adoption across general business functions such as input sourcing, inventory management, product pricing, accounting practices, marketing, and payment systems comes at a productivity cost for firms in any sector. The World Bank's FAT survey finds that the relationship between technology use in these general business functions and labor productivity is as strong among services firms as among manufacturing firms in Brazil, Senegal, and Vietnam (Cirera et al. 2020b).[28] And although the inherent role of labor remains important in most low-skill services, there is evidence of such productivity gains resulting from ICT-related automation.

In retail services, there is a positive association—beyond a threshold level—between the share of firms that used websites and labor productivity across a large cross-section of countries (figure 3.15). Similarly, informal enterprises in Senegal (the large of majority being in retail) that make greater use of basic software and other specialized apps to facilitate general business functions have higher labor productivity and total sales on average than those that do not use such software and apps (Atiyas and Dutz 2021). Similarly, Haller and Lyons (2019) use firm-level data across Ireland from 2006 to 2012 to find consistent evidence that broadband availability positively affects TFP in administrative and support service activities.

In tourism-related services, numerous studies have found that the positive relationship between ICT use and the industry's competitiveness increased between 1995 and 2018 (Villa Espinosa, Miñana Terol, and González-Ladrón-de-Guevara 2018). Using data from the hospitality industry in South Africa, Cohen and Olsen (2013) find that higher-performing establishments have better, more integrated IT systems in place.[29] The sample of responding firms was split about evenly between smaller (less than 100 rooms) and larger (over 100 rooms) establishments and between chains (60 percent) and nonchains (40 percent).

In transportation services, digital technologies have also boosted productivity by creating a single window for streamlining customs procedures. In Costa Rica, for example, a one-stop online customs system increased both exports and imports.

FIGURE 3.15 **Retail Services Exhibit a Positive Association between Website Use and Labor Productivity**

Share of retail firms using a website in relation to labor productivity, by country, 2016

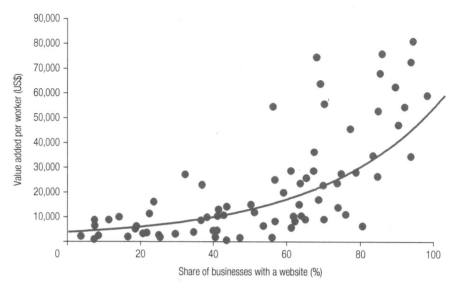

Sources: Calculations based on ILOSTAT, https://ilostat.ilo.org/; United Nations National Accounts, https://unstats.un.org/unsd /snaama/; World Bank Enterprise Surveys.

Note: Website data are for most recent available year (2013 onward).

Similarly, in Colombia, computerizing import procedures increased imports and accelerated the growth of firms most exposed to the new procedures. Although the empirical evidence on these impacts is limited, the use of new digital technologies in transportation and logistics services could reduce shipping and customs processing times by an estimated 16–28 percent (World Bank 2020).

Efficiency Gains from Scaling Up Based on Increasing Intangible Capital

This ability to scale production in a single establishment has been limited among the low-skill services that are less traded because there was typically little value in consolidating many restaurants or retail outlets in the same location. Yet, as described in chapter 2, there is a long history of retail "chains," especially in the United States, that typically scaled up through multiple establishments across different locations.[30]

The diffusion of ICT and associated intangible capital such as management practices and branding has further enabled firms in retail and food services, for instance, to replicate the same production process in multiple locations near consumers (Hsieh and Rossi-Handberg 2020). This standardization of production over many establishments is well illustrated by restaurant chains. Gawande (2012) cites the Cheesecake Factory, which has invested in information and communication technologies and management practices that determine the optimal staffing, daily food purchases for each restaurant, and a well-oiled process for introducing new menu items. Based on 1977–2010 data from the United States, Hsieh and Rossi-Hansberg (2020) suggest that top retail and wholesale firms have indeed become more efficient over time, as reflected in their increased industry market shares.[31]

Furthermore, much like tech companies among global innovator services, digital platform companies in the low-skill services sectors derive scale from valuable intangible assets based on network effects. Take food delivery services, for example. As more restaurants join a digital platform, the variety of choice increases, attracting more customers. And the more customers who join, the greater the value to restaurants of benefiting from the platform's brand because they are likely to get more orders. Among logistics and delivery services, the top "unicorn" firms—private start-up companies valued at US$1 billion or more—are DoorDash (a US-based food delivery platform), followed by Go-Jek (an Indonesia-based on-demand multiservice platform).

Examples in other services subsectors include Jumia, an e-commerce platform that is the first technology unicorn operating in Africa. Jumia serves 14 countries on the continent and has over 4 million customers, including in food delivery services. The unicorns with the highest valuation in the auto and transportation industry are ride-sharing companies, such as DiDi in China, Grab in Singapore, and Ola Cabs in India. In the travel industry, the unicorn with the highest valuation is, not surprisingly, the US-based Airbnb. Traveloka, an Indonesian company that facilitates airline ticketing and hotel booking services, is fourth on this list of travel unicorns (CBInsights 2020).[32]

Implications for Jobs and Inclusion

The use of ICT has not displaced labor in the services sector. Analyzing firm-level data from a large cross-section of countries across regions, Cusolito and Peña (2020) and Cusolito et al. (2020) find that adoption of websites and email is positively correlated with changes in the number of both skilled and unskilled workers across firms in wholesale trade, retail trade, and hotels and restaurants. For email adoption, they find this positive correlation to be biased in favor of skilled workers in both manufacturing and these low-skill services subsectors. However, the positive association between the use of websites and jobs is relatively stronger for unskilled workers in low-skill services' firms but not in manufacturing.

The scaling-up based on ICT-related intangible capital has also not replaced labor. Evidence from the United States shows that total employment has risen substantially, even in increasingly concentrated industries such as wholesale and retail (Hsieh and Rossi-Hansberg 2020). This rising intangible capital has also not increased the demand for skills among the users of these technologies. For example, Uber drivers do not need map-reading skills because the app does it for them. They also do not need numeracy skills because all payments are by credit card on the platform. With restaurant chains, data analytics helps predict meals, how to tweak menu offerings, and how to speed up customer turnaround, but it does not change the skill requirements for cooks or wait staff. This is good news for inclusion.

Furthermore, there is a host of new gig-economy workers in ridesharing, retail delivery, and food delivery whereby work obtained through digital platforms is executed in person. Back-of-the-envelope calculations estimate that there are 250,000 such gig workers in Africa, 30 million across Asian LMICs, and 2 million in Latin America (Heeks 2017). In a survey of such gig-economy workers across Southeast Asia and Sub-Saharan Africa, most of the respondents reported that it was their primary occupation and an important source of income for their households (Wood et al. 2019).

In the United States, establishments without paid employees in the ground passenger transportation sector grew by almost 250 percent from 2010 to 2016. That there were almost no Uber drivers in 2012 and 465,000 Uber drivers in 2015 suggests that job creation in the sector can indeed be attributed to online platforms (Abraham et al. 2019). Similarly, Airbnb is estimated to have supported more than 45,000 jobs across three destinations in Indonesia in 2016 (Ollivaud and Haxton 2019).

Digital platforms also enable market entry because they disproportionally benefit smaller firms and service providers by reducing verification costs.[33] Rating systems that signal product quality on these platforms further enhance buyers' trust in unfamiliar suppliers (Goldfarb and Tucker 2019).

As a result, digital platforms increase market competition as well. For example, Airbnb provides an alternative to hotels in the hospitality industry, while Uber can reduce the demand for incumbent taxi services. It is therefore possible that competition from these new entrants may reduce wages or displace labor among incumbent service providers.[34] Based on firm-level data from the United States and nine European countries,[35] Rivares et al. (2019) find that sharing-economy platforms such as Uber and Airbnb are associated with a decline in employment and wages among incumbent service providers. Similarly, the rise of digital platforms in travel-related industries coincided with a decline in the number of physical travel agencies in the United States from an estimated 25,975 establishments in 2000 to 14,797 in 2016, and a concomitant fall in employment from 183,143 to 108,985 (Lopez-Cordova 2020), with smaller firms being the most adversely affected (Lieber and Syverson 2012).

Ultimately, the entry of new service providers via digital platforms will increase overall employment if they create more jobs than those lost with the exit of incumbents. For example, e-commerce created 400,000 jobs, while retail jobs in brick-and-mortar firms declined by 140,000 between 2007 and 2017 in the United States (Mandel 2017). It is also important to note that market competition that spurs entry and reallocates resources from less- to more-productive service providers will provide better and more jobs in the long run.

Yet there are concerns about the quality of gig-economy jobs in retail, accommodation, and transportation services in terms of wages and nonwage benefits. In the United States, Uber divers earn much higher wages than taxi drivers (Hall and Kreuger 2018), and workers who provide personal services through digital platforms earn higher wages than their nonplatform counterparts (Sundarajan 2016). Similarly, in Cali, Colombia, ridesharing-platform workers typically earn more than double the minimum wage (Paredes and Reilly 2018).

However, these gig-economy jobs are also characterized by unstable contractual arrangements, no guaranteed minimum wage, a lack of employment-linked social security, and a lack of training opportunities (De Stefano 2016; Huws et al. 2017; Schwellnus et al. 2019). Once these benefits are considered, Friedman (2014) argues, gig workers' median wages in the United States are significantly lower than those of workers with traditional contracts. Notably, however, the nonpecuniary benefits among workers in retail, accommodation and food, and transportation services in LMICs were not high even before gig-economy work, owing to a large informal sector.

Skill-Intensive Social Services

Among the skill-intensive social services, the increasing opportunities for scale in telemedicine and e-learning have reduced the need for proximity between buyers and sellers. These opportunities are reflected in the cross-border exports of health and education services from high-income countries, which increased consistently between 2005 and 2017 (figure 3.16, panel a).

Telemedicine largely relates to remote medical diagnosis and testing that is enabled by telecommunications technology. Telepresence has also enabled expert surgeons to mentor other surgeons in surgery procedures from a distance via cameras and microphones (Wall and Marescaux 2013). Telesurgery that uses wireless networking and robotic technology can also enable surgeons to operate on distant patients (Choi, Oskouian, and Tubbs 2018). However, high costs, questions about the stability and security of internet networks, and a host of legal and regulatory issues pose challenges for the wider take-up of telesurgery anytime soon (Avgousti et al. 2016).

Similar trends can be seen in education, with the proliferation of e-learning platforms and massive open online courses (MOOCs) addressing a variety of educational needs, from those of primary school students to the furtherance of postgraduate degrees and diplomas. These platforms have emerged across the world, and Byju's (an online learning app, headquartered in India) is the top unicorn firm among education services globally. Furthermore, online distance-learning programs from many leading universities increasingly present cheaper and more flexible alternatives for students worldwide who, because of financial constraints or other reasons, cannot travel abroad to pursue higher education. The increasing possibilities for the remote provision of education services has been highlighted during the COVID-19 pandemic.

There is also scope for greater innovation through ICT investments. Enlisting several examples of digitalization in European health care services, Lapão and Dussault (2017) find that e-records and e-prescriptions make it possible for clinicians to be more productive by allowing easier access to information and reducing paperwork.

The same holds true for investments in labor-augmenting intangible capital such as software, big-data analytics, and branding, which have also enabled hospitals and schools to standardize and codify best practices and scale production over many locations. Gawande (2012) provides the example of hospitals in the United States, of which more than 60 percent are owned by for-profit chains or are part of a large network owned by an academic institution. The Steward Health Care Group, for instance, has used the "remote ICU" to provide consistent care in all the intensive care units (ICUs) in its hospitals and has adopted a common medical data platform in all its hospitals and outpatient clinics. By 2019, Steward had expanded from its 6 original hospitals in Boston to 38 hospitals and 271 outpatient clinics in 10 states and Malta. This franchising model can also be exported through foreign direct investment (FDI) that establishes affiliates abroad. FDI from high-income countries, especially for health services, increased considerably between 2005 and 2017 (figure 3.16, panel b).

FIGURE 3.16 **High-Income Countries Have Consistently Increased Their Exports of Skill-Intensive Social Services, Especially through FDI**

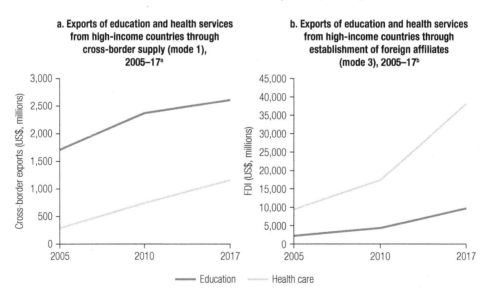

a. Exports of education and health services from high-income countries through cross-border supply (mode 1), 2005–17ᵃ

b. Exports of education and health services from high-income countries through establishment of foreign affiliates (mode 3), 2005–17ᵇ

Education — Health care

Source: Trade in Services data by Mode of Supply (TiSMoS) database, World Trade Organization (WTO).

Note: The service delivery "modes" refer to the classification of services trade applied in the WTO General Agreement on Trade in Services (GATS), as further described in chapter 1. FDI = foreign direct investment.

a. Mode 1 is "cross-border supply," whereby a provider delivers services to a customer in another country without any movement of persons or commercial presence, including through digital delivery.

b. Mode 3 is "commercial presence" or FDI, whereby a provider delivers services through its presence in the customer's country, such as through a locally established subsidiary or affiliate company.

Jobs for unskilled labor remain limited in these services, however, and indirect job creation in other sectors that are more intensive in low-skilled labor is constrained by having few linkages.

Conclusion

The spread of computerization and the internet enabled a set of global innovator services—comprising finance, ICT, and business services—to reap the productivity benefits of international trade, linkages with other sectors, and technology adoption. Digital platforms expand the scope for such services to be internationally traded by enabling new forms of online outsourcing. And although the advent of "software robots" and AI-enabled ML algorithms in high-income countries can affect the export competitiveness of LMICs in the market for offshored professional, scientific, and technical services (such as software, call centers, and other BPO processes) by making labor a smaller share of overall costs, there is little evidence of any reshoring as yet. Such automation is limited in LMICs and therefore poses less risk to direct labor substitution in these services. The rise of intangible capital has also enabled large scale economies among tech firms in these services but has also increased the emphasis on skills in the new jobs being created.

There are increasing opportunities to achieve scale and innovation in skill-intensive social services too. The reduced need for proximity between buyers and sellers has boosted e-learning and telemedicine services. Furthermore, school and hospital services can increasingly be scaled up by establishing more establishments, including abroad. Last but not least, digitalizing medical and student records can deliver considerable efficiency gains.

The group of low-skill (tradable and domestic) services are less amenable to remote delivery and remain more intensive in face-to-face interactions with consumers. Yet the importance of physical proximity has been reduced to the extent that digital platforms match demand and supply across these services. For example, travel-related digital platforms have boosted tourism-related accommodation and transportation services. The potential for AI- and ML-related automation in high-income countries to result in reshoring is also less relevant for these low-skill services that are not offshored to begin with.

Beyond exporting opportunities, the rise of intangible capital has created new opportunities for retail and food services firms to scale service provision over many locations. There is also significant productivity potential associated with low-skill-biased automation (the diffusion of computerization and the internet) that reduces the cost of computing across different business functions. Moreover, job prospects remain robust: ICT-related automation has not been labor-replacing, the scope for AI-related automation is limited in LMICs, and the digital economy has created new jobs in the gig economy.

A related question is whether the services sector, especially global innovator services and low-skill tradable services, *need* a manufacturing core to develop. To the extent that final demand contributes substantially to the growth of these services subsectors, opportunities can be created without a manufacturing base. Growth opportunities for services in the absence of a manufacturing core might be reinforced if intermediate demand for these services subsectors derives largely from sectors other than manufacturing. Furthermore, can the growing productivity potential of global innovator services translate into jobs for unskilled labor through greater linkages with other sectors? Chapter 4 assesses these possibilities.

Notes

1. Dingel and Neiman (2020) use survey data from the Occupational Information Network (O*NET), an online database of standardized and occupation-specific descriptors in the United States (https://www.onetcenter.org/), to develop a home-based work (HBW) measure. This occupation-level measure is combined with information from the US Bureau of Labor Statistics on the prevalence of each occupation in the economy. The authors also combine their measure with employment data, by occupation, from other countries and find a positive relationship between the share of jobs that can be done from home and levels of per capita income.

2. These trends reinforce the earlier findings of Kässi and Lehdonvirta (2018) based on all projects posted publicly to five of the largest English-language online work platforms: Freelancer, Guru, Amazon Mechanical Turk (Mturk), PeoplePerHour, and Upwork.

3. A World Bank (2018) report argues that user-generated content (UGC) on digital platforms is fast becoming the main source of tourism information. The country of Jordan, for example, relies heavily on UGC to illustrate that it is a safe and interesting tourism destination for potential travelers who live afar.

4. Retail sales data from "Quarterly Retail E-Commerce Sales, 4th Quarter 2020," *US Census Bureau News.*

5. Information from the Kunpa website: https://kunpa.co/en/home/.

6. Calculations using the Occupational Information Network (O*NET) database (https://www.onetcenter.org/) and US Bureau of Labor Statistics data.

7. Evidence from Cirera at al. 2020b; Cusolito and Peña 2020 (from World Bank Enterprise Survey Data); and the OECD ICT Access and Usage by Businesses database (https://stats.oecd.org/Index.aspx?DataSetCode=ICT_BUS).

8. On the basis of the FAT survey, Cirera et al. (2020a, 2020b) rank the technologies used by firms for both general and sector-specific business functions by their level of sophistication. In every case, the most sophisticated technologies rely on digital technologies and/or data.

9. In machine learning, a common task is the study and construction of algorithms that can learn from and make predictions based on data. Such algorithms function by making data-driven predictions or decisions, through building a mathematical model from input data. "Training data" are the data used to train an algorithm or *machine learning* model to predict the outcome that the model is designed to predict (Bishop 2006; Kohavi and Provost 1998).

10. The "EU-14" comprises the following pre-2004 EU member states: Austria, Belgium, Denmark, Finland, France, Germany, Greece, Ireland, Italy, the Netherlands, Portugal, Spain, Sweden, and the United Kingdom. It does not include one other pre-2004 member state, Luxembourg. The United Kingdom has since left the EU, as of January 31, 2020.

11. Data on R&D intensity in OECD economies are from the OECD STructural ANalysis (STAN) Database (https://www.oecd.org/industry/ind/stanstructuralanalysisdatabase.htm).

12. The difficulty of measuring intangible capital can raise measured total factor productivity (TFP). For instance, if branding as factor of production goes up but cannot be measured, it will increase TFP that is computed as a residual measure even if there are no true efficiency gains.

13. The United States is the dominant employer country of online freelancers, with a market share of 52 percent.

14. Survey results from the Online Labor Index Worker Supplement of the iLabor Project, Oxford Internet Institute at the University of Oxford, https://ilabour.oii.ox.ac.uk/online-labour-index/.

15. eBay Machine Translation (eMT) is an in-house ML system that statistically learns how to translate different languages. The eMT makes it easier for shoppers from other countries who speak another language to search for products, reducing their personal "cost" of translating.

16. The authors employ a difference-in-difference analysis to explore the effects of the eMT technology, whereby the comparison group is either (a) all other countries to which US sellers export on eBay, or (b) offline US exports to the same Latin American countries.

17. To promote intra-EU trade, US eBay pages were not translated.

18. Labor cost estimates from "Definition and Benefits," IRPA/AI website, http://www.irpaai.com.

19. In addition, a "software robot's" work is more consistent and leaves a digital trail that makes regulatory compliance reporting faster and more reliable. The RPA process can also scale up or down rapidly to address, for example, seasonal fluctuations in the paperwork flow—that is, software can be used more intensively in busy periods instead of hiring and training temporary workers (Baldwin 2019).

20. What is striking is that this substantial improvement has come not over the past 10 years but just since the summer of 2016.

21. However, only an estimated 3.63 percent of India's working population (approximately 13.5 million) were employed in these emerging occupations in 2012. This is attributable, at least in part, to the lack of technology-related skills among most workers (Khatiwada and Maceda Veloso 2019).

22. The OECD countries included Belgium, France, Germany, Hungary, Italy, Poland, Spain, Sweden, the United Kingdom, and the United States.

23. The authors develop a proxy for online platform development based on Google searches containing part of the name of 50 relevant platforms grouped within an industry and year (2004–17) for each country.

24. However, these productivity gains in incumbent service provider firms drop sharply if a single online platform dominates.

25. There are two potential effects at play in the case of restaurants. On the one hand, new delivery channels could substitute for dine-in service and thereby reduce offline profits. On the other hand, they might expand market reach and generate new and more customers, including at physical locations.

26. This conclusion reinforces Hoonsawat's (2016) finding that the internet helps mitigate travelers' lack of information about a given destination, thus increasing their demand for tourism services.

27. These three service categories consist largely of the kind of work contracted through the Amazon Mechanical Turk (MTurk) crowdworking website.

28. The coefficient of the technology adoption index, which measures the sophistication of the array of technologies across business functions in the regression on log value added per worker, is 0.61 for manufacturing and only slightly lower for services, at 0.49.

29. The most common IT applications used by the responding hospitality firms were (a) property management systems (PMS), reservations, and guest accounting; (b) room status and

housekeeping management; (c) hotel websites; (d) finance and accounting; (e) customer relationship management (CRM); (f) reports and statistical tools; (g) central reservation system (CRS); (h) personnel; (i) check-in, check-out kiosks; and (j) sales and catering.

30. This refers to the advent of big-box retailers such as supermarkets, hypermarkets, club stores, and supercenters or mass merchandisers in high-income countries, which are (as discussed in chapter 5) also becoming more commonplace in LMICs.

31. Hsieh and Rossi-Hansberg (2020) also find that rising concentration in the retail and wholesale sectors is entirely driven by an increase in the number of local markets served by top firms.

32. The unicorn companies are valued as of May 26, 2020.

33. Small firms can be unfamiliar to potential customers, and online platforms can, through their brand and reputation, enable market exchange in the presence of asymmetric information about the quality and trustworthiness of these suppliers.

34. This negative effect on jobs or wages among less-efficient incumbents may be reduced to the extent that incumbent firms meet part of the increased demand owing to lower market prices that result from the competition provided by new firms that enter (Schwellnus et al. 2019).

35. The countries include Belgium, France, Germany, Hungary, Italy, Poland, Spain, Sweden, and the United Kingdom.

References

Abraham, Katharine G., John Haltiwanger, Kristin Sandusky, and James Spletzer. 2019. "The Rise of the Gig Economy: Fact or Fiction?" *AEA Papers and Proceedings* 109: 357–61.

Andrews, Dan, Giuseppe Nicoletti, and Christina Timiliotis. 2018. "Digital Technology Diffusion: A Matter of Capabilities, Incentives or Both?" Economics Department Working Paper 1476, Organisation for Economic Co-operation and Development, Paris.

Apedo-Amah, Marie Christine, Besart Avdiu, Xavier Cirera, Marcio Cruz, Elwyn Davies, Arti Grover, Leonardo Iacovone, et al. 2020. "Unmasking the Impact of COVID-19 on Businesses: Firm-Level Evidence from across the World." Policy Research Working Paper 9434, World Bank, Washington, DC.

Araya, Daniel. 2019. "Top 10 Industries Transformed by Self-Driving Cars." *Forbes*, January 10.

Ariu, Andrea, and Giordano Mion. 2016. "Service Trade and Occupational Tasks: An Empirical Investigation." *World Economy* 40 (9): 1866–89.

Arvis, Jean-François, Paul E. Kent, Ben Shepherd, and Rajiv Nair. 2017. "Additive Manufacturing and the Diffusion of 3D Printing: Impact on International Trade." Unpublished manuscript, World Bank, Washington, DC.

Atiyas, Izak, and Mark Dutz. 2021. "Digital Technology Uses among Informal Micro-Sized Firms: Productivity and Jobs Outcomes in Senegal." Policy Research Working Paper 9573, World Bank, Washington DC.

Autor, David. 2014. "Polanyi's Paradox and the Shape of Employment Growth." Working Paper 20485, National Bureau of Economic Research, Cambridge, MA.

Autor, David H., and David Dorn. 2013. "The Growth of Low-Skill Service Jobs and the Polarization of the US Labor Market." *American Economic Review* 103 (5): 1553–97.

Autor, David H., Lawrence F. Katz, and Melissa S. Kearney. 2006. "Measuring and Interpreting Trends in Economic Inequality." *AEA Papers and Proceedings* 96 (2): 189–94.

Autor, David H., Lawrence F. Katz, and Melissa S. Kearney. 2008. "Trends in U.S. Wage Inequality: Revising the Revisionists." *Review of Economics and Statistics* 90 (2): 300–23.

Autor, David H., Frank Levy, and Richard J. Murnane. 2003. "The Skill Content of Recent Technological Change: An Empirical Exploration." *Quarterly Journal of Economics* 118 (4): 1279–1333.

Avdiu, Besart, and Gaurav Nayyar. 2020. "When Face-to-Face Interactions Become an Occupational Hazard: Jobs in the Time of COVID-19." *Economics Letters* 197: 109648.

Avgousti, Sotiris, Eftychios G. Christoforou, Andreas S. Panayides, Sotos Voskarides, Cyril Novales, Laurence Nouaille, Constantinos S. Pattichis, and Pierre Vieyres. 2016. "Medical Telerobotic Systems: Current Status and Future Trends." *BioMedical Engineering OnLine* 15 (1): 1–44.

Baldwin, Richard. 2019. *The Globotics Upheaval: Globalization, Robotics and the Future of Work.* New York: Oxford University Press.

Baldwin, Richard, and Rikard Forslid. 2020. "Globotics and Development: When Manufacturing Is Jobless and Services Are Tradable." Working Paper 26731, National Bureau of Economic Research, MA.

Basu, Susanto, John Fernald, and Miles Kimball. 2004. "Are Technology Improvements Contractionary?" Working Paper 10592, National Bureau of Economic Research, Cambridge, MA.

Baumol, William J. 1967. "Macroeconomics of Unbalanced Growth: The Anatomy of Urban Crisis." *American Economic Review* 57 (3): 415–26.

Bhatia, Abhishek, and Deepa Mani. 2020. "AI, Occupational Identity and Labor Markets: Evidence from India." Working Paper, Srini Raju Centre for IT and the Networked Economy (SRITNE), Indian School of Business, Hyderabad, India.

Bishop, Christopher M. 2006. *Pattern Recognition and Machine Learning.* New York: Springer.

Blinder, Alan S. 2009. "How Many US Jobs Might be Offshorable?" *World Economics* 10 (2): 41–78.

Blinder, Alan S., and Alan B. Krueger. 2013. "Alternative Measures of Offshorability: A Survey Approach." *Journal of Labor Economics* 31 (S1): S97–S128.

Bloom, Nicholas, Raffaella Sadun, and John Van Reenen. 2012. "Americans Do IT Better: US Multinationals and the Productivity Miracle." *American Economic Review* 102 (1): 167–201.

Bresnahan, Timothy. 2010. "General Purpose Technologies." In *Handbook of the Economics of Innovation*, vol. 2, edited by Bronwyn H. Hall and Nathan Rosenberg, 761–91. Amsterdam: Elsevier.

Bresnahan, Timothy F., and Manuel Trajtenberg. 1995. "General Purpose Technologies 'Engines of Growth'?" *Journal of Econometrics* 65 (1): 83–108.

Bronnenberg, Bart J., and Paul B. Ellickson. 2015. "Adolescence and the Path to Maturity in Global Retail." *Journal of Economic Perspectives* 29 (4): 113–34.

Brynjolfsson, Erik, and Lorin M. Hitt. 2000. "Beyond Computation: Information Technology, Organizational Transformation and Business Performance." *Journal of Economic Perspectives* 14 (4): 23–48.

Brynjolfsson, Erik, Lorin M. Hitt, and Shinkyu Yang. 2002. "Intangible Assets: Computers and Organizational Capital." *Brookings Papers on Economic Activity* 2002 (1): 137–98.

Brynjolfsson, Erik, Xiang Hui, and Meng Liu. 2019. "Does Machine Translation Affect International Trade? Evidence from a Large Digital Platform." *Management Science* 65 (12): 5449–5956.

Brynjolfsson, Erik, and Andrew McAfee. 2017. "What's Driving the Machine Learning Explosion?" *Harvard Business Review*, July 18.

Brynjolfsson, Erik, and Tom Mitchell. 2017. "What Can Machine Learning Do? Workforce Implications." *Science* 358 (6370): 1530–34.

Brynjolfsson, Erik, Tom Mitchell, and Daniel Rock. 2018. "What Can Machines Learn, and What Does It Mean for Occupations and the Economy?" *American Economic Review Papers and Proceedings* 108: 43–47.

Brynjolfsson, Erik, Daniel Rock, and Chad Syverson. 2021. "The Productivity J-Curve: How Intangibles Complement General Purpose Technologies." *American Economic Journal: Macroeconomics* 13 (1): 333–72.

Cathles, Alison, Gaurav Nayyar, and Désirée Rückert. 2020. "Digital Technologies and Firm Performance: Evidence from Europe." Working Paper 2020/06, European Investment Bank (EIB), Luxembourg.

CB Insights. 2020. "The Complete List of Unicorn Companies." Online company data as of May 26. CB Insights, New York.

Choi, Paul J., Rod J. Oskouian, and R. Shane Tubbs. 2018. "Telesurgery: Past, Present, and Future." *Cureus* 10 (5): e2716.

Cirera, Xavier, Diego Comin, Marcio Cruz, and Kyung Min Lee. 2020a. Technology Firm-level Adoption of Technologies in Senegal. Unpublished paper, World Bank, Washington, DC.

Cirera, Xavier, Diego A. Comin, Marcio Cruz, and Kyung Min Lee. 2020b. "Technology Within and Across Firms." Policy Research Working Paper 9476, World Bank, Washington, DC.

Cirera, Xavier, and William F. Maloney. 2017. *The Innovation Paradox: Developing-Country Capabilities and the Unrealized Promise of Technological Catch-Up.* Washington, DC: World Bank.

Cohen, Jason F., and Karen Olsen. 2013. "The Impacts of Complementary Information Technology Resources on the Service-Profit Chain and Competitive Performance of South African Hospitality Firms." *International Journal of Hospitality Management* 34 (1): 245–54.

Corrado, Carol, Jonathan Haskel, Cecilia Jona-Lasinio, and Massimiliano Iommi. 2018. "Intangible Investment in the EU and US Before and Since the Great Recession and Its Contribution to Productivity Growth." *Journal of Infrastructure, Policy and Development* 2 (1): 11–36 .

Corrado, Carol, Charles Hulten, and Daniel Sichel. 2005. "Measuring Capital and Technology: An Expanded Framework." In *Measuring Capital in the New Economy*, edited by Carol Corrado, John Haltiwanger, and Daniel Sichel, 11–46. Chicago: University of Chicago Press.

Cusolito, Ana P., Daniel Lederman, Fausto Patiño Peña, and Jorge Peña. 2020. "The Effects of Digital-Technology Adoption on Productivity and Factor Demand: Firm-Level Evidence from Developing Countries." Policy Research Working Paper 9333, World Bank, Washington, DC.

Cusolito, Ana P., and Fausto Patiño Peña. 2020. "How Digital-Technology Adoption Affects the Skill Composition of the Workforce: Firm-level Evidence for Manufacturing vs. Service Sectors in Developing Countries." Unpublished manuscript, World Bank, Washington, DC.

De Stefano, Valerio. 2016. "The Rise of the 'Just-in-Time Workforce': On-Demand Work, Crowdwork and Labour Protection in the 'Gig-Economy.'" Conditions of Work and Employment Series No. 71, International Labour Office, Geneva.

Demmou, Lilas, Irina Stefanescu, and Axelle Arquié. 2019. "Productivity Growth and Finance: The Role of Intangible Assets—A Sector Level Analysis." Economics Department Working Paper 1547, Organisation for Economic Co-operation and Development, Paris.

Dingel, Jonathan I., and Brent Neiman. 2020. "How Many Jobs Can Be Done at Home?" *Journal of Public Economics* 189 (2): 104235.

EY, FICCI, and NASSCOM (Ernst and Young, Federation of Indian Chambers of Commerce and Industry, and National Association of Software and Services Companies). 2017. "Future of Jobs in India: A 2022 Perspective." Report, Ernst and Young LLP, Kolkata.

Fraunhofer Institute. 2019. "Characterizing the New Data Economy: Big Shifts and Their Impact on Europe and the Wider Global Economy." Unpublished manuscript, Fraunhofer Institute, Munich.

Friedman, Gerald. 2014. "Workers without Employers: Shadow Corporations and the Rise of the Gig Economy." *Review of Keynesian Economics* 2 (2): 171–88.

Gawande, Atul. 2012. "Restaurant Chains Have Managed to Combine Quality Control, Cost Control, and Innovation. Can Health Care?" *New Yorker*, August 13.

GlobalWebIndex. 2018. "Social: GlobalWebIndex's Flagship Report on the Latest Trends in Social Media." Annual social media report, GlobalWebIndex, London. https://www.globalwebindex .com/hubfs/Downloads/Social-H2-2018-report.pdf.

Goldfarb, Avi, and Catherine Tucker. 2019. "Digital Economics." *Journal of Economic Literature* 57 (1): 3–43.

Goldman Sachs. 2019. "Music in the Air." Insights music industry report and infographics, Goldman Sachs, New York.

Goos, Maarten, and Alan Manning. 2003. "McJobs and MacJobs: The Growing Polarisation of Jobs in the UK." In *The Labour Market under New Labour: The State of Working Britain 2003*, edited by Richard Dickens, Paul Gregg, and Jonathan Wadsworth, 70–85. Basingstoke, UK: Palgrave Macmillan.

Hall, Jonathan V., and Alan B. Krueger. 2018. "An Analysis of the Labor Market for Uber's Driver-Partners in the United States." *ILR Review* 71 (3): 705–32.

Haller, Stefanie A., and Sean Lyons. 2019. "Effects of Broadband Availability on Total Factor Productivity in Service Sector Firms: Evidence from Ireland." *Telecommunications Policy* 43 (1): 11–22.

Hallward-Driemeier, Mary, and Gaurav Nayyar. 2018. *Trouble in the Making? The Future of Manufacturing-Led Development.* Washington, DC: World Bank.

Hallward-Driemeier, Mary, Gaurav Nayyar, Wolfgang Fengler, Anwar Aridi, and Indermit Gill. 2020. *Europe 4.0: Addressing the Digital Dilemma.* Washington, DC: World Bank.

Haskel, Jonathan, and Stian Westlake. 2018. *Capitalism without Capital: The Rise of the Intangible Economy.* Princeton, NJ: Princeton University Press.

Heeks, Richard. 2017. "Decent Work and the Digital Gig Economy: A Developing Country Perspective on Employment Impacts and Standards in Online Outsourcing, Crowdwork, Etc." Working Paper 71, Centre for Development Informatics, Global Development Institute, University of Manchester, UK.

Hoonsawat, Ratidanai. 2016. "Information Searching: The Case of Tourism Promoted through the Internet." *Global Economy Journal* 16 (1): 33–47.

Hortaçsu, Ali, and Chad Syverson. 2015. "The Ongoing Evolution of US Retail: A Format Tug-of-War." *Journal of Economic Perspectives* 29 (4): 89–112.

Horton, John, William R. Kerr, and Christopher Stanton. 2017. "Digital Labor Markets and Global Talent Flows." In *High-Skilled Migration to the United States and Its Economic Consequences*, edited by Gordon H. Hanson, William R. Kerr, and Sarah Turner, 71–108. Chicago: University of Chicago Press.

Hsieh, Chang-Tai, and Esteban Rossi-Handberg. 2020. "The Industrial Revolution in Services." Unpublished paper, Princeton University, Princeton, NJ.

Huws, Ursula, Neil H. Spencer, Dag S. Syrdal, and Kaire Holts. 2017. "Work in the European Gig Economy: Research Results from the UK, Sweden, Germany, Austria, the Netherlands, Switzerland and Italy." Report, Foundation for European Progressive Studies (FEPS), Brussels; UNI Europa, Brussels; and University of Hertfordshire, UK.

ITU (International Telecommunication Union). 2018. *Setting the Scene for 5G: Opportunities & Challenges.* Geneva: ITU.

Jullien, Bruno. 2012. "Two-Sided B to B Platforms." In *The Oxford Handbook of the Digital Economy*, edited by Martin Peitz and Joel Waldfogel, 161–85. Oxford: Oxford University Press.

Kässi, Otto, and Vili Lehdonvirta. 2018. "Online Labour Index: Measuring the Online Gig Economy for Policy and Research." *Technological Forecasting and Social Change* 137: 241–48.

Khatiwada, Sameer, and Mia Kim Maceda Veloso. 2019. "New Technology and Emerging Occupations: Evidence from Asia." Economics Working Paper 576, Asian Development Bank, Manila.

Kohavi, Ron, and Foster Provost. 1998. "Glossary of Terms." *Machine Learning* 30: 271–74.

Kuek, Siou Chew, Cecilia Paradi-Guilford, Toks Fayomi, Saori Imaizumi, Panos Ipeirotis, Patricia Pina, and Manpreet Singh. 2015. "The Global Opportunity in Online Outsourcing." Working paper, Report ACS14228, World Bank, Washington, DC.

Lapão, Luis Velez, and Gilles Dussault. 2017. "The Contribution of eHealth and mHealth to Improving the Performance of the Health Workforce: A Review." *Public Health Panorama* 3 (3): 463–71.

Lendle, Andreas, Marcelo Olarreaga, Simon Schropp, and Pierre-Louis Vézina. 2016. "There Goes Gravity: eBay and the Death of Distance." *Economic Journal* 126 (591): 406–41.

Lewis, Colin. 2014. "Robots Are Starting to Make Offshoring Less Attractive." *Harvard Business Review*, May 12.

Li, Wendy C. Y., Makoto Nirei, and Kazufumi Yamana. 2019. "Value of Data: There's No Such Thing as a Free Lunch in the Digital Economy." Discussion Paper 19-E-022RIETI, Research Institute of Economy, Trade, and Industry, Tokyo.

Lieber, Ethan, and Chad Syverson. 2012. "Online versus Offline Competition." In *The Oxford Handbook of the Digital Economy*, edited by Martin Peitz and Joel Waldfogel, 189–223. Oxford: Oxford University Press.

LinkedIn. 2018. "LinkedIn 2018 Emerging Jobs Report." Annual statistical report of Economic Graph team, LinkedIn, Mountain View, CA. https://economicgraph.linkedin.com/research/linkedin-2018-emerging-jobs-report.

Lopez-Cordova, Ernesto. 2020. "Digital Platforms and the Demand for International Tourism Services." Policy Research Working Paper 9147, World Bank, Washington, DC.

Maloney, William F., and Carlos Molina. 2016. "Are Automation and Trade Polarizing Developing Country Labor Markets, Too?" Policy Research Working Paper 7922, World Bank, Washington, DC.

Maloney, William, and Temel Taskin. 2020. "Determinants of Social Distancing and Economic Activity during COVID-19: A Global View." Policy Research Working Paper 9242, World Bank, Washington, DC.

Mandel, Michael. 2017. "How Ecommerce Creates Jobs and Reduces Income Inequality." Paper, Progressive Policy Institute, Washington, DC.

Manyika, James, Susan Lund, Michael Chui, Jacques Bughin, Jonathan Woetzel, Parul Batra, Ryan Ko, and Saurabh Sanghvi. 2017. "Jobs Lost, Jobs Gained: Workforce Transitions in a Time of Automation." Report, McKinsey Global Institute, McKinsey & Company, New York.

McAfee, Andrew, and Erik Brynjolfsson. 2012. "Big Data: The Management Revolution." *Harvard Business Review* 90 (10): 60–68.

Mohamed, Intan Salwani, Govindan Marthandan, Mohd Daud Norzaidi, and Siong-Choy Chong. 2009. "E-Commerce Usage and Business Performance in the Malaysian Tourism Sector: Empirical Analysis." *Information Management and Computer Security* 17 (2): 166–85.

Muñiz, Sandra. 2018. "Artificial Intelligence Causes BPO Jobs to Decline." *BPO News*, May 4.

Nielsen. 2014. "Global Consumers Embrace the Share Economy." Nielsen press release, May 28.

Nomura, Shinsaku, Saori Imaizumi, Ana Carolina Areias, and Futoshi Yamauchi. 2017. "Toward Labor Market Policy 2.0: The Potential for Using Online Job-Portal Big Data to Inform Labor Market Policies in India." Policy Research Working Paper 7966, World Bank, Washington, DC.

OECD (Organisation for Economic Co-operation and Development). 2010. *The OECD Innovation Strategy: Getting a Head Start on Tomorrow*. Paris: OECD.

OECD and Eurostat (Organisation for Economic Co-operation and Development and the statistical office of the European Union). 2005. *Oslo Manual: Guidelines for Collecting and Interpreting Innovation*. 3rd ed. Paris: OECD; Luxembourg: Eurostat.

Oldenski, Lindsay. 2012. "Export versus FDI and the Communication of Complex Information." *Journal of International Economics* 87 (2): 312–22.

Ollivaud, Patrice, and Peter Haxton. 2019. "Making the Most of Tourism in Indonesia to Promote Sustainable Regional Development." Economics Department Working Paper 1535, Organisation for Economic Co-operation and Development (OECD), Paris.

Paredes, Luis Hernando Lozano, and Katherine M. A. Reilly. 2018. "Decent Work for Ride Hailing Workers in the Platform Economy in Cali, Colombia." In *Urban Transport in the Sharing Economy Era*, edited by Cooperative Cities Program of the Center for the Implementation of Public Policies for Equity and Growth (CIPPEC), 92–127. Buenos Aires: CIPPEC.

Polder, Michael, George van Leeuwen, Pierre Mohnen, and Wladimir Raymond. 2010. "Product, Process and Organizational Innovation: Drivers, Complementarity and Productivity Effects." Working Paper 2010-035, Maastricht Economic and Social Research Institute on Innovation and Technology (MERIT), United Nations University, Maastricht, Netherlands.

Rivares, Alberto Bailin, Peter Gal, Valentine Millot, and Stéphane Sorbe. 2019. "Like It or Not? The Impact of Online Platforms on the Productivity of Incumbent Service Providers." Economics Department Working Paper 1548, Organisation for Economic Co-operation and Development, Paris.

Sáez, Sebastian, Ruchita Manghnani, Martin Kanz, Deepa Mani, Gaurav Nayyar, and Erik van der Marel. 2019. "Competitiveness of India's IT/ITeS Sector." Unpublished manuscript, World Bank, Washington, DC.

Schulte, Julius. 2019. "AI-Assisted Recruitment Is Biased. Here's How to Make It More Fair." *Agenda* article, May 9, World Economic Forum, Cologny, Switzerland. https://www.weforum.org /agenda/2019/05/ai-assisted-recruitment-is-biased-heres-how-to-beat-it/.

Schwellnus, Cyrille, Assaf Geva, Mathilde Pak, and Rafael Veiel. 2019. "Gig Economy Platforms: Boon or Bane?" Economics Department Working Paper 1550, Organisation for Economic Co-operation and Development, Paris.

Shankar, Venkatesh. 2018. "How Artificial Intelligence (AI) Is Reshaping Retailing." *Journal of Retailing* 94 (4): vi–xi.

Shead, Sam. 2017. "Londoners Are Turning to Apps So They Don't Have to Buy a Car." *Insider*, June 29.

Stapleton, Katherine, and Layla O'Kane. 2021. "Artificial Intelligence and Services Offshoring." Unpublished manuscript, World Bank, Washington, DC; and Burning Glass Technologies, Boston.

Sundarajan, Arun. 2016. *The Sharing Economy: The End of Employment and the Rise of Crowd-Based Capitalism*. Cambridge, MA: MIT Press.

Villa Espinosa, Diego Mauricio, José Luis Miñana Terol, and Fernando Raimundo González-Ladrón-de-Guevara. 2018. "Relationship between Information and Communication Technology and Competitiveness in the Tourism Industry: A Mapping Review." *RITUR-Revista Iberoamericana de Turismo* 8 (2): 143–73.

Wall, James, and Jacques Marescaux. 2013. "History of Telesurgery." In *Telemicrosurgery: Robot Assisted Surgery*, edited by Philippe A. Liverneaux, Stacey H. Berner, Michael S. Bednar, Sijo J. Parekattil, Gustavo Mantovani Ruggiero, and Jesse C. Selber, 15–18. Paris: Springer-Verlag.

Wood Alex J., Mark Graham, Vili Lehdonvirta, and Isis Hjorth. 2019. "Good Gig, Bad Gig: Autonomy and Algorithmic Control in the Global Gig Economy." *Work, Employment and Society* 33 (1): 56–75.

World Bank. 2018. "The Voice of Travelers: Leveraging User-Generated Content for Tourism Development." Report 130052, World Bank, Washington, DC.

World Bank. 2020. *World Development Report 2020: Trading for Development in the Age of Global Value Chains*. Washington, DC: World Bank.

Wu, Chunhua, Yanwen Wang, and Ting Zhu. 2016. "Mobile Hailing Technology Adoption, Digital Inequality, and Worker Productivity: A Case of the Taxi Industry." Working paper, University of British Columbia, Vancouver, Canada.

Zhang, Sha, Koen Pauwels, and Chenming Peng. 2019. "The Impact of Adding Online-to-Offline Service Platform Channels on Firms' Offline and Total Sales and Profits." *Journal of Interactive Marketing* 47 (2): 115–28.

4 Look Before You Leap: Services Before Manufacturing?

Introduction

Following the conventional structural change process, high-income countries and large emerging economies with a sizable industrial base have moved up the value chain of manufactured goods by diversifying out of "production" per se into services—either those "embodied" in goods as part of the manufacturing process (for example, design or research and development [R&D]) or those "embedded" in goods during postproduction (such as marketing, branding, and other add-on services). These services increasingly account for much of the value added in a manufactured product's supply chain, as illustrated by the "smile curve" (coined by Stan Shih, Acer's CEO in the early 1990s) and further discussed below.

In hitherto less industrialized lower-income countries, the relevant question therefore is whether services subsectors—especially those with higher productivity growth rates and longer-term potential for scale, innovation, and spillovers—*need* a manufacturing core to develop. Chapter 2 identified the "global innovators" (information and communication services; professional, scientific, and technical services; and finance) as services subsectors whose high productivity growth was underpinned by a greater incidence of scale, innovation, and spillovers, albeit with greater skilled-labor intensity. Further, chapter 3 showed that "low-skill tradable services" (transportation services, accommodation and food, and wholesale trade) increasingly provide *opportunities* to achieve scale economies and innovation while also absorbing low-skilled labor. Understanding where demand for these types of services is growing, and how demand may be shifting, also helps determine their contribution to growth and jobs.

Services often cater to final demand, including through direct exports. They also cater to intermediate demand from other sectors within a country. To the extent that final demand contributes substantially to the growth of these services subsectors, opportunities can be created independent of a country's manufacturing base. These opportunities might be reinforced if intermediate demand for a given services subsector derives largely from sectors other than manufacturing.

At the same time, the importance of these services to enable a strong manufacturing sector cannot be underemphasized. To the extent that services serve intermediate demand from the manufacturing sector, they are embodied in manufactured goods and hence important for manufacturers' productivity. Further, services are increasingly *embedded* in the postproduction of goods (such as through marketing, sales, and after-sales care) in ways that differentiate products in the market. These linkages between sectors can help alleviate the productivity-jobs dichotomy discussed in chapter 2.

The rest of the chapter is organized as follows. It first analyzes the diversification of more-industrialized countries into higher-value-added services, which has upgraded their positions in global value chains for manufactured goods. Subsequently, for less-industrialized countries, it explores two channels for high-productivity services to develop in the absence of a manufacturing core—by growing either exports (serving final demand in the world market) or sales to other sectors in the economy (serving domestic intermediate demand). It also examines the ways in which services are increasingly important for developing or strengthening a manufacturing base. Last but not least, it highlights how intersectoral linkages boost productive opportunities associated with services-led growth for low-skilled workers.

Services and Value Chain Upgrading in Industrialized Countries

Services increasingly account for much of the value added in the supply chain of manufactured goods. The "smile curve" alludes to a U-shaped relationship between the stage of production in a supply chain and its contribution to total value added. It suggests that upstream activities (such as R&D and product design services), together with downstream activities (such as branding and advertising services), constitute a large share of value added, but the intermediate production stages (such as component manufacturing and final assembly) do not.

Apple's iPhone illustrates a case in which merchandise components and their assembly constitute less than one-third of the product's total value, while services—such as R&D, design, software development, engineering, marketing, retail, and distribution—account for two-thirds (Drake-Brockman and Stephenson 2012). Ali-Yrkkö et al. (2011) produce a more detailed breakdown of the value-added contributions of services and manufacturing components for the Nokia N95 smartphone, among the most popular consumer-focused smartphones in the 2000s. The parts (including processors, memories, integrated circuits, displays, and cameras) accounted for 33 percent of the product's value, whereas assembly accounted for only 2 percent. The remaining two-thirds of the product's value came from Nokia's internal support services (30 percent), licenses (4 percent), distribution (4 percent), retailing (11 percent), and operating profit (16 percent).

Low and Pasadilla (2016) also take a firm-level case study approach to analyze a range of manufacturing value chains around the East Asia and Pacific region. They find that in the Chinese bread value chain, for example, approximately 30 different services categories are involved in production, contributing about 72 percent of the product's value. Similarly, West (2018) finds that services such as R&D, retail, logistics, and banking account for almost 90 percent of the total sales value of a jacket.

Servicification Trends in Industrialized Countries

For firms in industrialized countries, using their established manufacturing core to diversify into related but higher-value-added services is the natural progression. "Servicification" describes this development, whereby manufacturing firms increasingly produce, sell, and export more services as integrated activities (National Board of Trade of Sweden 2016).

An analysis of data across 23 countries for 2007, 2009, and 2011 finds that 30 percent of manufacturing firms, on average, sold services too (Neely, Benedettini, and Visnjic 2011). This share of servitized firms ranged from 55 percent of manufacturers in the United States to 19 percent in China. Other estimates show that in France, the share of servitized firms remained stable at 69 percent from 1997 to 2007 (Crozet and Milet 2017), while in Sweden nearly all firms are servitized (Lodefalk 2013, 2015).

The extent to which manufacturers sell services has also increased over time, as several cases illustrate: In Sweden, the share of services in the sales of manufacturing firms increased from 13.6 to 20.3 percent between 1997 and 2006 (Lodefalk 2013, 2015). In France, this share remained close to 17–18 percent between 1997 and 2007 (Crozet and Milet 2017). In the United Kingdom, this share increased from 5 percent in 1997 to slightly over 20 percent in 2007 (Breinlich, Soderbery, and Wright 2014).

This servicification of manufacturing is apparent specifically among exporters as well. Transactions data from Belgium show that manufacturers that export both goods and services accounted for about 44.8 percent of total manufactured goods exports and 42.3 percent of services exports (Ariu, Mayneris, and Parenti 2020). Further, among these firms, one-fourth of the exports of manufactured goods were triggered by services.

Evidence suggests that manufacturing firms offer a wide range of services that include both global innovator services and low-skill tradable services. Among them, based on evidence from 23 countries, Neely (2008) identified management consulting; design and development; financial leasing; repair and maintenance; and retail and distribution services. In Sweden, wholesale, retail, and repair are the top-selling services of manufacturing firms, while computer-related services represent a smaller share of sales (Lodefalk 2013). In the European Union (EU), more broadly, 55 percent of manufacturing firms offer distribution services, and 32 percent offer business services (National Board of Trade of Sweden 2016). In contrast, US manufacturers primarily offer business services such as R&D (Barefoot and Koncz-Bruner 2012).

High-tech manufacturing seems to be leading the trend toward servicification. In France, the mechanical and electrical equipment industries are the most servitized, with a service intensity (share of revenue from selling services) of 5 percent, in contrast to food, beverages, and tobacco, which collectively have the lowest service intensity, close to 1 percent (Crozet and Milet 2017). In the EU, the share of revenue from selling services is 6 percent in more technology-intensive industries, compared with 3 percent and 4 percent in medium- and low-tech manufacturing, respectively (National Board of Trade of Sweden 2016). Technology-intensive manufacturing has a higher service intensity because servicification often results from innovation; manufacturing industries that introduce new products are also more likely to sell complementary services (Biege et al. 2012; Dachs et al. 2012).

Shifts in Manufacturing Global Value Chains

This servicification of manufacturing in more-industrialized countries has been driven, in large part, by the fragmentation of production in global value chains (GVCs). Leading firms in high-income countries have typically retained the more skill-intensive parts of the chain, such as upstream and downstream services, while outsourcing the low-skill, labor-intensive assembly of manufactured goods to low- and middle-income countries (LMICs).

Where the Jobs Are Going

This trend is reflected in a compositional shift away from production jobs to services jobs within the manufacturing sector in high-income countries. In the United States, the share of professional and managerial service workers in the manufacturing sector increased by 6 percentage points between 1990 and 2012, while the share of production workers, operatives, and laborers declined (figure 4.1). Conversely, across LMICs since 2000, the average shares of machine operators and other elementary occupations (manual laborers) in the manufacturing sector increased, respectively, by 3 and 1.5 percentage points (figure 4.2).

These trends are consistent with the examples of traditional manufacturing firms such as Apple, Dyson, or H&M, which locate the R&D, design, and branding services at their headquarters in the United States or Europe while largely offshoring production jobs to lower-cost locations (Bernard and Fort 2015). In a seminal paper, Bernard, Smeets, and Warzynski (2017) show that a non-negligible portion of the relative and absolute declines in manufacturing employment and firms in Denmark between 1994 and 2007 is explained by firms switching industries—from manufacturing to services. By 2007, employment at these former manufacturers equaled 8.7 percent of manufacturing employment, accounting for half the sector's employment decline.

FIGURE 4.1 **The Share of Professional and Managerial Service Workers in the US Manufacturing Sector Has Increased Significantly since 1990**

Change in shares of occupations within the US manufacturing sector, by type, 1990–2012

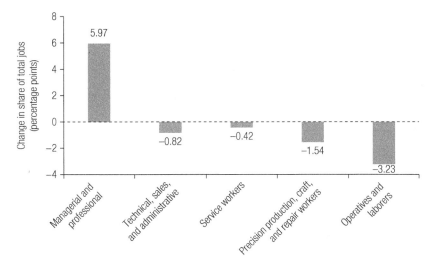

Source: Calculations based on Integrated Public Use Microdata Series (IPUMS) US database, Minnesota Population Center, University of Minnesota.

FIGURE 4.2 **In LMICs since 2000, the Share of Production Workers in Manufacturing Has Increased**

Change in shares of occupations within manufacturing sectors across LMICs, by type, 2000–14

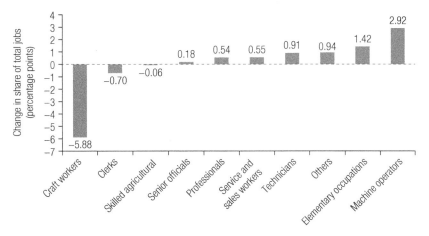

Source: Calculations based on World Bank's International Income Distribution Database (I2D2).

Note: Sample dataset includes 41 low- and middle-income countries (LMICs) across all regions. Graph shows the average percentage-point change in share of total manufacturing employment. LMICs, by World Bank income group classifications, had 1994 gross national income of less than US$8,955. "Elementary occupations" refers to manual laborers.

Country Readiness to Upgrade

Much like high-income countries, LMICs with a strong industrial base can benefit from upgrading their positions in GVCs by increasing the share of services-intensive tasks. But which countries are ready? Figure 4.3 identifies four groups of countries by (a) level of industrialization, and (b) whether their manufacturing base is expanding or shrinking.

The first cluster—the readiest to upgrade—comprises eight middle-income countries (as defined in 1994) in East Asia and Europe and Central Asia: China, the Czech Republic, Indonesia, the Republic of Korea, Malaysia, the Philippines, Thailand, and Turkey. In 1994, manufacturing value added made up 20–30 percent of GDP in these countries, and this share did not change substantially between 1994 and 2015. It increased by 1–2 percentage points in the Czech Republic, Korea, and Thailand but declined by 2–4 percentage points in China, Indonesia, Malaysia, the Philippines, and Turkey.

The second cluster comprises four countries, also in East Asia and Europe and Central Asia, that although relatively small in their share in global manufacturing, might increasingly benefit from diversifying into higher-value-added services. This cluster includes Hungary, Poland, the Slovak Republic, and Vietnam—countries

FIGURE 4.3   LMICs Can Be Grouped into Four Clusters Based on Their Level of Industrialization

Manufacturing value added as a share of GDP, 1994 relative to 2015

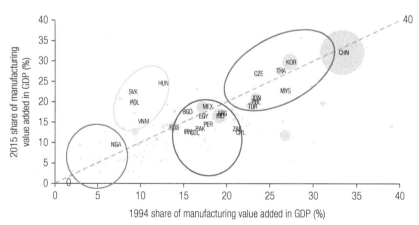

Sources: Calculations using data from the World Development Indicators and United Nations Industrial Development Organization (UNIDO) Manufacturing Value Added (MVA) databases.

Note: Bubble size represents a country's share in global manufacturing value added in 2015. Circle colors designate country clusters by two criteria—(a) level of industrialization, and (b) whether their manufacturing base is expanding or shrinking—that indicate readiness to upgrade their participation in global value chains (GVCs) by increasing their services intensity (share of revenue from selling services). Green indicates low- and middle-income countries (LMICs) with a large manufacturing base, albeit sightly diminished in some by 2015. Yellow indicates LMICs with the largest 1994–2015 increase in manufacturing's GDP share from a sizable base. Red indicates those with a moderately high, but shrinking, manufacturing base. Blue indicates those with the smallest manufacturing base. LMICs, by World Bank income group classifications, had 1994 gross national income of less than US$8,955. Countries are labeled using ISO alpha-3 codes.

whose share of manufacturing value added in GDP was 10–15 percent in 1994 and increased notably over the next two decades.

The third cluster comprises 11 countries spanning the Middle East and North Africa, Latin America, and South Asia: Argentina, Bangladesh, Chile, Colombia, the Arab Republic of Egypt, India, the Islamic Republic of Iran, Mexico, Morocco, Pakistan, and Peru. In these countries, manufacturing value added was 15–20 percent of GDP in 1994, although this share declined in most of the countries by 1–5 percentage points over the next two decades. By 2015, it had increased only in Bangladesh and Mexico, by 1–2 percentage points.

The fourth cluster comprises a large cross-section of countries, especially in Sub-Saharan Africa, that account for a negligible share in global manufacturing value added and whose share of manufacturing in GDP was as low as 5–10 percent between 1994 and 2015. Therefore—even in Botswana, Lesotho, Nigeria, and Uganda, where share of manufacturing value added in GDP increased by 2–4 percentage points between 1994 and 2014—this improvement was from very low base shares.

The central question for countries in the third and fourth clusters is the extent to which services with productivity potential can grow in the absence of a robust manufacturing base.

The scope for growth in the services sector beyond links to the manufacturing sector depends on the size of two channels: The first is the growth in final demand, especially the ability to export directly as a way to serve larger markets. The second is the growth in domestic demand from sectors other than manufacturing—that is, the role of services as inputs into agriculture, mining, construction, utilities, and other services. The next section looks at each in turn.

Services Growth without a Manufacturing Core

Growth in Final Demand: Expanding Services Exports

Services subsectors vary in the extent to which they serve either (a) final demand, comprising consumption, investment, and (net) exports; or (b) intermediate demand from other sectors in the economy. Growth opportunities linked to final demand will not depend directly on a country's manufacturing base.

Among these subsectors, "skill-intensive social services" (such as health and education) are almost entirely stand-alone services. Many "low-skill domestic services" (including retail trade, household activities, and other personal services) and certain "low-skill tradable services" (including accommodation and food services) also overwhelmingly serve final demand. Final demand accounts for smaller shares of output among other low-skill tradables (such as wholesale trade and transportation services) and among all the "global innovator services."

However, these smaller shares do not rule out the role of final demand in shaping growth opportunities for these subsectors. Among global innovator services, for example, a range of information and computer-related services are embedded in manufactured goods in ways that do not require countries to have a manufacturing base. For instance, local language and cultural considerations matter for mobile-phone applications, and technological solutions need to be adapted in areas with low communication coverage—for example, by using narrowband instead of broadband, mobile money instead of bank transfers, and so on. This market for apps development and start-ups is booming everywhere, including in Sub-Saharan Africa, where several incubators and accelerators have emerged and the development of local technological solutions and start-ups is supported (Bamber et al. 2017).

At the same time, the growth opportunities from final demand will be limited to the size of the domestic market *unless* exports account for a large share of final demand. And despite their lower share of final demand in total output, global innovator services and low-skill tradable services have higher shares of *exports* in total output, as shown in chapter 1. The share of exports in the total output of information and communication technology (ICT) services—on average, across 40 countries—was close to 20 percent in 2014. The corresponding shares were approximately 15 percent for wholesale trade and transportation services (low-skill tradables) and 10 percent for other global innovators: financial services and professional, scientific, and technical services (figure 4.4).

Among the global innovators (as chapter 1 showed), cross-border supply, including through digital delivery, accounted for a notable share of international trade. This has allowed countries to specialize in the production and export of offshore services—computer programming, software development, business process outsourcing (BPO), accounting, and architectural and engineering services—just like manufactured goods.

Among the low-skill tradable services, tourism-related accommodation and food services as well as passenger transportation services have also enabled such specialization. The exports of freight transportation and wholesale trade, in contrast, are closely linked to the export of goods.

The export intensity was lowest in skill-intensive social services and low-skill domestic services—the two groups in which the final-demand intensity was the highest. These services are less amenable to specialization, but this does not imply the absence of all exporting opportunities—especially for health and education.

The Big Exporters

Services in high-income economies. Trade costs in services are lowest among high-income economies (WTO 2019). It is therefore not surprising that the large majority of the top 10 exporting economies in each of the global innovator services and low-skill tradable services between 2005 and 2017 were high-income economies (varying by service): Australia; Canada; France; Germany; Hong Kong SAR,

FIGURE 4.4 **Services That Predominantly Serve Final Demand Are Less Exported**

Shares of final demand and exports in total output of selected services subsectors, by group, 2014

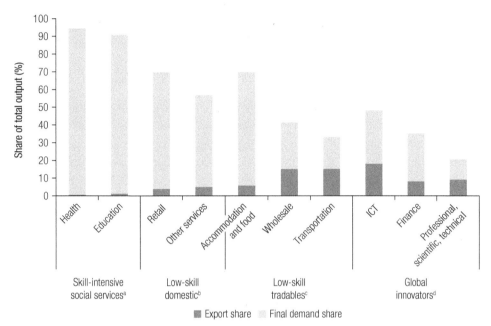

Source: Calculations based on World Input-Output Database.

Note: The dataset covers 40 countries—primarily high-income countries, but also large low- and middle-income countries (LMICs) such as Brazil, China, India, Indonesia, the Republic of Korea, Mexico, and Turkey, as well as several smaller European LMICs such as Bulgaria, Croatia, and Romania. The dataset covers all regions except the Middle East and North Africa and Sub-Saharan Africa. Final demand comprises consumption, investment, and (net) exports. ICT = information and communication technology.

a. Skill-intensive social services employ a relatively low share of low-skilled workers in services such as health and education. Although less traded internationally than other subsector groups, they can be exported through such means as foreign direct investment (FDI), enrollment of foreign students, and "medical tourism."

b. Low-skill domestic services employ mostly low-skilled workers (those with only primary education or less). With some exceptions, they have few linkages to other sectors and are less tradable internationally than other subsector groups. "Other services" refers to administrative and support services; arts, entertainment, and recreation services; and other social, community, and personal services.

c. Low-skill tradable services employ mostly low-skilled workers and are considered tradable in international markets. Some (such as transportation and warehousing) are relatively capital intensive, have linkages to other sectors, and may be amenable to offshoring.

d. Global innovator services employ mostly high-skilled workers (those with postsecondary education or more) and are highly traded in international markets. Collectively, they have the greatest linkages with other sectors and are particularly amenable to offshoring. Some are relatively capital intensive and also characterized by high research and development (R&D) intensity.

China; Ireland; Italy; Japan; the Netherlands, Singapore, Spain, Switzerland, the United Kingdom, and the United States.[1]

The share of exports from high-income countries across global innovator services remained high between 2005 and 2017, albeit declining over time. Their share of global exports of financial services was as high as 95 percent in 2005 but declined to 89 percent in 2017. Similarly, high-income countries exported 94 percent of ICT services globally in 2005, a share that declined to 86 percent in 2017. They also exported 90 percent of professional, scientific, and technical services globally in 2005, but this share declined to 75 percent in 2017 (figure 4.5).

High-income countries' share in world exports of transportation services and accommodation and food services was lower and declined further over time. In transportation services, they accounted for 80 percent of global exports in 2005, which declined to 75 percent in 2017. Similarly, these countries' share in world exports of accommodation and food services declined from 66 percent in 2005 to 61 percent in 2017.

Services in LMICs. As the high-income countries' collective share in global exports of services has declined, the resulting increase in the LMICs' share of world exports across different services subsectors has been concentrated among a few large emerging markets. In 2017, the top 10 exporting LMICs accounted for more than three-fourths of LMICs' total exports of global innovator services (finance, ICT, and professional services). These top 10 countries' corresponding shares of low-skill tradable services were lower—amounting to about 60 percent of transportation services and 50 percent of accommodation and food services (figure 4.6).

Across the global innovator services, the top 10 LMIC exporters between 2005 and 2017 typically included Brazil, China, Hungary, India, Indonesia, Korea, Malaysia, Mexico, the Philippines, Poland, the Russian Federation, South Africa, and Saudi Arabia (figure 4.7, panels a–c).[2]

Across the low-skill tradable services, the top 10 LMIC exporters between 2005 and 2017 was a similar group, typically comprising Brazil, China, Egypt, India, Indonesia, Korea, Malaysia, Mexico, Russia, Thailand, and Turkey (figure 4.7, panels d–f).[3]

FIGURE 4.5 **High-Income Countries Account for Declining Shares of Global Services Exports**

Share of high-income countries in global exports of selected services subsectors, 2005–17

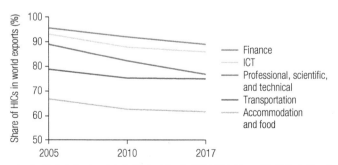

Source: Calculations using the Trade in Services data by Mode of Supply (TiSMoS) database, World Trade Organization.

Note: High-income countries (HICs) are those whose gross national income per capita was at least US$8,955 in 1994. ICT = information and communication technology.

At Your Service? The Promise of Services-Led Development

FIGURE 4.6 **A Few Large Emerging Markets Account for Most of the Services Exports from LMICs**

Share of the top 10 exporting LMICs in selected services subsectors, 2017

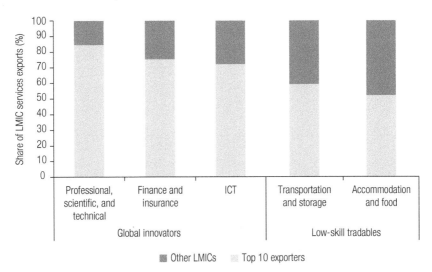

Source: Calculations using the Trade in Services data by Mode of Supply (TiSMoS) database, World Trade Organization.

Note: The top 10 exporting low- and middle-income countries (LMICs) in each services subsector are measured by the value of exports in US dollars. LMICs, by World Bank income group classifications, had 1994 gross national income of less than US$8,955. ICT = information and communications technology.

LMICs among the top 10 global exporters. A few LMICs were among the top 10 global exporters of services between 2005 and 2017. The rise of China as a manufacturing powerhouse often obfuscates its rising importance as an exporter of global innovator services. China in 2005 was already the 5th-largest exporter of professional, scientific, and technical services.[4] And although China was outside the top 10 exporting countries for financial services until 2010, it was the 10th-largest exporter in 2017. Furthermore, China was the 7th-largest exporter of wholesale and retail services in 2010 and 2017, and it went from being the 10th-largest exporter of transportation services in 2010 to the 7th-largest in 2017. China's success in exporting these low-skill tradable services is perhaps less surprising, given that its exports are closely linked to the export of goods.

Among the other most successful LMICs, India—much cited for its success in exporting software services—was the 8th-largest exporter of ICT services in 2017, having been outside the top 10 until 2010.[5] Korea, reinforcing its position as a global manufacturing hub, has become a leading global exporter of low-skill tradable services. Outside of the top 10 till 2010, Korea was the 8th-largest exporter of wholesale (and retail) services in 2017. Similarly, Korea was the 8th-largest exporter of transportation services in 2010, although it exited the top 10 in 2017. In accommodation and food services, Turkey was the 8th-largest exporter in 2010, and Thailand was the 4th-largest

FIGURE 4.7 **Large Emerging Economies Are the Biggest LMIC Exporters across Services Subsectors**

Top 10 exporting economies among LMICs, by services subsector, 2005–17

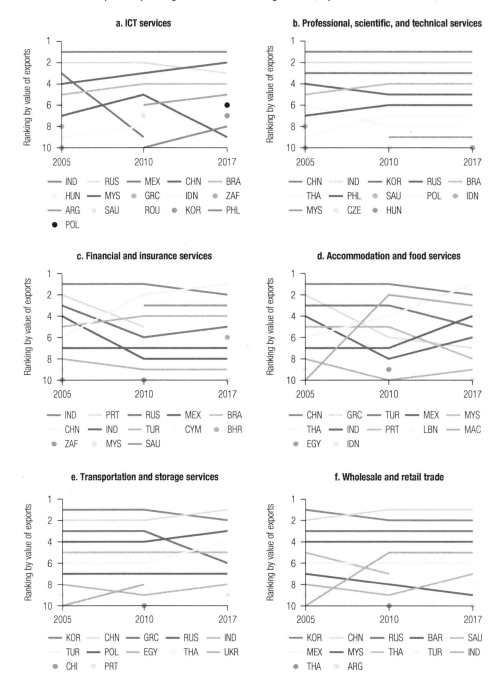

Source: Calculations using Trade in Services data by Mode of Supply (TiSMoS) database, World Trade Organization.

Note: The top 10 exporting low- and middle-income countries (LMICs) in each services subsector are measured by the value of exports in US dollars. LMICs, by World Bank income group classifications, had 1994 gross national income of less than US$8,955. Economies are labeled using ISO alpha-3 codes. ICT = information and communication technology.

At Your Service? The Promise of Services-Led Development

exporter in 2017 (having been outside the top 10 until 2010).[6] Notably, the export success of these large emerging economies was attributable, in large part, to firms establishing affiliates abroad (WTO 2019).

Export Diversification through Global Innovator Services

The share of global innovator services in total services exports is positively associated with per capita income (figure 4.8). This is consistent with the fact that the export of these services has been shown to depend on human capital, the quality of telecommunications networks, and the quality of institutions (Kimura and Lee 2006; Lennon, Mirza, and Nicoletti 2009; Shingal 2010).[7] Yet numerous LMICs, including those beyond the big exporters, have successfully diversified their export baskets through offshore global innovator services.

FIGURE 4.8 **Global Innovator Services Make Up Larger Shares of Total Services Exports in HICs Than in LMICs**

Share of global innovators in countries' services exports in relation to per capita income, 2017

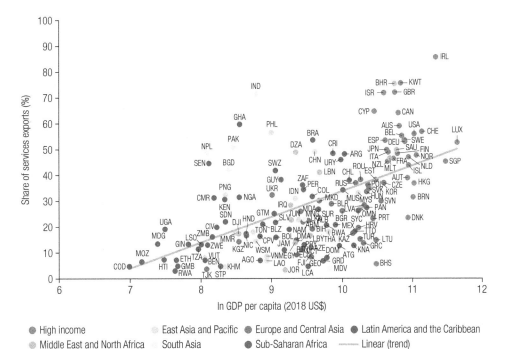

Sources: Calculations using the Trade in Services by Mode of Supply (TiSMoS) database, World Trade Organization; and World Development Indicators database.

Note: Data cover 162 countries across all regions. Global innovator services—including information and communication technology (ICT); professional, scientific, and technical services; and financial and insurance services—employ mostly high-skilled workers, are highly traded internationally, and are the most amenable to offshoring. Countries are labeled using ISO alpha-3 codes, and income groups are defined according to World Bank Group classification by gross national income in 1994. HIC = high-income country; LMIC = low- or middle-income country; ln = natural log.

Business process outsourcing (BPO). BPO services, for example, have been pivotal in the evolution of the Philippines from an agriculture-based economy where manufacturing has played only a limited role. Global innovator services accounted for more than half of the Philippines' services exports in 2017—considerably higher than the average for its level of per capita income—and that success is attributed to a large pool of relatively low-cost English-speaking workers, low telecommunications and internet costs, and similarities with the US legal and educational system (box 4.1).

Similarly, Costa Rica, where global innovator services accounted for about half of the country's services exports in 2017—considerably higher than the average for its level of per capita income—was a pioneer in attracting offshore BPO services to Latin America, drawing on its proximity to the United States' central time zone and largely bilingual population.

And at even a lower level of per capita income, the high share of global innovators in Ghana's 2017 services exports—60 percent—was also driven by its success in offshore business services. The Ministry of Communications' Accra Digital Centre, a BPO hub established in 2011, was an important enabler, and Ghana was ranked as the number one destination in Sub-Saharan Africa in A. T. Kearney's 2016 Global Services Location Index.[8]

ICT services. South Asian countries stand out. That the share of global innovator services in India's services exports was as high as 70 percent in 2017 is not surprising, given that it is one of the big global exporters. What is less discussed is the success of Bangladesh and Pakistan (box 4.2), whose corresponding shares were 40 percent and 50 percent, respectively—considerably higher than the average at their levels of per capita income. These countries' global innovator exports consisted largely of software and other ICT services, attributable to an abundant supply of skilled workers who are proficient in the English language (including a large pool of online freelancers, as discussed in chapter 3).

Financial services. The strong exporting performance of Kenya and Lebanon in global innovator services is attributable to financial services, which alone accounted for 20 percent of those countries' total services exports in 2017. Exploiting the potential for banking services in their own region, nine Kenyan banks have subsidiaries in other East African Community (EAC) countries.[9] From 2011 to 2016, the number of Kenyan bank branches abroad increased from 211 to 297 (WTO 2019). The subsector's liberalization has been an important driving factor where, at the end of 2017, fully foreign-owned banks accounted for one-third of Kenya's commercial banks (15 out of 42) and total banking assets (WTO 2019). Egypt and Lebanon have similarly emerged as regional hubs for exporting financial services in the Arab world, with banks establishing branches and wholly owned subsidiaries abroad.

The Philippines' Emergence in the Offshore Services Industry

The Philippines is a relative newcomer to GVCs among the countries in the Association of Southeast Asian Nations (ASEAN). Over the past few decades, its economy has evolved from being agriculturally based to being dependent on services, with manufacturing playing a more marginal role (Bamber et al. 2017).

Services in the Philippines have been dominated by the emergence of a strong call center base. Among the first firms to set up call center operations in the country were US-based America Online (AOL) and SYKES,[12] both in 1997. The country's cultural affinity with the United States rapidly gave it a competitive edge over India's call centers.

The resulting growth was explosive: in 2004, the sector employed approximately 100,000 people, generating US$1.4 billion in exports (Kleibert 2015). By 2015, the offshore services sector had over 1.2 million full-time employees, with an estimated US$22 billion in exports, which is 20 percent of the Philippines' total exports (Price, Francisco, and Caboverde 2016). This success also made the BPO sector the second-largest contributor to the Philippines' foreign-exchange earnings, after remittances (Shead 2017). In addition, the Philippine BPO sector tripled its share of the global BPO market—from 4 percent in 2004 to 12.3 percent in 2014 (Errighi, Bodwell, and Khatiwada 2016).

The country's participation has been predominantly in voice-based call center operations. These cover a wide range of tasks, such as negotiating credit card repayments, troubleshooting, and booking flights and hotel room services, among others. Having successfully established itself as the market leader in these voice-based services at the turn of the century, the country began upgrading into nonvoice procedures, including email, chat, and even social-media branding as well as back-office operations for finance and accounting and human resources. JP Morgan Chase, Citibank, Deutsche Bank, HSBC, Wells Fargo, and Bank of America are among the firms with fully owned back offices in the Philippines (Kleibert 2015). These back offices are typically quite large; for example, Accenture's operations employ 45,000 people, making it one of the largest employers in the country. Even many back-office finance and accounting services operations have up to 12,000 full-time employees each (Fernandez-Stark, Bamber, and Gereffi 2011).

In the late 2000s and early 2010s, service exports also began in the medical transcription sector and in gaming and animation. These higher-value services require more trained personnel, but they yield higher revenue per employee (Fernandez-Stark, Bamber, and Gereffi 2011). Nonetheless, call centers and back-office services still accounted for 66 percent of BPO exports in 2012 (Kleibert 2015).

The success of the Philippines as a strong competitor to India in the BPO industry is mostly attributed to its large, English-speaking youth population. Call centers draw on previously underutilized labor pools (youth and female workers), hiring many young workers with high school diplomas and, in some cases, basic tertiary education. This large labor force in the Philippines allows it to host big offshore services operations and to easily reduce costs for more transaction-intensive activities by developing cities beyond metropolitan areas. Also helping to drive competitiveness in the sector was a liberalized telecommunications sector, which drastically reduced costs in the 1990s, combined with effective export processing zones and strong incentives (Kleibert 2015).

Pakistan's ICT Services Boom

The Pakistan Software Export Board (PSEB) reports a currently registered total of 4,641 IT firms and 4,066 call centers.[a] The industry is primarily spread across three major cities—Karachi, Lahore, and Islamabad (Rahman et al. 2017)—and currently employs more than 300,000 IT professionals.

According to a survey of 300 IT firms by the National ICT R&D Fund (currently known as Ignite) under the Ministry of Information Technology and Telecommunication (MOITT), 14 percent of the firms had 50 or more employees, 17 percent had 25–50 employees, and the rest had fewer than 25 employees (National ICT R&D Fund 2014). The sector comprises mostly domestically owned firms with limited foreign operations. In addition, 13 percent of the surveyed firms were foreign, and of the top 10 exporters, only one is foreign. However, the country's multinational IT presence includes IBM, Oracle, and Cisco, among others. According to the Pakistan Software Houses Association for IT and ITeS (P@SHA), the largest private sector association for the IT industry, about 53.8 percent of the industry's revenue comes from the export market.[b]

Pakistan's ICT services exports have grown by a compound average growth rate of 10.8 percent per year, increasing from US$433 million in fiscal year (FY) 2009/10 to more than US$1 billion in FY2018/19—when more than half (52 percent) of Pakistan's telecommunications, computer, and information services exports went to the United States, followed by 8.8 percent to the United Arab Emirates and 7 percent to the United Kingdom (Sáez, Rizwan, and van der Marel 2020). The share of computer-related services within these ICT services exports increased from 44 percent to 73 percent between FY2009/10 and FY2018/19, with average annual growth of 17.3 percent.

Within computer-related services, exports are concentrated in low- to medium-value-added software services, which include enterprise planning, application development, and integration; there is limited activity in product development. Similarly, low-value-added services such as call centers lead the BPO segment, accounting for 90 percent of the export revenue in this segment (Sáez, Rizwan, and van der Marel 2020). A small number of firms supply offshore services in higher-value-added segments such as banking, finance, insurance, and health care. Still only accounting for less than 1 percent of world exports in computer-related services, there is ample room for Pakistan's exports in this subsector to grow in the future.

However, official statistics do not capture the full extent of Pakistan's export success. Industry experts believe that approximately US$1.5 billion worth of exports are not reported—US$1 billion by small and medium enterprises (SMEs) and US$0.5 billion by online freelancers (SBP 2019). Pakistan now has the third-largest number of freelancers among IT and IT-enabled services in the world, right after India and Bangladesh. About 42.4 percent of freelancers in Pakistan are in software development, making up about 10.5 percent of global freelancers in software development—much higher than in Bangladesh, Nepal, and Sri Lanka but lower than in India.

Source: Sáez, Rizwan, and van der Marel 2020.
a. Registration is optional for IT companies, but PSEB registration is mandatory for call centers to legally operate in Pakistan.
b. Export revenue data from the P@SHA website: https://www.pasha.org.pk/knowledge-center/industry-stats/.

Factors of LMIC success in global innovator exports. The success of these LMICs in exporting global innovator services might appear surprising, given their comparative advantage in unskilled-labor-intensive activities. There are two explanations: First, large countries can have large pools of skilled labor, even when average skill levels in the population are low. Second, their success often reflects their comparative disadvantage in labor-intensive manufacturing (Goswami, Mattoo, and Sáez 2012).

In India, for example, the market for skilled labor in services is relatively flexible, whereas that for unskilled labor in the formal manufacturing sector is rigid owing to regulation and unions. Moreover, the infrastructure for service delivery (telecommunications networks) has improved dramatically relative to the infrastructure for goods delivery (roads and ports). Last but not least, the regulatory and industry institutions governing trade in global innovator services have typically been of better quality than the institutions governing trade in goods (for example, customs authorities) (Goswami, Mattoo, and Sáez 2012).

On the flip side, the more-limited success of countries such as Chile, Malaysia, Mexico, and Thailand in exporting global innovator services may have less to do with their absolute disadvantage in these services than with their comparative advantage in exporting agricultural and manufactured goods—driven by either (a) high-quality physical infrastructure and customs regulations or management, (b) inadequate skills, or (c) a combination of the two (Goswami, Mattoo, and Sáez 2012).

Some of the export success for LMICs in exporting global innovator services is also attributable to the (temporary) "movement of natural persons" abroad—that is, "mode 4" of services trade under the General Agreement on Trade in Services (GATS) of the World Trade Organization (WTO).[10] Chapter 1 showed that this mode accounts for a non-negligible share of world trade in two services subsectors: ICT and professional services.

This mode is reinforced by trends in longer-term international migration, whereby the share of migrant workers in these global innovator services has increased across high-income countries. The share of migrant workers in ICT services was 33 percent, 29 percent, and 17 percent, respectively, in Canada, the United States, and Europe in 2018. In fact, highly skilled international migrants are disproportionately employed in ICT services across the Organisation for Economic Co-operation and Development (OECD) countries—this subsector, for example, accounting for approximately one-fourth of such migrants to the United States. In the United States, workers born in India accounted for 14 percent of employment in ICT services in 2018 and made up almost half of the foreign-born labor force in the subsector (OECD 2020).[11]

Export Diversification through Low-Skill Tradable Services

Accommodation and food services and transportation services make up a major part of the tourism sector, which many low-income countries have also used to help diversify their exports away from volatile primary sectors (Loungani et al. 2017). This specialization is reflected in a negative relationship between the share of these low-skill tradable services in total services exports and countries' per capita income (figure 4.9).

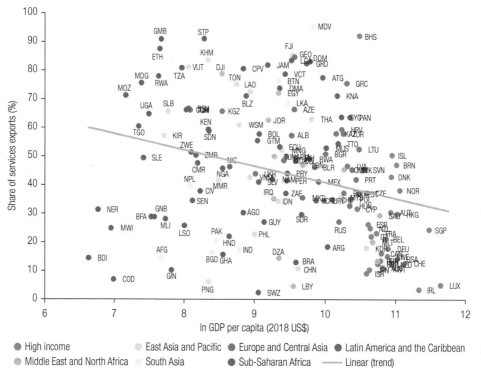

FIGURE 4.9 **Low-Skill Tradable Services Make Up Larger Shares of Total Services Exports in Lower-Income Countries Than in High-Income Countries**

Share of accommodation and food services and transportation services in countries' services exports in relation to per capita income, 2017

Sources: Calculations using the Trade in Services by Mode of Supply (TiSMoS) database, World Trade Organization; and World Development Indicators database.

Note: Low-skill tradable services—including accommodation and food services and transportation services—employ mostly low-skilled workers and are tradable in internationally, particularly in the tourism sector. Countries are labeled using ISO alpha-3 codes. "High-income countries" had gross national income per capita exceeding US$8,955 in 1994. ln = natural log.

Among low-income countries (as defined by 1994 gross national income), the share of low-skill tradable services in services exports—at two-thirds or more in 2017—was considerably higher than the average for their levels of per capita income in Bhutan, Cambodia, Egypt, Rwanda, Sri Lanka, Tanzania, and Uganda. Among middle-income countries, Jordan and Thailand similarly stand out.

The share of tourism-related low-skill tradable services in total services exports was also expectedly high (at more than three-fourths) relative to per capita income in island economies across regions and income levels in 2017. These economies ranged from the Bahamas and Jamaica in the Caribbean, Cabo Verde in Africa, and Maldives in South Asia, to Fiji and Vanuatu in the Pacific.

Two other countries stand out on account of their shares of transportation services in total services exports: Ethiopia (as high as 75 percent) and Panama (40 percent). This finding is not attributable to tourism-related travel but rather to these countries' emergence as regional hubs for transportation and logistics services because of the convergence of maritime and air cargo connectivity.

Aided by its location and tax regime, Panama has emerged as a logistics platform for the Americas, helping to reconcile long-haul and feeder maritime services and providing an air transportation hub to facilitate customization and distribution in global and regional value chains. This follows the earlier example of Dubai in the United Arab Emirates, which emerged as a world-class logistical platform for labeling and packaging goods manufactured in South Asia, Southeast Asia, and East Asia and mainly bound for European and North American markets (box 4.3). The growth of Ethiopian Airlines has similarly catapulted Ethiopia, at the crossroads of major trade routes, into becoming a passenger and air cargo hub in Africa.

It is worth noting that recent crises have disproportionately hit trade in low-skill tradable services. For example, even though services trade was less affected than manufacturing by the Global Financial Crisis of 2008–09 (when trade in goods fell by almost 30 percent), export opportunities in transportation-related services declined relative to global innovator services (business, telecommunications, and financial services), which continued growing at their precrisis rates (Ariu 2016). Transportation and accommodation and food services that are traded internationally largely through tourism-related travel have also been harder hit during the current COVID-19 pandemic because they are intensive in face-to-face interactions (as discussed in box 3.3).

Export Diversification by Leveraging Health and Education Services

Education and health services account for a negligible share of global services trade, but they are rising. And although there is little scope for specialization, given that all countries need to provide these social services, the possibility of exporting these services creates opportunities to access demand beyond the domestic market.

Education services. Thanks to over 5 million international students worldwide in 2017, trade in education services was estimated at US$111 billion, with a share of only 0.9 percent of world trade in services but recording annual average growth of 7 percent since 2005 (WTO 2019). High-income countries such as Australia, Canada, the United Kingdom, and the United States are the main destinations for foreign students (Beghin and Park 2019). However, China, India, and Malaysia, among others, are emerging as exporters of education services, attracting students mainly from other low- and middle-income countries where a growing young population will continue to fuel demand.[13]

Although education services are predominantly traded through consumption abroad (mode 2), as discussed in chapter 1, digital technologies will increasingly enable the cross-border supply of these services (mode 1) through e-learning platforms (see chapter 3).

Health services. Trade in health services was estimated at US$54 billion in 2017—only 0.4 percent of world trade in services but recording annual average growth of 11 percent since 2005 (WTO 2019). Globally, over 72 percent of health services were traded, primarily by high-income economies, through affiliated hospitals and medical centers in other countries (mode 3). Another 22 percent were exported to foreign patients during their stays abroad (mode 2).

Geography, Transportation Services, and the Emergence of Logistics Hubs

The Case of Panama

Panama has become an emerging logistics and manufacturing platform for the Americas. The growth of global trade (particularly intra-American trade) and the development of steamships provided an impetus for the construction of the Panama Canal, which was completed in 1914. This set the stage for Panama to become a "tollbooth country" that derived revenue from canal crossings. Within decades, Panama became an important connector within the global maritime transport system and imposed Panamax as a de facto standard in maritime shipping. However, investments related to this connectivity were limited as long as Panama remained a location where cargo was simply passing by. It could be said that Panama was a weak intermediary location since the cargo in transit was not "touched."

In the 1990s, a series of events began transforming Panama's conventional role as a transit country, culminating in 1999 as the Panama Canal Authority took full control of the canal. Port privatization reforms in 1995 were accompanied by significant investments in port infrastructure and the entry of major global terminal operators: Hutchison Port Holdings (HPH), SSA Marine, and Singapore Port Authority (PSA). Containerized traffic handled by the ports grew rapidly. The setting of post-Panamax ship services and the growth of trans-Pacific trade induced a new dynamic in Panama. It quickly became a trans-shipment hub helping to reconcile long-haul and feeder maritime services on both the Atlantic and Pacific sides of the canal. Of the 6.8 million 20-foot equivalent units (TEUs) that were handled at Panamanian ports in 2012, about 95 percent concerned trans-shipment activities.

As the first decade of the twenty-first century progressed, a new trend reinforced the role of Panama as a global trade platform. Increasing trans-shipment volumes, Panama's central position within the Americas, the growth of the country's finance sector, and its emerging function as an air transportation hub encouraged the setting up of logistics activities that were not present before. In such a scenario, Panama could become a logistics platform servicing global and regional supply chains by providing added-value activities for the region, such as customization and distribution.

This transition is far from complete, and several challenges must be addressed to ensure that Panama can develop world-class logistics capabilities. In particular, additional port capacity is necessary, particularly on the Pacific side, as well as portcentric logistics zones and a more extensive road system to support these new interactions.

Box continues on the following page

Geography, Transportation Services, and the Emergence of Logistics Hubs *(continued)*

The Case of Dubai

In the past two decades, Dubai has emerged as a world-class logistics platform, a role attributable in part to its geographical location at the crossroads of major trade routes between Asia, Europe, South Asia, and East Africa. This role began to take shape in the 1960s, when the growing availability of capital derived from oil exports in neighboring countries led to initial infrastructure investments such as the first modern port facilities (Port Rashid), completed in 1971. The 1980s and 1990s saw an acceleration of Dubai's hub status, with Asia-Europe trade booming and its role growing as a logistics platform.

Dubai used the sovereign wealth fund approach to finance state-sponsored enterprises to fulfill its strategic objectives. Emirates Airlines was established in 1985, and Dubai International Airport was gradually expanded and upgraded with new runways and terminals. Dubai soon became a passenger and air cargo hub for the Middle East. By 2014, it handled 70.5 million passengers and 2.2 million tons of cargo, making it the third-busiest in the world for passenger traffic and the sixth-busiest for cargo. The opening of the Jebel Ali Free Zone in 1985, a zone of 5,700 hectares beside the Jebel Ali container terminals, conferred the role of Dubai as a free port with incentives concerning foreign ownership and the taxation regime.

Source: Rodrigue 2016.

However, low- and middle-income economies—especially in Asia, the Middle East and North Africa, and Latin America—are emerging as medical tourism hubs, offering treatment on a par with high-income economies but at substantially lower prices (Dihel and Goswami 2016).[14] For example, dental care in Thailand costs about 85 percent less than in the United States, even when the cost of travel is included (Arunanondchai and Fink 2007). The top 20 exporters of health exports through "consumption abroad" (mode 2) in 2017 included, among other low- and middle-income economies, Turkey, Thailand, Costa Rica, Jordan, Mexico, India, and Malaysia (figure 4.10).

As demand for health care services outpaces supply in high-income countries with aging populations, LMICs with large working-age populations can also export these services through the movement of health workers (mode 4) and longer-term migration. Between 2010 and 2011, Germany, the United Kingdom, and the United States had a significant proportion of foreign-born nurses (over 10 percent) (OECD 2015). Asian economies, especially small and island economies, were the world's top suppliers of emigrant doctors and nurses. Between 2010 and 2011, doctors and nurses who had emigrated to OECD countries accounted for an estimated 20 percent of the health care workforce needs in their countries of origin (OECD 2015).

FIGURE 4.10   The Top 20 Health Tourism Destinations Include Many Low- and Middle-Income Economies

Top 20 exporters of health services through "consumption abroad" (mode 2), by income group, 2017

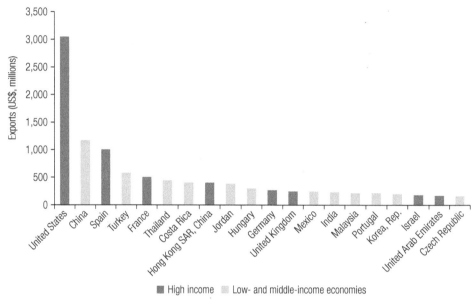

Source: Calculations using Trade in Services data by Mode of Supply (TiSMoS) database, World Trade Organization.

Note: Low- and middle-income economies, by World Bank income group classifications, had 1994 gross national income (GNI) of less than US$8,955. High-income economies had GNI exceeding US$8,955 in 1994.

Exports of Low-Skill Domestic Services through Migration

Low-skill domestic services (such as retail, personal services, and administrative and support services) can be exported to the extent that people move across national boundaries—either through short-term (mode 4 trade) or longer-term migration. In fact, as a share of sector-wise employment, migrant workers in high-income countries are most abundant across the low-skill domestic services.

In the United States, up to half of all domestic workers for private households in 2018 were migrants, having increased from 39 percent in 2005. The trend was even stronger in European countries, where this share increased from 36 percent in 2005 to 53 percent in 2018 (OECD 2020). In three-fourths of OECD countries, the share of migrants in domestic personal services is at least twice as high as in the economy over-all. The next-highest share is in accommodation and food services, where the shares of migrants in 2018 were 27 percent in Europe and 24 percent in the United States. The third most migrant-intensive sector was administrative and support services—which includes building security and cleaning services—with corresponding shares of 22 percent in Europe and 30 percent in the United States (OECD 2020).

The earlier section, on final demand, illustrated how global innovator services and low-skill tradable services have provided opportunities for productivity growth through exports, whereby transactions take place directly between a service provider and the final consumer (firm or household) in another country. These growth opportunities have been independent of a country's manufacturing base. Except for accommodation and food services, however, these internationally traded services are also more likely to serve intermediate demand from other sectors of the domestic economy.

Intermediate Sales in Total Output: Differences across Services Subsectors
The 2014 share of domestic intermediate sales in total output—on average, across 40 countries in all income groups—ranged from approximately 50 percent in wholesale trade and ICT services, and 60 percent in financial and transportation services, to 70 percent in professional, scientific, and technical services (figure 4.11).

FIGURE 4.11 **Global Innovator and Low-Skill Tradable Services Are More Likely Than Other Subsector Groups to Serve Domestic Intermediate Demand**
Average share of domestic intermediate sales in total output across 40 countries in selected services subsectors, by group, 2014

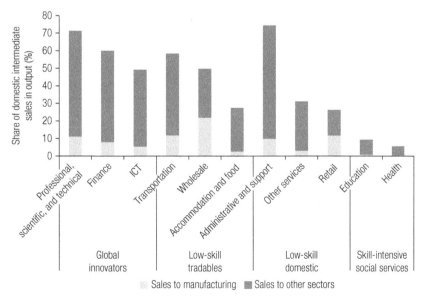

Source: Calculations based on the World Input-Output Database.

Note: The dataset covers 40 countries in all regions except the Middle East and North Africa and Sub-Saharan Africa. LMICs, by World Bank income group classifications, had 1994 gross national income (GNI) of less than US$8,955. High-income countries had GNI exceeding US$8,955 in 1994. "Other services" refers to arts, entertainment, and recreation services and other social, community, and personal services. ICT = information and communication technology.

Rising demand for these services from other sectors in the economy, domestically, is another important growth opportunity. The previous section, on services and value chain upgrading, already explored some of these linkages with manufacturing. Here we explore the extent to which sectors outside manufacturing—agriculture, mining, construction, utilities, and other services—can also be important drivers of demand for given services subsectors. Growth opportunities independent of a country's manufacturing base will be reinforced to the extent that intermediate sales to the manufacturing sector do not account for a disproportionate share of this rising demand.

In 2014, on average across 40 countries, the share of manufacturing in intermediate sales to other sectors was about 20 percent in wholesale trade; 10 percent in transportation, financial, and professional, scientific, and technical services; and 5 percent in ICT services.[15] The question is whether higher growth in intermediate sales to manufacturing has been associated with higher overall growth for these global innovator and low-skill tradable services over time.

Intermediate Sales of Low-Skill Tradable Services

Growth in wholesale and retail trade output between 2000 and 2014 was higher in the same countries where growth in intermediate sales from wholesale and retail trade to the manufacturing sector was also higher. However, growth in the share of these intermediate sales to manufacturing between 2000 and 2014 was not associated with a higher rate of growth of wholesale and retail trade output across countries (figure 4.12). In other words, selling relatively more to the manufacturing sector did not result in higher growth rates for wholesale and retail trade overall. This finding suggests that intermediate sales from wholesale and retail trade to other sectors matters too. The same holds true for transportation services (figure 4.13).

However, there may be differences across countries. Take the example of China, which experienced one of the highest rates of services output growth over this period. Intermediate demand accounted for more than 85 percent of the output growth in transportation services between 2000 and 2014 and, although sales to manufacturing was a sizable component, this rising intermediate demand also included increased sales to nonmanufacturing sectors: agriculture, mining, utilities, and construction, as well as other services. The growth of wholesale (and retail) services in China depended more than transportation services on a manufacturing core; sales to manufacturing accounted for 40 percent of the annual average output growth of wholesale and retail trade, while wholesale and retail sales to other sectors made a substantially smaller contribution (Nayyar, Cruz, and Zhu 2018).

Intermediate Sales of Global Innovator Services

Among global innovator services, growth in ICT services output between 2000 and 2014 was higher in the same countries where growth in the share of intermediate sales

FIGURE 4.12 **The Growth of Domestic Intermediate Sales to Manufacturing Matters for the Growth of Wholesale and Retail Trade Services, but Not Disproportionately So**

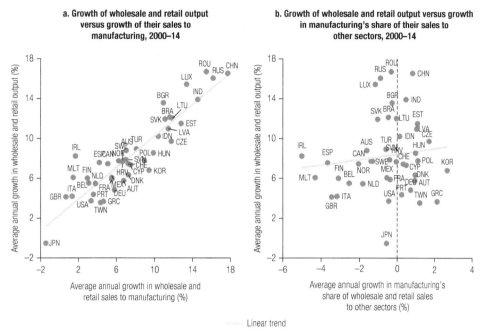

Source: Calculations based on the World Input-Output Database.

Note: Average annual percentage growth is plotted for 40 countries across global regions and income groups, labeled using ISO alpha-3 codes. Slanted lines designate fitted values.

of ICT services to manufacturing was also higher (figure 4.14, panel a). Less robust is the association between the 2000–14 growth in the output of financial services and professional, scientific, and technical services across countries and growth in their shares of intermediate sales to manufacturing (figure 4.14, panels b–c).

There are differences in this regard across countries too. Take the example of China, whose average annual growth in services output between 2000 and 2014 was the highest of the 40 countries in the World Input-Output Database. Although the contribution of intermediate domestic demand to the growth of professional, scientific, and technical services over the period was as high as 90 percent, this contribution was not driven only by links with the manufacturing sector. The inputs of professional, scientific, and technical services into mining, utilities, and construction as well as other services was equally if not more important than inputs into manufacturing (Nayyar, Cruz, and Zhu 2018). In fact, the growth of professional, scientific, and technical services output across countries is also positively associated with growth in their shares of intermediate sales to ICT services.[16]

FIGURE 4.13 **The Growth of Domestic Intermediate Sales to Manufacturing Matters for the Growth of Transportation Services, but Not Disproportionately So**

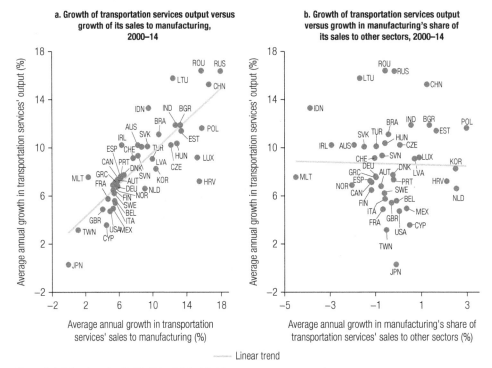

a. Growth of transportation services output versus growth of its sales to manufacturing, 2000–14

b. Growth of transportation services output versus growth in manufacturing's share of its sales to other sectors, 2000–14

Linear trend

Source: Calculations based on the World Input-Output Database.

Note: Average annual growth is plotted for 40 countries across global regions and income groups, labeled using ISO alpha-3 codes. Slanted lines designate fitted values.

Evidence from India shows that growth in manufacturing has accelerated growth in value added and worker productivity in services firms within the same geographic region, especially among global innovator services such as telecommunications and business services that are used as inputs in the manufacturing sector (Dehejia and Panagariya 2016). Furthermore, firm-level transactions data from Turkey show that the growth in sales to manufacturing firms in the same province particularly matters for the growth of firms in ICT and professional services (Avdiu, Demir, et al. 2021). The authors show that growth of 10 percentage points in such local linkages with manufacturing firms results in growth of 2.3 percentage points in the overall output of firms in these global innovator services. However, the growth in sales to local firms in the services sector does not have a significant effect economically or statistically.

At the same time, individual country experiences illustrate that global innovator services can grow without a manufacturing base and instead through

FIGURE 4.14   Global Innovator Services' Total Output Growth Is (Weakly) Associated with Growth in Their Shares of Domestic Intermediate Sales to Manufacturing

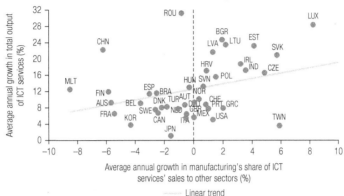

a. ICT services' output growth in relation to growth in share of its intermediate sales to manufacturing sector, 2000–14

Average annual growth in manufacturing's share of ICT services' sales to other sectors (%)

Average annual growth in total output of ICT services (%)

Linear trend

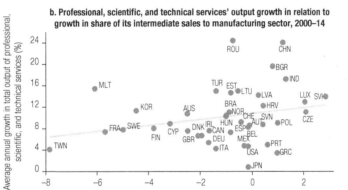

b. Professional, scientific, and technical services' output growth in relation to growth in share of its intermediate sales to manufacturing sector, 2000–14

Average annual growth in share of manufacturing in sales of professional, scientific, and technical services to other sectors (%)

Average annual growth in total output of professional, scientific, and technical services (%)

Linear trend

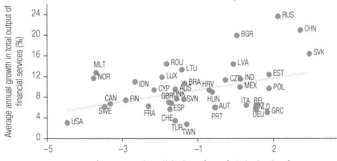

c. Financial services' output growth in relation to growth in share of its intermediate sales to manufacturing sector, 2000–14

Average annual growth in share of manufacturing in sales of financial services to other sectors (%)

Average annual growth in total output of financial services (%)

Linear trend

Source: Calculations based on the World Input-Output Database.

Note: Average annual growth is plotted for 40 countries across global regions and income groups, labeled using ISO alpha-3 codes. Slanted lines designate fitted values. ICT = information and communication technology.

linkages with other sectors. At the beginning of the twentieth century, copper mining in the United States engendered a knowledge network in chemistry and metallurgy (Maloney and Valencia Caicedo 2016). Likewise, Norway has created an innovative oil and gas industry with substantial links to knowledge-intensive services (Cappelen, Eika, and Holm 2000; Fagerberg, Mowery, and Verspagen 2009).

Much like Norway, Australia, and Canada, Chile has used its mineral resources and exports to diversify into providing sophisticated engineering and scientific research services. Multinational mining companies started out by providing lower-value design drawings for Chilean mining operations, and by 2010, five of them had established global engineering services centers for the copper industry in Chile (Arze 2009; Sanchez and Boolan 2009). Engineering service exports related to mining peaked at an estimated US$275 million in 2011 and was the largest offshore services export sector in Chile, accounting for one-third of services exports (Fernandez-Stark, Bamber, and Gereffi 2010). A wide range of Chilean firms are also involved in scientific R&D services to develop new, innovative technologies for process upgrading.

Global innovator services can also be embodied in agricultural production. Take the example of IT services in Uruguay that derived from the country's thriving beef exports. To mitigate the challenges of health and food safety standards on these exports, Uruguay has developed a sophisticated bovine traceability system that provides real-time data on the national cattle market. It now exports these advanced IT services for the broader livestock industry, such as to Colombia. Similarly, Chile has developed scientific R&D services that are exported through genetic material embodied in grape varieties that make them resistant to fungus, help them ripen faster, and simplify the cultivation process. Since the 2000s, Chile has positioned itself not only as the world's leading exporter of table grapes but also as a global provider of genetic material as a "club good" abroad by exporting the underlying scientific R&D services (Bamber et al. 2017).[17]

Growing Importance of Services to a Manufacturing Core

That services may benefit from a manufacturing core does not take away from the fact that many services, in turn, are vital inputs into the production and sale of manufactured goods. Hence, to the extent that services are either *embodied* in manufacturing (as inputs such as design, logistics, or e-commerce platforms) or *embedded* as postproduction complements (such as warranties, after-sales support, and marketing services), the growth of the manufacturing sector too will depend on a vibrant and robust services sector.

Services Embodied in Exports of Manufactured Goods

In 2015, about one-third of the value of gross manufactures' exports among OECD countries was attributable to the value added of embodied services, with distribution and business services making the largest contributions. The corresponding share for low- and middle-income economies was about 29 percent (figure 4.15). The aggregate services value added in exports of manufactured goods for high-income economies remained largely unchanged between 2005 and 2015, but it increased in Asia, particularly because of the higher domestic services content in China's manufactures' exports (WTO 2019).

These estimates of services value added embodied in manufactures' exports, based on arm's-length transactions, is a lower bound for the servicification of manufacturing since these services are often produced "in house" by exporting companies (Low 2013). Using a combination of labor force surveys and the OECD-WTO Trade in Value-Added (TiVA) database, Miroudot and Cadestin (2017) estimate for a sample of

FIGURE 4.15 **About One-Third of the Value of Gross Manufactures' Exports Is Attributable to Services Inputs**

Services value added in exports of manufactured goods, OECD and non-OECD economies, by services subsector, 2015

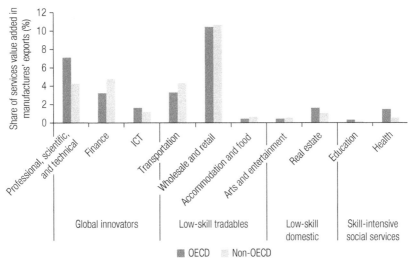

Source: Calculations based on the Trade in Value Added (TiVA) database of the Organisation for Economic Co-operation and Development (OECD).

Note: "Non-OECD economies" include Argentina; Brazil; Brunei Darussalam; Bulgaria; Cambodia; China; Colombia; Costa Rica; Croatia; Cyprus; Hong Kong SAR, China; India; Indonesia; Kazakhstan; Malaysia; Malta; Morocco; Peru; the Philippines; Romania; the Russian Federation; Saudi Arabia; Singapore; South Africa; Taiwan, China; Thailand; Tunisia; and Vietnam. ICT = information and communication technology.

31 economies[18] that the share of services value added in manufacturing exports increases from 37 percent to 53 percent when manufacturing firms' "in-house" services activities are added.

How Services Boost Manufacturing Productivity

A substantial body of evidence shows that the services "embodied" in manufactured goods have a significant impact on manufacturing productivity (Arnold et al. 2010; Arnold, Javorcik, and Mattoo 2011; Arnold, Mattoo, and Narciso 2008). This evidence spans a range of countries and relates mainly to the global innovator services and low-skill tradable services. A study of OECD countries, for example, finds that the density of telecommunications services makes them crucial inputs for the competitiveness of manufacturing (Nordås and Kim 2013). Similarly, access to financial services matters for manufacturing productivity, notably in LMICs (Bas and Causa 2013). In Colombia, the productivity of manufacturing firms increases with linkages to services firms (Alfaro and Eslava 2020). In Ethiopia, improvements in transportation services have enabled the time-sensitive cut flowers industry to flourish, increasing its exports from US$12 million in 2005 to US$662 million in 2014 (Hoekman and te Velde 2017).

Much of this productivity boost has been attributable to reforms that have liberalized upstream services. Firm-level data from the Czech Republic show a positive relationship between services sector liberalization and the performance of domestic firms in downstream manufacturing sectors (Arnold, Javorcik, and Mattoo 2011). Furthermore, liberalization in banking, insurance, telecommunications, and transportation services improved the productivity of manufacturing firms in India (Arnold et al. 2015). This result is reinforced by Bas (2014), who finds that the liberalization of telecommunications and transportation services in India resulted in a 6–8.5 percent increase in manufacturing firms' probability of exporting. And increased openness to services trade has increased manufacturing productivity among OECD economies (Francois and Woerz 2008).

Greater trade openness that facilitates the import of key enabling services—mainly through foreign direct investment (FDI)—is a key channel through which services liberalization helps improve the manufacturing sector's performance. For instance, FDI inflows (a proxy for foreign-owned firms' establishment of "commercial presence") in producer services enhanced the productivity of manufacturing firms in Chile (Fernandes and Paunov 2012). Similarly, Bas and Causa (2013) find that if the regulation of financial services in China were improved to the average level observed in OECD economies, the country's manufacturing productivity would increase by 6.5 percent. In fact, imported financial services can compensate, at least in part, for an underdeveloped domestic financial services sector to boost manufacturing productivity and exports (Liu et al. 2018).

The impact of liberalization that facilitates the import of key enabling services in lower-income countries on downstream manufacturing productivity can be further enhanced through improvements in the quality of institutions and complementary domestic regulatory policies (Van der Marel 2016). This is especially important because most imported services used as inputs in manufacturing are located in the country of production—in other words, imported through the establishment of "commercial presence" in the destination market (Andrenelli et al. 2018). The importance of differences in institutional quality is reflected in Beverelli, Fiorini, and Hoekman (2017), which finds that an identical reduction in services trade restrictiveness in Canada and Tanzania would increase manufacturing productivity by 16.7 percent in Canada but by only 3.9 percent in Tanzania.

How Technological Change Strengthens the Servicification of Manufacturing

The servicification of manufacturing will be further strengthened through "smart" production processes that transmit data through networks, machines, and computers connected to the internet (Hallward-Driemeier and Nayyar 2018). ICT services—such as custom computer programming services, software publisher services, telecommunications services, internet publishing, and data-processing services, including cloud computing—produce data for technology-intensive "smart" factories and share this information throughout the entire value chain.

At the same time, telecommunications, information services, and publishing services are also the most data-intensive users. Other services that are strong users of data include office support and business services, computer programming services, engineering services, advanced data analytics, advertising and market research, and R&D services. These services use real-time information through equipment logs, smart meters, or manufacturing sensors to optimize production processes (Dijcks 2013; Opresnik and Taisch 2015; Van der Marel 2021). ICT service sectors, as the predominant producers and users of data, can therefore play a crucial role in boosting manufacturing competitiveness through the Internet of Things (IoT).[19]

In fact, these increasing complementarities between services and production tasks (Grossman and Rossi-Hansberg 2008; Healey and Ilbery 1991) might influence location decisions in manufacturing GVCs. The possibility of reshoring production to where the professional services are located reflects the concern that separating production from R&D harms a firm's long-term ability to innovate. This might be more relevant for research- and skill-intensive manufactures (such as pharmaceuticals, semiconductors, and microprocessors) with little labor-intensive assembly. For example, the manufacture of certain capital goods and advanced inputs (such as semiconductors, doped wafers for semiconductors, and fiberoptic cables) stayed in high-income economies during the twentieth-century ICT revolution, while the assembly of high-tech goods such as laptops and mobile phones did move to low- and middle-income economies. Therefore, the production of advanced manufactured goods (such as wearable tech, autonomous vehicles, biochips and biosensors, and new materials) are most likely to colocate with R&D services facilities in high-income economies as they are being developed (Hallward-Driemeier and Nayyar 2018).

Embedded Services: "Downstream" Complement

The Bundling of Manufactured Goods and Services

Services are increasingly bundled with (or added to) manufactured goods, thereby adding value postproduction (Vandermerwe and Rada 1988). This close interaction of "manufacturing" and "services" means that the boundaries between these sectors in the broader production process are becoming increasingly blurred, to such an extent that it is difficult to assign firms exclusively to one sector.

Examples abound: Xerox has restructured itself into a "document solution" company, offering not only technologically advanced printer systems but also postsales services like document managing and consulting, equipment maintenance, and financing that represented about 75 percent of Xerox's total revenues in 2019 (Xerox 2020). Similarly, in 2012, these complementary postproduction services accounted for 15–20 percent of turnover in SSAB (steel producer), 20–30 percent in Volvo AB (automobiles), and 42 percent in Ericsson (telecommunication networks), and these firms expected their services shares in turnover to increase (National Board of Trade of Sweden 2012).[20]

Technological advancements are blurring these lines still further. For example, IBM has transformed itself from a producer of computer hardware to a service supplier of cloud computing and AI-enabled scientific and business modeling and customer services (McGregor 2019).

This bundling of manufactured goods and services is increasing among firms in LMICs too. In a new study on India, Grover and Mattoo (2021) find that the share of manufacturers offering services has increased threefold—from about 20 percent of manufacturing firms in 1994 to nearly 60 percent in 2013. At the same time, the intensity of this servicification has also tripled: the average share of services revenue in total revenue increased from 7 percent to 21 percent (figure 4.16).

Consistent with the trends in high-income countries, Grover and Mattoo (2021) find that firms in high-tech manufacturing industries are the most servitized in India. They also find that the diversification of manufacturing firms spans global innovator services as well as low-skill tradable services. For instance, the share of manufacturers offering financial and business services in India increased dramatically between 1994 and 2013, while a large share of servitized firms continue to offer retail and wholesale services.

FIGURE 4.16 **In India, the Share of Servitized Manufacturing Firms and Their Service Intensity Have Both Roughly Tripled**

Share of manufacturers that sell services and the share of services in their total revenue, India, 1994–2013

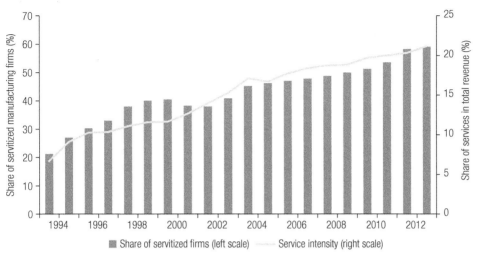

Source: Grover and Mattoo 2021.

Note: "Servitized" firms are those manufacturers that also sell services. "Service intensity" is the share of total revenue attributable to the sale of services.

What Explains the Bundling of Manufactured Goods and Services

The growing complementarity between manufactured goods and services described above is attributable to both supply- and demand-related factors (Grover and Mattoo 2021). The supply side relates to economies of scope in production. For example, a cell phone is a good, but it is tied to the use of telecommunications services, which allow the user to install apps with purchased content that can give rise to additional transactions such as audiovisual services (streaming movies or music), publishing (e-books), or computer services (video games). Apple's combination of iTunes with the iPod provides a relevant example whereby the company profited from pairing a music device with a service that allowed consumers to buy music instantly and remotely (Amit and Zott 2012).

Amazon's Echo—a music player that comes with an artificial intelligence (AI)-enabled digital assistant, "Alexa"—provides a more recent example. The embedded voice recognition technology, which enables the digital assistant to accomplish tasks such as creating a reminder for a certain activity or estimating the length of a commute, has improved the Echo speaker's profitability (Son and Oh 2018). ICT services and professional, scientific, and technical services are therefore increasingly complementary to the manufacture of computing machinery.

The demand-side explanation for this bundling of goods and services relates to consumer preferences that can enable a firm to differentiate its product from those of its competitors. Financial services such as credit and insurance offered by manufacturers of consumer durables are a case in point. In some instances, these production- and consumption-driven motivations come together. Traditional consumer durables, for instance, increasingly come with an assortment of after-sales services, such as advertising, warranties, and repair. By supplying these services with their goods, manufacturers can increase their market share since a product-service bundle is harder to compete against (Gebauer, Fleisch, and Friedli 2005).

A study of Indian manufacturers finds that the bundling of goods and services is positively associated with exposure to import competition (Grover and Mattoo 2021). Firm-level data from the United Kingdom also support the link between servicification and import competition: the increase in servicification of UK manufacturing between 1997 and 2007 was associated with a decline in import tariffs (Breinlich, Soderbery, and Wright 2014). Further evidence from Belgium suggests that such bundling has enabled manufacturers to differentiate their products and increase their sales in export markets by selling larger quantities at higher prices (Ariu, Mayneris, and Parenti 2020).

Although economies of scope in production and consumer preferences for bundling are more likely to push certain industries toward servicification, not all firms within an industry servitize. Servicification is likely to require organizational changes that impose additional fixed costs of bundling services with goods (Gebauer, Fleisch, and Friedli 2005). Given the large productivity differences across firms within narrowly defined industries (Syverson 2011), it is therefore likely that only the more productive firms servitize. In fact, the bundling of goods and services by manufacturing firms in India is positively associated with firm productivity and does not shield low-productivity firms from import competition (Grover and Mattoo 2021).

The Role of Linkages in Expanding Inclusion

Chapter 2 illustrated the dichotomy between productivity growth and unskilled-jobs creation in the services sector, in that they are less likely to occur together in the same subsector. Chapter 3 then showed that this productivity-jobs dichotomy within a given services subsector may be narrowing, especially among low-skill tradable services, owing to (a) the reduced importance of physical proximity in matching demand and supply, (b) innovation, and (c) combining labor with intangible capital. Access to larger markets, including through linkages, can further narrow this dichotomy.

Low-Skill Tradable Services: Indirect Productivity Gains

Trade in low-skill tradable services directly creates more and better jobs for low-skilled labor. For example, tourism brings significant benefits for employment and wages in Mexico (Faber and Gaubert 2019). Similarly, retail imports through FDI in Mexico (particularly through the entry of Walmart) increased real wages, while employment gains in new foreign-owned retail stores were canceled out by employment contraction in local stores (Atkin, Faber, and Gonzalez-Navarro 2018). Furthermore, evidence across 83 low- and middle-income economies from 2013 to 2018 shows that tourism and travel-related services such as travel agencies, tour operators, hotels and restaurants, and transportation are characterized by the highest contribution in exports by smaller firms and by women-owned firms (WTO 2019).

The impact of low-skill tradable services on economic inclusion is magnified through their intersectoral linkages. Increasing the productivity of wholesale trade and transportation services reduces transaction costs for all marketed products and is particularly beneficial for sectors, such as agriculture and manufacturing, that employ low-skilled labor. For example, in Tanzania, after accounting for linkages between sectors, the reduction of transportation costs is associated with a substantial increase in the incomes of unskilled and rural workers (Adam, Bevan, and Gollin 2018).

Low-skill services can also be indirectly exported through forward linkages with other traded sectors. For instance, although direct value added in the export of distribution (wholesale and retail trade) services is negligible across most countries, the sector's value added *embodied* in the exports of other sectors is considerably larger (figure 4.17). These forward linkages could either be with goods-producing sectors or other directly exported services.

Global Innovator Services: Indirect Job Creation

Linkages with other sectors can also help narrow the dichotomy between productivity growth and the absorption of low-skilled labor among global innovator services through indirect job creation. For example, for every US$1,000 of ready-made garment exports from Bangladesh, about US$160 can be attributed to unskilled-labor value added in gross exports (figure 4.18, panel a). For the same value of business services exports from the Philippines, less than US$90 can be ascribed to unskilled-labor value added.

However, when a sector's inputs to *economywide* production are included, the contribution of unskilled-labor value added for every US$1,000 of exports remains unchanged for apparel in Bangladesh but *increases* to US$130 for business services in the Philippines (figure 4.18, panel b). Even in a larger cross-section of countries, exports of business services are distinctly more intensive in unskilled labor when linkages with other sectors are also included (figure 4.19).

A recent study in India finds that employment growth in traded services at the district level contributes to employment growth in low-skill domestic services, with this effect being stronger in women-led firms and smaller firms (Avdiu, Bagavathinathan, et al. 2021). This evidence suggests that global innovator services can be inclusive and

FIGURE 4.17 **Indirect Exports of Wholesale and Retail Services through Forward Linkages with Other Sectors Exceeds Their Direct Exports across Most Countries**

Direct VA in exports of distribution services versus indirect VA embodied in exports of other sectors as a share of GDP, 2014

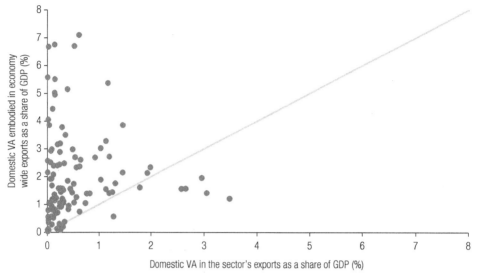

Sources: Calculations based on World Bank's Export Value Added (EVA) and World Development Indicators databases.

Note: The EVA dataset covers 111 countries across all regions and income levels. "Distribution services" refers to wholesale and retail trade. The y-axis measures *indirect* value added (VA) embodied in economy-wide exports as a share of GDP, and the x-axis, *direct* VA in the sector's exports as a share of GDP.

effective in creating demand for unskilled labor, either through spillovers or by generating demand for nontraded services that are intensive in unskilled labor.

Furthermore, to the extent that global innovator services are relatively skill-intensive, they raise the incentives for workers in LMICs to obtain more education. For example, evidence from India shows that employment growth in telecommunications, financial, and insurance services, boosted by liberalization in these subsectors, has raised educational attainment (Jensen 2012; Nano et al. 2021; Oster and Steinberg 2013). As a result, the increase in the skill premium was also less pronounced in India (Shastry 2012).

Conclusion

Leading manufacturing firms across the world are producing complex bundles of goods and services. The latter includes upstream services such as research and design as well as downstream services such as marketing, sales, and after-sales care that increasingly account for a large share of total value added in a product's supply chain. This has meant that manufacturing firms, especially in high-income countries, are increasingly

FIGURE 4.18 **Exports of Garments from Bangladesh and Business Services from the Philippines Have Similar Shares of Unskilled-Labor Value Added When Forward Linkages to Other Sectors Are Included**

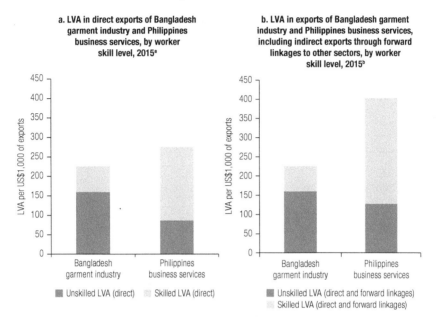

a. LVA in direct exports of Bangladesh garment industry and Philippines business services, by worker skill level, 2015[a]

b. LVA in exports of Bangladesh garment industry and Philippines business services, including indirect exports through forward linkages to other sectors, by worker skill level, 2015[b]

Unskilled LVA (direct)   Skilled LVA (direct)

Unskilled LVA (direct and forward linkages)
Skilled LVA (direct and forward linkages)

Source: Calculations based on World Bank's Labor Content of Exports (LACEX) database.

Note: "Unskilled" workers are those employed as clerks (group 4), service and sales workers (group 5), skilled agricultural and fishery workers (group 6), craft and related trade workers (group 7), plant and machine operators and assemblers (group 8), and elementary occupations (group 9) in the International Standard Classification of Occupations (ISCO), whereas "skilled" workers are those employed as legislators, senior officials, and managers (group 1), professionals (group 2), and technicians (group 3) in the ISCO.

a. Labor value added (LVA) of "direct" exports comprises wages paid directly for the production of the sector's exports.

b. LVA's inclusion of "indirect" exports through "forward linkages" adds those wages paid indirectly via the production of inputs for economywide exports.

servitized in their revenue streams and composition of employment, while their production tasks are offshored to lower-cost locations.

The question is the extent to which hitherto less industrialized countries can capitalize on growth opportunities in the services sector without a sufficiently large manufacturing base. All services subsectors with higher potential to achieve scale and innovation—professional services, finance, ICT, transportation, wholesale trade, and accommodation and food services—are linked to other sectors domestically but also serve consumers at home or export to the rest of the world.

Serving final demand, especially by exporting, can create development opportunities independent of a country's manufacturing base. Accommodation and food services and passenger transportation services cater primarily to final demand and provide export opportunities linked to tourism. Among the low-skill tradable services, the export of freight transportation and wholesale services is closely linked to goods trade, although hubs of logistics services highlight opportunities that are not linked to

FIGURE 4.19 **Business Services' Exports Are More Unskilled-Labor Intensive When Forward and Backward Linkages to Other Sectors Are Included**

Unskilled LVA in direct exports of business services versus unskilled LVA in their indirect exports through forward and backward linkages with other sectors, by region, 2015

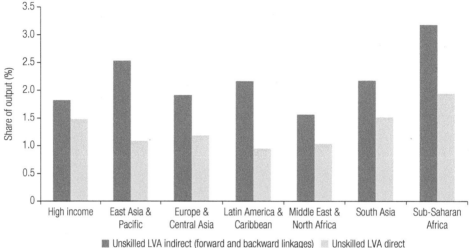

Unskilled LVA indirect (forward and backward linkages)   Unskilled LVA direct

Source: Calculations based on World Bank's Labor Content of Exports (LACEX) database.

Note: The dataset covers 141 countries across all income levels and regions. "Unskilled" workers are those employed as clerks (group 4), service and sales workers (group 5), skilled agricultural and fishery workers (group 6), craft and related trade workers (group 7), plant and machine operators and assemblers (group 8), and elementary occupations (group 9) in the International Standard Classification of Occupations (ISCO). Labor value added (LVA) refers to wages, of which "unskilled LVA direct" designates the wages paid *directly* to unskilled workers for production of the sector's exports. "Unskilled LVA indirect (forward and backward linkages)" designates the wages paid *indirectly* to unskilled workers through the production of either (a) inputs for economywide exports (forward linkages), or (b) economywide inputs for the sector's exports (backward linkages). High-income countries, by World Bank income group classifications, had gross national income exceeding US$8,955 in 1994.

production capacity in other sectors. Even among global innovator services that predominantly cater to domestic intermediate demand from other sectors, there are ample opportunities to export BPO and ICT services.

Evidence also suggests that growth opportunities for the services sector in the absence of a manufacturing core are reinforced because intermediate demand also derives from sectors other than manufacturing. Even in the case of global innovator services—where the share of intermediate sales to manufacturing is associated with higher growth—sales to mining, utilities, and construction as well as to other services has also contributed significantly to the sector's growth.

At the same time, the growing complementarities between manufacturing and services also mean that the importance of services to manufacturing cannot be emphasized enough. Manufacturers increasingly use services either for their own production needs (upstream services embodied in goods) or for their customers (downstream services, such as sales and after-sales services bundled with goods). As a result, services are growing in importance to develop a competitive manufacturing sector—a process expected to intensify, given the role that the generation and use of data will play in increasingly interconnected "smart" factories.

Last but not least, the services sector's impact on economic inclusion is magnified through its linkages with other sectors. This holds the potential to reduce the dichotomy between productivity growth and job creation for unskilled labor in certain services subsectors.

Notes

1. Calculations based on World Trade Organization's Trade in Services data by Mode of Supply (TiSMoS) database. Neither Singapore nor Hong Kong SAR, China, were among the top 10 exporters of global innovator services.

2. Other LMICs have also succeeded in particular subsectors. For ICT services among LMICs, Argentina went from the 6th position in 2005 to the 5th position in 2017, while Romania (outside the top 10 exporters of ICT services until 2010) occupied the 10th position in 2017. Turkey was the 8th-largest LMIC exporter of financial services in 2005 but slid to the 9th position in 2010 and 2017. Last but not least, Thailand figured among the top 10 LMIC exporters of professional, scientific, and technical services consistently in 2005, 2010, and 2017.

3. Among the other successful LMICs in particular subsectors, Poland was consistently one of the top 10 LMIC exporters of transportation services between 2005 and 2017, while Chile and Ukraine were among the top 10 in 2010. Furthermore, Saudi Arabia was among the top 10 LMIC exporters of wholesale and retail trade services until 2010, while Argentina was in 10th position in 2017.

4. China retained this position in 2010 but became the 10th-largest exporter of these services in 2017, falling behind Germany, France, the United Kingdom, Canada, and Ireland.

5. Final demand accounted for about 60 percent of the growth in professional, scientific, and technical services in India between 2000 and 2014, half of which was attributable to exports (Nayyar, Cruz, and Zhu 2018).

6. Calculations based on the WTO's TiSMoS database.

7. "Quality of institutions" is measured by the degree of corruption, complexity of export procedures, rigidity in employment law, or an index of economic freedom.

8. The 2016 Global Services Location Index ranked the top 55 countries for outsourcing based on metrics in three categories: financial attractiveness, people skills and availability, and business environment.

9. The EAC regional intergovernmental organization comprises six countries: Burundi, Kenya, Rwanda, South Sudan, Tanzania, and Uganda.

10. GATS, a WTO treaty, breaks down services trade into four "modes": (1) "cross-border supply," including digital delivery; (2) "consumption abroad," including services provided to foreign tourists or students; (3) "commercial presence" (or FDI), such as through locally established subsidiaries or affiliate companies; and (4) "movement of natural persons," when delivery involves the travel of the service provider to the consumer's country.

11. This migration of IT workers from Indian conglomerates, which began the software export industry by sending programmers to clients' sites overseas, originated as early as the mid-1970s (Dossani 2005).

12. SYKES set up operations in 1997; in 2015, the company had 13,000 employees in the Philippines: http://www.sykes.com/philippines/.

13. Data from the Institute for Statistics (UIS) database of the United Nations Educational, Scientific, and Cultural Organization (UNESCO): http://data.uis.unesco.org/.

14. Growing numbers of medical travel agencies and insurance companies are providing health coverage to facilitate this consumption abroad (WTO 2019).

15. These shares of intermediate sales are not notably different between high-income countries and LMICs in the sample.

16. Output and intermediate sales calculations based on the World Input-Output Database.

17. Twenty-four Chilean exporters—together with Chile's Instituto de Investigaciones Agropecuarias (INIA), the Innova Chile–CORFO initiative, and Universidad Católica de Chile—collaborated in the financing and development of four new grape varieties in Chile.

18. The sample of 31 countries comprised primarily OECD countries, in addition to Brazil, Bulgaria, India, and Romania.

19. The IoT is defined as "the use of sensors, actuators, and data communication technology built into physical objects"—from roadways to pacemakers—that enable those objects to be tracked, coordinated, or controlled across a data network or the internet (Manyika et al. 2013; UNIDO 2016).

20. At the same time, many services firms have diversified into manufacturing activity and have even introduced new goods, as Google has in the tablet market and Amazon has with its Kindle e-reader (Lopez-Bassols and Millot 2013).

References

Adam, Christopher, David Bevan, and Douglas Gollin. 2018. "Rural–Urban Linkages, Public Investment and Transport Costs: The Case of Tanzania." *World Development* 109: 497–510.

Alfaro, Laura, and Marcela Eslava. 2020. "Development and the Comparative Advantage of Services." Unpublished manuscript, Harvard Business School and University of the Andes (Uniandes), Bogotá, Colombia.

Ali-Yrkkö, Jyrki, Petri Rouvinen, Timo Seppälä, and Pekka Ylä-Anttila. 2011. "Who Captures Value In Global Supply Chains? Case Nokia N95 Smartphone." *Journal of Industry, Competition and Trade* 11 (3): 263–78.

Amit, Raphael, and Christoph Zott. 2012. "Creating Value through Business Model Innovation." *MIT Sloan Management Review* 53 (3): 41–49.

Andrenelli, Andrea, Charles Cadestin, Koen De Backer, Sébastien Miroudot, Davide Rigoi, and Ming Ye. 2018. "Multinational Production and Trade in Services." Trade Policy Paper 212, Organisation for Economic Co-operation and Development, Paris.

Ariu, Andrea. 2016. "Services versus Goods Trade: A Firm-Level Comparison." *Review of World Economics* 152 (1): 19–41.

Ariu, Andrea, Florian Mayneris, and Mathieu Parenti. 2020. "One Way to the Top: How Services Boost the Demand for Goods." *Journal of International Economics* 123: 103278.

Arnold, Jens, Beata Javorcik, Molly Lipscomb, and Aaditya Mattoo. 2010. "Services Reform and Manufacturing Performance: Evidence from India." Discussion Paper 8011, Centre for Economic Policy Research (CEPR), London.

Arnold, Jens Matthias, Beata Javorcik, Molly Lipscomb, and Aaditya Mattoo. 2015. "Services Reform and Manufacturing Performance: Evidence from India." *Economic Journal* 126 (590): 1–39.

Arnold, Jens M., Beata S. Javorcik, and Aaditya Mattoo. 2011. "Does Services Liberalization Benefit Manufacturing Firms? Evidence from the Czech Republic." *Journal of International Economics* 85 (1): 136–46.

Arnold, Jens Matthias, Aaditya Mattoo, and Gaia Narciso. 2008. "Services Inputs and Firm Productivity in Sub-Saharan Africa: Evidence from Firm-Level Data." *Journal of African Economies* 17 (4): 578–99.

Arunanondchai, Jutamas, and Carsten Fink. 2007. "Trade in Health Services in the ASEAN Region." *Health Promotion International* 21 (S1): 59–66.

Arze, Elias. 2009. "Chile Interview Series: Ara Worley Parsons S.A. Personal communication with K. Fernandez-Stark & G. Gereffi." January 27. Conducted for the Chile in the Offshore Services Global Value Chain project, Duke Center on Globalization, Governance & Competitiveness (Duke CGGC), Duke University, Durham, NC.

Atkin, David, Benjamin Faber, and Marco Gonzalez-Navarro. 2018. "Retail Globalization and Household Welfare: Evidence from Mexico." *Journal of Political Economy* 126 (1): 1–73.

Avdiu, Besart, Karan S. Bagavathinathan, Ritam Chaurey, and Gaurav Nayyar. 2021. "Services Trade, Gender and Jobs: Evidence from India." Unpublished manuscript, World Bank, Washington, DC.

Avdiu, Besart, Banu Demir, Umut Kilinc, and Gaurav Nayyar. 2021. "Does the Services Sector Benefit from a Manufacturing Core? Firm-Level Evidence from Turkey." Unpublished manuscript, World Bank, Washington, DC.

Bamber, Penny, Olivier Cattaneo, Karina Fernandez-Stark, Gary Gereffi, Erik van der Marel, and Ben Shepherd. 2017. "Diversification through Servicification." Unpublished manuscript, World Bank, Washington, DC.

Barefoot, Kevin, and Jennifer Koncz-Bruner. 2012. "A Profile of U.S. Exporters and Importers of Services: Evidence from New Linked Data on International Trade in Services and Operations of Multinational Companies." *Survey of Current Business* (June): 66–87.

Bas, Maria. 2014. "Does Services Liberalization Affect Manufacturing Firms' Export Performance? Evidence from India." *Journal of Comparative Economics* 42 (3): 569–89.

Bas, Maria, and Orsetta Causa. 2013. "Trade and Product Market Policies in Upstream Sectors and Productivity in Downstream Sectors: Firm-Level Evidence from China." *Journal of Comparative Economics* 41 (3): 843–62.

Beghin, John C., and Byung Yul Park. 2019. "The Exports of Higher Education Services from OECD Countries to Asian Countries: A Gravity Approach." Economics Working Paper, Department of Economics, Iowa State University, Ames.

Bernard, Andrew B., and Teresa C. Fort. 2015. "Factoryless Goods Producing Firms." *American Economic Review* 105 (5): 518–23.

Bernard, Andrew B., Valerie Smeets, and Frederic Warzynski. 2017. "Rethinking Deindustrialization." *Economic Policy* 32 (89): 5–38.

Beverelli, Cosimo, Matteo Fiorini, and Bernard Hoekman. 2017. "Services Trade Policy and Manufacturing Productivity: The Role of Institutions." *Journal of International Economics* 104: 166–82.

Biege, Sabine, Martin Borowiecki, Bernhard Dachs, Joseph F. Francois, Doris Hanzl-Weiss, Johan Hauknes, Angela Jäger, et al. 2012. "Convergence of Knowledge-Intensive Sectors and the EU's External Competitiveness." Research Report 377, Vienna Institute for International Economic Studies (wiiw), Vienna.

Breinlich, Holger, Anson Soderbery, and Greg C. Wright. 2014. "From Selling Goods to Selling Services: Firm Responses to Trade Liberalization." Discussion Paper 1303, Centre for Economic Performance, London School of Economics and Political Science, London.

Cappelen, Ådne, Torbjørn Eika, and Inger Holm. 2000. "Resource Booms: Curse or Blessing?" Paper presented at the Annual Meeting of American Economic Association, Statistics Norway, Oslo.

Crozet, Matthieu, and Emmanuel Milet. 2017. "Should Everybody Be in Services? The Effect of Servitization on Manufacturing Firm Performance." *Journal of Economics & Management Strategy* 26 (4): 820–41.

Dachs, Bernhard, Sabine Biege, Marcin Borowiecki, Gunther Lay, Angela Jäger, and Doris Schartinger. 2012. "The Servitization of European Manufacturing Industries." Paper 38995, Munich Personal RePEc Archive (MPRA), Austrian Institute of Technology, Vienna.

Dehejia, Rajeev, and Arvind Panagariya. 2016. "The Link between Manufacturing Growth and Accelerated Services Growth in India." *Economic Development and Cultural Change* 64 (2): 221–64.

Dihel, Nora, and Arti Grover Goswami, eds. 2016. "The Unexplored Potential of Trade in Services in Africa: From Hair Stylists and Teachers to Accountants and Doctors." Report 107185, World Bank, Washington, DC.

Dijcks, Jean-Pierre. 2013. "Oracle: Big Data for the Enterprise." White paper, Oracle Corp., Redwood Shores, CA.

Dossani, Rafiq. 2005. "Origins and Growth of the Software Industry in India." Paper, Walter H. Shorenstein Asia-Pacific Research Center, Freeman Spogli Institute for International Studies, Stanford University, Stanford, CA.

Drake-Brockman, Jane, and Sherry Stephenson. 2012. "Implications for 21st Century Trade and Development of the Emergence of Services Value Chains." Working paper, International Centre for Trade and Sustainable Development (ICTSD), Geneva.

Errighi, Lorenza, Charles Bodwell, and Sameer Khatiwada. 2016. "Business Process Outsourcing in the Philippines: Challenges for Decent Work." ILO Asia-Pacific Working Paper Series, International Labour Organization, Geneva.

Faber, Benjamin, and Cecile Gaubert. 2019. "Tourism and Economic Development: Evidence from Mexico's Coastline." *American Economic Review* 109 (6): 2245–93.

Fagerberg, Jan, David Mowery, and Bart Verspagen, eds. 2009. *Innovation, Path Dependency, and Policy: The Norwegian Case.* Oxford: Oxford University Press.

Fernandes, Ana M., and Caroline Paunov. 2012. "Foreign Direct Investment in Services and Manufacturing Productivity: Evidence for Chile." *Journal of Development Economics* 97 (2): 305–21.

Fernandez-Stark, Karina, Penny Bamber, and Gary Gereffi. 2010. "Chile's Offshore Services Value Chain." Technical report, Duke Center on Globalization, Governance, and Competitiveness (Duke CGGC), Duke University, Durham, NC.

Fernandez-Stark, Karina, Penny Bamber, and Gary Gereffi. 2011. "The Offshore Services Value Chain: Upgrading Trajectories in Developing Countries." *International Journal of Technological Learning, Innovation and Development* 4 (1): 206–34.

Francois, Joseph, and Julia Woerz. 2008. "Producer Services, Manufacturing Linkages, and Trade." *Journal of Industry, Competition, and Trade* 8 (3–4): 199–229.

Gebauer, Heiko, Elgar Fleisch, and Thomas Friedli. 2005. "Overcoming the Service Paradox in Manufacturing Companies." *European Management Journal* 23 (1): 14–26.

Goswami, Arti Grover, Aaditya Mattoo, and Sebastián Sáez, eds. 2012. *Exporting Services: A Developing Country Perspective.* Washington, DC: World Bank.

Grossman, Gene M., and Esteban Rossi-Hansberg. 2008. "Trading Tasks: A Simple Theory of Offshoring." *American Economic Review* 98 (5): 1978–97.

Grover, Arti, and Aaditya Mattoo. 2021. "Why Do Manufacturing Firms Sell Services? Evidence from India." Policy Research Working Paper 9701, World Bank, Washington, DC.

Hallward-Driemeier, Mary, and Gaurav Nayyar. 2018. *Trouble in the Making? The Future of Manufacturing-Led Development.* Washington, DC: World Bank.

Healey, Michael J., and Brian W. Ilbery. 1991. *Location and Change: Perspectives on Economic Geography.* Oxford: Oxford University Press.

Hoekman, Bernard, and Dirk Willem te Velde, eds. 2017. "Trade in Services and Economic Transformation: A New Development Policy Priority." Supporting Economic Transformation essay series, Overseas Development Institute, London.

Jensen, Robert. 2012. "Do Labor Market Opportunities Affect Young Women's Work and Family Decisions? Experimental Evidence from India." *Quarterly Journal of Economics* 127 (2): 753–92.

Kimura, Fukunari, and Hyun-Hoon Lee. 2006. "The Gravity Equation in International Trade in Services." *Review of World Economics* 142 (1): 92–121.

Kleibert, Jana. 2015. "Expanding Global Production Networks: The Emergence, Evolution, and Developmental Impact of the Offshore Service Sector in the Philippines." Doctoral thesis, University of Amsterdam.

Lennon, Carolina, Daniel Mirza, and Giuseppe Nicoletti. 2009. "Complementarity of Inputs across Countries in Services Trade." *Annals of Economics and Statistics* 93–94: 183–206.

Liu, Xuepeng, Aaditya Mattoo, Zhi Wang, and Shang-Jin Wei. 2018. "Services Development and Comparative Advantage in Manufacturing." Policy Research Working Paper 8450, World Bank, Washington, DC.

Lodefalk, Magnus. 2013. "Servicification of Manufacturing: Evidence from Sweden." *International Journal of Economics and Business Research* 6 (1): 87–113.

Lodefalk, Magnus. 2015. "Servicification of Manufacturing Firms Makes Divides in Trade Policy-Making Antiquated." Working Paper 2015:1, Örebro University, Örebro, Sweden.

Lopez-Bassols, Vladimir, and Valentine Millot. 2013. "Measuring R&D and Innovation in Services: Key Findings from the OECD INNOSERV project." Paper prepared for the Working Party of National Experts on Science and Technology Indicators (NESTI) and the Working Party on Innovation and Technology Policy (TIP), Organisation for Economic Co-operation and Development (OECD), Paris.

Loungani, Prakash, Saurabh Mishra, Chris Papageorgiou, and Ke Wang. 2017. "World Trade in Services: Evidence from a New Dataset." Working Paper 17/77, International Monetary Fund, Washington, DC.

Low, Patrick. 2013. "The Role of Services." In *Global Value Chains in a Changing World*, edited by Deborah K. Elms and Patrick Low, 61–81. Geneva: World Trade Organization.

Low, Patrick, and Gloria O. Pasadilla, eds. 2016. *Services in Global Value Chains: Manufacturing-Related Services.* Singapore: World Scientific.

Maloney, William F., and Felipe Valencia Caicedo. 2016. "The Persistence of (Subnational) Fortune." *Economic Journal* 126 (598): 2363–2401.

Manyika, James, Michael Chui, Jacques Bughin, Richard Dobbs, Peter Bisson, and Alex Marrs. 2013. "Disruptive Technologies: Advances That Will Transform Life, Business, and the Global Economy." Report, McKinsey Global Institute, McKinsey & Company, New York.

McGregor, Jim. 2019. "IBM Drives Watson AI Everywhere." *Forbes*, February 12.

Miroudot, Sébastien, and Charles Cadestin. 2017. "Services in Global Value Chains: From Inputs to Value-Creating Activities." Trade Policy Paper 197, Organisation for Economic Co-operation and Development, Paris.

Nano, Enrico, Gaurav Nayyar, Stela Rubínová, and Victor Stolzenburg. 2021. "The Impact of Services Liberalization on Education: Evidence from India." Staff Working Paper ERSD-2021-10, World Trade Organization, Geneva.

National Board of Trade of Sweden. 2012. "Everybody Is in Services: The Impact of Servicification in Manufacturing on Trade and Trade Policy." Stockholm: National Board of Trade.

National Board of Trade of Sweden. 2016. *The Servicification of EU Manufacturing: Building Competitiveness in the Internal Market.* Stockholm: National Board of Trade.

National ICT R&D Fund. 2014. "Pakistan IT & ITES Industry Survey 2014." Survey report by the National ICT R&D Fund, Ministry of Information Technology, Government of Pakistan, Islamabad.

Nayyar, Gaurav, Marcio Cruz, and Linghui Zhu. 2018. "Does Premature Deindustrialization Matter? The Role of Manufacturing versus Services in Development." Policy Research Working Paper 8596, World Bank, Washington, DC.

Neely, Andy. 2008. "Exploring the Financial Consequences of the Servitization of Manufacturing." *Operations Management Research* 2 (1): 103–18.

Neely, Andy, Ornella Benedettini, and Ivanka Visnjic. 2011. "The Servitization of Manufacturing: Further Evidence." Paper presented at the 18th European Operations Management Association Conference, Cambridge, July 3–6.

Nordås, Hildegunn K., and Yunhee Kim. 2013. "The Role of Services for Competitiveness in Manufacturing." Trade Policy Paper 148, Organisation for Economic Co-operation and Development (OECD), Paris.

OECD (Organisation for Economic Co-operation and Development). 2015. *International Migration Outlook 2015.* Paris: OECD Publishing.

OECD (Organisation for Economic Co-operation and Development). 2020. *International Migration Outlook 2020.* Paris: OECD Publishing.

Opresnik, David, and Marco Taisch. 2015. "The Value of Big Data in Servitization." *International Journal of Production Economics* 165: 174–84.

Oster, Emily, and Bryce Millett Steinberg. 2013. "Do IT Service Centers Promote School Enrollment? Evidence from India." *Journal of Development Economics* 104: 123–35.

Price, Nicholas A., Jamil P. Francisco, and Christopher E. Caboverde. 2016. "IT-BPO in the Philippines: A Driver of Shared Prosperity?" Working Paper 16-002, Rizalino S. Navarro Policy Center for Competitiveness, Asian Institute of Management, Manila, Philippines.

Rahman, Zia Ur, Izaz Ahmad Khan, Muhammad Shabbir Jan, and Sayyed Abbas Shah. 2017. "Evaluating Telecommunications in Respect to Offshore Software Industry of Pakistan." *International Journal of Research in Computer and Communication Technology* 6 (1): 14–18.

Rodrigue, Jean-Paul. 2016. "Logistics at the Crossroads: Panama and Dubai." Case study for the "Manufacturing Our Future: Cases on the Future of Manufacturing" white paper, World Economic Forum, Geneva.

Sáez, Sebastian, Nadeem Rizwan, and Erik van der Marel. 2020. "Digital Pakistan: A Business and Trade Assessment." Report AUS0001607, World Bank, Washington, DC.

Sanchez, John, and Hassan Boolan. 2009. "Chile Interview Series: Bechtel S.A. Personal communication with K. Fernandez-Stark & G. Gereffi." January 29. Conducted for the Chile in the Offshore Services Global Value Chain project, Duke Center on Globalization, Governance & Competitiveness (Duke CGGC), Duke University, Durham, NC.

SBP (State Bank of Pakistan). 2019. "The State of Pakistan's Economy." First Quarterly Report 2018–19, SBP, Karachi.

Shead, Bob. 2017. "Business Process Outsourcing in the Philippines." Op-ed article, ASEAN Briefing, April 17, https://www.aseanbriefing.com/news/business-process-outsourcing-philippines/.

Shastry, Gauri Kartini. 2012. "Human Capital Response to Globalization: Education and Information Technology in India." *Journal of Human Resources* 47 (2): 287–330.

Shingal, Anirudh. 2010. "How Much Do Agreements Matter for Services Trade?" Paper 32815, Munich Personal RePEc Archive (MPRA), University Library of Munich.

Son, Yoonseock, and Wonseock Oh. 2018. "Alexa, Buy Me a Movie! How AI Speakers Reshape Digital Content Consumption and Preference." Presentation, International Conference on Information Systems (ICIS), San Francisco, December 13–16.

Syverson, Chad. 2011. "What Determines Productivity?" *Journal of Economic literature* 49 (2): 326–65.

UNIDO (United Nations Industrial Development Organization). 2016. *Industrial Development Report 2016: The Role of Technology and Innovation in Inclusive and Sustainable Industrial Development.* Vienna: UNIDO.

Van der Marel, Erik. 2016. "Ricardo Does Services: Service Sector Regulation and Comparative Advantage in Goods." In *Research Handbook on Trade in Services*, edited by Pierre Sauvé and Martin Roy, 85–106. Cheltenham, UK: Edward Elgar Publishing.

Van der Marel, Erik. 2021. "Disentangling Data Flows: Inside and Outside the Multinational Company." In *Trade in the 21st Century: Back to the Past?* edited by Bernard M. Hoekman and Ernesto Zedillo, 331–64. Washington, DC: Brookings Institution Press.

Vandermerwe, Sandra, and Juan Rada. 1988. "Servitization of Business: Adding Value by Adding Services." *European Management Journal* 6 (4): 314–24.

West, John. 2018. "Getting Better Value Out of Global Value Chains." In *Asian Century . . . on a Knife-Edge: A 360 Degree Analysis of Asia's Recent Economic Development*, 91–123. Singapore: Palgrave Macmillan.

WTO (World Trade Organization). 2019. *World Trade Report: The Future of Services Trade.* Geneva: WTO.

Xerox. 2020. "2019 Annual Report: Making Every Day Work Better." Xerox, Louisville, KY.

5 Boosting Productivity to Keep Up the Good Work: Policy Imperatives

Introduction

The framework presented in chapter 1 emphasized the importance of achieving *scale*, fostering *innovation*, and expanding *linkages* across subsectors in raising productivity and creating better jobs for more people. Whereas these gains have traditionally come together in manufacturing, the longer-run evidence for services (as shown in chapter 2) has pointed to a dichotomy: Some services subsectors exhibit significant productivity gains, but they are not necessarily the ones creating many jobs. And the jobs that are being created are primarily in low-skill services subsectors. This still represents a productivity gain, in that many of these jobs are more productive than smallholder farming. However, the big questions center on (a) their potential to drive continued productivity gains over time, and (b) the scope for broader-based services growth to help lower-income countries catch up to higher-income countries.

Looking ahead, changes in technology and shifts in the nature of intersectoral linkages are modifying the potential for scale, innovation, and spillovers in ways that not only raise productivity in higher-skill services subsectors but also can expand the benefits to lower-skill services subsectors. Chapter 3 showed how technological change is expanding the scope for services to be automated, delivered remotely, and scaled up through a rise in intangible capital. Chapter 4 explored growth opportunities in the services sector due to the expanding role of services within manufacturing sector value chains and opportunities that are also independent of a manufacturing base—either through direct exports or through links with other sectors. The trends reinforce each other in part, since sectors with high linkages are among those benefiting most from technology. These sectors' expanded role as enablers means they can help magnify productivity gains and raise demand for jobs in labor-intensive, lower-skill sectors as well.

This chapter brings these findings all together to discuss the policy implications for expanding the services sector's productivity growth and its ability to create better jobs for more people. It does so in four steps: First, it identifies four policy areas—trade, technology, training, and targeting—that expand the potential for scale, innovation, and spillovers, emphasizing the growing potential that technological change and greater intersectoral linkages offer. It discusses what is at stake with each of the four policy areas and what the evidence says regarding the effectiveness of relevant reforms. Second, it measures how countries are performing on these four dimensions as a whole to show where countries currently stand in practice. Third, it examines the implications for policy, by subsector, to identify where the priorities and potential gains could be highest for different countries. Finally, it looks at some of the key issues concerning how policy makers can improve country performance in each of the four policy areas.

Overall, this chapter focuses on how policy makers and the development community can best respond to how different services subsectors are evolving to raise productivity and create more jobs. Policy choices can build on the momentum in technology and linkages to strengthen the services sector's contributions to development.

The Policy Agenda: Trade, Technology, Training, and Targeting (the 4Ts)

To expand services' contributions to development, policies must address their ability to achieve greater scale economies, raise labor productivity through innovation, and take advantage of greater spillover effects through linkages. Chapters 3 and 4 underscored how trends in technology and greater use of enabling services are contributing to these growth opportunities. The policy areas discussed here would build on that momentum along four dimensions: trade, technology, training, and targeting—the "4Ts."

Trade. Lowering barriers to services trade can expand access to larger markets and achieve greater scale. As digital technologies help reduce the need for physical proximity between producers and consumers, reforms could make increasingly tradable services *more* traded in practice. This has an international dimension, but expanded "trade" can also happen domestically. The reduced need for proximity allows businesses to reach customers beyond those in their immediate vicinity, but regulatory barriers and standards can restrict market contestability behind, and not just at, the border.

Technology. Expanding access to digital technologies can expand channels for innovation by reducing the inherent role of labor in services. It underscores the ability for software, big data, and machine learning to perform various tasks more efficiently and also drives new investments in innovation. This is not simply a matter of information and communication technology (ICT) infrastructure but of supporting the adoption and use of digital technologies—and updating the regulatory framework to address new features of data and digital business models.

Training. Improving training and skills development is central to raising both quality and productivity while enabling more workers to move to skill-intensive service subsectors. The agenda is reinforced with the spread of digital technologies to address the demand for digital skills as well as for new skills resulting from the increase in intangible capital associated with ICTs.

Targeting. Recognizing the potential for more linkages between enabling services and other sectors, a case can be made to target the growth of these enabling services subsectors to widen the benefits for productivity and jobs through these multiplier effects.

The increased scope for remote delivery, automation, the rise of intangible capital, and intersectoral linkages have a primary mapping to each of the 4Ts. However, this mapping is not always unique; some of the relationships overlap (table 5.1). The closest one-for-one association is between linkage-engendered intersectoral spillovers and *targeting*. In contrast, buying a *technology* license—even with the necessary infrastructure and regulatory frameworks in place to support the use of artificial intelligence (AI)–related automation—is not sufficient to be able to use it in practice. These capabilities also require the right skills *training* of firms' managers and workers. Furthermore, it is not the automation trend alone that necessitates the adoption of new technologies. For example, the reduced physical proximity between producers and consumers enabled in large part by digital platforms requires *technology* adoption by firms. The expansion of intangible capital to scale up is similarly predicated on *technology* adoption by firms. Last but not least, the expansion of intangible capital may necessitate a *trade*-related policy response if it increases industry concentration among a few firms.

Trade: Enabling Scale through Access to Larger Markets

To take advantage of the reduced need for physical proximity between producers and consumers, three dimensions of policy issues must be addressed to allow services to be traded beyond the local market:

- *Barriers to international trade in services.* Unlike trade in goods, trade in services often requires either (a) the firm (mode 3) or worker (mode 4) to enter the consumer's country to deliver the service, or (b) the customer to move across borders (mode 2)—each of which, in turn, means that regulations on the flow of people and capital matter too.[1]

- *Regulatory barriers.* Regulations affect not only barriers at the border but also domestic regulations that limit competition within sectors. Regulations can both impede international competition and also serve as barriers to the entry or expansion of domestic firms.

- *Data-related regulations.* If it is digital delivery of services that reduces the need for proximity, a regulatory environment that enables the trusted flow of data will be critical.

Physical infrastructure such as ports, roads, and broadband internet networks also matter in enabling services trade; in fact, this infrastructure is itself part of the services sector, such as in transportation and telecommunications.

TABLE 5.1 **The Increased Scope for Scale, Innovation, and Intersectoral Spillovers Can Be Mapped to Each of the 4Ts, but Some of the Relationships Overlap**

Impacts of the changing nature of services on productivity and jobs and resulting policy implications

Aspect	Features of the services sector			
	Scale	**Innovation**		**Spillovers**
Characteristics of traditional services	Simultaneity of production and consumption	Inherent role of labor and limited role for capital, hence reduced incentives for innovation		Multiplier effects from use of enabling services in goods-producing sectors
Trends	Due to ICT, reduced need for physical proximity	Potential for automation and data analytics to leverage labor	From increased intangible capital, more incentives to innovate and invest	Expansion of linkages with other sectors, including other services
Implications for productivity	More efficient matching of supply and demand, hence expanding tradability and widening market access to increase scale	Innovation boosted by gains in scale and efficiency in business processes	Improved service quality and incentives for innovation (with some impact on scale too)	Greater spillovers for other sectors, including other services
Implications for jobs	Potential expansion of job locations, with higher demand increasing the number of jobs	Likely greater substitution of labor and shifting mix of job tasks (as usually tasks rather than whole jobs can be automated)	Potentially higher demand for skills	Higher multipliers for employment growth
Policy implications to realize benefits of these trends	*Trade*—to lower barriers to services trade and competition, hence expanding access to markets	*Technology*—to improve access to ICT and technology adoption, with complementary policies to ensure competition and inclusion	*Training*—to raise digital and complementary interpersonal skills and management practices	*Targeting*—to expand spillovers

Source: Summary based on chapters 1–5.

Note: The arrows indicate the mapping of each forward-looking trend (reduced proximity, automation, intangible capital, and linkages) to the 4Ts agenda. ICT = information and communication technology.

At Your Service? The Promise of Services-Led Development

International Trade in Services: A More Complex Agenda Than Liberalizing Goods Trade

To date, much of the progress in trade liberalization has been for goods, owing to a dramatic reduction in quotas, quantitative restrictions, and tariffs through various rounds of multilateral negotiations. Nontariff barriers, including domestic regulatory requirements, are more common, but even here, trade barriers in services remain higher than for goods (Miroudot, Sauvage, and Shepherd 2013). Examples of restrictions in services can vary from outright bans on foreign ownership to national licensing requirements and local content requirements.

Measures of Services Trade Restrictiveness

Restrictions on services trade are more common in low- and middle-income countries (LMICs) than in high-income countries (figure 5.1). However, LMICs exhibit considerable variation. Countries such as Ecuador, Ghana, Mongolia, Nigeria, and Senegal are remarkably open. On the other hand, several LMICs—primarily in the Middle East and North Africa, South Asia, and East Asia and the Pacific—have some of the most restrictive policies. They include countries that have achieved fast growth, such as China, India, Indonesia, Malaysia, the Philippines, and Thailand.

FIGURE 5.1 **Services Trade Restrictions Show Considerable Variation but Are Higher in LMICs Than in HICs**

Services Trade Restrictiveness Index by country income level, 2016

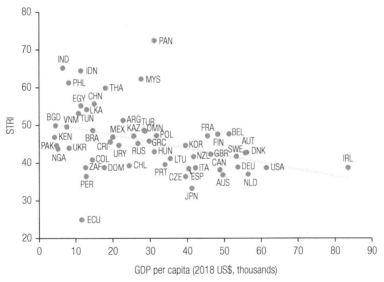

Source: Calculations based on Borchert et al. 2019 and World Development Indicators database.

Note: The 2016 Services Trade Restrictiveness Index (STRI), covering 55 countries across regions and income levels, is based on information in the Services Trade Policy Database, a joint initiative of the World Bank and the World Trade Organization (WTO). It covers three out of the four modes of supply in the WTO's General Agreement on Trade in Services (GATS): cross-border supply (mode 1), commercial presence (mode 3), and presence of natural persons (mode 4). The STRI score ranges from 0 to 100, where 0 is completely open and 100 is completely closed for foreign service suppliers. Low- and middle-income countries (LMICs), by World Bank income group classifications, had 1994 gross national income (GNI) of less than US$8,955. High-income countries (HICs) had GNI exceeding US$8,955 in 1994. Countries are labeled using ISO alpha-3 codes.

Services subsectors also vary considerably in trade restrictiveness. Professional, scientific, and technical services are among the most protected in both high-income countries and LMICs, reflecting in part national licensing requirements and a reluctance to recognize other countries' accreditation. Of the 73 countries with data available from 2016 to 2019, 62 have aggregate scores above 40 (on a 1–100 scale), and in 63 countries, the professional services restrictiveness score exceeds the national average for all the sectors for which data are available (Borchert at al. 2019).

It is therefore not surprising that among these professional services—where the potential for trade is high because the need for physical proximity between producers and consumers is less important—the level of international trade is low compared with goods-producing sectors (figure 5.2).

Variable Declines in Restrictions Across Countries

The good news is that restrictions on these professional services—which provide opportunities, much like goods, for international specialization (see chapter 4)—have declined across all countries between 2008 and 2016 (figure 5.3, panel a).

FIGURE 5.2 **Professional Services Are among the Least Traded Sectors, Despite High Tradability, Given Their Low Face-to-Face Interactions with Consumers**
Face-to-face interactions index in relation to trade-to-output ratio in the United States, by sector, 2018

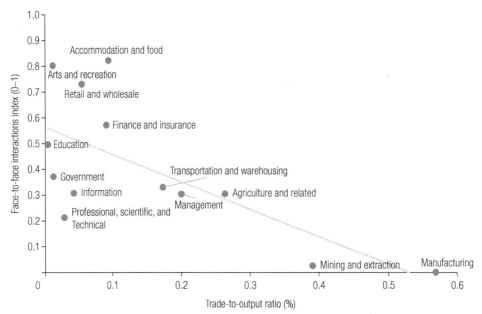

Source: Calculations based on US Bureau of Economic Analysis data and the US Department of Labor's Occupational Information Network (O*NET) database.

Note: The index of face-to-face interactions with consumers, developed by Avdiu and Nayyar (2020), measures the extent to which an occupation involves (a) establishing and maintaining personal relationships; (b) assisting and caring for others; (c) performing for or working directly with the public; and (d) selling to or influencing others. It ranges from 0 (none) to 1 (highest).

FIGURE 5.3 **Trade Restrictions Have Declined on Professional Services but Not on Retail Services**

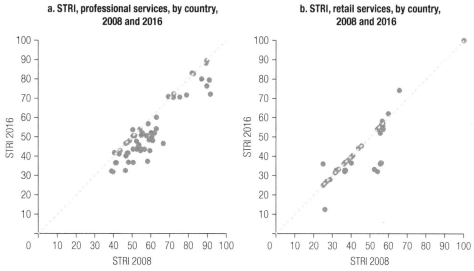

a. STRI, professional services, by country, 2008 and 2016

b. STRI, retail services, by country, 2008 and 2016

Source: Calculations based on Borchert et al. 2019.

Note: The 2016 Services Trade Restrictiveness Index (STRI), covering 55 countries across all regions and income levels, is based on information contained in the Services Trade Policy Database, a joint initiative of the World Bank and the World Trade Organization (WTO), and is constructed to be comparable to the 2008–11 World Bank STRI. It covers three out of the four modes of supply in the WTO's General Agreement on Trade in Services (GATS): cross-border supply (mode 1), commercial presence (mode 3), and presence of natural persons (mode 4).The STRI score ranges from 0 to 100, where 0 is completely open and 100 is completely closed for foreign service suppliers. In retail services (panel b), Panama scored 100 on both the 2008 and 2016 STRI.

Among low-skill services such as retail trade, few countries had higher rates of restrictions in 2016 than in 2008. Only 7 countries had greater restrictions in these sectors that they did overall, and only 17 of the 74 with updated Services Trade Restrictiveness Index (STRI) scores had values above 40. Large emerging markets (such as Argentina, India, Indonesia, Malaysia, Thailand, and Vietnam), together with high-income European countries (such as Belgium, Finland, France, and Greece) are among those with the highest restrictions in retail services and have made little progress in reducing these restrictions since 2008 (figure 5.2, panel b).

With retail services, the restrictions are most commonly through service delivery mode 3 ("commercial presence" in a foreign country). Restrictions on foreign retail chains or big-box stores are a case in point. These services are not subject to international specialization, owing to the importance of proximity, and are therefore large in all countries. As a result, trade liberalization promises enormous productivity gains through greater competition and lower prices for consumers. The impact on jobs would depend on whether the competition displaced local service providers and what types of linkages exist between the foreign service providers and other domestic firms (box 5.1).

Scaling Up Food Services Retail: The Role of Foreign Direct Investment

Food retail services have been largely transformed in higher-income economies, with mom-and-pop and corner stores having made way for larger-scale supermarkets, hypermarkets, big-box stores, and more recently e-commerce (Hortaçsu and Syverson 2015). Traditional small-scale forms of retail nevertheless remain commonplace in low- and middle-income economies, where they still account for 57 percent of sales, against 19 percent in high-income economies (Bronnenberg and Ellickson 2015). In some economies, such as India, Nigeria, and Pakistan, more than 90 percent of sales are conducted in small-scale food retail stores (figure B5.1.1).

The reallocation of market share from small-scale stores to larger supermarkets has been a major source of productivity gains in food retail in the United States (Foster, Haltiwanger, and Krizan 2006). These larger firms achieve scale not only through larger establishments (such as supermarkets) but also through establishments in multiple locations (see chapter 2)—that is, chain stores (Jia 2008). These large chains can also negotiate higher discounts from suppliers through bulk purchases. Big-box retail stores that combine a supermarket with a department store are even larger (for example, Walmart in the United States, Asda in the United Kingdom, and the hypermarchés in France). The e-commerce share of food retail has also grown, such as through Amazon Fresh in the United States and Ocado in the United Kingdom.

Foreign direct investment (FDI) has played an important role in expanding larger-scale retail across LMICs: the 100 largest global retailers operate, on average, in 12 countries (Bronnenberg and Ellickson 2015; Deloitte 2014). This expansion of large-scale retail has been associated with productivity gains. For example, Walmart's entry in Mexico resulted in lower prices and innovation among Walmart's suppliers, with a decline in market share for less-efficient producers (Iacovone et al. 2015). In Romania, retail multinational companies (MNCs) had similar productivity-enhancing impacts on local suppliers (Javorcik and Li 2013). There is a large benefit in terms of household welfare too. Atkin, Faber, and Gonzalez-Navarro (2018) argue that foreign entry of supermarkets in Mexico significantly lowered prices for consumers.

The question is what this means for jobs and their quality. The reallocation toward larger stores implies that new jobs are created but potentially are displacing those in traditional stores. For example, Walmart's entry into a given US county between 1977 and 1998 immediately created about 100 jobs in that county but over the subsequent five years displaced approximately 50 jobs in other retail establishments and 20 jobs in wholesale firms, for a net gain of 30 jobs (Basker 2005).[2] Neumark, Zhang, and Ciccarella (2008) suggest that the displacement might in fact be higher and not compensated by new jobs, while Haltiwanger, Jarmin, and Krizan (2010) find that the displacement is likely localized.

There is some evidence that the entry of larger-scale FDI retail has increased job quality in LMICs. For example, FDI firms in Romania pay higher wages than domestic retailers (Javorcik and Li 2013). Iacovone et al. (2015) highlight that the entry of Walmart in Mexico affected job quality throughout the supply chain, with wages in large upstream firms increasing, but those in smaller firms (which are less likely to supply to Walmart) decreasing.

Box continues on the following page

BOX 5.1

Scaling Up Food Services Retail: The Role of Foreign Direct Investment *(continued)*

FIGURE B5.1.1 **Traditional Food Retail Formats Are Predominant in Low- and Middle-Income Economies but Have Been Replaced by Supermarkets or Hypermarkets in High-Income Economies**

Share of food retail sales in selected economies, by retail format, 2014

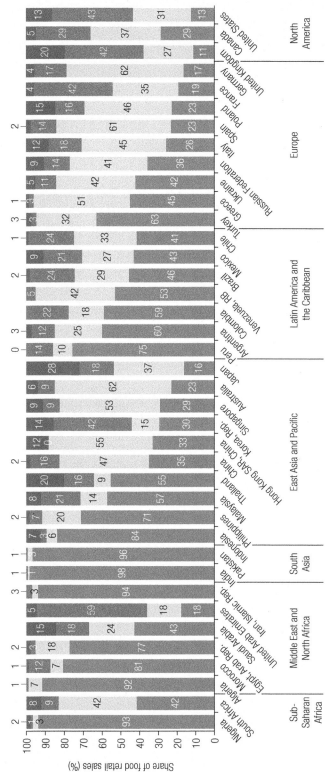

Legend: ■ Traditional ▨ Supermarkets ▨ Hypermarkets ■ Convenience

Source: Adapted from Bronnenberg and Ellickson 2015, originally based on Euromonitor International data.

Note: "Traditional retail formats" include small-scale stores and specialized food and beverage stores. "Supermarkets" include both traditional supermarkets and specialized food and beverage stores. "Supermarkets" include small-scale stores and specialized food and beverage stores. "Hypermarkets" include wholesaling clubs. Low- and middle-income economies are classified by their 1994 income levels. High-income economies are those whose gross national income per capita was at least US$8,955 in 1994.

Although much of the empirical literature has focused on the gains to liberalizing goods trade, the potential gains from liberalizing services trade should be even higher (Hoekman 2006). This is both because many countries are starting at a higher level of protection and because the spillover benefits of intersectoral linkages are much larger for services. Robinson, Wang, and Martin (2002) estimated that the gains from a 50 percent cut in protection would be five times higher for services than for goods. Furthermore, the liberalization of services trade can have direct and sizable effects on goods trade and vice versa (Ariu, Mayneris, and Parenti 2020). Gains also vary across countries. Progress is more evident among larger economies, whereas small economies have benefited relatively less (Anderson et al. 2018). Countries that have excelled in goods trade, such as those in East Asia, could also benefit from liberalization of services trade to expand opportunities in the services sector (Jensen 2013).

If a lower-income country were to move to the average openness of financial services seen in higher-income countries (roughly 50 percent higher), GDP per capita growth rates would increase by an estimated 0.4–0.6 percent annually (Eschenbach and Francois 2002). Similarly, Mattoo, Rathindran, and Subramanian (2006) find that with full financial services liberalization, LMICs and high-income countries, respectively, would grow 2.3 percent and 1.2 percent faster. Several studies also find a close link between telecommunications liberalization and higher GDP growth rates, especially in lower-income countries where FDI can complement relatively scarce physical capital (El Khoury and Savvides 2006; Eschenbach and Hoekman 2006; Mattoo, Rathindran, and Subramanian 2006).

Studies also examine different modes of service delivery. Borchert, Gootiiz, and Mattoo (2012) estimate the impacts of restrictions on foreign acquisitions, national discrimination in licensing, restrictions on the repatriation of earnings, and lack of legal recourse for foreign companies regarding FDI restrictions.[3] They find the expected value of FDI could be US$2.2 billion lower over a seven-year period in a country and sector characterized by a "closed" policy regime (STRI score of 75–100) than in an "open" policy regime (STRI score of 0–25). They also find that countries that restrict the establishment of foreign banks rather than imposing operational restrictions have a 3.3 percentage point lower credit-to-GDP ratio. In addition, Fernandes and Paunov (2008) find that opening FDI in services in Chile contributed 5 percent to manufacturing productivity growth from 1992 to 2004. And Nordås and Kox (2009) estimate that if all economies harmonized or recognized each other's regulations, a country's total services trade through commercial presence in another country could increase by 13–30 percent.

As for the mobility of factors, it is expected that liberalizing services trade would enable lower-income countries to attract more capital and skilled labor, which would benefit unskilled workers through expanded job opportunities and wages. The scale effects could even outweigh substitution effects, such that local skilled workers also gain (Markusen, Rutherford, and Tarr 2000). In Europe, allowing greater mobility of workers (equivalent to 3 percent of the European Union's labor force) would have greater benefits than the complete liberalization of all remaining restrictions on goods trade, with estimated gains exceeding US$150 billion (Walmsley and Winters 2005).

Domestic Regulations: At the Heart of Expanding Services Trade

As is clear from the discussion on the regulation of different modes of services trade, much of the agenda on "trade" in services is really about domestic regulations, which affect the trade not just internationally, but also domestically.

Balancing Public Interest with Effects on Competition

Services sectors are among the most regulated domestically. Some of them are regulated as natural monopolies, such as in communications or railway networks. Some are sectors that involve a sizable public provision of services (for example, health or education), with strong public interest dimensions on quality standards and a commitment to making access widely available. In other sectors, standards are regulated because of information asymmetries on quality and the need to demonstrate the significant human capital investments necessary to meet these standards (as in professional services). Still other sectors must comply with public safety requirements (for example, accommodation and food, as well as transportation).

One question is whether the regulations go beyond protecting such public interests and serve to raise barriers to entry that benefit incumbents (box 5.2). In some cases, regulations are indeed designed to protect segments from competition, particularly foreign competition—such as in retail trade, where restrictions on big-box stores or foreign retail chains are in place. One of the most restricted services is air transportation, whose regulation reflects national interests in maintaining national airlines.

Thus, the services trade agenda concerns not only the international mobility of capital and labor but also broader barriers to entry and competition, licensing requirements, and standards. Domestic regulations may not discriminate against foreign providers explicitly but can have that effect in practice. If all workers in licensed professions must be accredited by a domestic educational institution, the effect is to keep foreign service providers from entering the local market. In addition, market access can be unpredictable if the allocation of new licenses remains opaque and highly discretionary, as it is in many countries. Having clear and transparent criteria for licensing or permits is important, but the gaps between what is on the books and what happens in practice can be significant (Hallward-Driemeier and Pritchett 2015; World Bank 2020).

Beyond Border Restrictions: How Domestic Regulations Affect Potential for Competitiveness and Scale

Since 1998, the Organisation for Economic Co-operation and Development (OECD) has collected measures of product market regulations. The World Bank has collaborated to extend the coverage to 20 more LMICs. Together, they cover 70 countries: 33 high-income countries and 37 LMICs. These OECD–World Bank economy-wide product market regulation (PMR) Indicators cover three areas of regulation: (a) state control (including state ownership or price controls); (b) barriers to entrepreneurship (complexity of regulatory procedures, administrative burdens on start-ups, and regulatory protection of incumbents); and (c) barriers to trade and investment. The latter pillar overlaps with the STRI; the other two provide additional dimensions of interest.

As with trade restrictions, there is considerable variation in various measures of state control, but the levels are higher among LMICs than high-income countries. This holds especially true for the involvement of state-owned enterprises (SOEs) in network sectors (such as telecommunications and transportation), governance of SOEs, and price controls (figure B5.2.1).

In practice, this high degree of state control restricts not only the ability of foreign firms to enter (mode 3 services trade) but also the ability of more domestic firms to enter and invest. However, more high-income countries have converged in terms of allowing for more competition (Dauda and Drozd 2020). Furthermore, among both high-income countries and LMICs, some services subsectors are more regulated than others. For example, rail transportation services are the most protected among network sectors (figure B5.2.2, panel a) and legal services the most protected among professional services (figure B5.2.2, panel b).

FIGURE B5.2.1 **Regulatory Barriers from State Control in the Services Sector Are More Widespread in LMICs Than in HICs**

PMR scores on selected state control indicators, HICs and LMICs, 2013–17

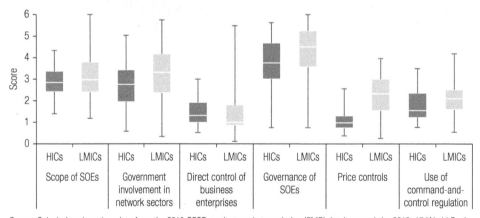

Source: Calculations based on data from the 2013 OECD product market regulation (PMR) database and the 2013–17 World Bank–OECD PMR database.

Note: The year of data varies by country, between 2013 and 2017. The product market regulation (PMR) score for each indicator of state control ranges from 0 (the most competition-friendly regulatory regime) to 6 (the least competition-friendly). White lines across bars indicate the median. Error bars indicate the range of country scores. The sectors covered here include electricity, gas, and water supply (classified under "Industry" in the International Standard Industrial Classification of All Economic Activities [ISIC] classification); as well as transportation, telecommunications, retail, and professional services. "Network sectors" include energy, transportation, and e-communications. Low- and middle-income countries (LMICs) are classified by their 1994 income levels. High-income countries (HICs) are those whose gross national income per capita was at least US$8,955 in 1994. OECD = Organisation for Economic Co-operation and Development. SOEs = state-owned enterprises.

Box continues on the following page

FIGURE B5.2.2 **Product Market Regulation in Network and Professional Services Is Higher in LMICs Than in HICs—and Highest in Rail Transportation and Legal Services in Both Groups of Countries**

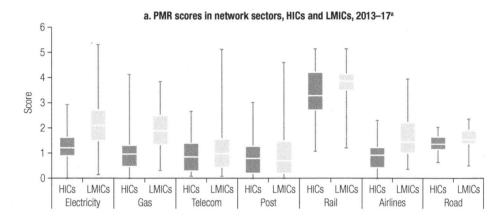

a. PMR scores in network sectors, HICs and LMICs, 2013–17[a]

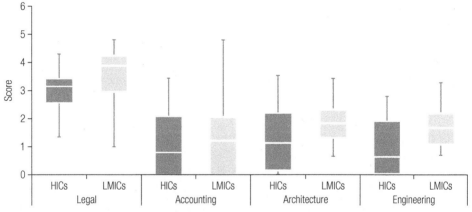

b. PMR scores in professional services, HICs and LMICs, 2013–17[b]

Source: Calculations based on data from the 2013 OECD product market regulation (PMR) database and the 2013–17 World Bank–OECD PMR database.

Note: The year of data varies by country, between 2013 and 2017. The product market regulations (PMR) scores for each sector are aggregate scores ranging from 0 (the most competition-friendly regulatory regime) to 6 (the least competition-friendly). White lines across bars indicate the median. Error bars indicate the range of country scores. Low- and middle-income countries (LMICs) are classified by their 1994 income levels. High-income countries (HICs) are those whose gross national income per capita was at least US$8,955 in 1994. OECD = Organisation for Economic Co-operation and Development.

a. "Network sectors" include electricity, gas, and water supply, transportation, and e-communications.

b. "Professional services" include lawyers, notaries, accountants, architects, engineers, and real estate agents.

Liberalizing trade is likely to bring bigger gains in some services subsectors than others, with the gains likely highest where the linkages are highest. For example, pro-competition reforms in India's banking, transportation, insurance, and telecommunications services were found to boost the productivity of both foreign and locally owned manufacturing firms. A 1 standard deviation improvement in the aggregated index of services liberalization resulted in productivity increases of 11.7 percent and 13.2 percent for domestic and foreign enterprises, respectively. The largest impacts resulted from transportation reforms, followed by telecommunications and banking reforms (Arnold et al. 2016).

The likely benefits of deep trade agreements that liberalize domestic regulations will depend largely on the extent to which they affect key enabling services, especially transportation and logistics (Hofmann, Osnago, and Ruta 2019) and financial and business services (Borchert and Di Ubaldo, forthcoming).

The Francois and Hoekman (2010) review of services trade looks at how many LMICs stand to benefit disproportionately from reforms that would improve service delivery. Many studies look at single sectors and show how the gains from reforms (or costs of the status quo) would be higher for LMICs relative to high-income countries—for example, Clark, Dollar, and Micco (2004) in maritime shipping; Doove et al. (2001) in air transportation; and Kalirajan et al. (2000) in banking services. Other studies did not show a disproportionate benefit, but that LMICs would still gain: Kalirajan (2000) on retail food distribution and Doove et al. (2001) on telecommunication services.

Data Flow Policies: Critical for Benefiting from Lower Proximity Needs

The third dimension of policies to expand services trade regard the exchange of data, particularly commercial data, across borders. This pertains most to mode 1 (cross-border) trade, with the digitalization of service delivery expanding the scope for services trade that does not need proximity of producers and consumers. It is also relevant for other modes, particularly mode 3 (foreign commercial presence), because the intangible assets and use of data to improve services are likely to be most effective if data can be shared across all units in a larger firm.

The impact of expanding access to digital technologies on trade expansion has been recognized for years. The internet contributed about 1 percentage point growth in global annual export growth from 1997 to 1999 (Freund and Weinhold 2002). Much of the earlier work focused on how the internet facilitated coordination in manufacturing global value chains (GVCs); more recently, the attention is on digitally provided services in their own right. Between 2000 and 2015, global data traffic over the internet rose by a factor of 863; far more is now possible in terms of using digital technologies to deliver services across borders (Ferracane, Kren, and van der Marel 2020).

Dimensions of Data Flow Issues

In looking at the policy issues, there are two dimensions to overseeing data flows. One concerns the approaches to data flows across borders. The other regards restrictions on *which* data can be collected, *how* they can be processed, *what* they can be used for, and *who* they can be shared with. These issues are more pressing for personal data than commercial data, although the increasing collection of data makes even commercial data increasingly identifiable and tied to personal data (Hallward-Driemeier et al. 2020).

Although countries' approaches to the domestic and international flows of data can be aligned, it is not necessarily so. Some countries put few restrictions (in some cases, no restrictions) on internal data flows but require data localization so no data can flow out of the country—a "limited transfer model." Other countries allow international flows as long as they meet other criteria on processing and uses of data—a "conditional transfer model." Still others provide minimal standards on either domestic or international flows—an "open transfers model." Outright bans on international data flows clearly limit the ability to gain from trade in services. But concerns about how other countries will respect the privacy of personal data can limit the willingness to let data flow across borders too.

Choosing Data Policies for Productivity and Trade

Based on data from 64 economies between 2006 and 2015, Van der Marel and Ferracane (2021) find that the imports of services over the internet would rise on average by 5 percent across all economies if they lifted their restrictions on cross-border data flows. Using more recent data, Ferracane and van der Marel (2020) categorize 116 countries' data policies on cross-border flows and domestic data processing to test their impacts on flows of cross-border services trade. They test whether countries sharing similar data policy approaches exhibit higher or lower digital services trade with each other than countries with different regulatory data approaches. Sharing a similar approach to domestic data flows is associated with higher international flows between partner countries in both open and conditional transfer models. However, countries with permissive sharing domestically and international localization, such as China, suffer a "double whammy," with fewer countries willing to send their data and, of course, with data not flowing out (Ferracane and van der Marel 2020).

Using a computable general equilibrium model, Bauer et al. (2013) estimate the economic impact of the General Data Protection Regulation (GDPR) of the European Union (EU) and find a reduction of trade between the EU and the rest of the world. Ferracane, Kren, and van der Marel (2020) also show that stricter data policies have a negative and significant impact on the performance of downstream firms in sectors reliant on electronic data. They also find that this adverse effect is stronger among countries with strong technology networks and among more servitized firms. More broadly, cross-border data flows can also contribute to the diffusion of knowledge and facilitate specialized production in GVCs that has contributed significantly to productivity growth in manufacturing (World Bank 2020).[4]

Technology: Improving Quality through Innovation

The Centrality of Adopting Digital Technologies

Digital technologies have an especially large role to play in the services sector.[5] As noted in chapter 3, the use of digital technologies is positively related to productivity gains, across the entire range of services subsectors, and is enabling new business models and new ways in which more firms can reach wider markets. These technologies include software applications, digital platforms, data analytics, and machine learning (ML) algorithms. They can be used to enable remote delivery, automate certain tasks, and raise the impact of intangible capital such that digital technologies enhance the ability and incentives of firms in the services sector to achieve scale and innovate.

Discoveries at the frontier tend to be concentrated in high-income countries, or even within certain regions or larger firms in high-income countries (Balland and Rigby 2017). For LMICs, most "innovation" entails the adoption of already existing technologies, with some possible adaptation to local conditions. There remains substantial variation in the adoption of technology not only across but also within countries. Even though new technologies reach lower-income countries sooner than before, the intensity in which these technologies are used in lower-income countries is much lower than elsewhere (Comin and Mestieri 2018). Despite the availability of newer technologies and their adoption by some frontier firms, many firms do not use them. The implication is not one of concern but rather that policies in LMICs should appropriately focus on encouraging adoption of the most-basic digital technologies. There can be tremendous gains to productivity from catching up (Cirera and Maloney 2017).

The Building Blocks: Broadband Internet, Data Regulations, and Firm Capabilities

Given the relevance of digital technologies, expanding access to the internet—and particularly broadband internet—is crucial. For instance, Hjort and Poulsen (2019) show that the arrival of internet cables in Africa predominantly benefited services firms, spurring market entry and boosting productivity. The internet is particularly relevant for services, for example, to be able to sell to clients (as through e-commerce) or to use distributed computing (such as cloud services). The internet has also enabled many services that once required face-to-face interactions to be delivered more remotely, as shown in chapter 3. The COVID-19 pandemic has shown that workers who perform certain services tasks (such as e-learning, telemedicine, and professional services) have been more able to work from home than those in the manufacturing or primary sectors (for example, Avdiu and Nayyar 2020; Bloom 2020). Internet access among the wider population has been crucial to enable such home-based work.

However, such access alone is not sufficient. Firms must make the most of the internet's potential, using it to upgrade and innovate how they do business. For most firms in most countries, this is about adopting technology—whether software applications, digital platforms, or more-advanced ML algorithms. The extent of unexploited potential here is underscored by the low use of even the most basic digital technologies. For example, as noted in chapter 3, the share of firms that have a website or use email to communicate with suppliers or customers varies considerably but is below 20 percent in many low- and middle-income countries.

The low shares of digital technology use can reflect gaps in the availability of affordable internet service, but they also reflect gaps in the capabilities of firms (as addressed below in the "training" section). Progress is needed on both fronts. The incentives and ability to use technologies are also affected by the regulation of digital markets. The potential scale and network effects of digital platform businesses raise new challenges for competition authorities. To ensure a level playing field for firms using digital platforms, it is critical to update data and competition polices (Hallward-Driemeier et al. 2020; World Bank 2021).

Training: Expanding Skills Development

The growing role for intangible capital associated with digital technologies places the improvement of workforce skills at the forefront. This does not mean that all the needed skills are "high end." Basic ICT skills, such as how to use email and word-processing software, relies on foundational cognitive skills, such as literacy and numeracy, as well as "soft" skills that foster adaptability, problem solving, and initiative. In addition to employee skills training, managerial and organizational practices that strengthen firm capabilities matter too.

High-End (Digital and Other) Technical Skills

The ability to design and work with complex information systems, especially in global innovator services, requires advanced skills in systems design, programming, and ML algorithms. However, many workers report that their lack of ICT skills is a constraint to employment and higher earnings (figure 5.4). For example, about 40 percent of workers in Vietnam report that deficient ICT skills prevent them from finding a job or getting a better-paying job. The shortage of such skills is an important barrier to growing these more productive services subsectors that provide higher-quality jobs.

FIGURE 5.4 **In Many LMICs, a Sizable Share of Working-Age Individuals Report That Their Lack of ICT Skills Is a Constraint to Employment or Higher Earnings**

Share of working-age individuals reporting lack of ICT skills as an employment constraint, selected LMICs, circa 2013

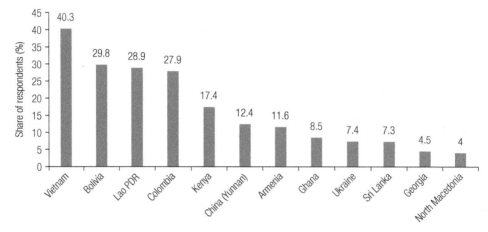

Source: Adapted from World Bank 2016, based on World Bank STEP household surveys.
Note: ICT = information and communication technology; STEP = Skills Towards Employment and Productivity.

While the expanding role of digital technology is putting a lot of attention on digital skills, a larger skills agenda is important for many services. Skill-intensive social services such as education and health require a great deal of traditional technical training, as do professional service providers. Education, and particularly tertiary education, plays a large role in equipping workers with many of the necessary advanced technical skills. It also fosters more-general skills—such as complex problem solving, critical thinking, and advanced communication—that are critical in these skill-intensive services. It is then not a surprise that countries with higher tertiary enrollment generally see a larger share of people employed in services subsectors that are intensive in using these skills (figure 5.5).

Beyond High-End Technical Skills

Not everyone using a computer or a smartphone needs to know how to code, but they do need basic cognitive skills such as literacy and numeracy. Building these skills means exposing children at a young age to basic digital technologies, such as how to use email and word-processing software, while also encouraging lifelong learning.

Beyond digital literacy, there is also a growing recognition of a wider set of skills associated with higher quality and customer satisfaction. Socioemotional and interpersonal skills play an especially important role in services characterized by a high degree

242   At Your Service? The Promise of Services-Led Development

FIGURE 5.5

Global Innovator Services Make Up a Higher Share of Total Employment in Countries with Higher Tertiary Enrollment Rates

Tertiary enrollment rates in relation to share of business and professional services in employment, by country, 2016

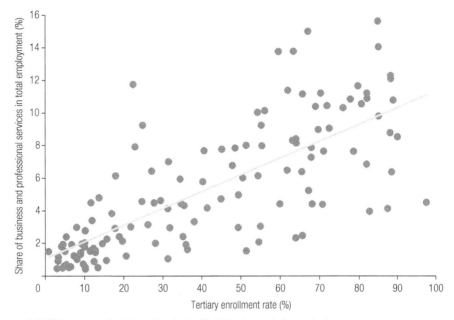

Sources: ILOSTAT data, International Labour Organization; World Development Indicators database.

Note: The dataset covers 129 countries across regions and income groups. For countries whose enrollment rates are unavailable for 2016, data are for 2015 or 2014.

of customization and the simultaneity of production and consumption that necessitates a close relationship with consumers. It is precisely these skills that slow down the automation of waiters in restaurants or hosts at event venues. In these industries, part of the value of the service would disappear if it were automated. Similarly, market research in the United States shows that the vast majority of consumers would be less likely to use a brand if there were no human consumer representative (Press 2019). The intangibility of many services, which often precludes the writing of complete contracts, also emphasizes these interpersonal skills where trust between the supplier and the buyer is crucial.

Managerial and Organizational Practices to Strengthen Skills within Firms
Beyond the capabilities of workers, management capabilities and practices also matter for firm performance (Bloom, Sadun, and Van Reenen 2012). They are crucial elements of the production process but cannot be bought "off the shelf" (Sutton 2012).

The importance of management practices for manufacturing firms has been well established. Among US manufacturing firms, the adoption of "structured" management practices[6] alone accounts for an estimated 22 percent of the total factor productivity (TFP) gap between a firm in the lowest and highest decile (Bloom, Brynjolfsson, et al. 2019). This is similar to the contribution of R&D and exceeds the contributions of ICT and human capital. Similarly, cross-country analyses show that roughly a third of differences in GDP could be related to differences in managerial practices (Bloom et al. 2014).

Many of the principles constituting good management practices, although developed with manufacturing firms in mind, also apply to services. For example, the concept of "lean manufacturing"—initially describing practices of Japanese carmakers to tie production more closely to demand—gave way to "lean retailing," whereby retailers minimize unsold stocks by carefully monitoring sales, allowing for lower inventories (see, for example, Abernathy et al. 1999; Evans and Harrigan 2005).

Sector-specific adaptations of the World Management Survey (WMS) applied to retail (Institute for Competitiveness & Prosperity 2010), health care (Bloom et al. 2020), or education (Bloom et al. 2015) show that measures of adoption of structured management practices—such as the importance to the firm of target setting, monitoring, and incentives—are associated with higher sales (figure 5.6).

Yet an analysis of new firm-level data from 2017–19 World Bank Enterprise Surveys suggests that the adoption of structured management practices is lower among services firms than manufacturing firms[7] in 36 of the 48 countries with available data (figure 5.7).[8] This finding reinforces new evidence from Mexico (illustrated in Bloom, Iacovone, et al. 2019) that management practices are less correlated with firm size in the services sector, especially in areas with small local markets.

Furthermore, the adoption of management practices in services tends to be higher in higher-income countries, even though the data show substantial variation.[9] A comparison of services sectors shows that low-skill sectors (such as retail and hotels and restaurants) exhibit low adoption of structured managerial practices relative to manufacturing firms. Meanwhile, transportation, wholesale, and information technology (IT) services exhibit such practices at levels similar to manufacturing firms (figure 5.8). This pattern holds for both LMICs and high-income countries.

Targeting: Enabling High-Linkage Services for Greater Spillovers

Industrial policy that targets specific sectors has been typically associated with the targeting of "complex goods" associated with the manufacturing sector (Maloney and Nayyar 2018). As LMICs turn increasingly toward the services sector, the

FIGURE 5.6 **In Most Countries, Services Firms' Adoption of Structured Management Practices Is Associated with Higher Sales per Employee**

Regression coefficient of log sales per employee on management scores of firms in services and manufacturing sectors, selected countries, late 2010s

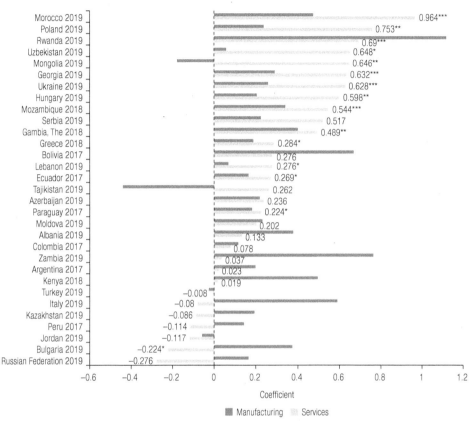

Source: Calculations based on World Bank Enterprise Survey data.

Note: The figures reported are the coefficients from a linear regression of log sales per employee on the management score (a sum of scores for operations, monitoring, targets, and incentives, with a maximum score of 12 and normalized for each country). No further controls have been applied. For roughly half (19) of the 48 countries with available data, the coefficient for services firms is also significantly different from zero at (at least) the 10 percent significance level. For manufacturing firms, the coefficient is positive for 42 out of 48 countries, and it is significantly different from zero at (at least) the 10 percent level for 25 countries. For 29 countries, the coefficient for services is higher than for manufacturing. Not all countries are shown in the figure because of space constraints.

Significance level: * = 10 percent, ** = 5 percent, *** = 1 percent.

conventional conception of targeting industrial development must address modern economic activities more broadly, including but not limited to manufacturing. This changing reality is already reflected in the use of terminology that ranges from "productive development policies," "structural transformation policies," and "productivity policies" to "learning, industrial, and technology policies" (Aiginger and Rodrik 2020).

FIGURE 5.7 **In 36 of 48 Surveyed Countries, the Adoption of Structured Management Practices Is Lower in Services Than in Manufacturing**

Relative average management scores of manufacturing and services firms, by country income group, late 2010s

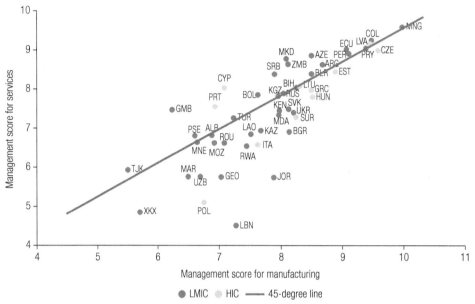

Source: Calculations based on World Bank Enterprise Survey data.

Note: Enterprise Surveys were conducted in 48 countries among firms with at least five employees between 2017 and 2019. Management scores are a sum of scores for operations, monitoring, targets, and incentives, with a maximum score of 12. The scoring methodology is based on Bloom, Sadun, and Van Reenen (2012), with adjustments for the targets and incentives scores due to non-availability of comparable data from Latin American countries for these indexes. Low- and middle-income countries, by World Bank income group classifications, had 1994 gross national income (GNI) of less than US$8,955. High-income countries had GNI exceeding US$8,955 in 1994. Countries are labeled using ISO alpha-3 codes.

The Risk Environment for Sector-Specific Interventions

Sector-specific interventions may be riskier now than in the past because of rapid changes and increasing uncertainty in the global economic landscape. The extent and pace of technological change is unknown, although diffusion has been accelerating. AI-enabled technologies are not new, but their applications have been expanding across sectors as they improve what they can do and as the associated costs fall. With advances in cognition and perception-related tasks, many services that were less automatable in the previous ICT revolution are increasingly suitable to ML.

With change happening so quickly, there is a risk of betting on and investing in sectors where the technology in use becomes obsolete. This risk is then further compounded by uncertainty about future demand, too, because obsolescence occurs on both the supply and demand sides. Recent events such as the COVID-19 pandemic further highlight how uncertainty makes sector-specific bets riskier, given the disproportionate effects on particular services subsectors due to social distancing.

FIGURE 5.8 **Transportation, Wholesale, and IT Services Firms Exhibit Managerial Practices at Levels Similar to Manufacturing Firms, While Adoption Is Lower in Retail and Hospitality Services**

Relative average management practices scores in manufacturing and selected services subsectors, by country income group, late 2010s

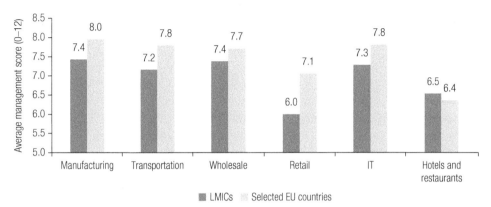

Source: Calculations based on World Bank Enterprise Survey data.

Note: Enterprise Surveys were conducted in 48 countries for firms with at least five employees between 2017 and 2019. These graphs are based on 28 countries with sufficient sectoral coverage: Argentina, Bolivia, Colombia, Cyprus, the Czech Republic, Ecuador, The Gambia, Greece, Hungary, Italy, Jordan, Kazakhstan, Kenya, Lao PDR, Latvia, Lithuania, Morocco, Mozambique, Paraguay, Peru, Poland, Portugal, Romania, Russian Federation, Rwanda, Slovakia, Turkey, and Zambia. Management scores are a sum of scores for operations, monitoring, targets, and incentives, with a maximum score of 12. The scoring methodology is based on Bloom, Sadun, and Van Reenen (2012), with adjustments for the targets and incentives scores due to nonavailability of comparable data from Latin American countries for these indexes. Low- and middle-income countries (LMICs), by World Bank income group classifications, had 1994 gross national income (GNI) of less than US$8,955. IT = information technology.

Yet, when faced with budget constraints and limits to government capacity, targeting remains an important tool to boost productivity. The merit in policies that target a sector's expansion will depend on its shifting desirability, as measured by spillovers, dynamic growth gains, and learning by doing. Chapter 4 showed how some services generate spillovers that benefit a wider set of economic actors through linkages. Because private investors tend not to take these multiplier effects into consideration, a case can be made for policies targeted to support their growth.

Input-Output Linkages That Emphasize Upstream Services

Evidence across more than 100 countries shows that the global innovator and low-skill tradable services have among the highest forward linkages (figure 5.9)—that is, the domestic value added of a sector embodied as inputs in economywide production (in US$, millions). Across all manufacturing and services subsectors, the value of these forward linkages was highest for information and professional services (shown in figure 5.9 as "Other business and ICT"). The value of these forward linkages in wholesale and retail trade (shown as "Distribution and trade"), finance, communication, and transportation services was also higher than in all manufacturing subsectors.

As a share of output, these forward linkages in information and professional services (67 percent) was surpassed only by paper products and mineral products (70 percent and 73 percent, respectively). The corresponding shares were also relatively high in financial services (55 percent), wholesale and retail trade (46 percent), communications (43 percent), and transportation (38 percent) (figure 5.9).

This comparison suggests that global innovator services and low-skill tradable services provide important inputs in a value chain. The removal of any distortion in these upstream services, such as telecommunications and finance, can therefore result in cascading benefits across many downstream sectors. In many countries, regulations in the trucking industry, are notorious for stifling competition and raising costs. In India, the productivity of downstream manufacturing firms increased following the liberalization of transportation services in the 1990s (Arnold et al. 2016). Beyond addressing regulatory barriers, tax holidays or subsidies that encourage more firms to be active in the same sector can lower concentration in that targeted sector and enhance incentives for firms to innovate (Aghion et al. 2015). In fact, because interventions in these markets affect many sectors at once, these are often considered ex ante horizontal rather than vertical policies specifically targeting the production of a good per se.

Liu (2019) takes the logic in the opposite direction, arguing for targeted support in upstream sectors when the downstream sectors are distorted. Under this analysis, the distortions in the downstream sectors magnify their market failures because the effects accumulate through backward demand linkages. Market imperfections cause less-than-optimal input use, thereby depressing the resources used by the input suppliers, which in turn purchase less from their own input suppliers. As a result, the most-upstream sectors become more "central" to market imperfections in the economy. Targeted support can compensate for this by giving upstream services the boost they otherwise should have.

Manelici and Pantea (2021) analyze the impact of such targeted support through the introduction of an unexpected personal income tax break for programmers with eligible bachelor's degrees and who work on software development for firms in Romania's ICT services sector. As a result of this policy change, the authors find that the ICT services sector grew faster in Romania than in otherwise similar countries and that downstream sectors relying more on ICT services also grew faster over time. This incentive provided to specific services providers had the desired multiplier effect of spreading benefits to a larger set of firms that use these services as inputs.

Where Countries Stand in the 4Ts Space

To illustrate how countries perform across the 4Ts, each of the 4Ts is described by a summary measure that aggregates relevant indicators. These indicators were selected to

FIGURE 5.9 **Global Innovator and Low-Skill Tradable Services Have among the Highest Forward Linkages across Sectors**

Domestic value added embodied as inputs in economywide production (as a share of output and as value in US$, millions) by industry, average across countries, 2015

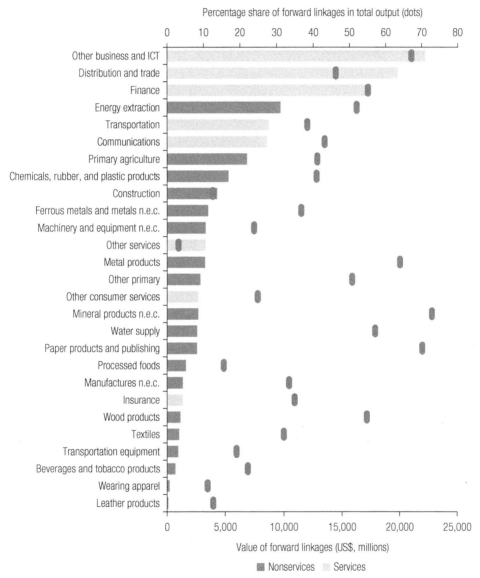

Source: Calculations based on World Bank's Export Value Added Database (EVAD).

Note: The dataset covers 118 countries across regions and income levels. The bars (measured by the bottom axis) represent the overall value of a sector's domestic value added embodied as inputs in economywide production. The green dots (measured by the top axis) represent the share of these forward linkages in total output. "Nonservices" includes agriculture and industry. "Other business and ICT" includes professional, scientific, and technical services. "Distribution and trade" includes wholesale and retail trade. "Other services" refers to social, community, and personal services. ICT = information and communication technology; n.e.c. = not elsewhere classified.

highlight the mix of policy areas discussed above that are either expected to have greater urgency or represent a new set of issues to be addressed. The list of indicators used here is not exhaustive; this exercise illustrates some of the key dimensions in this agenda.

Performance on the 4Ts: Relevant Indicators

Trade. A country's preparedness to engage in international trade in services combines measures of services trade restrictions, the ease of doing business, and restrictions on cross-border data flows. The World Bank's STRI measures policies that impose barriers on international trade transactions. The World Bank's *Doing Business* data capture the extent of regulatory burdens facing the private sector. To capture restrictions on cross-border data flows, countries are assigned a score of 0 if they have an open transfer model, 1 if they have a conditional transfer model, and −1 if they have a limited transfer model (data localization), based on findings from Ferracane and van der Marel (2020).

Technology. A country's capabilities to support technology diffusion and innovation combines the extent of internet use among the wider population and email use in firms. The share of the population with access to ICT gives a measure of the potential for a broader digital economy. Similarly, the share of firms that use email, drawn from the World Bank Enterprise Surveys, is a simple measure of how many firms are using basic digital technologies in their business operations. They reflect whether firms have the building blocks for the adoption of more sophisticated digital technologies, ranging from enterprise planning software and matching platforms to data analytics.

Training. A country's capabilities to respond to the rising demand for skills combines measures of tertiary education enrollment, digital skills, and firms' management practices. Tertiary school enrollment captures foundational skills that foster adaptability, critical thinking, and communication.[10] The digital skills index of the World Economic Forum (WEF) measures software programming, coding, or complementary skills in engineering that will be important to ensure that more people can access jobs that are likely to become increasingly cognitive with more technology-intensive business processes. Finally, measures of managerial practices that strengthen firms' capabilities for upgrading are captured from the World Bank Enterprise Surveys and the Centre for Economics Performance's WMS.

Targeting. A country's potential to target key upstream services scales the magnitude of forward linkages, drawn from the World Bank's Export Value Added Database, according to the size of the relevant sectors in the economy. It combines two elements: First, the shares of forward linkages in the outputs of ICT, professional, and financial services (the subsectors in which such shares are highest, on average, across countries) are multiplied by the shares of these services in total employment. Second, the shares of forward linkages in the outputs of wholesale and retail trade and transportation services (the subsectors with the highest linkages to the manufacturing sector, on average, across countries) are multiplied by the share of manufacturing in GDP.

Variations and Patterns in the 4Ts across Countries

In figure 5.10, the axes represent the summary measures of countries' trade and training landscapes, while the colors indicate the targeting landscape, and the bubble size

FIGURE 5.10 **Mapping Countries' Performance on Trade, Technology, Training, and Targeting (the 4Ts) Helps Identify Reform Priorities**
Country distribution in the space of trade, technology, training, and targeting, most recent year available

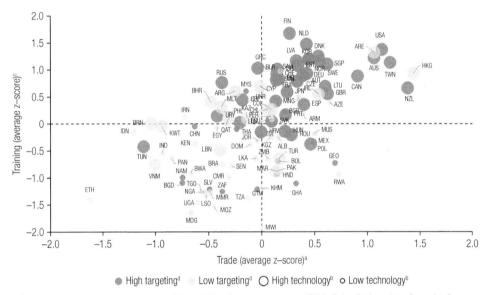

● High targeting[d]   ● Low targeting[d]   ○ High technology[b]   ○ Low technology[b]

Sources: Calculations based on World Bank's Services Trade Restrictiveness Index (STRI); *Doing Business* data, Enterprise Surveys, World Development Indicators, and Export Value Added Database (EVAD); Ferracane and Van der Marel 2020; World Economic Forum's digital skills index; Centre for Economic Performance's World Management Surveys; International Labor Organization's employment data; International Telecommunications Union's global and regional ICT data.

Note: The x- and y-axes represent the summary measures of countries' trade[a] and training[c] landscapes, respectively. Bubble size indicates the summary measure of technology[b] indicators, and colors indicate the summary measure of targeting.[d] The trade, training, technology, and targeting summary measures are derived from the relevant indicators and converted to z-scores to normalize their scales and are then averaged. Economies are labeled using ISO alpha-3 codes. The trade and training indexes are categorized as "high" or "low" based on the median z-score value (that is, whether they are above or below 0 on the x- or y-axes). The technology and targeting indexes are similarly categorized as "high" or "low" and shown, respectively, by the size (large versus small) and color (blue versus yellow) of the markers. ICT = information and communication technology.

a. Trade (x-axis) refers to a country's preparedness to engage in international trade in services and combines measures of the STRI, the ease of doing business, and restrictions on cross-border data flows.

b. Technology (large or small bubble size) refers to a country's capabilities to support technology diffusion and innovation and combines the extent of internet use among the wider population as well as measures email use in firms.

c. Training (y-axis) refers to a country's capabilities to respond to the rising demand for skills and combines measures of tertiary education enrollment, digital skills, and management practices in firms.

d. Targeting (blue for high, yellow for low) combines the share of forward linkages in the output of ICT/professional/financial services multiplied by share of these services in total employment; and the share of forward linkages in the output of wholesale/retail and transportation services multiplied by share of manufacturing in GDP.

indicates the technology landscape. For each summary measure, the relevant indicators are converted to z-scores to normalize their scales and are then averaged. To facilitate the discussion, countries are plotted using continuous variables for the trade and training indexes but categorized as "high" or "low" based on the median z-score value (that is, whether they are above or below a z-score of 0 on those respective axes). On the targeting and technology indexes, countries are similarly categorized as "high" or "low" (shown by the color or size of the markers) based on whether they are above or below the median z-score.

This variation in the 4Ts across countries is striking and brings out several complementarities across all four dimensions. Four patterns stand out:

- Trading and training are correlated; most countries are in the upper-right or lower-left quadrants.

- Most high-tech countries (big markers) are above the median z-score in training; countries with higher training or human capital scores tend to have high technology.

- Most highly targeted countries (blue markers) are to the right of the median z-score in trading; countries that are more open to trade in services are more likely to have a higher potential for linkages.

- Most of the small yellow markers are in the bottom-left quadrant and need to work on all 4Ts; most of the large blue markers are in (or near) the upper-right quadrant and are strong in all areas.

Variations in these patterns can provide insights for understanding the relative performance of countries and identifying dimensions on which they may be falling behind or where they are performing better.

Strong in all 4Ts. In the upper-right quadrant, many economies also have large blue markers—indicating they are strong on all four dimensions. Many are high-income economies, but several are middle-income economies, including some (such as Azerbaijan or Mongolia) that, while strong on trade and training, have room to improve their access to technology and better target linkages. Since the measured linkages encompass both services and manufacturing, the concentration on services in, for example, the United Arab Emirates or Hong Kong SAR, China, results in yellow markers for those economies.

Low in trade and training. The lower-left quadrant (indicating low trade and low training) includes several LMICs, especially in Africa. In this quadrant, most of the blue markers (for those with greater linkages) tend to be middle-income countries (China, South Africa, and Tunisia). But other middle-income countries (Brazil, India, Indonesia, and Vietnam) have yellow markers. Many of these middle-income countries may rely at least partly on their large economies and populations for both scale and a reasonable number (if not share) of skilled workers. China is in the lower-left quadrant less for its capabilities than for its restrictions on services trade and its data localization requirements.

High in training and technology, low in trade. Countries in the upper-left quadrant are high in skills-related training but low in services trade openness. These are largely middle-income countries in Eastern Europe and Central Asia (Belarus, Kazakhstan, the Russian Federation, and Ukraine); Latin America (Argentina and Uruguay); and East Asia (Malaysia and the Philippines). They are also relatively strong in technology (two-thirds having large markers). The Islamic Republic of Iran has the lowest STRI score among countries in this quadrant.

High in trade, variable in targeting and technology, low in training. Countries in the lower-right quadrant are low in skills-related training but high in services trade openness, spanning many regions and income levels. They are also relatively weak in technology adoption (most having smaller markers). Hungary, Poland, and Romania stand out in terms of their strong access to technology and high targeting (large blue markers), which perhaps reflects strong linkages through their participation in European manufacturing value chains. On the other hand, Mauritius and Rwanda stand out for their relative openness to trade in services, including on openness to flows of data. Rwanda has, for example, invested heavily in its ICT sector and will need more digital capabilities in terms of skills to be able to take greater advantage of this.

Effects of Variations in Technology and Intersectoral Linkages' Trends across Subsectors on Prioritization in the 4Ts across Countries

The relevance of countries' performance on the 4Ts will vary in part by the sectoral composition within a country. As described in chapters 3 and 4, the impacts across sectors of changing technology and intersectoral linkages are not even. Figure 5.11 shows how these trends of remote delivery, automation, intangible capital, and forward linkages affect services subsectors differentially. Amenability to home-based work (x-axis) shows potential for scale; suitability for machine learning (y-axis) shows potential for more technology adoption; software and R&D per worker shows potential for the greater accumulation of intangible capital (size of bubble); and forward linkages (color) shows where targeted support could deliver larger multiplier effects. Together, they help reinforce how policy priorities can vary across sectors.

Depending on the combination of the trends a services subsector is expected to face, the demands across the 4Ts will vary. Thus, countries, depending on the sizes of these subsectors, will then also face pressures to reform across different policy areas to be able to leverage the potential of the services sector to deliver the twin gains of productivity growth and job creation.

FIGURE 5.11 **Reduced Need for Proximity, Suitability for Automation, Intangible Capital, and Forward Linkages Are Changing the Scope for Scale, Innovation, and Spillovers across Services Subsectors**

Share of jobs amenable to home-based work, suitability for machine learning, expenditure on R&D and software per worker, and share of intermediate sales in output across services subsectors, 2017–18

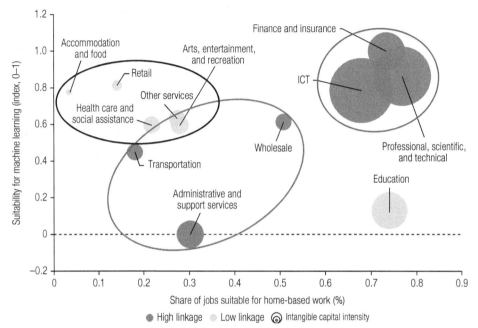

Source: Calculations based on Brynjolfsson, Mitchell, and Rock 2018; Dingel and Neiman 2020; OECD.Stat; World Input-Output Database; World Bank's Export Value Added Database (EVAD).

Note: Bubble size indicates the expenditure per worker on software and research and development (R&D) and bubble color the relative share of intermediate sales to other sectors in total output. The subsectors with the blue bubble color also experienced the largest increase in these forward linkages since the 1990s. "Other services" refers to other social, community, and personal services. ICT = information and communication technology.

Table 5.2 links these sets of trends to what they are likely to imply for priorities in the 4Ts agenda. Categorizing the impacts of these "future trends" as "high," "medium," or "low" (on the left side), the table shows various combinations of the trends (on the right side) to illustrate how clusters of policies can work together to enable different subsectors to benefit from the trends they face. This matrix helps reinforce how policy priorities in the 4Ts can vary across the services subsectors. For example, subsectors affected by all four trends have an interest in the full 4Ts policy agenda, whereas those affected by only one or two trends will benefit most from the policies that focus on those trends.

Most of the subsectors cluster in ways similar to the groups described in chapter 1. However, the difference between the ability for remote delivery (what could be traded

TABLE 5.2 Mapping the Impacts of Trends—Reduced Proximity, Increased Automation, Intangible Capital, and Forward Linkages—by Services Subsectors Can Inform the Priorities in the 4Ts Agenda

Impact of future trends				Priority within 4Ts agenda				
Reduced proximity (scope for home-based work)	Potential for automation (suitability for machine learning,[a] data analytics)	Intangible capital (expenditure per worker on software and R&D)	Intersectoral linkages (share of forward linkages in total output)	Trade (if H/M in reduced proximity)	Technology (if H/M in increased automation)	Training (if H/M in intangible capital)	Targeting (if H/M in sectoral linkages)	Subsectors likely affected in this combination of policy priorities
High	High	High	High	Yes	Yes	Yes	Yes	ICT, finance, and professional services
High	Medium	Medium	Low[c]	Yes	Yes	Yes	No	Education services
Medium[b]	High	Low	Low[c]	Yes	Yes	Yes	No	Health services[d]
Medium[b]	Medium	Low	High	Yes	Yes	No	Yes	Transportation, wholesale trade, and administrative and support services
Low	High	Low	Low	No	Yes	No	No	Accommodation and food; retail trade; arts, entertainment, and recreation; and other services

Source: Elaborations based on chapters 3, 4, and 5.

Note: H/M = high or medium. ICT = information and communication technology.

a. Most services subsectors have similar scores on the suitability for machine learning (SML) index, which reinforces the relative evenness of SML scores across occupations (Brynjolfsson, Mitchell, and Rock 2018). In figure 0.16, administrative and support services and education stand out as being notably lower on the SML index than all other services subsectors. Here, however, these subsectors are classified as "medium" instead of "low" because the manufacturing sector has a distinctly lower SML score (as shown in the full volume, chapter 3).

b. Some portions can be done remotely (through platforms that facilitate matching and telemedicine), but final delivery has more of a need for proximity.

c. Linkages will be there in the longer run with more-educated, healthier workers.

d. Health services is already a high-skill sector, and so training is relevant despite the "low" level of intangible capital. This categorization might reflect the fact that health-related R&D is either captured in pharmaceutical manufacturing or in universities (included under education services).

through mode 1, cross-border supply) and overall international tradedness aligns somewhat differently. For example, accommodation and food services join low-skill domestic services; administrative and support activities join low-skill tradable services; and education is far more suited to remote delivery if needed than health services.

ICT, finance, and professional services are characterized by all four trends described above: reduced proximity, increased automation, intangible capital, and forward linkages. They are most amenable to remote work that enables greater offshoring. At the same time, they are most suitable for ML that can provide efficiency gains related to data analytics. To the extent these offshored services can be automated through ML algorithms in high-income countries where wages are higher, this will place an even greater premium on investing in labor-augmenting digital technologies that help retain the labor cost advantage that the export of these services from LMICs is predicated upon. Global innovator services are also characterized by the largest magnitude of intangible capital per worker and the highest incidence of forward linkages to other sectors.

Given these trends, a strong performance on each of the 4Ts is needed for countries to leverage the potential of global innovator services. All countries in the upper-right quadrant of figure 5.10 (high training, high trade) that are blue (above the median in targeting) and with a large bubble (above the median in technology) are already well positioned to address all the trends because they are strong in all of the 4Ts. The countries least well positioned are those that are not strong on any of the 4Ts, of which 20 are in the lower-left quadrant with small, yellow markers. So, most countries have a mix; some characteristics are strong, but not all. Looking at the combination of their 4Ts should help identify their priorities.

It is not that countries must be strong in all 4Ts to strengthen their global innovator services, but being below the median in any one dimension will likely make it harder for firms in these services subsectors to take full advantage of the trends to raise their productivity and expand. With the two strongest correlations among the 4Ts being between training and technology, and between trade and targeting, improving either complementary pair would likely have the biggest impact. So, the countries most open to services trade (such as Azerbaijan or Mauritius) could seek to expand the scope for linkages. Countries that are stronger in training (such as Egypt or Thailand) could leverage it with more technology.

Among the low-skill tradable services, transportation and wholesale trade share in several trends with administrative and support services in the low-skill domestic services category. These subsectors are characterized by relatively low levels of intangible capital, but they require only moderate physical proximity between producers and consumers. They are also characterized by moderately high suitability to AI-related automation and strong forward linkages with other sectors, especially manufacturing. They would therefore benefit from policies addressing trade, technology, and targeting. Other low-skill tradables—such as accommodation and food services and retail trade—have more in common with low-skill domestic services in terms of recent trends and are discussed below.

Those countries least likely to benefit from trade, technology, and targeting are those (in figure 5.10) to the left of the median on the x-axis that perform below the average in trade with yellow markers (having limited linkages) as well as small markers (having little technology). Many Sub-Saharan African countries (including Botswana, Ethiopia, Kenya, Lesotho, Madagascar, Mozambique, Nigeria, Tanzania, and Uganda) are in this category—with lost opportunities for spillovers to their agricultural and nascent manufacturing sectors too.

Skill-Intensive Social Services: Trade, Technology, and Training

Education and health services experience expanded opportunities to separate production and consumption, including internationally—particularly for education services, which are highly amenable to remote work. And although health services, overall, remain less amenable to remote delivery, certain tasks such as medical diagnosis and testing can be increasingly delivered through digital tools and platforms.

Education services, in which nonroutine cognitive tasks dominate, are least suitable for ML across services subsectors but are characterized by a high incidence of intangible capital. Health services, which are moderately suitable for ML-related automation and data analytics, can deliver efficiency gains that in turn can help raise a country's competitiveness in the market for medical tourism. And although these services provide spillovers through more educated and healthier workers, there is a considerable lag before they benefit other sectors.

Both education and health services will therefore benefit from policies that advance technology and increase trade (a combination pertaining to countries on the right side of figure 5.10 that have large markers). Given the higher human capital requirements to take advantage of the data analytics and intangible capital in these skill-intensive social services, training is also likely to matter. Therefore, those countries in the upper-right quadrant with large markers are best suited to take advantage of current trends. Chile, Colombia, Latvia, and Slovenia are well positioned in this regard.

Low-skill domestic services are least amenable to remote work, especially in the final delivery of services. Accommodation and food services as well as retail services can make more sales through digital platforms, but the delivery of these services demands proximity and makes up a large share of jobs in these subsectors. The same holds true for personal services such as hairdressing that remain predicated on the physical proximity between producers and consumers.

However, some of these sectors have greater potential for big-data- and ML-related automation, such as through platforms that facilitate matching, e-commerce that reduces the need for physical retail space, and automated checkouts. If technology is the area that can contribute to productivity gains, these sectors in countries with large markers in figure 5.10 should benefit, but those in countries with small markers have limited opportunities to leverage technology even in these low-skilled services. Among the countries more open to services trade (such as Ghana, Honduras, Rwanda, and Zambia), scaling up access to technology should boost the performance of these services subsectors intensive in the use of low-skilled labor.

Leveraging the 4Ts Agenda for Growth and Productivity: Three Caveats

There are three caveats to keep in mind in interpreting how much countries can or cannot leverage growth and productivity opportunities in different services subsectors with their performance on the 4Ts.

First, the mapping of expected changes to these 4Ts is not exact. For example, that a subsector is expected to have higher levels of intangible capital does not necessarily mean countries must be in the top half of the training index to be successful in the subsector; the threshold could be lower—or higher. And the choice of variables used are proxies; using a conceptually similar indicator could shift country positions. But this mapping is useful as a starting point to identify where countries likely need to strengthen their performance.

Second, the discussion above used quadrant boundaries as cutoffs for the trade and training indexes; many countries are close to the middle and thus not far from meeting or exceeding the thresholds. Where they lie on the continuum is what is important in the end. For example, Chile and Croatia are above the median on three of the 4Ts and are close on the fourth—placing them in a good enough position on all 4Ts to leverage the potential of global innovator services.

Third, a country's aggregate performance on the 4Ts does not necessarily reflect its ability to develop solutions in particular locations, even if not, on average, across the country. This may be particularly true for large countries such as China, India, Indonesia, and the Philippines, where aggregate numbers conceal pockets of skills, international connectedness through FDI, or subnational locations with stronger linkages. For example, India's successful foray into the export of software services was indeed catalyzed by a range of policies that boosted the 4Ts, albeit not for the country as a whole (box 5.3).

The Way Forward: How to Improve the 4Ts

Clearly, many countries would benefit from improving their performance on one or more of the 4Ts. This section provides additional guidance on issues to consider, informed by lessons of what has worked.

Trade: Minimizing Barriers, Weighing Trade-Offs

Assess the Scope of Relevant Trade Policies across Modes of Delivery
Reform efforts should recognize that sectors vary in their most prevalent mode of delivery and thus in which types of restrictions are most likely to be constraining. For mode 1 trade (direct cross-border supply of services), restrictions are greatest in auditing, maritime transportation, commercial banking, and insurance services. For tourism and the education of foreign students under mode 2, countries can require

---

BOX 5.3

India's Software Revolution and the 4Ts

The growth of the India's software services exports did not occur in a policy vacuum. In fact, proactive policy changes spanning the areas of trade, training, technology, and targeting (4Ts), starting in the 1980s, were a major catalyst. These policy changes were driven, at least in part, by software technology parks (STPs) that were export-processing zones exclusively for software services.

The number of firms in STPs increased from 400 in 1995 to 8,455 in 2008–09, of which 7,214 were registered as exporters. And the share of these firms in India's software exports increased dramatically, from 8 percent in 1992–93 to 81 percent 10 years later (Goswami, Gupta, and Mattoo 2012).

Trade

The new Computer Policy of 1984 reduced import duties from 135 percent to 60 percent on relevant hardware and from 100 percent to 60 percent on software. It also liberalized the production of high-performance computers by allowing the private sector, including foreign-owned firms, to compete with SOEs. Similarly, software production was opened to firms with up to 40 percent foreign ownership (covered by the Foreign Exchange Regulation Act of 1973) as well as to very large companies (covered by the Monopolies and Restrictive Trade Practices Act of 1969).

The STPs, established in 1986, provided one-stop shops for project approvals, import and export certification, and duty-free imports of computer hardware. Furthermore, full foreign ownership was made conditional on 100 percent of production being exported. India's 1991 economic reforms further reinforced this liberalization of international trade and foreign investment in India's software services sector (Goswami, Gupta, and Mattoo 2012).

Box continues on the following page

India's Software Revolution and the 4Ts *(continued)*

Technology

The Computer Policy of 1984 placed software under the Copyright Act, thereby rendering software piracy punishable by law. This was reinforced by the Agreement on Trade-Related Aspects of Intellectual Property Rights (TRIPS), which came into effect with the establishment of the World Trade Organization (WTO) in 1995. The Copyright Act spurred the domestic and foreign sales of Indian software products and packaged software. The STPs provided firms with all the relevant digital infrastructure, such as reliable electric power, data communication facilities, high-speed satellite links, and core computer facilities (Goswami, Gupta, and Mattoo 2012).

Training

Investment in engineering education played a big role in developing a large pool of skilled labor. The world-renowned Indian Institutes of Technology provided the early momentum. The number of engineering colleges in India increased from 246 in 1985 to more than 1,100 in 2003. The result was an increase in the number of engineers from about 59 per million (45,000 engineers) in 1985 to 405 per million (440,000 engineers) in 2003 (Arora and Bagde 2010). The Computer Policy of 1984 also established several research institutes, private training institutes, and technical organizations for software development.

By the late 1990s, several programs leveraged the technical expertise of the Indian diaspora. For example, the United Nations Development Program's Transfer of Knowledge through Expatriate Nationals (TOKTEN) initiative—in collaboration with the government of India and industry associations—enabled 650 expatriate professionals to undertake short-term assignments in India across 250 technical institutions from 1980 to 2001 (Mathur 2007). Furthermore, the government—in collaboration with professional associations—facilitated the placement of many nonresident Indians in honorary fellowships at universities.

Targeting

Industry-government information flows facilitated by the National Association of Software and Services Companies (NASSCOM)—the industry association for India's software services firms—played an instrumental role in guiding the industrial policy process (Kapur 2002). The flow of information between the private sector and government also benefited from alumni networks for the government-funded Indian Institutes of Technology. The same holds true for expert advisory panels, established by the government and composed of eminent nonresident Indians in the software industry. As for financial support, firms in the STPs received a range of tax exemptions (Goswami, Gupta, and Mattoo 2012).

visas. For retail and wholesale trade, transportation, and telecommunications, restrictions on foreign investment restrict commercial presence in another country (mode 3). And firms' ability to employ foreign workers in their country (mode 4) is highly restricted for all professional services, particularly legal services. But many countries also have quotas for lower-skilled workers, including for domestic personal services (WTO 2019). Hence, the trade in services agenda is both more complex—and politically charged.

The overall impact of restrictions on services trade depends, in part, on whether different modes act as complements or as substitutes. If they are substitutes for each other, restrictions may lead to a less efficient mode of delivery, but overall trade may not be affected too much. However, if they are complements to each other, the impact can be that much bigger. As digital technologies allow more professional services to be delivered digitally, it could be possible to move from a mode 3 or 4 (commercial presence or employment of foreign workers) to mode 1 (cross-border supply). However, restrictions on foreign entry or foreign workers would then likely apply to services being delivered via mode 1 as well. Quantifying these types of restrictions that are not outright bans is challenging. Measuring the potential substitutability and complementarity across modes complicates these efforts further.

Use International Trade Agreements to Reduce Barriers to Services Trade

Much as in goods trade, countries can control regulatory barriers that limit imports of services, but they cannot lower the restrictions other countries impose on their exports. The export of services through mode 2 (for example, tourism-related travel) is an exception to the norm. There can still be gains from liberalizing restrictions unilaterally; allowing more imports of services could raise competitive pressures, productivity, and innovation as more foreign know-how and investment could enter the home country (Fernandes, Rocha, and Ruta, forthcoming; World Bank 2020). Furthermore, deep trade agreements offer the opportunity for reciprocal reforms.[11]

At the multilateral level, the General Agreement on Trade in Services (GATS) was launched at the Uruguay Round of negotiations and came into force in 1995 along with creation of the WTO. However, its progress at the WTO has slowed in recent years, with less consensus on moving forward to expand the GATS (Francois and Hoekman 2010; Mattoo, Stern, and Zanini 2008; World Bank 2020).[12]

More progress is being made through bilateral or regional deep trade agreements, which can cover not only trade but also multiple policy areas such as investment, labor flows, and intellectual property. Just under 60 percent of all preferential trade agreements (PTAs) filed with the WTO through 2017 covered the services sector. This coverage in PTAs varies across services-related areas; only 10 percent address labor regulations, about 25 percent address visas and asylum, 40 percent address investment, and 50 percent address public procurement (Hofmann, Osnago, and Ruta 2019).

The increasing coverage of public procurement—which represents a sizable share of GDP and most of it in services—is particularly noteworthy because regulations have traditionally exhibited strong home bias. The inclusion in PTAs of provisions that liberalize procurement contracts has been associated with a strong increase in services trade[13] (Mulabdic and Rotunno, forthcoming).

Further, even though provisions governing the movement of labor remain less prevalent, there are some signs of progress:

- The Chile-Singapore Free Trade Agreement (FTA) and the 2007 US-Korea FTA (which entered into force in 2012) include chapters to liberalize trade in key services subsectors. The latter also established a working group to develop criteria for the licensing of professional service providers (Page and Plaza 2006).

- The Association of Southeast Asian Nations (ASEAN) member states have a framework of Mutual Recognition Arrangements (MRAs) for eight high-skill professions.[14] Architectural and engineering services have made more progress, with recognized professionals registering at the ASEAN level (Kikkawa and Suan 2019).

- In Africa, the Common Market for Eastern and Southern Africa (COMESA) has adopted the Protocol on the Free Movement of Persons, Labour, Services, Right of Establishment and Right of Residence. The East African Community (EAC) also has a Protocol on the Free Movement of Persons and is working to expand the mutual recognition of skills.

- The Africa Continental Free Trade Agreement (AfCFTA), launched on January 1, 2021, aims to create a single free trade area with free movement of goods and services, although not all countries have signed its Protocol on Free Movement of Persons.

When the benefits of deepening existing trade agreements to cover additional policy areas such as services, foreign investment, intellectual property rights, and labor mobility are compared with those of signing new, "shallower" trade agreements with more countries, evidence shows that the benefits to trade are greater for the former (Fernandes, Rocha, and Ruta, forthcoming; Fontagné et al. 2021). Using the count of provisions in PTAs, Dhingra, Freeman, and Huang (2021) find that find that deep PTAs boost services trade by about 30 percent more than shallow agreements. Deep trade agreements also increase GVC activity by addressing trade in both goods and services (Andrenelli et al. 2018; Dhingra, Freeman, and Mavroeidi 2018; Laget et al. 2020; Orefice and Rocha 2014).

Strengthen Trust in Data Flows

Too many LMICs still have no regulations in place regarding data flows. Rather than an affirmative choice, it reflects uncertainty on the implications of different choices and concerns about the capacity of implementing policies. A lack of restrictions on cross-border trade flows in data could maximize services trade, but there are legitimate privacy concerns on how data can be used, from exposure of personal medical information to concerns about manipulation or surveillance.

Consumers' trust in how their data are used can be critical to their willingness to participate in the digital economy, and so implementation of data policies must be prioritized (World Bank 2021). And more research is being done to show the implications of different choices—for cross-border trade, potential disincentives on smaller firms' ability to comply with required data protocols, and innovation—as well as on whether protection of privacy itself could be a source of comparative advantage (Ferracane and van der Marel 2020; Hallward-Driemeier et al. 2020; World Bank 2021).

Countries can well differ on how they value the potential trade-offs associated with privacy, but sufficient trust in the system will be important for the growth of services trade. More work is still needed to develop standards and mutual recognition agreements in areas of data protection to give domestic regulators confidence that allowing data to leave their jurisdiction will not undermine their regulatory goals (Meltzer 2019). The share of trade agreements with provisions related to data flows increased from just under 40 percent in 1995 to almost 70 percent in 2015 (Hofmann, Osnago, and Ruta 2019).

Technology: Enabling More Adoption of Digital Technologies

Technology adoption in the services sector, much like any other sector, requires an enabling environment that encompasses the appropriate infrastructure, regulatory frameworks, and firm (management) capabilities (Cirera and Maloney 2017). Many of the policy prescriptions relevant to innovation in manufacturing—including good country-level infrastructure and institutions supporting innovation—are also relevant to innovation in the services sector. Given the relevance of digital technologies in enabling services firms to achieve scale and innovation, expanding access to broadband internet connectivity and regulatory frameworks that govern the use of data will be increasingly important. The next section, on training, will further discuss firm capabilities. Beyond the enabling environment, more-tailored innovation policy support will also benefit technology adoption in the services sector.

Expand Access to Digital Infrastructure

Access to the internet must be reliable and affordable if it is to be inclusive. Although countries have been accelerating their rollout of internet access, reliable and affordable access to broadband internet remains insufficient in many LMICs—and for the poor in both high-income countries and LMICs. Fiber optic cables now reach most countries in the world, but there are bigger gaps across countries in their provision of "last mile" connectivity and in their investments in data centers and cloud computing that would enable greater use and exchange of data.

To expand access to the digital infrastructure, it is important to ensure competition between providers (including through FDI), target subsidies carefully, and develop performance requirements to ensure coverage of more-remote locations and lower-income areas (World Bank 2021).

The network effects and scale economies associated with digital business models raise issues that many competition and tax authorities are ill equipped to address. With some services offered "for free," prices are a poor indicator of anticompetitive behavior. Issues of self-preferencing on platforms or cross-subsidization across features can be other forms of abuse of market dominance. Ownership over data and the portability of such data have issues for privacy—another area where regulations are being updated—as well as implications for competition, innovation, and inclusion. Having data-sharing policies are important for new firms and for small and medium enterprises (SMEs) that would otherwise lack access to the same volume of information.

Digital trade of services also poses new challenges for taxation because traditional tax treaties tend to focus on having a physical presence. Firms that have "presence without mass" can avoid significant tax payments, and governments can be denied a growing source of revenues. International negotiations are seeking to address these issues, including possible formulas for minimum tax payments from multinationals that serve markets only virtually (World Bank 2021).

Select the Right Instruments to Support Innovation

Beyond the enabling environment, innovation policies require the right mix of instruments where services often form a "blind spot" (Cirera et al. 2021). Many science, technology, and innovation (STI) policies focus predominantly on agriculture and manufacturing firms, both in terms of their choice of instruments and their outreach efforts. For example, a recent analysis of policy instruments to support innovation in Indonesia, the Philippines, and Vietnam highlighted a distinct lack of instruments targeting services subsectors (Cirera et al. 2021).

However, not all instruments targeting agricultural farms and manufacturing firms may be equally suitable for the services sector. For example, grants that facilitate the acquisition of technologies embedded in machinery and equipment are more suitable for manufacturers because services firms tend to rely less on investments in physical capital. In contrast, incubators and accelerators can foster innovation among young firms in the services sector that can scale up quickly owing to lower fixed costs.

Making entrant firms more productive could lead to substantial productivity growth, especially because (as noted in chapter 2) although firm entry tends to be high in the services sector, many of these new firms tend to have productivity levels below the industry average. In addition, STI agencies should broaden the scope of their outreach and ensure that they screen innovation policy support programs for their potential to benefit firms in the services sector.

Training—in the broad meaning of acquiring skills rather than just receiving instruction—plays a crucial role in boosting workers' capabilities. In this regard, a distinction needs to be made between high- and low-skill services tasks, however. Although the former require an advanced set of cognitive and technical skills, the latter do not, and basic digital literacy and socioemotional skills would typically suffice. For firms seeking to upgrade their production processes and innovate, a growing body of evidence emphasizes organizational and managerial practices beyond worker skills.

Make Higher Education More Dynamic and Establish Foundational Cognitive Skills

For higher-skill services tasks, university education and skill development programs must become more responsive to changing industry demands, including for ICT-related skills such as software programming and coding or complementary engineering skills that are often in short supply across LMICs. The use of private providers and incentive contracts (whereby payment is conditional on participant placement) can help to align incentives. Having private sector actors involved in setting curricula can also help reflect the types of skills future employees will need.

At the same time, establishing foundational cognitive skills such as literacy and numeracy, as well as the "soft" skills that foster adaptability, problem solving, and initiative from an early age, deserves emphasis. These foundational cognitive and socioemotional skills will benefit a far larger share of the population. These skills can also be bolstered through more-informal forms of learning such as on-the-job training and continued acquisition of skills through lifelong learning (World Bank 2019).

Upgrade Management Skills

The training agenda also needs to encompass management skills. This type of support has often been overlooked (Cirera and Maloney 2017). Adopting new technologies can be disruptive, and managers must be able to plan for and address change processes. They also need to know how to take advantage of the potential that new technologies bring, and policy support can help overcome the information gaps in the returns to technology acquisition. Addressing these information gaps could also help resolve challenges in financing investments in training and technology (Bloom et al. 2013). The adoption of structured management practices can be enhanced through either the direct provision of training and other business advisory services or through vouchers and awards.

However, not all firms will be positioned to take advantage of management training. Efforts to include informal enterprises show that only a relatively small fraction have the capabilities to use the training or the purchases of external consulting services to raise performance significantly or to a level that would let them formalize. (See, for example, De Mel, McKenzie, and Woodruff [2010] in Sri Lanka; Bruhn [2011] in Mexico; Aga et al. [2019] in Mozambique; and Anderson and McKenzie [2020] in Nigeria). Programs with successive rounds of filtering that combine training, performance responses, and access to finance seem most effective. This is also an area where innovative uses of data are being employed to see whether new techniques—from structured data on utility bills to unstructured data on social media and internet use—can be effective in identifying enterprises with higher growth potential (Óskarsdóttir et al. 2019; Pazarbasioglu et al. 2020).

Targeting: Supporting Upstream Enabling Services

When some services provide positive spillovers, such as enabling linkages, or are characterized by information or coordination failures, there can be a case for more directed support to target their growth. The question then is what an "industrial policy" for services should look like.

The traditional conception of industrial policy encompassed top-down policy making, targeting preselected sectors, and employing a standard list of subsidies and incentives. The contemporary conception and practice of industrial policy is instead increasingly much more about (a) engagement with the private sector, which facilitates the collection of information; (b) transparency and accountability through experimentation with an iterative evaluation process and the use of digital technologies; and (c) recognizing the larger connections across the value chain to be effective.

Improve Government-Industry Information Flows

Aiginger and Rodrik (2020) argue that establishing an institutional framework that improves government-industry information flows in an inclusive and transparent way is key to assessing the changing desirability and feasibility dimensions of targeted approaches. Since the private sector is likely to better understand the location and nature of the market failures that inhibit industrial development, a fluid dialogue with the government is an important source of policy-relevant information.

"Public-private coordination councils" could seek out and gather information on investment ideas, achieve coordination among different state agencies, push for regulatory changes to eliminate unnecessary transaction costs, and generate a package of relevant financial incentives for new activities when needed (Rodrik 2004). Harrison and Rodríguez-Clare (2010) argue that governments should create a "social process" whereby different industry organizations submit proposals to compete for government support.

An example of such public-private dialogue from Ecuador highlights the importance of complementarities between services and other sectors. The lack of reliable air transportation services to major markets led the association of flower exporters in Ecuador during the 1980s to convince the government to set up the required number of cargo flights for this activity (Hernández et al. 2007).

In approaches that emphasize public-private information flows, ensuring that a wide range of private sector actors are included is important for the process to lead to more inclusive outcomes and to avoid potential capture from a few more connected players.

Prioritize Experimentation and Evaluation

Making experimentation and iterative evaluation processes a central feature of targeted policies both reveals information on which interventions work and develops a performance-oriented mindset. An experimental approach that establishes search processes in the face of uncertainty and inadequate information can help governments discover where the market failures lie and how the targeting can be most effective. Fernandez-Arias, Hausmann, and Panizza (2020) illustrate this new approach in the context of financial services, which they argue should extend beyond traditional public banking functions such as subsidized lending for SMEs to directly search for nascent economic activities whose takeoff is blocked by market or government failures.

Inducements to firms for investment and risk taking through this search process can be more effective when combined with monitoring and evaluation, whereby governments allow nonproductive firms to fail and exit the market. This approach can address long-standing concerns that targeted policies may enable chosen sectors to capture the political process to guarantee continued special treatment.

Several researchers have proposed using "problem-driven iterative adaptation" (PDIA), an approach that combines experimentation with solutions to particular problems with iterative feedback while engaging a broad set of actors to ensure that reforms are viable and relevant (Andrews 2011; Andrews, Pritchett, and Woolcock 2013).

Use Technology to Support Effective Policy Making

Related to prioritizing evaluations, authorities should take advantage of digital technologies to improve policy making. This advice is applicable across the set of policy recommendations but is particularly relevant for targeting. Using ICT and Web-based platforms can improve the inclusivity, transparency, and communication strategies with the private sector, which can help to address governance concerns with targeted approaches (World Bank 2016).

Similarly, big-data analytics aided by ML algorithms can be effective as a means of disseminating information, sharing public data with more service providers, or coordinating market players in helping address certain market failures. And digital technologies that help with collecting data during the production process can provide needed feedback loops for monitoring and evaluation purposes. This provides the possibility for real-time adjustment in policies to improve their effectiveness.

Take a Value Chain Approach

The growing interdependence between sectors—especially between manufacturing and services—means that GVCs for goods are increasingly services intensive. For hitherto less industrialized countries, such as those in Sub-Saharan Africa, future success in basic labor-intensive manufacturing cannot be separated from the quality of certain enabling services. While many firms may be competitive at the factory gate, they face large costs in getting goods to markets. Investments and regulatory reform that improve their competitiveness in transportation, logistics, and distribution services are therefore critical for the delivery of manufactured goods (Gelb et al. 2020).

Lin and Wang (2020) argue that the availability of global innovator services at sufficient scale and low-enough cost becomes increasingly important as production structures become more advanced. Hallward-Driemeier and Nayyar (2018) similarly emphasize inputs from professional, scientific, and technical services into more-advanced manufacturing industries such as pharmaceuticals, automotive, electronics, and machinery and equipment. Liberalization that boosts competition in business services and in telecommunications can therefore be enormously influential for digital business models in the manufacturing sector.

These linkages between services and manufacturing mean that "picking" manufacturing sectors without the relevant complementary services sectors might not be effective. Instead, a policy approach that targets all relevant industries in a particular value chain seems more fruitful in a world where the boundaries between services and manufacturing are increasingly blurred.

Conclusion

This chapter has discussed the policy choices (the 4Ts) that can reinforce the trends in technology and in increasing intersectoral linkages to raise productivity and to create jobs in the services sector, as follows:

- *Expanding trade in services* by reducing barriers to trade, competition, and trustworthy data can help achieve scale. This is particularly important for global innovator services but also for other services subsectors where digital technologies are expanding how trade can happen, such as in education and health.

- *Strengthening technology adoption* is critical to encourage higher-quality services—not just in high-skill services but in also in other subsectors where technology is enhancing the matching of supply and demand and where low-skilled workers can still benefit from improved access to information.

- *Training workers and managers* to equip them with the requisite skills, including those necessitated by the rise of intangible capital, will also matter, especially in high-skill services subsectors.

- *Targeting enabling services* can have larger benefits, particularly if they address underlying market failures that would otherwise limit the provision of the service.

While each of the 4Ts was linked in the first instance to addressing scale or innovation or spillovers, there are important synergies across them. Take the example of *technology* and *training*. Access to the internet matters, but attention to socioemotional skills, digital skills, and management capabilities is also important to unlock the potential for digital applications in practice. The same holds true for *trade* and *targeting*. Targeted policies that seek to expand spillovers also need to pay attention to how contestable the enabling services are if the targeted policies seek to expand the use of these services.

As the evidence on where countries stand in this 4Ts policy space shows, some countries perform relatively better on some dimensions than others. As a first step, mapping where a country lies in the 4Ts space indicates where the potential may be greatest for reforms to strengthen the prospect of services-led development. But priorities will also differ across subsectors in terms of the relative importance of improving trade, technology, training, and targeting. For countries with (or seeking to establish) larger manufacturing or agriprocessing sectors, transportation and warehousing services may be a priority. In such cases, addressing contestability and applications of technology in these sectors may matter more than raising digital skills more widely. Countries with relatively high shares of skilled workers may see greater gains in expanding trade in global innovator services.

The diffusion of digital technologies and deepening of intersectoral linkages imply that the possibilities of services-led productivity growth and job creation are expanding. Policy makers can choose to build on their momentum to help realize this potential for services-led development by emphasizing trade, technology, training, and targeting. Countries' performance across each of the 4Ts and consideration of how these matter for different services should be part of the process of identifying policy priorities. The evidence shows that reforms in these areas can make a lasting difference.

Notes

1. The General Agreement on Trade in Services (GATS) of the World Trade Organization (WTO) breaks down services trade into four "modes": (1) "cross-border supply," including digital delivery; (2) "consumption abroad," involving the travel of the consumer, such as foreign tourists or students; (3) "commercial presence" (or FDI), such as through locally established subsidiaries or affiliate companies; and (4) "movement of natural persons," when delivery involves the travel of the service provider to the consumer's country.

2. Basker (2005) found no effect of Walmart's entry on two retail-related sectors in which Walmart does not compete directly: restaurants and automobile sales and service.

3. Borchert, Gootiiz, and Mattoo (2012) distinguish between three broad stages of investor comfort: (a) the right for foreign enterprises to appeal decisions issued by the regulating authority;

(b) requirements that the regulator provide reasons for a decision, such as the rejection of a license request; and (c) in addition to the first two requirements, independence of the regulating authority from the relevant sector ministry.

4. Dimensions other than privacy concerns matter in how digital services are encouraged or discouraged. One is the tax treatment of digital services, particularly when markets can be served without having a physical footprint in the country. New issues are also being raised for competition authorities regarding the potential abuse of market dominance by global tech giants. Many LMICs are not included in how these rules will be formulated (World Bank 2021).

5. More "physical" technologies still play a role in certain services sectors, such as transportation and medical services, albeit often with ICTs of increasing importance. ICTs often require significant physical infrastructure, including computers, network links, and data centers.

6. "Structured management practices" typically include practices related to *operations* (such as whether operations are "lean," or the adoption of continuous improvement techniques); *monitoring* (tracking performance of units and workers); the setting of *targets* (what type of targets are set and whether they are set throughout the organization); and the use of *incentives* in people management (such as performance-based pay, promotion policies, and dealing with low performance). The most common instruments for measuring management practices are (a) the Centre for Economics Performance's World Management Survey (WMS), which scores practices using a double-blinded methodology (https://worldmanagementsurvey.org/); and (b) the US Census Bureau's Management and Organizational Practices Survey (MOPS), which relies on self-reported adoption of practices, allowing for inclusion in firm-level surveys (https://www.census.gov/programs-surveys/mops.html). Despite different methodologies, the scores of the two instruments have been found to be correlated (Bloom, Brynjolfsson, et al. 2019). An alternative measure, targeting micro and informal enterprises, is the survey of business practices by McKenzie and Woodruff (2016).

7. The World Bank Enterprise Surveys are a global set of surveys of manufacturing and services establishments, covering formal establishments with more than five employees. The services subsectors covered include retail, wholesale, hotels and restaurants, transportation, and information technology (IT). For more information, see the Enterprise Surveys website: https://www.enterprisesurveys.org/en/enterprisesurveys.

8. When the number of employees is controlled for, management practices in services are lower in 33 out of 48 countries, although differences narrow a bit. It is expected that structured management practices might matter less for smaller firms. For example, setting up an elaborate system to monitor the output of each worker has lower returns when there are fewer employees. The Enterprise Survey only includes firms with five or more employees.

9. The MOPS questionnaire (adapted in the Enterprise Survey) relies on self-reported answers to questions about management practices, while the WMS uses a double-blind scoring mechanism. Despite a strong correlation between MOPS and WMS scores within a country (see Bloom, Brynjolfsson, et al. 2019), cultural biases could play a larger role in the differences between MOPS scores across countries. Such cultural biases have been found in self-reported innovation surveys (Cirera and Muzi 2016).

10. It is not that all skills will need tertiary education, but this variable better differentiates across countries than secondary enrollment rates, and there will be an increased need for some skilled workers to support less-skilled workers.

11. Policy responses to COVID-19 raise new concerns on whether barriers will hurt services trade in ways that disproportionately hurt lower-income countries. Many countries have restricted Mode 2 and Mode 4 trade as a way of trying to contain the spread of the virus (Mattoo, Rocha, and Ruta, forthcoming).

12. With services trade negotiations established on a case-by-case basis, there remains considerable variation in the interpretation and application of GATS across countries.

13. This result holds true even when removing EU countries from the analysis.

14. The professions within the ASEAN MRA framework include engineering, nursing, architecture, medicine, dentistry, tourism, surveying, and accountancy.

References

Abernathy, Frederick H., John T. Dunlop, Janice H. Hammond, and David Weil. 1999. *A Stitch in Time: Lean Retailing and the Transformation of Manufacturing—Lessons from the Apparel and Textile Industries*. New York: Oxford University Press.

Aga, Gemechu, Francisco Campos, Adriana Conconi, Elwyn Davies, and Carolin Geginat. 2021. "Informal Firms in Mozambique: Status and Potential." Report 138991, World Bank, Washington, DC.

Aghion, Philippe, Jing Cai, Mathias Dewatripont, Luosha Du, Ann Harrison, and Patrick Legros. 2015. "Industrial Policy and Competition." *American Economic Journal: Macroeconomics* 7 (4): 1–32.

Aiginger, Karl, and Dani Rodrik. 2020. "Rebirth of Industrial Policy and an Agenda for the Twenty-First Century." *Journal of Industry, Competition and Trade* 20 (2): 189–207.

Anderson, James E., Ingo Borchert, Aaditya Mattoo, and Yoto V. Yotov. 2018. "Dark Costs, Missing Data: Shedding Some Light on Services Trade." *European Economic Review* 105: 193–214.

Anderson, Stephen J., and David McKenzie. 2020. "Improving Business Practices and the Boundary of the Entrepreneur: A Randomized Experiment Comparing Training, Consulting, Insourcing and Outsourcing." Policy Research Working Paper 9502, World Bank, Washington, DC.

Andrenelli, Andrea, Charles Cadestin, Koen De Backer, Sébastien Miroudot, Davide Rigo, and Ming Ye. 2018. "Multinational Production and Trade in Services." Trade Policy Paper 212, Organisation for Economic Co-operation and Development, Paris.

Andrews, Matt. 2011. "Which Organizational Attributes Are Amenable to External Reform? An Empirical Study of African Public Financial Management." *International Public Management Journal* 14 (2): 131–56.

Andrews, Matt, Lant Pritchett, and Michael Woolcock. 2013. "Escaping Capability Traps through Problem Driven Iterative Adaptation (PDIA)." *World Development* 51: 234–44.

Ariu, Andrea, Florian Mayneris, and Mathieu Parenti. 2020. "One Way to the Top: How Services Boost the Demand for Goods." *Journal of International Economics* 123: 103278.

Arnold, Jens Matthias, Beata Javorcik, Molly Lipscomb, and Aaditya Mattoo. 2016. "Services Reform and Manufacturing Performance: Evidence from India." *Economic Journal* 126 (590): 1–39.

Arora, Ashish, and Surendrakumar Bagde. 2010. "Human Capital and the Indian Software Industry." Working Paper 16167, National Bureau of Economic Research, Cambridge, MA.

Atkin, David, Benjamin Faber, and Marco Gonzalez-Navarro. 2018. "Retail Globalization and Household Welfare: Evidence from Mexico." *Journal of Political Economy* 126 (1): 1–73.

Avdiu, Besart, and Gaurav Nayyar. 2020. "When Face-to-Face Interactions Become an Occupational Hazard: Jobs in the Time of COVID-19." *Economics Letters* 197: 109648.

Balland, Pierre-Alexandre, and David Rigby. 2017. "The Geography of Complex Knowledge." *Economic Geography* 93 (1): 1–23.

Basker, Emek. 2005. "Job Creation or Destruction? Labor Market Effects of Wal-Mart Expansion." *Review of Economics and Statistics* 87 (1): 174–83.

Bauer, Matthias, Hosuk Lee-Makiyama, Erik Van der Marel, and Bert Verschelde. 2014. "The Costs of Data Localisation: Friendly Fire on Economic Recovery." ECIPE Occasional Paper 3/2014, European Centre for International Political Economy, Brussels, Belgium.

Bloom, Nicholas. 2020. "How Working from Home Works Out." Policy brief, June, Stanford Institute for Economic Policy Research (SIEPR), Stanford University, Stanford, CA.

Bloom, Nicholas, Erik Brynjolfsson, Lucia Foster, Ron Jarmin, Megha Patnaik, Itay Saporta-Eksten, and John Van Reenen. 2019. "What Drives Differences in Management Practices?" *American Economic Review* 109 (5): 1648–83.

Bloom, Nicholas, Benn Eifert, Aprajit Mahajan, David McKenzie, and John Roberts. 2013. "Does Management Matter? Evidence from India." *Quarterly Journal of Economics* 128 (1): 1–51.

Bloom, Nicholas, Leonardo Iacovone, Mariana Pereira-López, and John Van Reenen. 2019. "Management in Mexico: Market Size, Frictions and Misallocation." Unpublished working paper, Stanford University, Stanford, CA.

Bloom, Nicholas, Renata Lemos, Raffaella Sadun, Daniela Scur, and John Van Reenen. 2014. "JEEA-FBBVA Lecture 2013: The New Empirical Economics of Management." *Journal of the European Economic Association* 12 (4): 835–76.

Bloom, Nicholas, Renata Lemos, Raffaella Sadun, and John Van Reenen. 2015. "Does Management Matter in Schools?" *Economic Journal* 125 (584): 647–74.

Bloom, Nicholas, Renata Lemos, Raffaella Sadun, and John Van Reenen. 2020. "Healthy Business? Managerial Education and Management in Health Care." *Review of Economics and Statistics* 102 (3): 506–17.

Bloom, Nicholas, Raffaella Sadun, and John Van Reenen. 2012. "The Organization of Firms Across Countries." *Quarterly Journal of Economics*, 1663–1705.

Borchert, Ingo and Mattia Di Ubaldo. Forthcoming. "Scoping Services Trade Agreements: What Really Matters." In *The Economics of Deep Trade Agreements*, edited by Ana M. Fernandes, Nadia Rocha, and Michele Ruta. Washington, DC: World Bank.

Borchert, Ingo, Batshur Gootiiz, Joscelyn Magdeleine, Juan A. Marchetti, Aaditya Mattoo, Ester Rubio, and Evgeniia Shannon. 2019. "Applied Services Trade Policy: A Guide to the Services Trade Policy Database and the Services Trade Restrictions Index." Staff Working Paper ERSD-2019-14, World Trade Organization, Geneva.

Borchert, Ingo, Batshur Gootiiz, and Aaditya Mattoo. 2012. "Policy Barriers to International Trade in Services: Evidence from a New Database." Policy Research Working Paper 6109, World Bank, Washington, DC.

Bronnenberg, Bart J., and Paul B. Ellickson. 2015. "Adolescence and the Path to Maturity in Global Retail." *Journal of Economic Perspectives* 29 (4): 113–34.

Bruhn, Miriam. 2011. "License to Sell: The Effect of Business Registration Reform on Entrepreneurial Activity in Mexico." *Review of Economics and Statistics* 93 (1): 382–86.

Brynjolfsson, Erik, Tom Mitchell, and Daniel Rock. 2018. "What Can Machines Learn, and What Does It Mean for Occupations and the Economy?" *American Economic Review Papers and Proceedings* 108: 43–47.

Cirera, Xavier, and William F. Maloney. 2017. *The Innovation Paradox: Developing-Country Capabilities and the Unrealized Promise of Technological Catch-Up.* Washington, DC: World Bank.

Cirera, Xavier, Andrew Mason, Francesca de Nicola, Smita Kuriakose, Davide S. Mare, and Trang Thu Tran. 2021. *The Innovation Imperative for Developing East Asia.* Washington, DC: World Bank.

Cirera, Xavier, and Silvia Muzi. 2016. "Measuring Firm-Level Innovation Using Short Questionnaires: Evidence from an Experiment." Policy Research Working Paper 7696, World Bank, Washington, DC.

Clark, Ximena, David Dollar, and Alejandro Micco. 2004. "Port Efficiency, Maritime Transport Costs, and Bilateral Trade." *Journal of Development Economics* 75 (2): 417–50.

Comin, Diego, and Martí Mestieri. 2018. "If Technology Has Arrived Everywhere, Why Has Income Diverged?" *American Economic Journal: Macroeconomics* 10 (3): 137–78.

Dauda, Seidu, and Maciej Drozd. 2020. "Barriers to Competition in Product Market Regulation: New Insights on Emerging Market and Developing Economies." Finance in Focus note, World Bank, Washington, DC.

Deloitte. 2014. "Global Powers of Retailing 2014: Retail Beyond Begins." Research report, Deloitte, London.

De Mel, Suresh, David McKenzie, and Christopher Woodruff. 2010. "Who Are the Microenterprise Owners? Evidence from Sri Lanka on Tokman versus De Soto." In *International Differences in Entrepreneurship*, edited by Josh Lerner and Antoinette Schoar, 63–88. Chicago: University of Chicago Press.

Dhingra, Swati, Rebecca Freeman, and Hanwei Huang. 2021. "The Impact of Deep Trade Agreements on Trade and Welfare." Discussion Paper 1742, Centre for Economic Performance, London School of Economics and Political Science.

Dhingra, Swati, Rebecca Freeman, and Eleonora Mavroeidi. 2018. "Beyond Tariff Reductions: What Extra Boost from Trade Agreement Provisions?" Discussion Paper 1532, Centre for Economic Performance, London School of Economics and Political Science, London.

Doove, Samantha, Owen Gabbitas, Duc Nguyen-Hong, and Joe Owen. 2001. "Price Effects of Regulation: International Air Passenger Transport, Telecommunications and Electricity Supply." Staff Research Paper 1682, Productivity Commission, Australian Government, Melbourne.

El Khoury, Antoine C., and Andreas Savvides. 2006. "Openness in Services Trade and Economic Growth." *Economics Letters* 92 (2): 277–83.

Eschenbach, Felix, and Joseph Francois. 2002. "Financial Sector Competition, Services Trade, and Growth." Discussion Paper 2002-089/2, Tinbergen Institute, Amsterdam.

Eschenbach, Felix, and Bernard M. Hoekman. 2006. "Services Policy Reform and Economic Growth in Transition Economies." *Review of World Economics* 142 (4): 746–64.

Evans, Carolyn L., and James Harrigan. 2005. "Distance, Time, and Specialization: Lean Retailing in General Equilibrium." *American Economic Review* 95 (1): 292–313.

Fernandes, Ana M., and Caroline Paunov. 2008. "Foreign Direct Investment in Services and Manufacturing Productivity Growth: Evidence for Chile." Policy Research Working Paper 4730, World Bank, Washington, DC.

Fernandes, Ana M., Nadia Rocha, and Michele Ruta, eds. Forthcoming. *The Economics of Deep Trade Agreements*. Washington, DC: World Bank.

Fernández-Arias, Eduardo, Ricardo Hausmann, and Ugo Panizza. 2020. "Smart Development Banks." *Journal of Industry, Competition and Trade* 20 (2): 395–420.

Ferracane, Martina Francesca, Janez Kren, and Erik van der Marel. 2020. "Do Data Policy Restrictions Impact the Productivity Performance of Firms and Industries?" *Review of International Economics* 28 (3): 676–722.

Ferracane, Martina Francesa, and Erik van der Marel. 2020. "Regulations on Personal Data: Differing Data Realms and Digital Services Trade." Background paper for *World Development Report 2021: Data for Development*. Washington, DC: World Bank.

Fontagné, Lionel, Nadia Rocha, Michele Ruta, and Gianluca Santoni. 2021. "A General Equilibrium Assessment of the Economic Impact of Deep Trade Agreements." Policy Research Working Paper 9630, World Bank, Washington, DC.

Foster, Lucia, John Haltiwanger, and Cornell J. Krizan. 2006. "Market Selection, Reallocation, and Restructuring in the US Retail Trade Sector in the 1990s." *Review of Economics and Statistics* 88 (4): 748–58.

Francois, Joseph, and Bernard Hoekman. 2010. "Services Trade and Policy." *Journal of Economic Literature* 48 (3): 642–92.

Freund, Caroline, and Diana Weinhold. 2002. "The Internet and International Trade in Services." *American Economic Review* 92 (2): 236–40.

Gelb, Alan, Vijaya Ramachandran, Christian J. Meyer, Divyanshi Wadhwa, and Kyle Navis. 2020. "Can Sub-Saharan Africa Be a Manufacturing Destination? Labor Costs, Price Levels, and the Role of Industrial Policy." *Journal of Industry, Competition and Trade* 20 (9): 335–57.

Goswami, Arti Grover, Poonam Gupta, and Aaditya Mattoo. 2012. "A Cross-Country Analysis of Services Exports: Lessons from India." In *Exporting Services: A Developing Country Perspective*, edited by Arti Grover Goswami, Aaditya Mattoo, and Sebastian Sáez, 81–119. Washington, DC: World Bank.

Haltiwanger, John, Ron Jarmin, and Cornell John Krizan. 2010. "Mom-and-Pop Meet Big-Box: Complements or Substitutes?" *Journal of Urban Economics* 67 (1): 116–34.

Hallward-Driemeier, Mary, and Gaurav Nayyar. 2018. *Trouble in the Making? The Future of Manufacturing-Led Development.* Washington, DC: World Bank.

Hallward-Driemeier, Mary, Gaurav Nayyar, Wolfgang Fengler, Anwar Aridi, and Indermit Gill. 2020. *Europe 4.0: Addressing the Digital Dilemma*. Washington, DC: World Bank.

Hallward-Driemeier, Mary, and Lant Pritchett. 2015. "How Business Is Done in the Developing World: Deals versus Rules." *Journal of Economic Perspectives* 29 (3): 121–40.

Harrison, Ann, and Andres Rodríguez-Clare. 2010. "From Hard to Soft Industrial Policies in Developing Countries." Column, *VoxEU.org*, June 27.

Hernández, Iván, Nathalie Cely, Francisco González, Ernesto Muñoz, and Iván Prieto. 2007. "The Discovery of New Export Products in Ecuador." Final report, STRATEGA Business Development Services, Quito, Ecuador.

Hjort, Jonas, and Jonas Poulsen. 2019. "The Arrival of Fast Internet and Employment in Africa." *American Economic Review* 109 (3): 1032–79.

Hoekman, Bernard. 2006. "Liberalizing Trade in Services: A Survey." Policy Research Working Paper 4030, World Bank, Washington, DC.

Hofmann, Claudia, Alberto Osnago, and Michele Ruta. 2019. "The Content of Preferential Trade Agreements." *World Trade Review* 18 (3): 365–98.

Hortaçsu, Ali, and Chad Syverson. 2015. "The Ongoing Evolution of US Retail: A Format Tug-of-War." *Journal of Economic Perspectives* 29 (4): 89–112.

Iacovone, Leonardo, Beata Javorcik, Wolfgang Keller, and James Tybout. 2015. "Supplier Responses to Walmart's Invasion in Mexico." *Journal of International Economics* 95 (1): 1–15.

Institute for Competitiveness & Prosperity. 2010. "Management Matters in Retail." Working Paper 13, Institute for Competitiveness & Prosperity, Toronto.

Javorcik, Beata S., and Yue Li. 2013. "Do the Biggest Aisles Serve a Brighter Future? Global Retail Chains and Their Implications for Romania." *Journal of International Economics* 90 (2): 348–63.

Jensen, J. Bradford. 2013. "Tradable Business Services, Developing Asia, and Economic Growth." In *Developing the Service Sector as an Engine of Growth for Asia*, edited by Donghyun Park and Marcus Noland, 148–76. Manila: Asian Development Bank.

Jia, Panle. 2008. "What Happens When Wal-Mart Comes to Town: An Empirical Analysis of the Discount Retailing Industry." *Econometrica* 76 (6): 1263–1316.

Kalirajan, Kaleeswaran. 2000. "Restrictions on Trade in Distribution Services." Staff research paper, Labor and Demography Series, Productivity Commission, Australian Government, Adelaide.

Kalirajan, Kaleeswaran, Greg McGuire, Duc Nguyen-Hong, and Michael Schuele. 2000. "The Price Impact of Restrictions on Banking Services." In *Impediments to Trade in Services: Measurement and Policy Implications*, edited by Christopher Charles Findlay and Tony Warren. London: Routledge.

Kapur, Devesh. 2002. "The Causes and Consequences of India's IT Boom." *India Review* 1 (2): 91–110.

Kikkawa, Aiko, and Eric B. Suan. 2019. "Trends and Patterns in Intra-ASEAN Migration." In *Skilled Labor Mobility and Migration: Challenges and Opportunities for the ASEAN Economic Community*, edited by Elisabetta Gentile, 1–24. Manila: Asian Development Bank; Cheltenham, UK: Edward Elgar Publishing.

Laget, Edith, Alberto Osnago, Nadia Rocha, and Michele Ruta. 2020. "Deep Trade Agreements and Global Value Chains." *Review of Industrial Organization* 57 (6): 379–410.

Lin, Justin Yifu, and Yong Wang. 2020. "Structural Change, Industrial Upgrading, and Middle-Income Trap." *Journal of Industry, Competition and Trade* 20 (2): 359–94.

Liu, Ernest. 2019. "Industrial Policies in Production Networks." *Quarterly Journal of Economics* 134 (4): 1883–1948.

Maloney, William F., and Gaurav Nayyar, 2018. "Industrial Policy, Information, and Government Capacity." *World Bank Research Observer* 33 (2): 189–217.

Manelici, Isabela, and Smaranda Pantea. 2021. "Industrial Policy at Work: Evidence from Romania's Income Tax Break for Workers in IT." *European Economic Review* 133 (490): 103674.

Markusen, James, Thomas F. Rutherford, and David Tarr. 2000. "Foreign Direct Investment in Services and the Domestic Market for Expertise." Working Paper 7700, National Bureau of Economic Research, Cambridge, MA.

Mathur, Somesh Kumar. 2007. "Indian IT Industry: A Performance Analysis and a Model for Possible Adoption." Paper 2368, Munich Personal RePEc Archive (MPRA), University Library of Munich, Germany.

Mattoo, Aaditya, Randeep Rathindran, and Arvind Subramanian. 2006. "Measuring Services Trade Liberalization and Its Impact on Economic Growth: An Illustration." *Journal of Economic Integration* 21 (1): 64–98.

Mattoo, Aaditya, Nadia Rocha, and Michele Ruta. Forthcoming. "Why Deep Trade Agreements May Shape Post-COVID-19 Trade." in *The Economics of Deep Trade Agreements*, edited by Ana M. Fernandes, Nadia Rocha, and Michele Ruta. Washington, DC: World Bank.

Mattoo, Aaditya, Robert M. Stern, and Gianni Zanini, eds. 2008. *A Handbook of International Trade in Services.* New York: Oxford University Press.

McKenzie, David, and Christopher Woodruff. 2016. "Business Practices in Small Firms in Developing Countries." *Management Science* 63 (9): 2967–81.

Meltzer, Joshua P. 2019. "Governing Digital Trade." *World Trade Review* 18 (Special Issue 1): S23–S48.

Miroudot, Sébastien, Jehan Sauvage, and Ben Shepherd. 2013. "Measuring the Cost of International Trade in Services." *World Trade Review* 12 (4): 719–35.

Mulabdic, Alen, and Lorenzo Rotunno. Forthcoming. "Trade Barriers in Government Procurement." In *The Economics of Deep Trade Agreements*, edited by Ana M. Fernandes, Nadia Rocha, and Michele Ruta. Washington, DC: World Bank.

Neumark, David, Junfu Zhang, and Stephen Ciccarella. 2008. "The Effects of Wal-Mart on Local Labor Markets." *Journal of Urban Economics* 63 (2): 405–30.

Nordås, Hildegunn K., and Henk Kox. 2009. "Quantifying Regulatory Barriers to Services Trade." Trade Policy Paper 85, Organisation for Economic Co-operation and Development (OECD), Paris.

Orefice, Gianluca, and Nadia Rocha. 2014. "Deep Integration and Production Networks: An Empirical Analysis." *World Economy* 37 (1): 106–36.

Óskarsdóttir, María, Cristián Bravo, Carlos Sarraute, Jan Vanthienen, and Bart Baesens. 2019. "The Value of Big Data for Credit Scoring: Enhancing Financial Inclusion Using Mobile Phone Data and Social Network Analytics." *Applied Soft Computing* 74: 26–39.

Page, John, and Sonia Plaza. 2006. "Migration Remittances and Development: A Review of Global Evidence." *Journal of African Economies* 15 (2): 245–336.

Pazarbasioglu, Ceyla, Alfonso Garcia Mora, Mahesh Uttamchandani, Harish Natarajan, Erik Feyen, and Mathew Saal. 2020. *Digital Financial Services.* Washington, DC: World Bank.

Press, Gil. 2019. "AI Stats News: 86% of Consumers Prefer Humans to Chatbots." *Forbes*, October 2. https://www.forbes.com/sites/gilpress/2019/10/02/ai-stats-news-86-of-consumers-prefer-to-interact-with-a-human-agent-rather-than-a-chatbot/.

Robinson, Sherman, Zhi Wang, and Will Martin. 2002. "Capturing the Implications of Services Trade Liberalization." *Economic Systems Research* 14 (1): 3–33.

Rodrik, Dani. 2004. "Development Strategies for the Twenty-First Century." In *New Development Strategies: Beyond the Washington Consensus*, edited by Akira Kohsaka, 13–38. London: Palgrave Macmillan.

Sutton, John. 2012. *Competing in Capabilities: The Globalization Process*. Oxford: Oxford University Press.

Van der Marel, Erik, and Martina F. Ferracane. 2021. "Do Data Flows Restrictions Inhibit Trade in Services?" *Review of World Economics*. Published ahead of print, April 29, 2021.

Walmsley, Terrie L., and L. Alan Winters. 2005. "Relaxing the Restrictions on the Temporary Movement of Natural Persons: A Simulation Analysis." *Journal of Economic Integration* 20 (4): 688–726.

World Bank. 2016. *World Development Report 2016: Digital Dividends*. Washington, DC: World Bank.

World Bank. 2019. *World Development Report 2019: The Changing Nature of Work*. Washington, DC: World Bank.

World Bank. 2020. *World Development Report 2020: Trading for Development in the Age of Global Value Chains*. Washington, DC: World Bank.

World Bank. 2021. *World Development Report 2021: Data for Better Lives*. Washington, DC: World Bank.

WTO (World Trade Organization). 2019. *World Trade Report: The Future of Services Trade*. Geneva: WTO.

6 Conclusion: In the Service of Development?

Introduction

The debate on the prospect of services-led development in hitherto less-industrialized countries needs to go beyond sector fetishism. *How* a good or service is produced has as important a potential impact on development—if not more so—as *what* is produced.

The ability to achieve greater scale economies, leverage labor with intangible capital, and enable spillovers across firms and sectors is what drives productivity growth and the creation of better jobs. These features, once thought of as unique to manufacturing, are increasingly shared by the services sector—which greatly expands the range of activities that can accelerate positive spillovers for development. This concluding chapter summarizes the findings that support that proposition.

The Promise of Services-Led Development

The Services Sector Can Increasingly Drive Economic Transformation

First, services can increasingly achieve scale economies through access to larger markets, enabled by branching or franchising and by expanding opportunities to sell remotely. This implies that scaling up services production beyond the limits of local demand would not push down prices and therefore profitability.

Second, services are increasingly characterized by innovation that improves labor productivity. This derives largely from the diffusion of digital technologies—both the wider adoption of computerization and internet-based technologies and the advent of machine learning, where advances in cognition- and perception-related tasks are most relevant to the services sector. The rise in intangible assets associated with adoption of these digital technologies is also driving a new kind of labor-augmenting capital accumulation.

Third, services are increasingly linked to other sectors, primarily by providing intermediate inputs. These linkages mean that services productivity has important spillovers for overall productivity.

Less-industrialized countries have capitalized on these transformative opportunities in the services sector as demand patterns shift, beyond links to a manufacturing base, through two channels: growth of exports (and other components of final demand) and sales to other sectors in the economy (domestic intermediate demand).

In the first instance, "stand-alone" transactions take place directly between a service provider and the final consumer. These include exports to larger markets, such as through offshore business services and tourism-related travel. Domestically, digital technologies have increasingly embedded services in goods—services for which the demand is independent of a manufacturing base. For example, local language and cultural considerations matter for mobile-phone applications and therefore provide an advantage to domestic firms that do not manufacture the phone itself.

Rising demand from other sectors in an economy matters too. And while a domestic manufacturing sector creates demand for a given services subsector, so too do agriculture, mining, construction, utilities, and other services. For example, Chile has used its mineral resources to diversify into the provision of sophisticated engineering services, and Uruguay now specializes in advanced information technology (IT) services for the livestock industry.

The services sector is not monolithic; services subsectors that are characterized by higher rates of labor productivity growth (relative to manufacturing) account for a lower share of jobs in low- and middle-income countries (LMICs) than in high-income countries. These are *global innovator services*—information and communication technology (ICT), finance, and professional services—that are internationally traded and offshored, research and development (R&D)– and technology-intensive, and linked to other sectors much like manufacturing. Yet, unlike manufacturing, they are typically also relatively skill intensive.

Low-skill domestic services such as retail, entertainment, and personal services are exactly the opposite: they absorb unskilled labor but provide little by way of scale, innovation, and linkages to other sectors. *Low-skill tradable services*—transportation, wholesale trade, and accommodation and food services—stand out in that they both create jobs for unskilled labor *and* provide some opportunities for scale, innovation, and spillovers to other sectors.

The absence of the twin benefits of productivity and jobs from the same activities may risk increased inequality since the higher-paying productive jobs of global innovator services benefit from scale, innovation, and spillovers, while unskilled services jobs do not.

The characteristics that contribute to productivity growth and job creation are changing over time, especially with the diffusion of digital technologies, thereby narrowing the productivity-jobs dichotomy in a given services subsector. *Global innovator services* remain intensive in skilled labor but can deliver the benefits of scale and innovation more widely through their linkages with sectors more intensive in low-skilled labor.

Low-skill (tradable and domestic) services will continue to *employ low-skilled labor* but with (a) *enhanced opportunities for accessing larger markets* (such as through digital platforms that match demand and supply for travel-related accommodation and transportation services as well as through streaming platforms for entertainment services); (b) *benefits from the digitalization of business processes* (such as through accounting apps in small-scale retail services and one-stop customs clearance for freight transportation services); and (c) *opportunities to scale up based on intangible capital* (such as in restaurant and retail chains).

At the same time, new technologies and changing globalization make export-led manufacturing a less powerful strategy than before. Scale economies in established centers of manufacturing, together with industrial automation, make it harder for latecomers to industrialization to compete based on lower labor costs. And even if successful, the twin wins of productivity and jobs associated with manufacturing are eroding as the diffusion of labor-saving processes lowers the job potential.

Many less-industrialized countries have capitalized on export opportunities in the services sector. These opportunities include offshore business services—ranging from software development to back-office operations for finance, accounting, marketing, customer support, and other professional services—as well as travel-related transportation and accommodation and food services. Some less-industrialized countries have also leveraged their health sectors to export services through health tourism.

Offshore business services. Although the share of global innovator services in total services exports is positively associated with per capita income, numerous LMICs have diversified their export baskets through offshore business services. India's success in exporting software services is much cited. Business process outsourcing (BPO) services have been similarly pivotal in the evolution of the Philippines from an agriculture-based economy, while Costa Rica was a pioneer in attracting offshore BPO services to Latin America, and Ghana has emerged as the top BPO destination in Africa. Last but not least, Kenya and Lebanon stand out as regional hubs for exporting financial services.

The success of these LMICs in exporting global innovator services that are relatively intensive in skilled labor is attributable to (a) large pools of skilled labor, even when average skill levels in the population are low; and (b) their comparative disadvantage in labor-intensive manufacturing due to the relatively low labor market flexibility, quality of (transportation and logistics) infrastructure, and quality of regulatory institutions that characterize the sector.

Accommodation and food services, transportation services. Accommodation and food services and transportation services that provide export opportunities linked to tourism have also enabled many low-income countries—including many in Sub-Saharan Africa and across small island economies in all regions—to diversify their exports away from volatile primary sectors.

Further, although the export of transportation and distribution services outside of tourism is closely linked to merchandise trade (whether manufactured goods or agricultural commodities), transportation and logistics services hubs have emerged based on geography but independent of a country's production capacity. For example, Panama has emerged as an air and maritime logistics hub for the Americas, helping facilitate distribution in regional value chains.

Health tourism. Skill-intensive social services (health and education) are not amenable to international specialization and will continue to need a substantial domestic presence owing to a significant face-to-face component. However, they also benefit from exporting opportunities, such as through health tourism. Costa Rica, India, Jordan, Malaysia, Mexico, Turkey, and Thailand have emerged as destinations for world-class health care at lower prices.

The Services Sector Is an Important Enabler in a Multisector Growth Strategy

If export-led manufacturing will likely contribute less to inclusive growth than it did during the past "miracles" of many current high-income economies—particularly those in East Asia—latecomers to industrialization will need a multisector strategy that can approximate its success. This will entail not only improving the productivity of the services sector but also modernizing agriculture, leveraging natural resources where available, and exploiting niches in manufacturing where entry remains more possible.

For all these sectors, the role of services either as *inputs* (for example, as design, marketing, or distribution costs included in the value of a good) or as *enablers* (such as through logistics services or e-commerce platforms) cannot be emphasized enough. In fact, the enabling services—ranging from ICT and finance to transportation and distribution—have experienced the largest increase in forward linkages among all sectors and will therefore be increasingly important for future growth opportunities associated with export-led manufacturing. And with the advent of "smart" production processes across the agriculture, mining, and manufacturing sectors, ICT services (as the predominant producers and users of data) will play an especially crucial role in boosting economywide productivity.

Ultimately, services-led development perhaps cannot deliver rapid productivity growth and good jobs within the same activity in the way that manufacturing once did. Yet these equations are changing. Global innovator services that are already highly productive and pay high wages stand to benefit even more through additional opportunities for scale and innovation. Raising skills should make more workers eligible to work in these higher-productivity services. At the same time, spillovers through their linkages with other sectors, and increasing demand as incomes rise, should still have benefits for less-skilled or poorer workers. Similarly, low-skill services that absorb much of the surplus labor in LMICs can benefit from digital technologies and intangible capital, and some can even benefit from scale, especially when linked to other traded sectors.

In contrast, manufacturing will likely continue to deliver on productivity, scale, trade, and innovation—just not with the same numbers of jobs as in the past, at least in some industries. So, the services sector could well offer more promise than some manufacturing subsectors, especially as it assumes the all-important enabling role for economywide productivity.

This promise of services-led development can be realized through identifying policy priorities that improve countries' performance across the 4Ts: Expanding *trade* in services is central to expanding scale. Expanding the use of digital *technologies* can further improve scale and widen the scope for intangible capital to raise quality and efficiency. *Training* will enable more workers to move to higher-skill jobs and reinforce the ability to absorb technologies. And *targeting* enabling services can expand the gains from spillovers, hence raising productivity and creating more jobs.

Better data, no doubt, will help researchers and the policy community crystallize the contribution of the services sector to productivity growth and job creation across LMICs.

A Data Agenda for Services

Better Capturing the Heterogeneity of Services

Services are inherently heterogeneous. And although lumping particular services into categories is often useful for summarizing data across countries, making data available at less-aggregated levels can be important to better understand how individual services differ from each other.

For one thing, getting a consistent harmonized time series of value added and employment in the services sector across countries is itself difficult, even at the level of broad subsectors: wholesale and retail trade; transportation and storage; accommodation and food; information and communication; finance; real estate; professional, scientific, and technical services; administrative and support services; education; health; arts and entertainment; and personal services.

Further, making such key statistics available at the International Standard Industrial Classification (ISIC) two-digit level would be crucial to differentiate further between services. For example, grouping together wholesale and retail trade—even though they are similar in function—ignores the fact that firms in wholesale trade, unlike those in retail, tend to operate on larger scales and function mostly as intermediaries rather than selling to final consumers. Similarly, air transportation services are distinct from road transportation services. Some datasets even continue to rely on older industrial classifications (for example, ISIC Revision 3.1) that group together services as disparate as ICT and transportation and storage.

In addition, it is far from straightforward to match international trade data, which primarily draw on balance of payments statistics, with ISIC sectoral classifications. International trade data by services subsector also need greater coverage across the different modes of delivery.

Moving Services Out of the Shadows in Firm-Level Data

This book has shown that only one-third of labor productivity differences between firms in the services sector, relative to manufacturing, can be explained by differences across subsectors. This heterogeneity (even within narrowly defined industries at the two-digit ISIC sector level) means that underlying firm dynamics are key to understanding broader sector performance.

Even though the coverage of the services sector has significantly improved in firm censuses and surveys in high-income countries, the same does not hold true in most LMICs. Further, even where such microdata on the services sector are available, they seldom track the same firms over time.

Simply improving the coverage of the services sector in firm-level data, however, is insufficient. Understanding the productivity dynamics of firms requires more-granular information to be available, for several reasons:

- As the role of intangible capital expands in raising the quality and productivity of services through the diffusion of data-based business models, the ability to measure it is increasingly important.

- Although full quality adjustment at the firm level might be difficult, capturing the prices that individual firms charge for services—an intermediary step—can significantly improve the estimation of performance.

- Because services are increasingly linked to other sectors of the economy, an account of transactions between firms in different sectors can improve our understanding of demand for intermediate inputs and spillovers.

- Unlike customs-level data for the manufacturing sector, firm-level information on exports and imports for services-related transactions is often missing.

Recognizing the Fading Border between Manufacturing and Services

The distinction between manufacturing and service activities within the same firm is increasingly blurred. Many services are *embodied* in manufactured goods and, with new digital technologies, increasingly more services are *embedded* in them too. Yet most data sources characterize all of a firm's activities within a single sector. Although outsourced activities are easier to capture in input-output tables, services provided in house by manufacturing firms are often subsumed in manufacturing value added. The analysis of firms that are increasingly multisectoral must therefore distinguish between services and manufacturing activities at the firm level in terms of both revenues and occupations.

This book has provided a framework to assess the development potential of the services sector. It has brought together new evidence on patterns of firm growth and on new trends that are expanding the contributions of services to scale, innovation, and spillovers. However, better data that enable more-granular research are needed to further expand the evidence base on how these trends develop, how inclusive the opportunities are, and which policies will be most effective in realizing that services-led development is indeed in the service of development.

Appendix A. Summary Measures for Trade, Technology, Training, and Targeting (the 4Ts)

TABLE A.1 Summary Measures for Trade, Technology, Training, and Targeting (the 4Ts), by Economy, Most Recent Year Available

Economy	Trade — Doing Business index (0–100)	Trade — Services trade restrictiveness index (0–100)	Technology — Restrictions on cross-border data flows	Technology — Percentage of firms using email	Technology — Percentage of individuals using the internet	Technology — Digital skills index (0–100)	Training — Tertiary enrollment rates (%)	Training — Management practices index in the services sector (1–5)	Targeting — Magnitude of forward linkages for global innovator services (%)	Targeting — Magnitude of forward linkages for low-skill tradable services (%)
Albania	67.7	19.4	—	57.4	69.6	49.9	55.0	1.7	1.3	2.8
Argentina	59.0	17.0	Medium	97.1	74.3	50.2	90.0	2.2	4.4	3.7
Armenia	74.5	11.4	Medium	87.7	68.2	59.0	54.6	—	0.9	2.2
Australia	81.2	17.0	Low	—	86.5	67.0	113.1	2.0	10.3	3.5
Austria	78.7	17.8	Medium	68.7	87.8	63.0	85.1	2.2	7.5	3.8
Azerbaijan	76.7	—	—	—	79.8	68.2	27.7	2.2	1.7	2.0
Bahrain	76.0	50.8	—	—	99.7	65.7	50.5	—	0.8	1.3
Bangladesh	45.0	44.2	Low	18.2	12.9	42.5	20.6	—	1.4	8.2
Belarus	74.3	35.1	—	86.5	82.8	—	87.4	2.1	4.1	9.7
Belgium	75.0	22.5	Medium	—	90.4	63.8	79.7	—	6.7	4.7
Bolivia	51.7	13.8	Low	72.4	44.3	37.0	24.9	1.9	2.3	7.4
Botswana	66.2	41.7	—	82.4	41.4	44.9	—	—	—	—
Brazil	59.1	22.5	Medium	76.7	70.4	34.8	51.3	1.7	3.6	4.9
Brunei Darussalam	70.1	—	High	—	95.0	64.3	31.4	—	2.9	1.7
Bulgaria	72.0	15.5	Medium	88.2	67.9	60.9	71.0	1.7	6.9	8.5
Cambodia	53.8	23.7	Low	61.6	40.5	42.8	13.7	—	1.3	7.6
Cameroon	46.1	26.4	Low	52.0	23.2	48.3	12.8	—	0.7	7.0
Canada	79.6	21.6	Low	—	92.7	67.9	68.9	2.2	—	—
Chile	72.6	23.4	Medium	98.0	82.3	54.4	88.5	1.8	—	—
China	77.9	36.6	High	83.6	54.3	61.0	50.6	1.7	—	—
Colombia	70.1	18.3	Medium	98.5	65.0	46.6	55.3	2.3	—	—
Costa Rica	69.2	29.3	Medium	87.6	81.2	64.8	55.2	—	—	—
Croatia	73.6	—	Medium	93.8	79.1	45.3	67.9	—	6.6	4.9
Cyprus	73.4	—	Medium	—	86.1	64.3	75.9	2.0	7.5	0.6
Czech Republic	76.3	16.6	Medium	93.5	80.9	63.0	64.1	2.3	5.1	14.2
Denmark	85.3	21.0	Medium	—	98.0	73.6	80.6	—	6.6	4.1
Dominican Republic	60.0	12.3	Medium	75.1	74.8	43.1	59.9	—	4.6	2.5
Ecuador	57.7	6.2	—	98.6	54.1	46.0	44.9	2.3	2.6	4.4
Egypt	60.1	52.1	Low	68.5	57.3	61.0	35.2	—	1.2	1.8
El Salvador	65.3	—	—	79.5	33.8	36.0	29.4	—	2.8	10.8

Table continues on the following page

Economy	Trade			Technology			Training		Targeting	
	Doing Business index (0–100)	Services trade restrictiveness index (0–100)	Restrictions on cross-border data flows	Percentage of firms using email	Percentage of individuals using the internet	Digital skills index (0–100)	Tertiary enrollment rates (%)	Management practices index in the services sector (1–5)	Magnitude of forward linkages for global innovator services (%)	Magnitude of forward linkages for low-skill tradable services (%)
Estonia	80.6	—	Medium	98.7	89.5	73.8	69.6	2.2	5.4	5.6
Ethiopia	48.0	88.2	Low	78.6	18.6	45.8	8.1	1.3	0.9	4.6
Finland	80.2	25.6	Medium	—	89.6	80.5	88.2	—	7.6	4.8
France	76.8	26.4	Medium	74.4	83.3	58.2	65.6	2.0	8.0	3.8
Georgia	83.7	11.5	Medium	—	68.8	44.3	63.9	1.3	—	—
Germany	79.7	17.5	Medium	64.7	88.1	67.8	70.2	2.2	7.3	7.6
Ghana	60.0	18.4	Low	—	37.9	53.5	15.7	1.3	1.7	13.7
Greece	68.4	18.0	Medium	—	75.7	51.8	136.6	2.0	5.0	2.3
Guatemala	62.6	17.7	—	90.0	40.7	39.1	21.8	—	2.2	10.1
Honduras	56.3	21.1	Low	83.0	32.1	43.9	26.2	—	2.6	12.1
Hong Kong SAR, China	85.3	—	Low	—	91.7	—	76.9	—	5.4	0.9
Hungary	73.4	17.5	Medium	84.1	80.4	49.5	48.5	1.9	5.6	7.5
India	71.0	65.7	Medium	73.2	20.1	57.2	28.1	1.6	1.1	6.3
Indonesia	69.6	50.0	High	31.3	47.7	58.5	36.3	—	1.4	7.8
Iran, Islamic Republic of	58.5	63.3	Low	—	70.0	51.8	68.1	—	1.8	5.9
Ireland	79.6	12.4	Medium	—	84.5	66.5	77.8	1.8	4.0	3.2
Israel	76.7	—	Medium	98.7	86.8	75.0	63.4	—	10.0	4.0
Italy	72.9	26.9	Medium	—	74.4	52.9	61.9	1.6	9.0	5.5
Japan	78.0	23.4	Medium	—	91.3	57.2	—	2.2	6.6	6.1
Jordan	69.0	48.2	Low	59.1	66.8	65.3	34.4	1.5	—	—
Kazakhstan	79.6	17.0	High	88.8	81.9	61.5	61.7	1.7	4.6	3.0
Kenya	73.2	29.5	High	69.5	22.6	59.1	11.5	1.9	—	—
Korea, Rep. of	84.0	23.1	Medium	—	96.2	66.5	94.3	—	5.3	9.0
Kuwait	67.4	51.8	—	—	99.5	53.5	54.4	—	0.5	2.8
Kyrgyz Republic	67.8	15.2	Medium	85.7	38.2	47.6	41.3	2.0	1.8	1.6
Latvia	80.3	—	Medium	92.6	86.1	63.1	88.1	2.4	6.4	5.3
Lebanon	54.3	42.3	Low	83.1	78.2	67.5	—	1.3	—	—
Lesotho	59.4	27.3	—	43.3	29.8	41.5	10.2	—	—	—
Lithuania	81.6	12.6	Medium	97.8	81.6	64.2	72.4	2.1	4.9	4.6
Luxembourg	69.6	—	Medium	—	97.1	69.8	19.2	—	9.1	1.1

Table continues on the following page

TABLE A.1 Summary Measures for Trade, Technology, Training, and Targeting (the 4Ts), by Economy, Most Recent Year Available (continued)

Economy	Trade			Technology			Training		Targeting	
	Doing Business index (0–100)	Services trade restrictiveness index (0–100)	Restrictions on cross-border data flows	Percentage of firms using email	Percentage of individuals using the internet	Digital skills index (0–100)	Tertiary enrollment rates (%)	Management practices index in the services sector (1–5)	Magnitude of forward linkages for global innovator services (%)	Magnitude of forward linkages for low-skill tradable services (%)
Madagascar	47.7	18.7	Medium	59.6	4.7	35.5	5.4	—	0.3	2.1
Malawi	60.9	34.2	Low	78.3	13.8	30.7	0.8	—	—	—
Malaysia	81.5	46.1	Medium	40.4	84.2	72.8	45.1	—	4.3	9.7
Malta	66.1	—	Medium	—	85.8	62.0	54.3	—	4.6	1.8
Mauritius	81.5	16.9	Medium	68.4	64.0	55.7	40.6	1.9	2.6	1.8
Mexico	72.4	29.5	Low	81.9	70.1	46.0	40.2	1.9	3.3	6.1
Mongolia	67.8	13.7	—	67.5	51.1	46.3	65.6	2.4	3.9	3.4
Morocco	73.4	21.0	Medium	98.4	74.4	48.0	35.9	1.4	—	—
Mozambique	55.0	18.6	—	50.8	20.8	29.0	7.3	1.6	0.3	3.3
Myanmar	46.8	—	Low	20.3	23.6	—	18.8	1.4	—	—
Namibia	61.4	37.0	—	76.5	36.8	43.9	22.9	—	4.3	5.9
Netherlands	76.1	12.3	Medium	—	93.3	77.1	85.0	—	8.3	3.2
New Zealand	86.8	11.0	Low	—	90.8	65.5	82.0	1.9	10.2	3.6
Nigeria	56.9	27.1	Medium	24.1	7.5	40.4	10.2	1.5	—	—
Norway	82.6	—	Medium	—	98.0	71.6	82.0	—	6.8	3.1
Pakistan	61.0	28.3	Low	52.1	17.1	52.4	9.0	—	0.7	5.2
Panama	66.6	47.8	—	66.0	63.6	42.0	47.8	—	2.6	4.4
Peru	68.7	16.4	Medium	96.2	60.0	39.3	70.7	2.2	3.0	3.8
Philippines	62.8	53.5	Low	79.4	43.0	67.7	35.5	—	1.2	3.7
Poland	76.4	11.0	Medium	88.4	84.5	54.5	67.8	1.4	4.4	9.3
Portugal	76.5	21.8	Medium	—	75.3	58.7	63.9	1.8	5.0	4.1
Qatar	68.7	60.1	Low	—	99.7	72.2	17.9	—	0.9	1.1
Romania	73.3	14.5	Medium	88.1	73.7	58.2	49.4	1.6	3.7	9.0
Russian Federation	78.2	25.7	High	94.9	82.6	65.8	81.9	2.0	4.9	6.3
Rwanda	76.5	25.0	Low	74.1	21.8	49.4	6.7	1.6	0.8	1.7
Saudi Arabia	71.6	42.5	Low	—	95.7	72.1	68.0	—	1.5	1.0
Senegal	59.3	19.0	Medium	67.0	29.6	53.4	12.8	—	0.9	5.6
Singapore	86.2	—	Medium	—	88.9	76.4	84.8	2.0	7.2	2.2
Slovak Republic	75.6	—	Medium	99.7	82.9	59.8	46.6	1.9	4.2	12.2
Slovenia	76.5	—	Medium	97.7	83.1	63.8	78.6	—	6.9	8.6

Table continues on the following page

TABLE A.1 Summary Measures for Trade, Technology, Training, and Targeting (the 4Ts), by Economy, Most Recent Year Available (continued)

Economy	Trade			Technology			Training		Targeting	
	Doing Business index (0–100)	Services trade restrictiveness index (0–100)	Restrictions on cross-border data flows	Percentage of firms using email	Percentage of individuals using the internet	Digital skills index (0–100)	Tertiary enrollment rates (%)	Management practices index in the services sector (1–5)	Magnitude of forward linkages for global innovator services (%)	Magnitude of forward linkages for low-skill tradable services (%)
South Africa	67.0	34.5	Medium	54.2	56.2	37.9	22.4	—	—	—
Spain	77.9	16.1	Medium	—	90.7	55.7	88.9	1.8	7.0	3.3
Sri Lanka	61.8	38.2	Low	34.8	34.1	53.8	19.6	—	1.5	5.4
Sweden	82.0	15.5	Medium	—	94.5	77.8	67.0	2.2	8.7	3.5
Switzerland	76.6	—	Medium	—	93.1	74.4	59.6	—	7.6	4.8
Taiwan, China	80.9	—	Low	—	88.8	69.8	—	—	5.8	13.2
Tanzania	54.5	30.7	Low	29.1	16.0	47.8	4.0	1.3	0.6	1.4
Thailand	80.1	48.0	Medium	55.4	66.7	54.3	49.3	—	2.0	7.9
Togo	62.3	—	Medium	80.4	12.4	—	14.5	—	0.5	7.9
Tunisia	68.7	44.5	High	93.2	66.7	53.9	31.7	—	0.5	10.7
Turkey	76.8	25.0	Medium	86.5	74.0	42.1	—	1.8	3.1	5.5
Uganda	60.0	34.5	Medium	39.2	23.7	40.4	4.8	—	0.5	4.4
Ukraine	70.2	27.2	Medium	87.8	62.6	57.5	82.7	1.9	4.0	4.2
United Arab Emirates	80.9	—	—	—	99.1	72.0	—	—	1.4	0.6
United Kingdom	83.5	14.4	Medium	—	92.5	65.6	60.0	2.0	8.7	2.8
United States	84.0	17.7	Low	—	88.5	72.2	88.2	2.3	8.6	4.5
Uruguay	61.5	28.4	Medium	98.3	76.9	54.4	63.1	—	6.4	2.8
Vietnam	69.8	41.5	High	91.6	68.7	46.1	28.5	1.7	1.2	6.7
Zambia	66.9	21.0	—	55.8	14.3	41.7	4.1	2.1	—	—

Source: Calculations based on the World Bank's Services Trade Restrictiveness Index (STRI), Doing Business data, Enterprise Surveys, World Development Indicators, and Export Value Added Database (EVAD); the World Economic Forum's digital skills index; the Centre for Economic Performance's World Management Surveys; the International Labour Organization's employment data; the International Telecommunications Union's Global and Regional information and communication technology data; and Martina Francesa Ferracane and Erik van der Marel, "Regulations on Personal Data: Differing Data Realms and Digital Services Trade" (background paper for *World Development Report 2021*, World Bank, Washington, DC, 2020).

Note: The magnitude of forward linkages for global innovator services is the share of intermediate sales in the output of information and communication technology, finance, and professional, scientific and technical services multiplied by the share of these services in total employment. The magnitude of forward linkages for low-skill tradable services is the share of intermediate sales in the output of transportation and wholesale and retail trade multiplied by the share of manufacturing in GDP. For economies covered in the World Management Survey, the management practices index is derived for the services sector by applying the ratio of the index of the manufacturing sector to the index of the services sector, averaged across countries for which both sectors are covered in the World Bank Enterprise Survey. Economies for which data are available for at least one variable within each of the 4Ts—trade, technology, training, and targeting—are included. — = no data available. SAR = Special Administrative Region.